WOMEN RISING

Women Rising

In and Beyond the Arab Spring

Edited by

Rita Stephan *and* Mounira M. Charrad

NEW YORK UNIVERSITY PRESS

New York

NEW YORK UNIVERSITY PRESS
New York
www.nyupress.org

References to Internet websites (URLs) were accurate at the time of writing. Neither the author nor New York University Press is responsible for URLs that may have expired or changed since the manuscript was prepared.

Library of Congress Cataloging-in-Publication Data
Names: Stephan, Rita, editor. | Charrad, M. (Mounira), editor.
Title: Women rising : in and beyond the Arab Spring /
edited by Rita Stephan and Mounira M. Charrad.
Description: New York, NY : New York University Press, 2020. |
Includes bibliographical references and index.
Identifiers: LCCN 2019041958 | ISBN 9781479846641 (cloth) |
ISBN 9781479801046 (paperback) | ISBN 9781479856961 (ebook) |
ISBN 9781479883035 (ebook)
Subjects: LCSH: Women—Political activity—Arab countries. | Women's rights—Arab countries. | Feminism—Arab countries. | Women—Arab countries—Social conditions—21st century.
Classification: LCC HQ1236.5.A65 W65 2020 | DDC 320.082/0974927—dc23
LC record available at https://lccn.loc.gov/2019041958

New York University Press books are printed on acid-free paper, and their binding materials are chosen for strength and durability. We strive to use environmentally responsible suppliers and materials to the greatest extent possible in publishing our books.

Manufactured in the United States of America

10 9 8 7 6 5 4 3 2 1

Also available as an ebook

*To all strong Arab women who have risen
and continue to rise.*

*To the next generation of strong women,
may you continue the journey.*

CONTENTS

FOREWORD

SUAD JOSEPH

The activism of Arab women for political transformation is over a century old. A major scholarly library of research now exists to document Arab women's activism from the nineteenth century to the present. This literature tackles a variety of issues, including voting rights, nationality rights, citizenship, family law, children's advocacy, the environment, education, civil liberties, and democratic governance. Indeed, one can argue that there has never been a period in which Arab women did not express agency through a variety of political pathways. Yet, the representation of Arab women in Western news, social media, popular culture, and even in some scholarship often continues to reproduce the Orientalist tropes of Arab women as apolitical, as having no access to politics, or as politically silent/silenced. The Arab Spring of 2011 is often represented as an apparition, a fleeting moment of female activism that sparked an awakening only to be crushed. *Women Rising: In and Beyond the Arab Spring* attends to Arab women's activism in the Arab Spring not as a fleeting moment, but as one moment in a long genealogy of Arab women's activism.

Women Rising is a volume of hope grounded in history and in the lived present. The editors, Rita Stephan and Mounira M. Charrad, argue that "there is no going back" and that democracy in the Arab region is not dead. Rather, they remind us, political transformations are "messy, lengthy, and problematic." Change is not just coming, they contend, but it is occurring in the daily lives of women who stand up and fight for themselves, their families, and their people through engagements that become readily visible to the public, as well as through enactments that, while not recorded, nevertheless contribute to the small streams that eventually turn into rivers of change.

Women Rising brings together voices of women across the nations of the Arab region—from Libya, Egypt, Lebanon, Palestine, Iraq, Morocco, Algeria, Bahrain, Yemen, Jordan, and Syria—and on and on. The editors bring forward voices from different religious and ethnic groups, across religious "divides" that they expose for their misrepresentation of women's conditionalities. They attend to voices of women across class, regional, and urban/rural arenas. They recognize the importance of transnational Arab women's voices, as these Arab women, spread across the globe, continue to invest in the transformations of their home countries. They intentionally trespass into and through topics less voiced, including sexual rights and sexual minorities—and protests, which are often ignored, such as "garbage" protests. They engage the many debates animating women activists across the region—constitutional reform, personal status laws, "Islamism" and "democracy," movements of nonviolence, militarism, authoritarianism, and sectarianism. They create spaces for the many forms in which these debates voice themselves—through art, photography, films, popular culture, cyberspace, blogging, graffiti, soundscapes, poetry, journalism, and the like. They track the many spaces that are created by women activists—universities, streets, villages, checkpoints, public plazas designated as "male" terrain, city centers, courtyards, and homes. They analyze the methods and tactics used by women activists to disrupt, unsettle, undo the structural, the institutional, the given, the normative, and the hegemonic.

In capturing these spaces, Stephan and Charrad mean to do some undoing themselves. They critique transnational feminists who homogenize Arab women's activism within a unifying subaltern frame that manages to gaze only through a single lens. They challenge the ahistorical rendering of Arab women as having only "woken up" with the Arab Spring. They offer a correction to much scholarship, as well as popular culture, that finds comfort in the reproduction of the Arab woman as "victim" needing Western rescue. They take on sisterly Third World feminist literature, which is largely based on Latin America, Africa, and East Asia, by making the case for the specificity of the contexts of Arab women as countries that are generally not poor, have oil wealth unevenly distributed, and have a vast range of political and cultural experiences. They offer theoretical perspectives on resistance, revolution, and reform to inform the readings of the many voices brought forth in the volume.

Women Rising quilts together the stories, the views, the values, the experiences, the approaches, the styles, and the analyses of Arab women throughout the Arab region and beyond. The stitching together of stories designed from so many fabrics of life is precisely what is needed to resist and undo the essentialism that continues to plague the representation of Arab women. Here, Stephan and Charrad assemble many pieces held together by threads of history into the present and beyond—the many spools, the many fabrics, the many colors—vibrant and alive to the lived realities. The totality is not one cover, but a patchwork—always in the making, always doing and undoing, always moved by agency and intent going forward and not back, and, despite the messy unfinished business, continuing to unfold as full of promise.

Introduction

Advancing Women's Rights in the Arab World

RITA STEPHAN AND MOUNIRA M. CHARRAD

When women flamed in protests from Tunisia to Yemen calling for political reforms, the world was quick to proclaim that Arab women had finally risen. Some claimed that "this was the first time so many women from so many different backgrounds had joined demonstrations."[1] Unfortunately, the world had not paid attention to Arab women protesting, voting, running for office, and leading organizations since the 1920s, through the Arab Spring years, and up until today. The events of the Arab Spring, a period during which women's activism intensified, were only a historical marker that brought women's activism to the forefront.

The Arab Spring gained prominence in international politics with the 2011 Egyptian protests in Tahrir Square against the Mubarak regime, following the protests in Tunisia, where the Arab Spring started. After a month of protest, much of which was captured on social media, Mubarak fled Egypt and both the Parliament and the constitution were dissolved (Clarke 2011). For many casual Western observers, Tahrir Square events were unique, if not surprising. However, for those who have been following the region's history, the 2011 Egyptian revolution marks only one dynamic part of a larger series of events known as the Arab uprisings. These uprisings, arguably, accumulated the social tension that has been rising in the region since the 2004 Kefaya Egyptian Movement for Change (Clarke 2011) and the 2005 Lebanese Cedar Revolution (Stephan 2018). Frustration heightened by the end of 2010, and spread quickly throughout the region.

The spark that started the Arab Spring was the one with which the young Tunisian man, Mohamed Bouazizi, set himself on fire in response to police brutality, on December 17, 2010. This event triggered notable public agitation and drove supporters to protest and topple the regime in Tunisia. The domino effect of protests followed in Bahrain, Egypt, Jordan, Kuwait, Libya, Morocco, Saudi Arabia, Syria, and Yemen, with shy endeavors in Algeria, Iraq, Oman, and Palestine. Some protests achieved a change of regimes, as in Tunisia, Egypt, and Lebanon (in 2005). Others developed into violent encounters that left the protesters in a deadlock with their governments, as in Bahrain; and others turned into bloody civil wars, as in Yemen, Libya, and Syria. In some countries, major reforms were implemented, as in Morocco, Kuwait, and Jordan. Minor reforms were also introduced in Algeria, Oman, and Saudi Arabia—ending these protests shortly thereafter,[2] though they reignited in 2019 in Algeria, Iraq, Lebanon, and Sudan.

Several years after the Arab Spring, Tunisia, a budding democracy, continues to fight corruption and extremism; Syria, Libya, and Yemen are torn between war and Islamic extremism; Egypt is slowly sliding into becoming a dictatorship and a sexually dangerous environment for women; and the Gulf countries continue to be preoccupied with their crowns' stability and with containing dissident voices. Morocco, Jordan, Lebanon, and Algeria are trying to appease their constituents by introducing social, economic, political, and legal reforms, on the one hand, while managing their financial crises and curbing the appeal of extremism and emigration on the other.

Some have been quick to write democracy's obituary in the region, but we argue that the democratic transition to consolidation is messy, lengthy, and problematic. Like us, however, the contributors to this volume believe that there is no going back. Social and political norms that have traditionally rewarded compliance are now changing to encourage innovation; male-dominated social structures and powers are now shaken; and women have gained confidence in their ability to influence politics and to challenge the secular-Islamist power poles. We believe that a social revolution has made women more self-assured of their collective power to fight exclusion, silence, and oppression.

Women Rising: In and Beyond the Arab Spring features women fighting for *reforms*; *resisting* oppression; and engaging in protests and *revolutions* to change the status quo. The volume also takes these terms *beyond* the chronological, geographical, and thematic spaces of the Arab Spring and explores women's agency before and after the events of the Arab Spring themselves. While the majority of the pieces in this volume focus on women's activism during the Arab Spring uprisings, ten chapters emphasize the expressions of women's agency that predate this era. By providing historical context for women's political activism long before the Arab Spring, these contributions shake the claim that Arab women just "woke up" in 2011. In the same vein, women's struggle for rights extends beyond this historical marker, and seven pieces continue into the aftermath of the Arab Spring, viewing subsequent events from a variety of angles.

The voices of *Women Rising* include those of activists, politicians, scholars, and many others. We bring to the fore voices we rarely hear, such as those of filmmakers, poets, students, and artists, as well as those who have been silenced, like rural women, queer feminists, and housewives. In their own voices, women give testimony on how their activism shaped the fight for democracy, liberty, and human rights. This volume creates a space for multiple forms that include literary expression, street art, photographic discourse analysis, interviews, critical biography, testimonies, ethnographic interpretation, and political commentary.

The forty essays in this volume bear witness to women's activism, and to the way women mitigated the threats and obstacles that they faced in Algeria, Bahrain, Egypt, Iraq, Jordan, Kuwait, Lebanon, Libya, Morocco, Palestine, Saudi Arabia, Sudan, Syria, Tunisia, Yemen, and even the Arab diaspora. The essays combine analysis and testimony by authors from diverse communities in the region as well as Australia, Japan, Canada, Europe, and the United States. The forty chapters reflect questions posed by local, national, and transnational activists on the topics of beliefs, identity, agency, mobilization, and resistance.

The pieces vary in the type of discourse with which they engage, the type of data they use, and the type of subjects they address. While Western media and the world community have focused on popular political topics such as the toppling of regimes and the occupying of popular places like Tahrir Square, contributions to this volume take readers to remote spaces and introduce them to unusual topics. Contributors tell their stories from their personal experiences as activists or participant observers, and analysts weave first-hand accounts of activism with analytic commentary to answer important questions, such as what Arab women fought for or believed in and how they expressed their agency, mobilized through space, and organized these movements.

Theoretical Contributions of *Women Rising*

We present resistance, revolution, and reform as three theoretical concepts that correspond to three bodies of literature. The Arab Spring events brought new challenges to the fields of feminism, social movements, and gender politics, as we know them.

Resisting Feminist Narrative

Just as Arab women resisted oppressive regimes, their activism was also a form of resistance to the ways they have been portrayed in the narrative of Western, transnational, and even Third World feminisms. Their actions during the uprisings revealed the shortcomings of Arab women's overwhelming misrepresention as "victims" and as subordinate by nature (Mohanty 1991); who operate in a highly patriarchal setting (Enloe 2013; Peterson and Runyan 2010); and whose activism is limited to "bargaining with patriarchy" (Kandiyoti 1988). This misrepresentation strips Arab women from their feminism and denies them agency and "the ability to exercise their own approaches to local and global problem solving" (Peterson and Runyan 2010, 127). Western scholars who claim expertise on global and Middle Eastern gender politics often misinterpret Arab women's activism as lacking feminist consciousness or identification (Ray and Korteweg 1999). Other Western feminists tend to believe that gender struggle is universal; in other words, women everywhere tend to face similar oppression merely by virtue of their sex/gender, and regardless of their cultural or geopolitical context (Tong and Botts 2009). Therefore, these feminists assume that they can play a leadership role in saving, and speaking on behalf of, Third World, minority, and Arab women.

Equally misrepresentative of Arab women's activism are transnational feminists who view gender inequality from a single global lens that focuses on the intersection of nationality, sex, class, and race. They assume that a unified subaltern identity exists among all victims of colonialism and imperialism (Alexander and Mohanty 1997; Enloe 2000). While colonial powers are indeed oppressive, past and present, Arabs' relations with them have been complicated, before and after the Arab Spring. Internal conflicts and unusual alliances have made Western forces the lesser of two evils in some instances, and have aided Arab women's resistance to their corrupt regimes, oppressive laws, and restrictive social norms. In their position of rejecting nation-states and viewing national- ism as detrimental to feminism, transnational feminists have claimed hegemony over the discourse on Third World women (Herr 2014). The Arab Spring showed that women's struggle within the context of the nation-state is still relevant, and that the nostalgic feelings of global sis- terhood were shaken even within the region's boundaries.

The literature on Third World feminism does not fully represent Arab feminists either. Despite sharing a colonial heritage with East Asia, Latin America, and sub-Saharan Africa, Arab women view their experience as hybrid (Tzoreff 2014). Moreover, Third World feminist literature, which is based mostly on the experience of these East Asian, African, and Latin America women (Mohanty 1991; Tong and Botts 2009), assumes that, by extension, their struggles apply to Arab women (Golley 2007). But this is not the case. Arab women see themselves living in a geography that is hybrid economically, politically, and socially.

Economically, one third of Arab countries are high income, and the rest are either high-middle or lower-middle income.[3] Politically, Arab countries range among oil-rich monarchies, dictatorships, and quasi democracies. Socially, Arab norms vary between conservative Saudi Arabian and westernized Lebanese. With these diverse characteristics, Arab women tend to construct their feminism vis-à-vis Western, trans- national, and Third World feminisms, on an intersectional understand- ing of nation, patriarchy, and Islam as both resources for mobilization and grounds for revolution and reform.

Social Revolutions

Numerous experts argue that the Arab Spring uprisings were failed revolutions that have instead produced violence and renewed state repression. They claim that a true shift in politics, institutions, and identities did not occur (Cook 2017) and that "most rulers of the Mid- dle East managed to survive the uprisings of 2011 . . . [and] dictators have strengthened their grip on power" (Kurzman 2013, 14–15). Typi- cally, democratic transitions are multicausal, notoriously difficult, and unpredictably nonlinear. Goldstone (2011) reminds us, "Revolutions are just the beginning of a long process. Even after a peaceful revolution, it generally takes half a decade for any type of stable regime to consolidate," and Kurzman further posits, "Most new democracies fail. They dissolve into civil wars, or are overtaken by coups or collapse under authoritarian bureaucrats and demagogues" (2016).

We propose to shift the evaluation of the Arab Spring to a different spectrum and caution against declaring the game "over." The uprisings of the Arab Spring did not produce revolutions in the sense of "rapid, basic transformations of a society's state and class structures" as defined by Skocpol (1979, 4). However, they did raise citizens' awareness of the power of collective action. We believe that while the foundations for democratic transition were not present before the Arab Spring, they certainly emerged with it. What we see as irreversible after the Arab Spring is the fact that citizens now realize the power of collective action: protest and campaigning. At the very least, the Arab Spring uprisings produced a political environment amenable to advancing women's political participation and contentious collective action.

Simply put, the revolution of Arab women resulted in their increased participation in public life, increased representation in decision making, and emboldened leadership of women's organizations. The rising rates of women's participation in the public sphere also led them to assume a larger role in governance (IRI 2016). In December 2016, the Inter-Parliamentary Union (IPU)[4] reported that women's representation in Parliament (single or lower house) in the Arab states reached 19.1 percent, compared to 12.5 percent in 2010 (the lowest in the world then). This advancement, however, does not reflect improving conditions for women in all Arab countries. Arab women continue to face "obstacles toward achieving parity in elected legislative bodies," and despite many great achievements, "stark variations across the region in terms of the numerical presence of women in Arab parliaments" remain (Shalaby 2016).

Since 2011, women have also infiltrated the contentious collective space en masse. They fought for women's rights and representation as parts of the larger effort to achieve greater political and economic reforms. They made their claim not only through women's organizations but also in nongovernmental, nonprofit, governmental, and for-profit entities. Although, to the best of our knowledge, no comprehensive data has been collected on women's organizations in the region, the chapters in this volume provide evidence of the activism that is taking place. In a nutshell, however diverse their geographies and societies might have been, women's participation in the Arab Spring has elevated their ability to influence the decision-making process. Despite being underrepresented in the new political order, women are refusing to take the back seat.

Reforms in Gender Politics

Historically, liberalization of women's rights in the region has been initiated primarily from above. In exploring the process of expanding women's rights in the Tunisian Law of Personal Status in 1956, Charrad (2001 and 2011) shows that reforms were a state-building strategy, initiated in the absence of on-the-ground activism, designed to weaken tribal governance, and to contribute to the formation of a "modern" centralized state. This top-down model locates power as it relates to gender in the state, rather than in civil society or the public. Whereas the bottom-up, grassroots model suggests that people's dissatisfaction with the gendered social order results in pressure and social change, the top-down model demonstrates how the agency of the state shapes power as it relates to gender. Since the Arab Spring, women have intensified pressure from below in efforts to introduce reforms in gender politics.

Women collaborated with international actors, civil society organizations, private sector partners, and "willing" state actors to pass a number of legal reforms that protect women's rights, combat gender-based violence, and promote gender equality. Most notable were laws (listed in chronological order from most recent) criminalizing gender-based violence in Jordan, Lebanon, Morocco, Tunisia, and Algeria and laws advancing social and political rights in Saudi Arabia and Tunisia:

IN 2019,
- Saudi Arabia passed a law allowing women to travel without male consent.[5]

IN 2017,
- Saudi Arabia passed a law allowing women to drive and ending a long-standing policy that has become a global symbol of the oppression of women in the ultraconservative kingdom.[6]
- the lower house of Parliament in Jordan removed Penal Code Article 308, which had made rape permissible if the rapist marries the victim. The

redaction is still waiting to be approved by the Upper House and signed by King Abdullah II.[7]

- the Lebanese Parliament agreed to abolish Penal Code Article 522, the infamous "rape law" or "rape-marriage" law, which exempted a rapist from punishment if he married his victim.[8]

- the Tunisian Parliament passed a law on "Eliminating Violence against Women," which stipulates that gender-based crimes of a physical, moral, sexual, or economic nature are punishable offenses. A first-of-its-kind law, it eliminated the loophole for rapists to avoid punishment by marrying their victims.[9]

- Iraq allowed women to apply for a passport in the same way as men, passed legislation on sexual harassment in employment, imposed criminal penalties or civil remedies for sexual harassment in employment, and gave women at least fourteen weeks of paid maternity leave.[10]

IN 2016,

- Algeria passed a law that punishes violence against women and sexual harassment.[11]

- Egypt passed legislation on sexual harassment in employment, and imposed criminal penalties or civil remedies for sexual harassment in employment.[12]

IN 2014,

- Tunisia passed the first constitution in the Arab world to use the language of equality between men and women, in addition to safeguarding the rights won by Tunisian women in 1959, including the right to divorce, marriage by mutual consent, and the banning of polygamy.[13]

- the Moroccan Parliament unanimously amended Article 475 in the Penal Code, which allowed a rapist to escape prosecution if he married his underage victim.[14]

- Bahrain amended labor laws to require nondiscrimination based on gender in employment.[15]

IN 2013,

- King Abdallah of Saudi Arabia allowed women to run for the 2015 municipal election and to join the Shura Council and hold at least one fifth of its 150 seats.[16]

While the passage of all these laws can be dismissed as an attempt by "liberalizing" states to appease the international community and appear democratic, one cannot deny that on-the-ground activism was influential in the passing of so many gender laws in the region. Major transformations occurred in Arab women's ability to respond to existing and new challenges. They gained momentum to personalize their agency and make their voices heard, as the chapters in this volume reveal.

Women's Voices in This Volume

Building on their experiences in mobilizing for women's rights, and on their analyses of women's activism, the authors in this volume provide a rich and nuanced understanding of women's agency and mobilization before, during, and following the Arab Spring. They offer the reader a unique perspective on what may be one of the most significant historical developments of our times. We aim for this volume, with women's agency as its central focus, to give voice to Arab women as they tell their own stories of activism for democracy, social justice, and women's rights.

NOTES
1 Belinda Goldsmith, "Arab Spring to Take Years to Improve Women's Rights: Activists," Reuters, December 4, 2012, https://www.reuters.com.
2 Blight Garry, Sheila Pulham, and Paul Torpey, "Arab Spring: An Interactive Timeline of Middle East Protests," *Guardian*, March 22, 2011, https://www.theguardian.com/world.
3 "The World by Income and Region," World Bank, https://data.worldbank.org.
4 "About Us," Inter-Parliamentary Union, 2018, https://www.ipu.org.
5 Associated Press, "Saudi Arabia Law Change Allows Women to Travel without Male Consent." NBC News, August 9, 2019, https://www.nbcnews.com.
6 Ben Hubbard, "Saudi Arabia Agrees to Let Women Drive," *New York Times*, September 26, 2017, https://www.nytimes.com.
7 Shannon Bradford, "Positive Steps in the Fight to Prevent Violence against Women in the Middle East and North Africa," George W. Bush Presidential Center, August 7, 2017, http://www.bushcenter.org.
8 "Historic Day for Women in Lebanon as Parliament Repeals Rape Law," UN Women, August 18, 2017, http://www.unwomen.org.
9 "Tunisia Passes Historic Law to End Violence against Women and Girls," UN Women, August 10, 2017, http://www.unwomen.org.
10 World Bank Group, *Women, Business, and the Law 2019*, https://wbl.worldbank.org/.

11 "New Law in Algeria Punishes Violence against Women," *CBS News*, February 2, 2016, https://www.cbsnews.com.

12 World Bank Group, *Women, Business, and the Law 2019*, https://wbl.worldbank. org/.

13 "Tunisia's New Constitution: A Breakthrough for Women's Rights," UN Women, February 11, 2014, http://www.unwomen.org.

14 "Morocco Repeals 'Rape Marriage Law,'" Al Jazeera, January 22, 2014, http://www. aljazeera.com.

15 World Bank Group, *Women, Business, and the Law 2019*, https://wbl.worldbank. org.

16 "Saudi Arabia's King Appoints Women to Shura Council," *BBC News*, January 11, 2013, https://www.bbc.com.

BIBLIOGRAPHY

Alexander, M. Jacqui, and Chandra Talpade Mohanty, eds. 1997. *Feminist Genealogies, Colonial Legacies, Democratic Futures*. New York: Routledge.

Charrad, Mounira M. 2001. *States and Women's Rights: The Making of Postcolonial Tunisia, Algeria, and Morocco*. Berkeley: University of California Press.

———. 2011. "Gender in the Middle East: Islam, States, Agency." *Annual Review of Sociology* 37, no. 1 (August): 417–37.

Clarke, Killian. 2011. "Saying 'Enough': Authoritarianism and Egypt's Kefaya Movement." *Mobilization: An International Quarterly* 16, no. 4 (December 1): 397–416. https://doi.org/10.17813/maiq.16.4.m728m673p7340l23.

Cook, Steven. 2017. *False Dawn: Protest, Democracy, and Violence in the New Middle East*. Oxford: Oxford University Press.

Enloe, Cynthia. 2000. *Bananas, Beaches, and Bases: Making Feminist Sense of International Politics*. Berkeley: University of California Press.

———. 2013. *Seriously! Investigating Crashes and Crises as if Women Mattered*. Berkeley: University of California Press.

Goldstone, Jack. 2011. "Understanding the Revolutions of 2011: Weakness and Resilience in Middle Eastern Autocracies." *Foreign Affairs* 90, no. 3 (June): 8–16.

Golley, Nawar Al-Hassan. 2007. "Is Feminism Relevant to Arab Women?" *Third World Quarterly* 25, no. 3 (January): 521–36.

Herr, Ranjoo Seodu. 2014. "Reclaiming Third World Feminism; or, Why Transnational Feminism Needs Third World Feminism." *Meridians* 12, no. 1: 1–30.

IRI—International Republican Institute. 2016. "Women's Political Empowerment, Representation, and Influence in Africa." Washington, DC: IRI, September. http://www.iri.org.

Kandiyoti, Deniz. 1988. "Bargaining with Patriarchy." *Gender and Society* 2, no. 3: 274–90.

Kurzman, Charles. 2013. "Winter without Spring." *Contexts* 12, no. 2 (Spring): 14–15.

———. 2016. "Waves of Democratization, Waves of Disillusionment: The Arab Spring in Historical Perspective." In *From Mobilization to Counter-Revolution: The Arab*

Spring in Comparative Perspective. Washington, DC: Project on Middle East Political Science, May 3. https://pomeps.org.

Mohanty, Chandra Talpade. 1991. "Under Western Eyes: Feminist Scholarship and Colonial Discourses." In *Third World Women and the Politics of Feminism*, edited by Chandra Talpade Mohanty, Ann Russo, and Lourdes Torres, 51–80. Bloomington: Indiana University Press.

Peterson, V. Spike, and Anne Sisson Runyan. 2010. *Global Gender Issues in the New Millennium.* Boulder, CO: Westview.

Ray, R., and A. C. Korteweg. 1999. "Women's Movements in the Third World: Identity, Mobilization, and Autonomy." *Annual Review of Sociology* 25 (August): 47–71.

Shalaby, Marwa. 2016. "Women's Political Representation and Authoritarianism in the Arab World." Elliott School of International Affairs, Project on Middle East Political Science, Women, and Gender in Middle East Politics, March 11, https://pomeps.org.

Skocpol, Theda. 1979. *State and Social Revolutions.* Cambridge: Cambridge University Press.

Stephan, Rita. 2018. "Lebanese Women's Rights beyond the Cedar Revolution" In *Arab Women's Activism and Socio-Political Transformation: Unfinished Gendered Revolutions*, edited by Sahar Khamis and Amel Mili, 73–88. London: Palgrave.

Tong, Rosemarie, and Tina Fernandes Botts. 2009. *Feminist Thought: A More Comprehensive Introduction.* Boulder. CO: Routledge.

Tzoreff, Mira. 2014. "The Hybrid Women of the Arab Spring Revolutions: Islamization of Feminism, Feminization of Islam." *Journal of Levantine Studies* 4, no. 2: 69–111.

PART I

What They Fight For

The chapters in this section feature women's demands before and during the Arab Spring for political, economic, legal, sexual, and social rights. Activists made political claims of their status as citizens, women, workers, political actors, queer activists, nonviolent resisters, and advocates against sexual violence. Political claims are "morally-legitimated demands" that become recognized as rights through persuasive interactions.[1] Activists use claim making as the "purposive and public articulation of political demands, calls to action, proposals, criticisms or physical attacks."[2] The chapters in this section show how women used claim making to challenge the status quo and fight against violence, oppression, and injustice.

Rula Quawas encourages her students to claim their voice in the cultural transformation of Jordan while Nadine Naber documents women workers' struggles over class oppression in Egypt. Former Kuwaiti parliamentary member Aseel Alawadhi shares her personal fight for political participation, and Amal Amireh searches for the voice of Palestinian queers in the claim for nationalism. Lina Abirafeh and ABAAD bring men into the effort to combat violence against women, and Ginger Feather carries Najia Adib's voice in breaking the silence on pedophilia in Morocco. Finally, Syrian American activist and scholar Mohja Kahf highlights Syrian women's nonviolent resistance against militarism and fundamentalism, and Aminah Ali Kandar features the leadership role of women in the nonviolent uprisings in Yemen.

This collection starts with Rula Quawas, the prominent champion of women's advancement in Jordan, who passed away on July 27, 2017. Rula was the founder of the Women's Studies Centre at the University of Jordan. Her journey embodies the theme of this collection, and her lifelong goal was to empower young women and challenge patriarchal structures.

NOTES

1 Malcolm Spector and John I. Kitsuse, *Constructing Social Problems* (New Brunswick, NJ: Transaction, 2001).

2 Ruud Koopmans, *Contested Citizenship: Immigration and Cultural Diversity in Europe* (Minneapolis: University of Minnesota Press, 2005), 24.

1

Barefoot Feminist Classes

A Revelation of Being, Doing, and Becoming

RULA QUAWAS

Graduate and undergraduate students who sign up for feminist theory and literature modules in the English Department at the University of Jordan engage in an exercise of unlearning and re-visioning beyond the patriarchal perspective through which Arab women have been trained to see the world. They not only wrestle with difficult and dense texts that deal with the history of feminism and theories of gender that create emotion, tension, and conflict, but they also come to engage with, and analyze, the Arab culture in which they live outside the classroom. Through a feminist lens, they rigorously and seriously engage with issues that directly affect them, and, through debate and argument, they sharpen their opinions and address tangential questions that affect the very core of their beingness, doingness, and becomingness.

My twenty years of teaching literature and feminist theory at the University of Jordan, and my activism in movements on women's rights, on social justice, and on cultural and social transformation in Jordan, have taught me that Arab women believe education to be their weapon. They believe that transformative education is substantively good for them, and evidence shows that they are right. An educated woman has what it takes to live and lead an informed and empowered life and to seek employment and be financially independent. Even though her education does not solve all her problems and, at times, fails to eliminate her subordination to man, it enhances and builds her capacities and creativities.

Admittedly, feminist discourse is not part of my thinking; rather, it is my thinking, connecting me to my students and to the *global* world. As we know, feminist thinking and practice emphasize a vision wherein

Figure 1.1. Rula Quawas in 2016 at the University of Jordan

everyone's needs are respected, everyone has rights, and no one needs to fear subordination or abuse. This vision runs counter to the male domination most of us have experienced or will experience in our lives. During the fall semester of 2011, I taught a feminist theory class in which my students produced a video addressing the sexual harassment experienced by female students on campus and uploaded it to YouTube in June 2012. The video, which is revolutionary and heterodox in more than one way, created a controversy storm not only in Jordan but also all over the world. Little did I know that months later, I would be relieved of my post as dean of the faculty of foreign languages and that I and my students would be demonized and deprecated.[1]

In the spirit of feminist discourse, I would like to share this saga poem, a narratological testimonial, which reflects the intellectual development and nourishment of my students, who come to harvest feminist knowledge, to challenge commonly held views about Muslim women as passive objects of patriarchal structures, and to midwife active speech. Their vivid voices are incorporated within the poem I have crafted to show their ontological desire to be, do, and become. This is their Arab Spring, or better still, their Arab Renaissance. The students emerge as active agents in their own learning, and they develop an authentic voice that bears witness to their lives and minds. As independent subjects, they rip into feminist texts and speak in their own active voices with certainty, becoming midwife learners, delivering their own ideas to the world, and engaging in conversations with other voices—past and present—in the culture. Through dialogue, they cross barriers and bridge private and shared experience. They not only rise; they go beyond.

Testimonial Poem:

The Democracy of the Human Spirit

> *I speak*
> I was born into an ancient sarcophagus,
> but when I looked closer, the sarcophagus was made of glass,
> and I could break it if I wished.
> Inside I was an instar,
> waiting to become an imagine.
> Inscribed on the walls of my tomb,
> expectations and dreams.
> Staring in from outside my tomb—a multitude of eyes.
> It is all a mosaic,
> constructed on a foundation of polyphonic voices.
> In the orange-scented soiled familial depths,
> I send down my roots to seek
> the knowledge of my ancestors,
> absorbing my inheritance, my right to grow up,
> to expand, ascend, simply to stand.
> Branching,
> my tendrils extend, seeking cracks
> in the walls of the glass womb.
> Finding air, sunlight, water.
> I give a little push, the crack becomes a chasm.
> I am imagined.

Students Speak

> Oh!
> Name is guttering, choking, drowning . . .
> Raw dirt catching strong ribs.
> Tears of shame and fear in splintered eyes.

A mask of sorrow
that bitterly hides
shrouds of darkness,
webs of silence,
nets of failure.
Alone, afraid as a sinner of exile.
A vortex of confusion in my veins,
a mesh of seaweed in my being,
a giant ripping hole in my canvas,
intolerable pain hidden in my veil,
patiently hiding in his shadows.

Tired, yet eager for sunlight,
violently shaking my head, asking
What should I do? Who should I be?
Self-perception distorted by bent power.
The burden of dutiful obligations,
An uncomfortable journey stunted by restriction.
This tangled and gruesome coexistence—wasted potential.
An ebbing fire tied up in copper, inner knots reaching my very fiber.
The torch of conformity painlessly cuts
through glory.
Paper bearing paper in the posture of departure.
The light at the end of a furnace,
not a tunnel.

I'm a stranger, displaced, and tired of everything.
I'm nothing,
    Absolutely nothing.
    No I, me, myself.
    Nada, a cipher, nonexistent.
Why couldn't I have been a boy?
    A female . . . What is my sin?
My crime?
A piece of luggage,
    Numb,
    Hollow,
    Shriveled.

Who will solve my problems?
Who will put an end
to my fractured dreams,
to my excruciating pain,
to my slow suicide, living death.
What will become of me?

The Awakening

Something snaps.
Something sheds.
Something surfaces.
Are you mad, woman? I laugh and
laugh loudly.
I am stronger than sin.
I know my defiant soul.
I am here,
self-present and beautiful.
I exist.
I will live.
How well I breathe now!
Mabrouk, pure one.
I am an Arab woman.
Ana Imra'ah Arabiya
I own my identity,
    My virginity,
    My voice,
    My self.
I am no longer a tenant of my body.
I am no longer enthralled in snares of silences.
I am ME,
birthing a new life into my soul,
catalyzing change,
and becoming an agent of change.
I am ready to sail,
to brave the horizon
and go beyond.

I am an Arab woman.
Ana imra'ah Arabiya

The Revelation

A journey of truth telling,
of voyaging in and
diving within
my nooks and crannies,
my ifs and buts,
my doubts and certainties,
discovering my innermost self,
unearthing a real self,
branded and labeled,
dominated and misrepresented,
subjugated and objectified,
negated, even canceled,
by societal restrictions,
forged by a culture of *'eib and haram.*

For the first time in forever,
I am okay.
My feelings are okay.
My thoughts are okay.
My life choices are okay.
I use myself, let nothing and no one use me.
I am not alone.
Other women are with me
in feminist courses,
awakening to our newfound selves,
infused with feminist knowledge and
with feminist consciousness,
birthing ourselves anew and afresh,
rehumanizing ourselves,
putting ourselves
into the text,
into the world,

into history,
embracing our solidarity
and singing our songs of freedom.
Unbuttoning our hearts,
which throb and beat with internalized misogyny.
Unlocking our muted voices,
and speaking back to the patriarchy.
Our language is not phallocentric,
shaped by socialization.
Our language is our verbal weapon
through which we unlearn our mindsets,
shaped by the male stream.
We become resistant readers,
refusing to be *immasculated*.[2]
We think, choose, and act.
We herald a new age of change,
and move on,
onward and forward.

I now call myself a woman.
A victor, rather than a victim.
I am no longer encapsulated in the image of
the Angel of the House.
No longer hiding behind Anon,
as Virginia Woolf has once said.
No longer confined in a doll's house,
or trapped behind aged yellow wallpapers,
or locked up in attic rooms,
labeled mad and bad.
I am free, body and soul.
Unveiling, unmasking, and unraveling
leaves of imposed cultural scripts
and religious myths about the inferiority of women.
Now, I love me,
A Promothea, with a handful of words
telling my story,
in gynocentric language,

in white ink.
Living my telling life,
one day at a time,
and sharing it with
my daughters
and also with my sons.
I have had enough.
My duty is to honor myself.
Owning and honoring it.
I am not an appendage,
Bint flan, always referenced and cross-referenced:
The daughter of my father,
the wife of my husband,
and the mother of my son.
I am not a blank page to be written upon.
I am a creator of art
and of life.
Bent on unlearning what it means to be a tenant in my very body,
undoing and rewriting patriarchal precepts,
shedding socially assumed fictitious garments,
ready-made cultural scripts,
written about and for me
in dark ink
thick and morose,
ink committing deadly sins
against me, the me-myself,
and my humanity.

I speak passion to my voice,
which has been buried under layers and layers
of Dos and Don'ts,
dictates of my Arab society,
of my family,
and of myself,
lampooning my existence and life.
I speak my truth,
speaking it to power.

I own my space,
a room of my own,
and furnish it, too,
with confidence, strength, and hope,
with education, ambitions, and aspirations;
A niche which fits me, all of me,
all of my contradictions and ambivalences,
all of my scars and wrinkles,
all of my positionalities and standpoints,
all of my pain and anguish,
all of my modalities of enunciations,
all of me,
Regardless.

I have made peace with my new reality.
Gaping holes have made me whole again.
It is a new beginning of enlightenment and self-exploration.
Feminist knowledge transforms me.
Feminist knowledge empowers me.
It gives me a new pair of eyes,
opens a wide gate to my heart, soul and mind.
I'm no longer a passive entity which lives to give birth as a machine.
no longer caught in a deadly either/or.
I am not an "other"
His other,
to be propertized, marginalized, or ridiculed.
I have broken through many barriers,
changed the landscape of the conversation
and reclaimed my voice and my life.
I have studied feminist literature.
Too long.
Long Enough.
Empowering and empowered women:
Edna, Nora, Celie, Jane,
and Zahra, Firdaus, Najwa, Khadra.
Women whose stories reflect a conscious,
subjective point of view,

or interpretation of reality.
Distinctive women's ways of knowing.
Stories that have served me well,
and many, many more.
I no longer see people.
I read their faces,
which are no object masks,
and each face has a wonderful story to tell.

I know how to be woman-oriented
and how to abound
in everything and in all things.
I have learned how to be fulfilled rather than filled.
I can do all things through Me,
Me, who strengthens me,
A stronghold in lived experiences.
I name myself,
and I own it, too.
I am an Arab woman,
Ana Imra'ah Arabiya,
realizing the potentials
I sense for myself as a woman,
through an act of re-vision,
re-calling, re-membering, and re-claiming,
I give voice to my deepest fears and hopes,
through unleashing my spirit
upon the world,
infusing my entire life
with renewed synergy,
with meaning,
with self-worth,
with love,
with purpose,
with abundance,
and full of things that
have never been.
Imagining a new path

toward the future,
maintaining and sustaining my gains
and achieving further progress.

Song of Praise

A song of praise I write for myself.
I give myself a new birth today.
I reclaim self-celebration.
I celebrate all that is my life.
I am unique and unrepeatable.
I am full of myself.
I believe in myself.
I can do everything and anything.
Hooray. Hip hip, hooray.
I am worthy of praise.
I am forgiven,
for every craze and phase,
for every haze and chase.
I love myself generously,
and nurture the seeds within me.
Over the big high mountains,
across the deep wide rivers,
across the expansive Sahara,
around bumpy and winding roads,
I step on through,
yes, step on through.
I am happy to be me,
heart and soul, body and mind,
the whole package, pink and blue.
Born to be special all by myself.
I am my own,
one of a kind, and I don't mind.
I am happy to be ME,
to celebrate ME.
There is nothing wrong with me.
I am in charge.

I am in control. So that I can reach my every goal.
I love being me.
I am enough.
Enough
I
Am.

Reflections

This saga poem is a string of vignettes that are designed not so much to supply solutions as to provide insight into the social challenges that Jordanian students experience, and to offer ways of addressing them that are open to discussion, rejection, acceptance, and/or revision. The students' feelings, thinking, and action provide grounding for my poems, and their experiences nurture the value of a feminist discourse, which aims to promote and support women's voices and agency. A feminist classroom is open, safe, and liberating in terms of students speaking up and teachers encouraging debate. Within this site of resistance and contestation, students find their voices and take ownership of their feminist education, question what they are taught and how it is relevant to them, dialogue about sensitive topic areas in feminism, such as sexism, politics, and identity issues, and engage in actions that change personal and political realities.

The majority of students come to feminist theory classes with little knowledge about the subject, and sometimes they come with preconceptions about feminism that make them apprehensive about their decision to enroll. Throughout their feminist education, they discover, many for the first time, the rich details of women's lives and experiences and learn to make sense of this knowledge. They say again and again, "This course is nothing like we thought it would be; it is so much better." Indeed, it is. Feminism, which pushes against and beyond boundaries, is a fight not only for the benefit of all women but for the benefit of all beings.

As a professor of literature and feminist theory, I have always glimpsed the possibility of a world that could be much more for Arab women. When I teach, I always ask myself, What is it that I can do within the domain of my classrooms to make this world a living reality? What kind of future do I want to create with my students? The last twenty years have been fiercely intense on the issue of teaching feminist theory classes to graduate and undergraduate students. Intense such teaching is, but it is also liberating, democratizing, and empowering for me and for my students. Together, we become part of a teaching-learning process in which we create the opportunity to dare or to brave into unconventional forms of doing research and giving voice to women who have been marginalized and, at times, ridiculed. Together, we live our lives forward.

NOTES

1 The sexual harassment video and a mesh of articles and stories on the reactions of the local and the international communities can be accessed at the blog *Supporting Social and Academic Freedom*: see "Yes to Harassment," *Supporting Social and Academic Freedom*, https://fortheloveoffreedom.wordpress.com/the-story.

2 In *The Resisting Reader: A Feminist Approach to American Fiction*, Judith Fetterley (1978) says that "the cultural reality is not the emasculation of men by women but the *immasculation* of women by men" (xx). She explains that women are taught to think as men and to identify with their points of views. In itself, this is misogyny (xx).

BIBLIOGRAPHY

Fetterley, Judith. *The Resisting Reader: A Feminist Approach to American Fiction*. Bloomington: Indiana University Press, 1978.

2

The Labor Strikes That Catalyzed the Revolution in Egypt

NADINE NABER

Two kinds of stories have been consolidated as predominant representations of women's activism within the Egyptian revolution in both dominant US and Egyptian corporate media discourses: (1) stories about how Egyptian women activists rose up to fight sexual harassment; and (2) stories about how Egyptian women mobilized en masse only to be pushed out of political participation afterwards (Naber and Said 2016). Mona Ezzat, labor organizer and human rights activist, points out that both cases reify the Western fixation on Egyptian women as if there is no broader context or political struggle (beyond "sexism") shaping their activism. All too often, she notes, it was as if outside commentators were exclaiming, "'Wow, the women of Egypt!' without any discussion of why they came to protest. We need a true understanding of the reality of women's lives and what brought them out to the street en masse. . . . I'm stunned by this fixation" (Ezzat 2013).

Ezzat's critique reflects the limitations of the liberal feminist lens that shapes dominant US and Egyptian discourses about Egyptian women's activism, as though their activism is simply a response to sexism. These discourses have assumed that women activists and protesters rose up to fight either against sexual violence enacted by Egyptian men or for equal political participation in official and unofficial politics. Meanwhile, these dominant stories relegate to the background the demands of the revolution for which women risked their lives—bread, dignity, and social justice—and the structural violence inflicted upon Egyptian women by neoliberalism, militarism, corruption, and authoritarianism, out of which these demands emerged.

In this chapter, I focus on the six-year period preceding the official revolution of 2011, when Egypt witnessed a series of workers' strikes wherein women were central actors. As Egyptian feminists have been doing all along, this chapter contributes to efforts committed to providing alternatives to both the liberal feminist (singular gender-based) and masculinist "unite and fight" (singular class-based) narratives by mapping the gendered socioeconomic conditions and grievances that inspired the participation of many women in the political actions that catalyzed the revolution. This chapter shows that women workers' struggles over class oppression and authoritarianism were co-constituted with struggles over gender injustice and that even when women protesters or strikers did not assert an explicitly "feminist" agenda, gender injustice and gender demands persisted. Of course, women workers' activism emerges out of the broader conditions in Egypt related to class and gender oppression, including the interrelated structures of authoritarianism, neoliberal economics, militarism, and the US's imperial alliance with Egypt, as Paul Amar (2011) and El Said, Meari, and Pratt (2015) have shown.

This chapter recognizes that, given the complex ways in which multiple oppressions have structured the lives of women workers, women involved in either the strikes of 2005–2008 or the revolution of 2011 may not have accorded all oppressions the same saliency in their activism all the time. It simultaneously acknowledges the potential dangers of attaching lesser value to different valences of oppressions (such as sexism) at different points in time. I am interested in what we can gain from reflecting back on the implicit structures of gender oppression that haunted the workers' strikes of 2005–2008, especially as they relate to dominant demands of the Egyptian labor movement, the Egyptian revolution, and the future Egypt revolutionaries have been fighting for.[1]

This study is based upon ethnographic, collaborative, and participatory research I conducted in 2012, 2013, and 2016 with twenty Egyptian women activists who participated in the revolution, have dedicated their lives to struggles for gender justice, and worked together in the coalition of revolutionary feminist organizations that formed in February 2011. Here, I focus on conversations with Mona Ezzat, a labor organizer and director of the Women and Labor Program at the New Women Foundation. Ezzat has been at the forefront of activism and research related to women workers, women's economic and social rights, and the right to organize for Egyptian women.

The Conditions of Twenty-first-century Egypt

At the turn of the twenty-first century, social movements against the interconnected forces of neoliberalism, authoritarianism, and imperialism peaked in Egypt. Spring 2005 was a key moment in this history when activists mobilized against a referendum on constitutional reform that made it impossible for candidates to run for the presidential election unless Mubarak's governing party (the National Democratic Party—NDP) permitted them to do so. Government supporters and security forces targeted women protesters, attacking their bodies and chasing them through the streets. The story of journalist Nawal Ali, attacked and nearly stripped by NDP, made international headlines—yet no one was held accountable despite protests (Slackman 2010). Such events have increasingly directed the attention of Egyptian anti-authoritarian/pro-democracy movements to the state's use of systematic gender violence. On the ground, grassroots initiatives that combine principles of both gender justice and anti-authoritarianism continued to develop (Amar 2011). During this period, women workers stood at the forefront of a series of mobilizations leading up to the revolution of 2011 (el-Hamalawy 2008). Workers' strikes between 2006 and 2011 catalyzed the official revolution of 2011 (generally understood as the eighteen days prior to the ousting of Hosni Mubarak), and women were heavily active in these strikes (El-Mahdi and Marfleet 2009; Slackman 2010). Ezzat contends that the conditions inspiring women's participation in the labor strikes of the early twenty-first century developed over the preceding thirty years:

> Egyptians have suffered from economic policies whose feature was to showcase the Egyptian market on the grounds that it had cheap labor. We witnessed the acceleration of the pace of privatization, leading to the sale of a number of factories at low prices. Government policies supported deals to sell companies and factories for profit and labor laws disadvantaged workers. These forces inspired a workers' movement, including many women. It escalated because these economic policies led to an increase in impoverishment, driving large segments of women into the labor market. The industrial sector absorbed many women workers—in spinning, weaving, pharmaceuticals, the food and electronics industries,

among others. These are the same factories whose workers opposed privatization and saw financial and administrative corruption. Numerous protests emerged, with women in large numbers. (Ezzat 2013)

By 2004, as the outcome of years of mounting frustration and struggles with bureaucracy and financial and administrative corruption in the public and private sectors, a wide movement of workers from different sectors was consolidated in Egypt. Women workers, heavily impacted by the policies Ezzat describes, were active in the major strikes of this period, as well as specific protests. They were especially active organizing within women-dominated sectors, such as nursing or education, or even the information sector, where they walked door to door collecting information and census data. She explains,

> Women and men joined protests because they were struggling with the same problems. Although the media and society were surprised women were participating in protests, their participation was a natural action. They were motivated by financial need and wanted to secure their families. They were under threat of being fired because their companies were being sold to privatization or because of corruption so women protested like men to defend their jobs and their workplace and this is a continuation of the long fight of women in the labor movement since the forties. Women were supporters and organizers. They prepared and participated in the negotiation process with the government. (Ezzat 2013)

These realities inspired mobilizations that came to be celebrated worldwide, such as those within Mahalla Spinning and Weaving textile mill in 2006, the largest industrial strike between 2004 and 2010. Mahalla Spinning and Weaving is one of the largest textile mills in the Middle East, with a labor force of twenty-seven thousand. In 2006, after a series of injustices, the company refused to grant workers a bonus the prime minister had promised to them. Egyptian police cracked down on workers who went on strike. This synopsis, composed from various interviews, represents the dominant narrative that circulated among activists in Egypt and internationally about the strike of December 7, 2006: Three thousand women garment workers left their posts. In some instances, women inspired men to join the strike. Production slowed almost to a halt. Workers rejected a twenty-one-day pay bonus from the factory management. The strike continued for two more days, reaching a total of all twenty-seven thousand workers present. On the fourth day, government officials offered a new compromise and promised a twenty-one-day bonus in addition to LE89 (equivalent to five US dollars) for each worker, one month worth of bonuses, and a half salary for January.

Many Egyptian and international activists have recognized women like labor activist Wedad Al-Damrdash. In a 2013 interview, Egyptian labor organizer (coordinator of labor communications at the Egyptian Center for Economic and Social Rights and member of the Popular Alliance Party) Dalia Moussa told me, "One of the most prominent activists in Egypt's labor movement is Wedad from Mahalla Spinning and Weaving. . . . She mobilized co-workers who feared that taking action would land them in jail." The *Washington Post* also covered Wedad's activism: "Wedad led women out of the building onto the mill grounds when the strike was supposed to begin but most men had not joined them" (Sly 2011). In Egypt and internationally, dominant narratives recognized women's labor activism not only in Mahalla, but in Asfoor, in Alexandria, and across Egypt.

While these stories identify women labor activists as "heroes" of class struggle, they obscure the gender injustices that shaped their labor activism. Stories of the Mahalla women fail to address the struggles of sexual harassment that women workers faced as they participated in public space. In an interview, Ezzat told me, "Like Mahalla, international stories have also narrated the well-known sit-in against Mansoura-Spanish Company through the story of a woman named Maryam—who played a key role inside the factory—or with references to the numerous women workers who participated in the sit-in. Mansoura-Spanish Company is in the Nile Delta province of Daqahliya, where women make up 75 percent of the labor force" (Ezzat 2013).

The tax collectors' strikes of 2007 (the largest collective of actions of the 2000s, involving fifty-five thousand real estate tax collectors employed by local authorities) have been remembered similarly (Beinin 2011). For three months, the property tax collectors went on strike to demand improvement in their working conditions. In progressive Egyptian and international discourse, the story of the tax collectors' strike tends to appear as follows:

The strike culminated in an 11-day sit-in when 8,000 tax collectors, including many women, camped out together with their children. They slept in front of the Ministers' Council building and won a 325 percent wage increase. This laid the groundwork for Egypt's first independent trade union. Women labor activists convinced their husbands they had to leave their families, fight the battle and sleep in the street even if they knew they would be beaten and arrested there. Even if their husbands did not agree, they were determined and they would go. They knew they had to go because they were getting paid 90 pounds a month and believed it was not a choice—even though they were negotiating with families to go and still had to stay on top of their housework, child-care, and so on but they were not making enough to stay alive. (el-Hamalawy 2008)

Fatma told me that Egyptian labor organizers collectively acknowledge the crucial contributions of women workers who participated in the tax collectors' strike (2013). She told me, for example, that they refer to Aisha Abu Sammad as "the amazing trade unionist"; that they acknowledge the contributions of Mervat, who, "with the land improvement workers was sleeping in the street in front of the Parliament building for many days in 2010 and standing chanting to encourage and lead her colleagues"; and that they referred to a woman from the rural Beheira area as one of "those who left her children and husband at the peak of the struggle!" (2013). Leftists and labor organizers have affirmed that women formed an important component of the matrix of forces propelling the mobilization that toppled President Hosni Mubarak in February of 2011. But feminist labor organizers like Ezzat have been insisting upon a gender analysis of women's labor and labor activism:

While women and men are struggling shoulder to shoulder, they do not have the same power in decision making. It is not only the factories, corporations, or government that are oppressing women (and men), but it is also workers (men), the unions (led by men), and the structures of family, community, and society that shape women workers' lives and work. While women participated with men, shouldn't that make her also a partner in the decision making? Here you will find them say, well, it is because her role is with the family. She is his partner as long as she is protesting and striking. They do not deny the role of the women but who will come and work with her on the issues of day care or sexual harassment or equal wages? We have a large gap in wages, up to 27 percent advantage to men! (2013).

Ezzat is referring to conditions whereby 20.2 percent of women participate in (formal) economic activities compared to 79.8 percent of men; and a gap in salaries between women and men continues to grow, despite the ways women and men came together within joint labor struggles. Official government data reveals that men workers make 13.8 percent more than women, and that women are relegated to jobs that align with patriarchal assumptions equating womanhood with mothering and home-making, including a concentration of women in the fields of education, health, and social work. Some sectors employ a particularly high number of women, such as nursing, where women workers live in what Ezzat calls "slave like conditions," including extremely low pay, discrimination in salaries, sexual harassment, an unsafe work environment, constant punishment at work such as pay deductions, long hours without overtime pay, and a lack of childcare and other crucial services (2013).

By assuming that the kinds of jobs where women work in larger numbers are "women's jobs" and therefore less important, patriarchal assumptions help to sustain the disproportionately low salaries women receive. Women are virtually nonexistent in trades such as mining and construction, and the percentage of men in managerial roles is double that of women (68.8 percent for men and 31.2 percent for women). Generally, more men occupy higher-level jobs compared to women (Ezzat 2012), and a gap in salaries exists between men and women workers for conducting the same work despite similar levels of education and experience (Shaaban 2014).

Even though women workers were not articulating gender-specific demands in their labor activism of this period and women and men workers share similar struggles, their life conditions (which inspired their actions) cannot be reduced to class struggle alone. Gender injustices such as the interconnected forces of (1) patriarchal family structures, (2) patriarchal structures at work, and (3) sexualized harassment permeate women workers' lives.

While the percentage of women working in Egypt is high, dominant family structures have marginalized the women who were involved in the major strikes of 2005–2008 in the area of decision making at home. Women workers are primarily responsible for housework in addition to their paid work. New Women Foundation is currently developing a program (started in 2010 and continuing) about the power imbalances that emerge in such contexts, calculating and balancing the time for un-paid work and protecting women working in the unofficial work sector. Women's problems as workers—from inequality in pay to the need for childcare at work—are not taken seriously, given the dominant assump-tion that women are primarily mothers. In other words, a patriarchal logic constructs the normative worker as a man (and women as moth-ers) and therefore excludes women from crucial decision making within labor activism. According to Ezzat, "When I talked to the men about women's participation in a union vote they say we cannot give women a vote as a member because she is home and cannot make a union meet-ing at night. And they act like they are being considerate to their woman comrades" (2013).

Yet while the gendered components of class struggle tended to be left out of the strikers' demands, the gendered components of class struggle were primarily responsible for a dynamic in which women's massive participation in these mobilizations often remained invisible and unrec-ognized. In a 2013 interview, labor organizer Fatma Ramadan (execu-tive board member of the Egyptian Federation of Independent Trade Unions and member of the Socialist Popular Alliance Party) told me, "Even though they are working, they are also primarily responsible for household care and childrearing. They work so many hours and then leave to do housework and deal with family commitments." Ezzat simi-larly explained,

> Because workplaces don't abide by the law and don't provide nurseries, the woman is still the one who wakes up on her own at five or six in the morning to see that her child is taken to the nursery or to her mother or neighbor. Then she turns around to go to work. Then she picks up her child and stays up all night doing housework. She is discriminated against based on the type of work she does and on the basis of gender and she often doesn't know that the law guarantees her the right to child leave,

maternity leave, nurseries, time for breastfeeding, and that she should receive equal wages. Also, even under poor working conditions and with unfair work requirements, depressed wages and [an] unstable labor market, and not having qualifications for decent work—women's work does not improve a woman's situation within her family, nor her rights within her extended family (2013).

Because the combined effects of class and gender co-constitute women workers' life conditions, men workers are more visible, because they do not have to leave strikes to return home to do housework or childrearing. An exclusive lens of class struggle limits our analyses of women's life conditions by ignoring the co-constitution of multiple oppressions that women workers in Egypt face and privileges the realities of men workers. An exclusive lens of class struggle also obscures the conditions that have prevented women from being as visible as men. Alternatively, the predominant feminist frameworks that center upon the struggles of middle-class women fail to account for the deeply intertwined conditions of gender and class oppression and do not account for the struggles of women workers.

An analysis of the gendered and sexualized underpinnings of authoritarianism and neoliberal economics that give rise to sexualized violence in Egypt is beyond the scope of my analysis. (See Amar 2011 for more information.) However, it is well established that sexualized violence in the workplace is an outgrowth of dominant ideals that equate women with motherhood and gendered conditions in the workplace. For instance, since many women workers lack stable contracts, they can be easily reprimanded or fired for reporting sexual harassment. Ezzat explains,

Because women were in the financial districts and were working without contracts, it made it very easy to fire them or face harassment from their boss or coworker. She cannot prove this and it leads to attacks against her. She is forced to remain quiet or she does not know the law and procedures she can take. This is tied to the lack of policies that would protect women at work and make them feel safe to report harassment. Sexual harassment also happens inside the government sector. But even among leftists, there is talk about government-led violence but not about the violence committed by the worker against the worker or the violence that comes out of living in poverty.

In 2013, Ezzat told me about recent efforts to establish independent unions related to gender equality in the workplace; the successful formation of childcare in particular factories; and how women's participation has increased in unions, the workplace, and political parties.[2] She explained how these efforts are taking place within a larger environment where government officials constantly refer to the role of women in economic growth projects but fail to establish policies, laws, or projects that support the distinct struggles of women workers. Discussing future visions, she said,

> What would truly shake up [authoritarianism] would be the arrival of a broad social movement made up of all the marginalized sectors of society, among the workers and the farmers, men and women, so we can build a foundation in the heart of these villages, that could truly shake up the voting blocs. I see the coming battle as a battle of economic rights and social rights, a battle for people's livelihoods, a battle for all people's wages, because we need to bring in the people who, because of the political reality, are absent. If we could draw them in on the grounds of their economic and social rights, we would be doing something very important. At the center of this are the issues of women because of the questions of justice, equality, citizenship. You can't just talk about them and exclude the rights and issues of women within them.

Conclusion

Ezzat's words capture the multidimensionality of Egyptian women workers' realities. Classism and authoritarianism are gendered, and their struggles cannot be reduced to either the struggles of women *or* the struggles of workers. Orientalist and liberal feminist paradigms, which single out women's activism in the Arab region only when it can be explained as a response to "cultural" or "religious" forms of oppression and masculinist paradigms that conceptualize the normative worker or activist as a man, do little to further women workers' struggles for social justice. But given the complex ways in which gender, class, authoritarianism, and neoliberal economics co-constitute one another, the dominant voices of the workers' strikes of 2006–2008, like the eighteen days of the revolution of 2011, did not accord all oppressions the same saliency all the time.

There is no magic formula for how much gender analysis is enough in a given context, but we must remain attentive to questions of power, history, and context. The extent to which women activists might hold each axis of power—of race, of class, of gender, and of sexuality—in view will vary depending on who we are talking about, what they are doing at the time, what the historical and political context is, what is at stake, and who their audience is. What is important is that we do not flatten our analyses of gender and/or class or make universal proclamations about either. We need flexible analyses that will vary their focus, just as different valences of power become more or less salient at different points in time. At the same time, there is a danger in ending the analysis of the saliency of oppressions here—especially since the socially inscribed gendering of women's bodies becomes more salient than ever in moments of intense violence. The point is not that priorities do not have to be selected or that postponing certain issues and agendas is not sometimes necessary and important—yet it is urgent that we carefully consider how these decisions get made, what kinds of criteria are used, and what their implications are for truly inclusive social movements and meanings of freedom.

NOTES

1 See, for example, the position paper Egyptian feminists wrote, insisting on the interconnections between sexualized violence and state violence in Egypt: "Position Paper on Sexual Violence against Women and the Increasing Frequency of Gang Rape in Tahrir Square and Its Environs," Nazra for Feminist Studies, Nazra, February 4, 2013, http://nazra.org.

2 "New Woman Foundation Congratulates Faraj Allah Company's Workers Union Success on Providing Nursery," New Woman Foundation, http://nwrcegypt.org.

BIBLIOGRAPHY

Amar, Paul. 2011. "Turning the Gendered Politics of the Security State inside Out? Charging the Police with Sexual Harassment in Egypt." *International Feminist Journal of Politics* 13, no. 3: 299–328.

Beinin, Joel. 2011. "Egypt at the Tipping Point?" *Foreign Policy*, January 31, https://foreignpolicy.com.

el-Hamalawy, Hossam. 2008. "Egypt's Tax Collectors and the Fight for Independent Trade Unions." *Socialist Review*, http://socialistreview.org.uk (accessed May 12, 2015).

El-Mahdi and Philip Marfleet, eds. 2009. *Egypt: The Moment of Change*. Chicago: University of Chicago Press.

El Said, Maha, Lena Meari, and Nicola Pratt. 2015. *Rethinking Gender in Revolutions and Resistance: Lessons from the Arab World*. London: Zed.

Ezzat, Mona. 2012. "Economic and Social Rights of Women in Egypt." In *Arab Watch on Economic and Social Rights*. Beirut: Arab NGO Network for Development, http://www.annd.org (accessed June 25, 2016).

———. 2013. Conversation with Nadine Naber, December 20. New Woman Foundation, Cairo, Egypt.

Moussa, Dalia. 2013. Conversation with Nadine Naber, December 6. Egyptian Center for Economic and Social Rights, Cairo, Egypt.

Naber, Nadine, and Atef Said. 2016. "The Cry for Human Rights: Violence, Transition, and the Egyptian Revolution." *Humanity: An International Journal of Human Rights, Humanitarianism, and Development* 7, no. 1 (Spring): 71–90.

Ramadan, Fatma. 2013. Conversation with Nadine Naber, December 6. Egyptian Center for Economic and Social Rights, Cairo, Egypt.

Shaaban, Adel. 2014. "Employment Policies from the Gender Perspective of Women and Employment in the Formal Sector." New Woman Foundation, http://nwrce-gypt.org (accessed June 25, 2016).

Slackman, Michael. 2010. "Labor Protests Test Egypt's Government." *New York Times*, April 28, http://www.nytimes.com (accessed May 12, 2015).

Sly, Liz. 2011. "An Act of Courage That Launched a Revolution." *Washington Post*, December 30, http://www.washingtonpost.com (accessed May 12, 2015).

3

From a Smear Campaign to the Kuwaiti Parliament

My Resolve Persists Despite Rumors

ASEEL ALAWADHI

Translated by Samyah Alfoory

In her 2009 race for the Kuwaiti Parliament, Aseel Alawadhi was accused of opposing Islam and the veil. With a PhD from the United States, Alawadhi was a political philosophy professor at Kuwait University who taught critical thinking. The scandal, referred to as "Fadihat Aseel Alawadhi," was based on amalgamated clips from her lectures to female students in which she appeared to argue that a well-known interpretation of the Quranic verse on the veil was applicable to the Prophet's wives rather than to all women. Six days before the elections, Aseel gave the following interview to journalist Bushra Al-Zain.[1]

Why was the YouTube accusation held against you and what's your reaction?

Election campaigns rarely happen without rumors. Many result from misunderstandings and misinterpretations, but the YouTube campaign was an organized and deliberate rumor leveled against me. This premeditated action violated the university rules and used three different segments from my lectures to frame me as urging students to drop the veil. In my lectures, I try to compel students to think about a range of views on a particular subject and consider contexts that give rise to one particular view over others. I propose ideas to my classes to stimulate their thinking. I take certain phenomena and apply them to a concept to stimulate a friendly and fun discussion. I think that overall these accusations are immoral, stemming from a misunderstanding of the democratic process. We are not in a state of war in which our ethical standards are being abandoned. As one community, of brothers and sisters, we agree and disagree.

I was very dismayed by this smear campaign. The focus of the election should be on my competence to reach Parliament, not my lectures. We have many more urgent issues impacting our nation and its citizens that must be prioritized. Citizens who embrace reform expect me to defend their issues as their representative, and they care less about my attitude towards the hijab. With these altercations, we, as politicians, send the wrong message to our citizens indicating that we are removed from their concerns and are only interested in battling each other. Efforts put into the YouTube video would have been better spent being directed towards finding solutions for the difficulties facing Kuwaitis' everyday life. This type of political action, which is beneath us, explains the poor services from which people suffer nationwide.

Are you leading students to abandon Kuwaiti society's conservative principles?

As much as anyone else, I am embedded in my conservative family and society. Yet, as a philosophy professor, I believe teaching critical thinking is fundamental at every educational level. Kuwait needs people to think critically in order to contribute to our national development. Learning is not merely regurgitating what's known, but rather questioning and examining knowledge in a critical manner, and understanding the reasoning and evidence that support each viewpoint. During Kuwait's Golden Era, we had freedom of thought and were an enlightened culture—two elements that go hand in hand to achieve development. We have since had waves of governance that impose restrictive ideologies, repress others, paralyze civil society and the Parliament, and produce a generation that is unreceptive to others' views. Because we have become a fertile ground for fanaticism, our social progress has been halted. This is why I try to push students in critical thinking courses to use their minds, to justify their opinions with logical reasoning, and to refrain from attacking each other. In these discussions, numbers and research are essential. Teaching students in this way does not challenge traditions and customs but serves them. Repressing freedom of expression is the real challenge to our society whereas the solution lies in strengthening our critical thinking skills.

Were you victimized because of your education?

I began my college education in architecture but later chose philosophy in order to answer the many questions I have had since childhood. In my academic experience, I was surprised to see students interested in gossip more than logic, and allegations over facts. My specialization in philosophy refined my character and taught me wisdom. My silence during the negative campaigns was the result of self-discipline and logical thinking. I truly believe that in disagreements there is progress and I am now more tolerant and accepting of others' views.

Are you "Americanized," as they accuse you?

Anyone in Kuwait who offers different ideas is labeled "Americanized." I do not imitate other cultures or people. I choose what works for me and discard what does not, according to my convictions, which I form according to logical reasoning. In my lectures, I purposely speak positively about the West because I want my students to learn about this world's progress. Embracing other cultures does not mean that I reject our great heritage. But we need to be realistic. In previous eras, our civilizations were more progressive. Specifically, we had freedom of thought that was fostered and knowledge was shared, translated, and produced. However, we have fallen behind in science, technology, weaponry, education, and human rights. Acknowledging this does not mean that we underestimate ourselves. But we must be honest about our own reality and willing to change it—this is why they say I'm "Americanized."

Is your hope to enter Parliament broken by these rumors?

Women have been absent from political life in Kuwait for a long period. Now, we have a legacy of this exclusively male practice and I refuse to accept women's continuous absence. Since the beginning of the election, I have encountered several rumors and ignored them. Some use the fact that I am not veiled as a basis for accusing me of being against

Islam and the hijab. These accusations aim to dissuade my religious supporters from voting for me. Others use my education in the United States to dissuade educated and open-minded Kuwaitis by appealing to their position against American dominance over Arab countries. In my doctoral thesis, I criticized American interference in the region, especially in regards to governance. Others refuse to allow women into the Parliament and attempt to undermine the role of women in politics in general. And of course, there are some Parliament members who fear losing their seat to someone who is more qualified than they; therefore, having a PhD could be perceived as a threat to them. My priorities are clear towards Kuwaiti voters. My first and most important concern is being a voice for Kuwaiti citizens in the halls of Parliament.

NOTE

1   A 2009 interview with *Al-Anbaa* Kuwaiti newspaper.

4

Palestinian Queerness and the Orientalist Paradigm

AMAL AMIREH

The intersectionality between queer studies on the one hand and the (neo-)orientalist vis-à-vis postcolonial studies on the other frames the debate about queer issues in the Middle East in two paradigms: universal and local. The first understands queer Middle Eastern identities as an expression of a universal gay identity that is progressing toward full expression, with the West as its model; the second understands them as products of local cultures and histories, which sets them apart from Western expressions of gayness. While these paradigms have been used to study queerness in other non-Western societies, they have been particularly crippling when applied to the Middle East. They inevitably have become enmeshed with the (neo-)orientalist and colonialist discourses that still dominate discussions of Arab and Muslim sexualities and, to a lesser extent, with the anticolonial discourses that resist them.

Focusing on queer issues as they relate to Palestine/Israel, we must be well aware of the colonialist context within which the discourse about sexuality is deployed. As Gil Hochberg states, we must "situate questions regarding LGBTQ rights, homophobia, and sexual policing, in direct relation to questions concerning the ethnonational and colonial politics that currently define the relationship between Israel and its occupied Palestinian population" (2010, 495). Indeed, "discussions of queerness (and sexual politics more extensively) are essential for our understanding of national movements, colonial oppression, new technologies of state surveillance, and new modes of racial/ethnic/religious segregation" (Hochberg 2010, 495). In fact, queer sexualities, as both discourses and practices, are entangled, in the context of the Palestine-Israel conflict, with colonialism and nationalism in fundamental and complex ways that cannot be ignored. The rest of this essay elaborates on some of these entanglements.

Palestinian Queers: Now You See Them, Now You Don't . . .

The visibility of Palestinian queers in Israeli discourse is determined by Israel's colonial project, the core of which is the denial of Palestinian national rights. In Israeli discourse and consciousness, Palestinian queers occupy two extreme locations: either they are hypervisible or they are invisible. In both cases, it is their Palestinianness, not their queerness, that determines whether and how they are seen, as illustrated in the two examples below.

In 2004, the Zionist Organization of America helped the Georgetown Israeli Alliance bring a Palestinian man to speak at the Georgetown campus. Hiding behind a wig, sunglasses, and a fake mustache, "Ali" claimed he was a gay Palestinian and spoke about the difficulties that he faced as a gay man in Palestinian society. But that was only part of his mission. He went on to sing the praises of the Israeli state as a haven for gay rights and to elaborate, as a good native informant, on the cultural differences between the repressive Palestinians and the liberal Israelis regarding homosexuality (Tehranian 2004). Ali's performance should be seen as one more in a long line of staged performances, where "others" are exhibited to propagandize for a colonial, racist agenda. Coming at the height of the Israeli repression of the Al Aqsa Intifada, Ali's cultural performance had one purpose only, which was to discredit the Palestinian people and their culture at a time when they were under assault by the Israeli military machine.

However, this hypervisibility turns into invisibility when another Palestinian queer demands to speak. As Hochberg shows (2010a, 2010b), during the Tel Aviv demonstration to protest the homophobic killing of two young gay Israelis, Palestinians were denied the right to speak. Both the former Knesset member Issam Makhoul and a representative of Aswat, a lesbian Palestinian organization, were not allowed to address the crowd on their own terms. According to some reports, the organizers felt that "they could not go so far," and as a result, on that day, no Palestinians were visible on the national stage (Nisreen and Dayna 2009). Those queer Palestinians demanding to speak were not the gay Palestinians the Israeli establishment likes to parade around. They do not present themselves as victims of Palestinian culture but as activists articulating a queer political agenda that is, simultaneously, anticolonial, antiracist, and antihomophobic.

Alisa Solomon (2010, 153) charts the altered value of queerness for the state of Israel. "In today's Israeli culture war," she notes, "queerness—or at least the tolerance of queerness—has acquired a new rhetorical value for mainstream Zionism: standing against the imposition of fundamentalist religious law, it has come to stand for democratic liberalism." The positive rhetorical function of queerness for Zionism, however, goes beyond those internal culture wars (between secular Jews and religious Jews) into the wider culture wars between Israelis and Palestinians, where it functions to consolidate a fractured Zionist consensus by casting Palestinians as the ultimate "Other" for their alleged essentialist homophobia.

Does the Palestinian Queer Exist?

And Can She Speak?

Palestinian queerness exists, but its discourses and practices are entangled in the context of colonialism, nationalism, religion, and patriarchy. Let me illustrate through using lessons from two Palestinian queer groups, Aswat and Al-Qaws. As explained on its website, Aswat is "a group of lesbian, bisexual, transgender, intersex, questioning and queer Palestinian women that came together in 2002 and established a home for Palestinian LBTQI women to allow safe, supportive and empowering spaces to express and address their personal, social and political struggles as a national indigenous minority living inside Israel; as women in a patriarchal society; and as LBTQI women in a wider hetero-normative culture." Alternatively, Al-Qaws for Sexual & Gender Diversity in Palestinian Society is a grassroots group, formed in November 2007 to create what its website describes as "a sustainable, visible, and truly impactful Palestinian LGBTQ movement that focuses on fostering the unity of the Palestinian LGBTQ community; connecting the local/global, anti-colonial, and queer feminist; and defying borders created by Israeli occupation." While Aswat's approach centers on advancing lesbian women's rights and empowering them, Al-Qaws has adopted a universalist queer activism agenda that transcends political, ideological, and social divisions.

Three major challenges restrict Palestinian queer women from setting their own discourse. The first challenge to forging a queer Palestinian agenda is the context of occupation and racism. Al-Qaws refuses to prioritize the issue of nationalism over the issue of advancing the rights of Palestinian queers living between Israel, the West Bank, Gaza, and sometimes the diaspora. As a political choice dictated by the lived realities of Palestinian queers, Al-Qaws's approach is the best alternative to the "prioritizing model" of struggle that has dominated the Palestinian national movement for decades and that had crippled the progressive forces within this movement. As a consequence of this prioritizing paradigm, leftist and women's groups could not forge a connection between what they called a "social agenda" and "a national agenda." Issues relating to sexuality, for instance, were meant to be dealt with after (national) liberation. Despite its youth, Al-Qaws, in my opinion, has already much to teach the more established Palestinian women's movement and leftist groups.

Another challenge facing Palestinian queer organizations is that of building a safe community where LGBTQ Palestinians can grow personally and politically. Again, homophobia and patriarchy are only part of the story—almost the easy part, as Samira Saraya explains: "For a Palestinian lesbian citizen of Israel, it will likely take a lot of maneuvering for her to successfully attend one of Aswat's meetings; for a lesbian living in the West Bank this 'mission' is almost impossible, and for the one in Gaza, it is not even remotely conceivable" (Hochberg 2010b, 610). But despite this fragmentation, both Aswat and Al-Qaws include members who live in Israel, the West Bank, and Gaza. In and of itself, that is an important political achievement that insists on Palestinianness as a primary category of identification.

The community Aswat and Al-Qaws create by being "out"—in the political sense—is crucial for loosening the grip that the trope "homosexuality as collaboration" has on Palestinian society. One Palestinian queer activist told me that the main reason for his decision to return to the West Bank and not continue his graduate studies abroad was Al-Qaws' decision to work in Ramallah. Although this is an individual story, I do believe it reflects the difference local queer Palestinian activism is already making and has the potential to make.

The third challenge, which is particularly frustrating, is that these queer activists have to contend with accusations that they are embracing an "inauthentic" identity that is foreign to Arab and Muslim culture. It is not that such accusations are anything new. Palestinian (and Arab) feminists and leftists had always to justify themselves against charges launched at them by Islamists and conservative nationalists that their ideologies, lifestyles, and political agendas are marks of contamination by either an imperialist West or a communist East.

The newness of these queer organizations, the small number of members, and their NGO status in some cases have been used against them to discredit their rootedness, relevance, and loyalties. They have been seen as tools of what Joseph Massad (2007) calls the "Gay International" that seeks to impose a heterosexual-homosexual regime on the Middle East as the continuation of the colonial, orientalist project in the area. For Palestinian queers, the Gay International, if relevant at all, is much less relevant than the realities of occupation, racism, and homophobia with which they have to contend daily. Yet, scholars like Joseph Massad (2007) are unable to see anticolonial queer Arab activists outside the orientalism paradigm.

The Misapplication of Orientalism

I contend that positions such as Massad's are a misapplication of models drawn from Michel Foucault's *History of Sexuality* (1984) and Edward Said's *Orientalism* (1978). As David Halperin (1998) reminds us, when Foucault wrote about the invention of the "homosexual," he was "speaking about discursive and institutional practices, not about what people really did in bed or what they thought about it. He was not attempting to describe popular attitudes or private emotions, much less is he presuming to convey what actually went on in the minds of different historical subjects when they had sex" (97). The accusations that Arab gays are inauthentic and that the "homosexual" is an "invention of the West" tend to collapse the differences between Arab and Western discourses, practices, ideas, and emotions. Yes, there is a Western discourse that invents the Arab homosexual as a victim of her culture, but that does not mean that all those who identify as gay, lesbian, or queer are "inventions."

The desire to defend against orientalism as the dominant paradigm by which the West represents the East has encouraged the privileging of orientalism as the main paradigm by which we seek to understand what is happening in the Arab world. It is important to remember that

Said never claimed his book had anything to say about the lived realities of Arabs or Palestinians. Again, like Foucault, he was dealing with discourses and representations, specifically, Western ones. What I am calling the orientalism paradigm privileges the power of the West's discourse to a degree that obscures resistances to this discourse, other competing discourses, and material realities.

Edward Said was well aware of the misuses of orientalism in the context of the Arab world (Hafez 2004). Perhaps he had these misuses in mind when he wrote, "All cultures are involved in one another; none is single and pure, all are hybrid, heterogeneous, extraordinarily differentiated and unmonolithic. This, I believe, is as true of the contemporary United States as it is of the modern Arab world" (Said 1994, xxix). I would suggest keeping these words in mind when we debate issues of identity, authenticity, and culture in relation to queer issues in the Arab world.

BIBLIOGRAPHY

Foucault, Michel. 1984. *History of Sexuality*. Paris: Gallimard.

Hafez, Sabry. 2004. "Edward Said's Intellectual Legacy in the Arab World." *Journal of Palestine Studies* 33, no. 3 (Spring): 76–90.

Halperin, David M. 1998. "Forgetting Foucault: Acts, Identities, and the History of Sexuality." *Representations*, no. 63 (Summer): 93–120.

Hochberg, Gil Z. 2010a. "Introduction: Israelis, Palestinians, Queers: Points of Departure." *GLQ: A Journal of Lesbian and Gay Studies* 16, no. 4: 493–516.

———. 2010b. "No Pride in Occupation: A Roundtable Discussion." *GLQ: A Journal of Lesbian and Gay Studies* 16, no. 4: 599–610.

Massad, Joseph. 2007. *Desiring Arabs*. Chicago: University of Chicago Press.

Nisreen and Dayna. 2009. "Palestinian Gays under the Hijab." *Aswat*. http://joannestle. blogspot.com/2009/08/palestinian-gays-under-hijab-by-nisreen.html (accessed July 2018).

Said, Edward. 1978. *Orientalism*. New York: Pantheon.

———. 1994. *Culture and Imperialism*. New York: Vintage.

Solomon, Alison. 2010. "Viva la Diva Citizenship: Post-Zionism and Gay Rights." In *Queer Theory and the Jewish Question*, ed. Daniel Boyarin, Daniel Itzkovitz, and Ann Pellegrini, 149–65. New York: Columbia University Press.

Tehranian, Alex. 2004. "Gay Man Criticizes Palestinian Society." Gay and Lesbian Archives of the Pacific Northwest, October 22, http://www.glapn.org.

5

"With All My Force . . ."

Men against Domestic Violence in Lebanon

LINA ABIRAFEH AND GHIDA ANANI

Arab men are rising to the challenge as advocates against violence in society and at home. ABAAD (أبعاد—"dimensions" in Arabic) began promoting men's role in eliminating violence through creative audiovisual material, created by men themselves. In these audiovisual advocacy materials, men and boys are not only the subject matter and target audience; they are also the producers. It goes without saying that messages are more likely to resonate with men if they are created *by* men.

As a resource center for gender equality based in Lebanon and serving the Middle East and North Africa, ABAAD aims to inspire men and boys to champion women's empowerment and to end violence. To this end, we have undertaken campaigns, studies, and programs that build on indigenous understandings of gender issues and engage males in a positive, proactive manner. We have learned that blaming and shaming does little to bring women and men together. Rather, ABAAD seeks to engage men and boys as equals.

In October 2011, we organized "With all my force. . . . against violence," a nationwide campaign driven by men, for men. Through advertisements on TV, YouTube, billboards, newspapers, flyers, posters, text messages, and awareness-raising activities, this campaign supported men who, like their female counterparts, refuse to remain silent about violence against women and gender inequalities in Lebanon. This media campaign began Lebanon's revolutionary journey towards using positive psychology to foster male allies in the fight for women's rights and to justify framing these rights as human rights and in terms of equality for all. The campaign portrays men not exclusively as perpetrators but also as partners whose engagement is critical to ending intimate partner violence—and violence against women more broadly.

Recognizing that change should start early, we began training Lebanese youth on gender equality, masculinities, and filmmaking. Participants who expressed interest in using media for equality applied for the training. We selected sixteen through a competitive process and trained participants on gender issues, including understanding masculinities and femininities and how they manifested in inequality. The young men produced and acted in these advertisements, which aired on Lebanese national television throughout the 16 Days of Activism to End Violence against Women in November. In December 2011, they were featured in ABAAD's "Beating Is Shameful" campaign. This campaign was influential not just in its message but also in its messengers: men who crafted and delivered a message targeted towards other men.

The media campaign led to the creation of a Men's Center, a space where men receive free, anonymous, individual counseling and support and participate in workshops and events, such as the multimedia advertising campaign against violence. As a joint venture between ABAAD and the International Medical Corps (IMC), the center began to offer help to young men and to address issues of violence in their homes and communities. Participants self-identify the causes of violence in the home, and use this experience as a launch pad to address communication and behavior and, ultimately, nonviolent problem-solving strategies. The center helps these young men build healthy relationships and contributes to building a healthy society. By letting participants select the issues they wish to address, ABAAD gives them ownership of sustainable solutions. The Men's Center is being promoted as part of a nationwide media campaign entitled "We are willing—and here—to listen." And it is working.

Building on these gains and to inform their continued efforts, ABAAD, in partnership with the IMC, launched a nationwide study in 2012 on perceptions of masculinity and domestic violence. One thousand Lebanese women and men of various religious and social backgrounds participated in this study and helped us identify how women and men perceive their gender roles and what ideas of masculinities guide this understanding. This groundbreaking research also set out to determine the extent of knowledge of violence against women and to see what role men believed they have in ending violence against women. As the first of its kind in Lebanon, this study revealed that change is underway. Men's perceptions of gender roles have become more flexible. They no longer view women's roles as limited to giving birth, raising children, and performing household tasks. Thus, Lebanese women have gained considerable power in terms of household decision making and in gainful employment in various fields. Their increased financial independence has opened doors for change both inside and outside the home. Moreover, perceptions of masculinity by both women and men have been transformed; while old perceptions of masculinity were widely associated with being firm and violent, these aspects no longer achieve significant rankings in modern understandings of masculinities. Respondents viewed masculine traits in terms of having a decisive and confident personality, personal values, and an ability to generate harmony in relationships. They expressed that masculinities are characterized by good communication skills, which are necessary to foster an environment of understanding. Including communication skills as a trait of masculinity reveals an interest in opting for peaceful resolution to conflict rather than force or coercion. These understandings are shared to a large extent by both females and males in Lebanon.

In 2012, ABAAD took a unique approach to activism by soliciting Muslim and Christian religious leaders to condemn violence against women in what became the "We Believe. . . . Partners to End Violence against Women" campaign. We asked religious leaders to cite holy texts to promote a culture of respect for the dignity of women, rejecting all forms of violence and condemning violence as sacrilege. Given the significance of religion in the Lebanese history of surviving conflict, partnership with these religious men brought a new dimension to ending violence against women, especially when they all agreed to become voices for Lebanese women of all faiths. They consented to highlight how all religions agree that all women are entitled to a life of dignity free from violence. This campaign inspired vast dimensions of solidarity and support. In this way, ABAAD explored new dimensions of activism and continued to redefine the positive ways men can be engaged in advocating for positive change for Lebanon and beyond.

6

"Ne Touche Pas Mes Enfants!"

A Woman's Campaign against Pedophilia in Morocco

GINGER FEATHER

Twelve years ago, Najia Adib broke the silence on pedophilia in Morocco after her own three-year-old child was abused while at his nursery school. Adib grew suspicious when her son stopped wanting to go to school and she later discovered semen on his underwear. She took the clothing to the Royal Gendarmerie for testing, and the DNA analysis linked the semen to the school director, who confessed to molesting multiple children during his eighteen years at the school. Despite the director's confession and the evidence against him, the judge sentenced him to only two years in prison. Angry at the lenient decision, Adib exposed the scandal in the media and knocked on many doors until the sentence was eventually increased to eight years. Adib was the only parent to speak out and was shocked to learn that no national association existed in Morocco to defend the victims of child sexual abuse. Resolved to raise awareness of the problem of pedophilia, help victims pursue justice through the legal system, and advocate for tougher sentencing for predators, she founded Don't Touch My Child in 2004 and Don't Touch My Children for Child Protection in 2006. In 2010 the Arab League recognized Adib as the first Muslim Arab woman to speak out against child rape, and appointed her as ambassador of the Arab child for her efforts in the fight to end sexual violence against children at the national and international levels.

Speaking out against pedophilia has been taboo in Moroccan society, and cases are frequently dismissed. In general, victims of sexual abuse are hesitant to come forward due to fear of reprisal, guilt, and shame, according to Meriam Othmani, former president of the Casablanca-based National Institute of Solidarity with Women in Distress (INSAF) ("La Lutte"

2011). Moroccans view the loss of virginity among unmarried girls—even in rape cases—as a social stigma that dishonors the entire family. Although rape is a criminal offense with tough penalties, according to Article 486 of the Moroccan penal code, Article 475 had been an escape clause for rapists because, until its repeal in 2014, it allowed families and judges to force girls to marry the accused rapist in order to restore the family honor. The ramifications of this law came to the forefront in 2012 with the case of Amina Filali. Amina was raped at fifteen by a twenty-three-year-old assailant and was later forced to marry him. Continuing to be abused by her now husband, Amina took her own life by drinking rat poison and dying in the street. Public outrage and massive demonstrations over her suicide demanded a change to article 475, and the article was amended on January 23, 2014, to allow the victim greater voice in the decision of whether or not to marry the alleged rapist.

Pedophilia is also a taboo topic because child sexual abuse is often a crime close to home in that family members, family friends, or neighbors are often the perpetrators. The World Health Organization indicates that, worldwide, 90 percent of child sexual abusers are parents, teachers, family friends, or mentors. Likewise, 75 percent of child sexual abuse victims in Morocco are assaulted by a family member, according to the Moroccan-based Coalition Against Sexual Abuse of Children (COCASSE) spokesman Khalid Cherkaoui Semmouni ("La Lutte" 2011). As a result, families are hesitant to prosecute their own members and therefore never officially report the crime. These families often ignore the Moroccan penal code, which was reformed in 2003 and clearly protects the rights of children. Articles 484, 485, and 486 stipulate that the sexual assault of an adult using violence or the rape of an adult carries a five- to ten-year sentence, while similar crimes against a child carry a ten- to twenty-year sentence. It is noteworthy that rape is narrowly defined in the 2003 Moroccan penal code as "the act by which a man has sex with a woman against the will of the latter."

Adib contends that the laws themselves are not the problem. Instead, the problem lies with the judges who do not fully apply the laws. In the case of the Hay Riad district in Rabat, a pedophile had raped two children and was released without a conviction or sentence because his sobs at the hearing moved the judge to leniency (Jazouani 2013). In May 2012, a man received a three-year sentence for raping two young sisters although the maximum sentence for the rape of a minor is up to twenty years ("Morocco Jails Rapist" 2012).

In terms of sexual violence against children, Adib estimates that seventy-one child sexual abuse cases are reported daily to authorities; however, the Ministry of Social Development officially registered only ninety-four cases in 2008 ("Najia Adib" 2010). This discrepancy is the result of families deciding not to continue with legal proceedings against the accused. Adib advocates for the victims' families, helping them pursue criminal charges against those accused of the crimes and ensuring that perpetrators are prosecuted and held accountable (Adib 2013). In May 2012, Maryam bin al-Shaikh was raped and killed by a shopkeeper in Mohamedia. The shopkeeper then put her body in a refrigerator and later cut her up and scattered her remains in an attempt to avoid detection. Adib attended al-Shaikh's funeral and organized public demonstrations to ensure that the shopkeeper was brought to justice (Jazouani 2012).

Child predation is a more recent systemic phenomenon that plagues Morocco. In 2003, UNICEF estimated that in Marrakech, which is known for its tourist influx, 71 percent of the customers of child prostitutes were Moroccans while 29 percent were foreign tourists or foreigners residing in Morocco ("La Lutte" 2011). More recently, high-profile child sexploitation cases in Morocco have involved Europeans as the perpetrators, underscoring that this issue may involve global systemic factors that make Morocco more susceptible to such illicit activity (Hofmann 2013; "Morocco Jails British Pedophile" 2014).

In August 2013, in Kenitra, Spanish national Daniel Galvan was convicted of abusing eleven children and in an unprecedented court decision received a thirty-year prison sentence. Adib went to court with several of Galvan's victims and helped them prepare their cases against Galvan. Human rights advocates celebrated this ruling across Morocco until Galvan received a royal pardon along with forty-seven other Spanish prisoners following a visit of Spanish king Juan Carlos. This reversal sparked public outrage that sexual predators could commit their crime with impunity in Morocco; the pardon was later revoked, a first in Morocco, and Galvan is serving the remainder of his sentence in Spain (Alami 2013).

Part of the increase in child predation in Morocco may be due to the traditionally lighter sentencing of those convicted of crimes against children. In addition, legal reforms in European countries have also heightened Morocco's risk of becoming a safe haven for pedophilia, child predation, prostitution, and human trafficking. Many European countries are passing stricter laws against the johns, pimps, and traffickers, forcing European sexual predators to move south to commit their crimes. Adib's advocacy raised public awareness and outrage, provoking demonstrations to stop toleration of these crimes in Morocco.

Adib contends that Morocco lacks the political will to address the problem of pedophilia adequately, allowing financial and legal constraints to persist. The problem of pedophilia is not adequately addressed by the Moroccan government, from whom Adib's organization receives minimal funding. Aicha Ech-Channa's Association Feminine Solidarity in Casablanca, however, received a donation from the monarchy for helping and housing unwed mothers, a group often ostracized by their families and shunned by society. "Without adequate resources, all we do is yell in the streets," insists Adib (2013).

Adib identifies overnight shelters or safe houses for victims of pedophilia as an urgent need. Harboring a married woman, even someone escaping abuse, was a criminal offense based on Article 496, which Parliament repealed in 2013. As a consequence, before this article was repealed, Adib cites a case in which a mother sued her husband for abusing their child, but while waiting for the court date, they had no place to go because no legal provisions existed to remove the child from the family home. Hence, the victim was forced to remain living under the same roof as the accused abuser.

As Adib confronts pedophilia in Morocco, she criticizes the lack of rehabilitation and monitoring of convicted pedophiles, who are simply released into society after serving their prison sentence. Adib argues that since many pedophiles were themselves the victims of sexual abuse, rehabilitation and preventive measures are needed to break the cycle and reduce the chances of recurrence.

Najia Adib's activism has lifted the taboo against speaking of pedophilia, and has raised public awareness among Moroccans that silence does not provide immunity to such crimes but rather inhibits prevention. Adib has worked tirelessly for the victims of such crimes and their families, for adequate application of existing laws against sexual predation on children, and for the proper rehabilitation and monitoring of pedophiles.

Sadly, Adib learned that the pedophile who had molested her child was released in 2013 without rehabilitation, probation or monitoring, and has opened a daycare center in another town under a slightly different name (Adib 2015). Pedophilia being a problem that affects not only Morocco but all societies at all socioeconomic levels, Adib believes that much work remains to convince Morocco and the world to view pedophilia as a cycle of abuse and to change the legal and structural barriers to break this vicious cycle.

BIBLIOGRAPHY

Adib, Najia. July 1, 2013. Personal interview with author in Rabat, Morocco.

———. June 1, 2015. Personal interview with author in Rabat, Morocco.

Alami, Aida. 2013. "Moroccans Protest Pedophile Pardon." Al Jazeera, August 3, https://www.aljazeera.com (accessed October 9, 2015).

Hoffman, Pauline. 2013. "Un pédophile français avait déjà été gracié au Maroc." Franceinfo, August 5, https://www.francetvinfo.fr (accessed October 9, 2015).

Jazouani, Hanane. 2012. "Je demande la peine de mort pour les violeurs d'enfants!" Yabiladi, May 18, http://www.yabiladi.com (accessed October 7, 2015).

———. 2013. "Projet de loi sur la pédophilie au Maroc: 'Ce sont les juges qui ont besoin d'être jugés!'" Yabiladi, January 17, https://www.yabiladi.com (accessed October 7, 2015).

"La Lutte contre la Traite des Personnes." 2011. Conseil National des Droits de l'Homme. Avis du CNDH sur le projet de loi N° 27–14, https://www.cndh.org.ma (accessed July 5, 2018).

"Morocco Jails British Pedophile for 20 Years." 2014. Al Arabiya, English edition, April 15, http://english.alarabiya.net (accessed October 9, 2015).

"Morocco Jails Rapist of Two Minor Sisters for 3 Years, Verdict Slammed as Too Soft." 2012. Al Arabiya, English edition, May 18, https://english.alarabiya.net (accessed October 10, 2015).

"Najia Adib Élue Ambassadrice de L'enfance Arabe." 2010. L'Opinion, January 4, http://www.lopinion.ma (accessed May 30, 2015).

Tennent, James. 2013. "Moroccans Are Sick of Their Country's Pedophile Problem." Vice, September 3, https://www.vice.com (accessed October 9, 2015).

7

Two Nonviolence Campaigns Initiated by Women in Syria

MOHJA KAHF

Among the activities that women initiated in the Syrian revolution are the "Stop the Killing" campaign of 2012 and the "Brides of Freedom" stand on November 21, 2012. To assess the significance of these two campaigns promoting nonviolent resistance, I seek to understand their context within a specific phase of the Syrian revolution. While in 2011 nonviolent protest was the norm, the consensus for nonviolence had disintegrated by 2012 among the grassroots protesters of the Syrian revolution. The militarized struggle left little room for nonviolent protest. Literally, streets where peaceful protests had occurred became battle zones. Further, while protesters had initially organized on the basis of civic unity across religions and sects, by early 2012 the Syrian revolution witnessed the rise of Islamist extremists. Both militarization and Islamist radicalization marginalized women activists. These developments also increased the influence of foreign powers in the revolution, further marginalizing Syrian activism. The "Stop the Killing" and "Brides of Freedom" campaigns worked uphill to reinvigorate the central role of women, boost local participation, and reassert Syrian agency in the revolution. Led by women from religious minority groups, these campaigns reaffirmed the nonsectarian civic unity of the initial protest movement. The "Stop the Killing" and "Brides of Freedom" campaigns revived, for a brief but significant moment, the values and methods of the initial protest movement begun in Syria in 2011.

Stop the Killing

The "Stop the Killing" campaign commenced on April 8, 2012, with a one-woman stand by thirty-two-year-old lawyer Rima Dali.[1] Dressed in a red raincoat, she held a large red banner at an intersection near the Parliament building in Damascus. White lettering on her banner said, "Stop the Killing, We Want to Build a Nation for All Syrians." A security agent who accosted Rima asked her, "Which side are you on?" Rima declined to answer, except to say, "I am a Syrian" (Ghadbian and Thiong 2014). Given that all nouns are gendered in Arabic, she was also saying, "I am a Syrian woman."

Between April and July 2012, twenty-six events in the "Stop the Killing" campaign swept Syria, mobilized by activists supportive of Rima's initial stand.[2] These activists spread the campaign through an underground network of grassroots civil resistance groups formed in the early months of the Syrian revolution. Despite the regime's detentions and bombardments, many of these civil resistance groups continued to exist and communicate with one another. Several "Stop the Killing" planning meetings were conducted on Skype, including one that I was permitted to attend. "Stop the Killing" signs flew that spring and summer of 2012 in Aleppo, Kurdish areas in north Syria, south in Suwayda, a historically Druze minority area, as well as in Tal and Douma.[3] Activists held a "Stop the Killing" street theater at City Mall in Kafr Soussa in which two women and two men lay on the ground representing civilians killed by the regime's lethal fire on nonviolent protesters, killings that had become a regular occurrence in Syria since March 2011.[4]

The Brides of Freedom

In the "Brides of Freedom" March, four women dressed in wedding gowns entered Medhat Pasha market in Damascus at midday on November 21, 2012.[5] The "Brides" silently displayed red banners with white words. Two women held the large middle banner, which said, "For the sake of Syrian human beings, civil society declares, stop all military operations in Syria. 100% Syrian." Signs on the left and right, each held by one woman, respectively, read, "You're tired. We're tired. We all want to live. 100% Syrian"; and "Syria is for all of us. 100% Syrian."[6] With an associate surreptitiously filming, the four "Brides" soon were accosted by security personnel.[7] They were imprisoned for forty-nine days, until January 9, 2013, subjected to subhuman conditions typical of Syria's detention system.[8] Videos of their stand were uploaded almost

Figure 7.1. "Brides of Freedom" March

immediately to the YouTube channel Freedom Days Syria, a consortium
of civil resistance groups formed in September 2011.[9] From there, the
videos were posted to various Syrian revolution social media pages. I
was among those who received links to the videos from then-director
of Freedom Days Syria, Dr. Alaa Zaza, within two hours after the stand,
with the request to post them widely.

Strategies, Similarities, and Challenges

The "Stop the Killing" and "Brides of Freedom" campaigns show the
creativity of women's nonviolent resistance. The campaigns' street theater transformed passive bystanders into active witnesses. Evoking the
"theater of the oppressed," as conceived by Augusto Boal (2000), both
campaigns created dramatic situations in which "one knows how these
experiments will begin but not how they will end, because the spectator is freed from his chains, finally acts, and becomes a protagonist"
(2000, 472). Participants risked detention, as public assembly and political statements not approved by the state are punishable offenses in Syria.

The red and white colors used in both the "Stop the Killing" and the
"Brides of Freedom" campaigns evince a neutrality strategized to draw
in all onlookers. Use of the Syrian revolution's green-topped flag was
off-limits at these events; calls for regime change and ridicule of Syrian

President Bashar al-Assad were also verboten. This restraint was key to both campaigns' strategies. The call to stop violence was stripped of any other message that might allow the regime to reframe the event to fit its narrative of the uprising. This neutrality is what stumped the security officer who accosted Rima in front of the Parliament building, and his moment of hesitation shows what is most powerful about these campaigns. They disrupt the familiar routine of protesters shouting, army shooting. They have the power to produce that instant of bewilderment on the face of authoritarian power, an instant that organized people could leverage.

The "Stop the Killing" campaign and the "Brides of Freedom" March faced challenges. First, they were nonviolent in a phase when the Syrian revolution had become militarized. The rise of a militarized discourse within a social movement contributes to patronizing attitudes toward nonviolent resistance. Secondly, women led both campaigns in a period when, due to militarization, women were being marginalized in the struggle. Militarization reinforces women's positions as victims instead of social actors capable of resisting the state. When a social movement militarizes, it relies on patriarchal logic that replicates oppressive systems through violent, gendered expressions of dominance. When women resist in creative and gender-specific ways, they subvert patriarchal power dynamics within a movement (Kuumba 2001).

Thirdly, the campaigns were initiated by members of religious minorities in a period when both the regime and the militarized rebels were escalating sectarian divides among Syrians, with extremist Islamist rebels recruiting Syrians to a Sunni "jihad." Rima Dali, a key organizer of "Stop the Killing" and "Brides of Freedom," comes from an Alawite family of Latakia. The other three members of the "Brides of Freedom" are also from minority sects: the youngest "Bride," Rowa Jafar, is from Salamiya, a city with large Ismailia Shia demographics, and the Zaour sisters, Lubna and Kinda, are Druze. Kinda Zaour's prison testimonial, which she published on her social media page after her release, indicated that during interrogation, she and her sister were threatened with excommunication from the Druze. Alawites in "Stop the Killing" events include Mais Mubarak and her brother Samir (each imprisoned for two months for participating); Sufana Baqleh, imprisoned for the "Stop the Killing" action in Kafr Sousa, is Christian.[10] Cities with large Christian and Alawite populations, such as Misyaf, participated in "Stop the Killing," as did minority-initiated civil resistance groups such as Atyaf and Nabd.[11] Minority activists face multifaceted pressures, including from those in the Syrian revolution who tokenize them. Minority activists simultaneously faced the regime's wrath for publicly refuting the regime's claim that Assad received the support of minority religious communities. Alawite activists faced especially bitter reprisals from the regime, as documented by Samar Yazbek throughout her memoir, *A Woman in the Crossfire: Diaries of the Syrian Revolution* (2011).

Led by women, both campaigns contested the increasing gender polarization that characterized this phase of the Syrian revolution. However, the "Stop the Killing" campaign differed from the "Brides of Freedom" with respect to mobilization of gender. Gender-specific resistance emerges when women create civil disobedience strategies utilizing feminized activities that express social dissent but are typically undervalued in larger movement dynamics (Kuumba 2001). The "Stop the Killing" campaign was not gender-specific in its rhetorical strategy. The "Brides of Freedom" March, in contrast, subversively mobilized the gender-specific role of the bride.[12] The bride costuming appealed to women and men across all sects and ethnicities. At the same time, the "Brides" encountered sexist belittlement because they used feminized symbols (bridal gowns). One male observer tweeted dismissively, "Cooking for the refugees (e.g.) would've been more beneficial than the 'Brides' stand," relegating women to traditionally feminized auxiliary roles. While those roles should not be devalued either, the comment misses the "Brides'" subversion of patriarchal logic.[13]

Though men participated, the "Stop the Killing" campaign was perceived by some of the wider revolutionary population as a "feminine" campaign—perhaps because of its frequent use of flowers, even though male protesters early in the Syrian revolution also used flowers. While most "Stop the Killing" events did not strategically mobilize gender the way "Brides of Freedom" did, there are exceptions. At a busy intersection on Damascus's mercantile Hamra Street, four young women distributed red and white flowers to passersby on April 30, 2012. Tied to each flower was a handwritten note saying, "Stop the Killing; the nation fits all of us," echoing notes tied to protest flowers by Ghiyath Matar (a male nonviolent protest leader who died in regime custody in September 2011). The women wore sleeveless tops and capri shorts, not atypically for many

Figure 7.2. "Stop the Killing" protester

Damascene women who do not practice veiling. Their appearances were helpful as the young women tripped about the avenue winning attention for their message. They hailed puzzled policemen and won over apathetic Damascene shop owners and municipal laborers (such as garbage collectors, who are often recruited as regime informants).

Such flirtatiousness flies on Hamra Street, but would not have gone well in the conservative town of Tal. There, local women in the "Stop the Killing" event of May 17 wore headscarves and long dresses typical in the town. Wielding banners through traffic, the women directed teenaged boys to lie down in a tableau evoking protesters killed on the street. The way they dressed helped them to marshal their cheering townspeople, in a strategized use of gender. "Stop the Killing" activists did not impose a uniform model, as long as events adhered to the call to end violence.

The Campaigns' Legacy

The campaigns' legacy is threefold. First, they reemphasized a significant value that had initially been part of the grassroots movement but had deteriorated: the insistence on a homegrown Syrian answer to the crisis, implying a rejection of foreign agendas with the phrase "100% Syrian" on each "Brides of Freedom" banner. Secondly, the campaigns reasserted the value of women's activism in spite of women's marginalization in that stage of the Syrian revolution. Thirdly, strong minority presence in the campaigns brought the spotlight back to civic unity, a core value of the initial protest movement. At a time when Islamist extremist militias were increasingly active in the Syrian revolution, this minority presence was significant. Minority activists of "Stop the Killing" and the "Brides of Freedom" resisted multiple intersecting oppressions simultaneously—increased militarization, Islamist extremism, the regime's sectarian manipulations—sacrificing any supposed privilege they enjoyed in the ostensibly minority-led authoritarian regime.

The campaigns' calls for an end to all violence provoked criticism from within the Syrian revolution. A well-known male Syrian revolution activist posted a picture of himself to Facebook holding a placard stating, "Stop the Soap Opera of the Stop the Killing Girls." A woman tweeted, "'Jihadists' have done more for us than a girl standing in a brides [sic] dress in a souq [market] has done."[14] In light of the regime's brutal response to nonviolent protesters throughout 2011, defending the right to armed self-defense had in 2012 become the most popular stand among Syrian revolution participants. Militarization proponents did not see, at that juncture, that militarization would increase rather than decrease risk to civilian victims.

Both campaigns are often dismissed as ineffectual. Certainly, neither campaign brought down the regime. Armed struggle, too, failed to bring down the regime. Armed rebellion gave the regime cover to escalate its violent response massively, at huge cost to civilians who were supposed to benefit from "self-defense" by rebel brigades. The Syrian death toll rose 161 percent after regime airstrikes began in January 2012.[15] No one was killed at a "Stop the Killing" or "Brides of Freedom" event, nor did regime airstrikes on civilians ensue from these actions. The campaigns' well-strategized accessibility allowed for inclusive participation and creative collaboration across gender lines, regional divides, and ethnoreligious sects. Calling the campaigns ineffective ignores the transformative way they moved beyond the framework of militarized resistance to create new forms of protest.

The "Stop the Killing" and "Brides of Freedom" campaigns did not restore the consensus to nonviolence, but offered a stunning reminder of the power of nonviolence when it had been all but forgotten. They forced the regime to return, however momentarily, to the defensive posture it had assumed during the nonviolent phase of the uprising. They reoccupied the moral high ground initially held by the nonviolent uprising. Regime violence is obscured behind the violence of the armed resistance. By calling for nothing but an end to killing, and being detained as people watched, these activists focused publicity on the regime's oppression.

Some think that only more massive weaponry can save Syrians from this ruthless regime and the Islamist militias that its violence has spawned. This is a hunchbacked illusion. Replicating the same structure of violence that the regime uses to subjugate people does not build a solid foundation for a future Syria. It is civil resistance that shattered the existential base of the regime in the early phase, and it is armed resistance that has failed. Change—real change, not just the ousting of a regime, but the Syria we want, with pluralistic democracy, government accountability, equal rights for all, an independent judiciary, sovereignty, and geographic integrity—comes from within, "100 percent Syrian." It comes most powerfully from voices on the margins— women, minorities, minority women—those caught in the crosshairs of the multiple oppressive forces of regime authoritarianism, Islamist extremism, and patriarchal forces within the revolution, all of which work to dismiss their powerful activist labor. After the romance of armed liberation fades—a process escalated by the authoritarianism of the Islamists who have taken the lead in it—and after people dig out of the rubble of indiscriminate regime bombing, the people power of civil resistance will still be there, renewed every day from the grassroots. People power continues to birth nonviolent resistance against oppressive authoritarianisms in Syria, and it is this kind of resistance that the "Stop the Killing" and "Brides of Freedom" campaigns model and mother.

NOTES

1 "اعتصام أمام مبنى مجلس الشعب في دمشق August 4, 2012." "I'tisam Amam Mabna Majlis al-Sha'b fi Dimashq August 4, 2012." YouTube video, 1:22, posted by "Syrian Rice," April 8, 2012.

2 "دمشق—اعتصام أوقفوا القتل عند وزارة الداخلية July 16, 2012." "Dimashq—I'tisam Awqifu al-Qatl 'ind Wizarat al-Dakhiliya July 16, 2012." YouTube video, 0:54, posted by "AllforSyria," April 17, 2012.

3 "حلب—الجامعة: وقفة احتجاجية للحرائر (أوقفوا القتل)" April 29, 2012." "Halab—al-Jami'ah Waqfah Ihtijajiyah lil Hara'er (Awqifu al-Qatl) April 29, 2012." YouTube video, 0:44, posted by "AleppoRevo's channel," April 29, 2012.

4 Stop the Killing, we want to build a country for all Syrians (English) Facebook Page, " Stop the Killing;" "مشاهد حملة أوقفوا القتل في مدينة التل." "Mashahed Hamlat 'Awqifu al-Qatl' fi Madinat al-Tal." YouTube video, 6:54, posted by "أيام الحرية | Freedom Days," April 13, 2012; "أحرار ثورة الكرامة: دوما 24 حملة أوقفوا القتل." "Ahrar Thawrat al-Karama: Duma 24 Hamlat Awqifu al-Qatl." YouTube video, 2:15, posted by "Freedom Dignity," May 24, 2012.

5 "الأسبوع السوري: حملة أوقفوا القتل محافظة السويداء" "Al-Usbu' al-Suri—Hamlat Awqifu al-Qatl—Muhafadhat al-Suwayda." YouTube video, 1:19, posted by "الاسبوع السوري" April 28, 2012; "تقرير سكاي نيوز: عرائس الحرية 21 نوفمبر 2012." "Taqrir Sky News 'an I'tiqal 'Ara'is al-Hurriyah | 21 November 2012," YouTube video, 0:16, posted by "SyriaUntold," February 22, 2013.

6 Stop the Killing, We Want to Build a Country for All Syrians Page (English-language support page for the campaign's Arabic-language page) post, November 21, 2012, Facebook. Version with translation posted on the page on November 25, 2012.

7 "لحظة اعتقال اعتصام العرائس ج 1 November 21, 2012." "Lahdhat I'tiqal I'tisam al-'Ara'is November 21, 2012 jiz' 1." YouTube video, 1:54, posted by "أيام الحرية | Freedom Days," November 21, 2012.

8 "لحظة اعتقال اعتصام العرائس ج2 November 21, 2012." "Lahdhat I'tiqal I'tisam al-'Ara'is November 21, 2012 jiz'2." YouTube video, 0:24, posted by "أيام الحرية | Freedom Days," November 21, 2012.

9 أيام الحرية Freedom Days Facebook Page, last modified August 18, 2015.

10 "[264] Damascus-al-Baramkah: stop killing" campaign in front of engineering faculty April 22, 2012." YouTube video, 0:29, posted by "TheSyrianrev2011," May 3, 2012; "دمشق كفرسوسة شام سيتي سيبرت: وقفة صامتة لوقف القتل"; April 11." "Dimashq Kafr Susa Sham City Center Waqfah Samitah li Waqf al-Qatl 4 April 11." YouTube video, 0:19, posted by "KafarSousah Revolt," April 11, 2012.

11 "شباب مصياف الثورة الرجل البخاخ القدموس: أوقفوا القتل" "Shabab Misyaf al-Thawra al-Rajul al-Bakhkhakh al-Qadmus—Awqifu al-Qatl." YouTube video, 0:43, posted by "شباب الثورة مصياف," May 15, 2012.

12 Stop the Killing, we want to build a country for all Syrians (English-language support page for the campaign's Arabic-language page) Facebook Page, "Solidarity for Syria's Brides of Freedom" photo album, last modified November 27, 2012.

13 @FadiMqayed, Twitter. December 10, 2012.

14 @Covert Politics_ سمية, Twitter. December 10, 2012.

15 The Violations Documentation Center in Syria. "Latest Martyrs." Accessed September 4, 2015.

BIBLIOGRAPHY

Boal, Augusto. 2000. *Theater of the Oppressed*. London: Pluto Press.

Ghadbian, Banah, and Janiene Thiong. 2014. "Rima's Red Raincoat." YouTube video, https://www.youtube.com/watch?v=86sHQcBWOYo.

Kuumba, Bahati M. 2001. *Gender and Social Movements*. Lanham, MD: AltaMira Press.

Violations Documentation Center in Syria. N.d. "Reports and Testimonies." Douma, Syria: Violations Documentation Center, https://vdc-sy.net/en/ (accessed September 4, 2015).

Yazbeck, Samer. 2011. *A Woman in the Crossfire: Diaries of the Syrian Revolution*. London: Haus Publishing.

8

Refusing the Backseat

Women as Drivers of the Yemeni Uprisings

AMINAH ALI KANDAR

"The people want the fall of the regime" is a slogan that reverberated throughout the Arab Spring uprisings, demanding freedom, economic equality, and democracy. As seen in video footage, photos, news reports, and eyewitness accounts, women were front-line drivers of the uprisings that swept across Yemen. The term "driver" indicates that women pushed, directed, and guided the protests with vigorous determination. They were key organizers and leaders from the onset of the protests and throughout their duration.

This chapter assesses the extent to which women drove Yemen's uprisings, by highlighting the contributions of four women: Tawakkol Karman, Afrah Nasser, Atiaf Alwazir, and Rasha Jarhum. It explores the role that these women played as drivers of the uprisings by examining how they initiated, organized, and led protests as well as how they managed communications and social media campaigns throughout these protests.

Women's participation in the Yemeni uprisings is important for three reasons. First, women used the opportunity to combine their growing intolerance of women's rights violations with that of socioeconomic inequalities—two issues at the forefront of the global development agenda. Second, women's activism in these protests challenged misconceptions about Arab women's perceived political apathy (Coleman 2011, 21). This examination of women's activism contributes to defining women's framing of their political participation during civil unrest. Third, analyses of the methods and impact of women's protest have been limited, particularly in an Arab context. Therefore, conclusions from this analysis provide insight into the nature of Arab women's participation in political protests. I focus on individual women rather than drawing broad conclusions about women as a social group, and I examine women as a segment of society that participated in protests, without reflecting on the level of engagement of Yemeni women in general. I employ a qualitative approach primarily focusing on the first year of the Yemeni uprisings, between January 2011 and January 2012. I use primary documents as the basis of this study, but include interviews and social media venues such as Facebook, Twitter, YouTube, and blogs.

Women in Yemen before the Uprisings

Globally, Yemen has one of the highest population growth rates and is among the most food insecure. In 2009, a staggering 42 percent of Yemenis lived below the poverty line (World Bank 2014). Health, reproductive issues, and lack of education are among the biggest challenges that Yemeni women face. Because schools are often inaccessible and have a mixed-gender setting, many girls are not allowed to attend school because of Yemeni society's traditional views on gender segregation. As a result of widespread early child marriage, many young women are stripped of educational opportunities and drop out of school early. In fact, two out of every three Yemeni women remain illiterate (UNICEF 2012). According to the Global Gender Gap Index, Yemen's female adult unemployment rate in 2012 was 41 percent, one of the highest worldwide. While women can work, societal norms have led to weaker female economic participation. Yemeni women are disenfranchised by their economic dependence, societal status, and low levels of education.

Women's political presence in Yemen mirrors their disenfranchised societal status. Though women received the right to vote in 1967, only 61 percent exercised that right in 2006, and fewer have run for political office (SWMENA 2011). According to the United Nations' assessment of Yemen's progress towards the 2015 Millennium Development Goals, women's political membership is "very low" and "deteriorating" (MCC 2012). In 1990, only four women were in Parliament, with only one in 2000 and zero since 2010 (World Bank 2016). In contrast, women voters increased from 15 percent in 1993 to 61 percent in the parliamentary election of 2006 (Basha, Ghanem, and Abdulhafid 2005). This increase suggests that while women's representation in Parliament is limited, their desire to be political participants through voting and activism has increased.

Civil society has offered a platform for Yemeni women to be politically active, despite the limitations they face. The first, and most prominent, women's organization in Yemen is the General Union of Yemeni Women. It was created in the 1940s and 1950s by the British, and later taken over by women from middle-class families. Approximately two hundred women's NGOs exist throughout the nineteen Yemeni governorates, ranging in specialization from service and charity to advocacy (Soul for Development 2002, 2).

Yemen's civil society operates in an illiberal and restrictive political environment. Because freedom of speech and assembly are highly repressed, Yemen scores low on the civil liberties scale. Political activism, and women's political participation in particular, were greater during the revolutionary struggle for independence from the British mandate in 1967. However, women have not been involved in many large-scale revolutionary protests since then, with the exception of smaller-scale human rights and free-speech protests that were organized throughout the first decade of the twenty-first century, which had minimal impact (Shackle 2012, 11).

Technological penetration in Yemen is equally low, especially Internet connectivity. In 2010, Yemen's Internet connection rate was among the lowest in the Arab world at 1.8 percent for Yemen's population of 23,495,361 (Internet World Stats 2010). Nonetheless, activists in the uprisings did not spare any tech-based mobilization efforts. Protesters used Facebook, Twitter, and cell phone–generated SMS messages to network, disseminate protest information, and circumvent the connectivity problem. In fact, mobile users received tweets directly through SMS, utilizing a service offered by Twitter for times when users were disconnected.

Women's political activism until the 2011 uprisings was restricted by social norms and repressive political discourses, which aimed at keeping women confined to the private sphere. While previously championing women's rights, former president Ali Abdullah Saleh attempted to garner support from traditional tribal leaders to deter women from protesting, by accusing them of "mingling with men" during the protests (Finn 2011). Despite his stance, women and other protesters managed to depose President Saleh, who had been in power for over thirty years. After a year of protests, his vice president, Abd Rabbuh Mansur Al-Hadi, served as interim president until the 2014 elections. However, the struggle for women's rights had just begun.

Women as Drivers of the Yemeni Uprisings

The Yemeni uprisings began on January 16, 2011, and continued until February 27, 2012 (Evens, Harb, and Jones 2012). The first protests were initiated by female protesters and were advanced by women's leadership and activism. One of the unique features of Yemen's uprisings was that media coverage focused on women's mobilization and their organization into women-only protests. Despite their poor socioeconomic status and low political participation, Yemeni women were vivid examples of women's indispensable leadership role.

Dr. Khaled Fattah of Lund University argues that "in Taghir ["Change"] Square, women were among the most energetic participants in the protests." In his analysis of what he calls Yemen's "social *intifada*" (uprising), Dr. Fattah asserts that "for the first time in decades, there was mixed, public interaction between men and women," making the breaking of gender barriers one of the most impressive achievements of the protests (2011, 81). Through the analysis of female protesters presented in this chapter, it is clear that Yemeni women not only supported and sustained the protests but also initiated and drove the popular uprisings, keeping them alive for a year.

The Igniting Activism of Tawakkol Karman

Described as the "mother" and "face" of the revolution, Tawakkol Karman is widely recognized as an icon of resistance and change. In 2005, Karman founded Women Journalists without Chains (WJWC), a human rights organization that focuses on democratic rights and freedom of expression. Prior to the peaceful protests that WJWC held from 2007 until the uprisings, Karman held weekly protests at the Girl's College of Sana'a University (Taman 2011). She was the first to camp in protest in Yemen's Taghir Square in 2011 but was arrested and imprisoned shortly after. As a result, approximately two hundred female supporters gathered and demanded her release. This incident was key to the uprisings and was one of the main factors that caused "the tide . . . to turn against Saleh." The next day, January 24, 2011, Karman was released, and she launched another protest that afternoon (Al-Haj and El Deeb 2011).

After her release from prison, Karman called for a "Day of Rage" protest, and over twenty thousand people responded in a mass civil uprising on February 3, 2011 ("Profile" 2011). Her activism and leadership in initiating the first protest of such magnitude helped ignite and direct the uprising. With nearly eighty thousand followers on Twitter (@TawakkolKarman) and 375,000 Facebook followers (Karman 2014), Karman was among the leading female figures of the uprisings, and her popularity spread rapidly. Her status granted her the leverage needed to continue her struggle in advocating for peaceful protests, towards the ultimate goal of democracy. She became an icon of the uprisings as her photo was displayed throughout the protests, in tents, and even held and hailed by men. This is especially remarkable in Yemen, as photos of women are not usually displayed publicly. Karman is a member of Yemen's leading opposition party, Al-Islah, making her an influential yet controversial political figure. She succeeded in becoming the youngest person, and first Arab woman, to win the Nobel Peace Prize, an achievement that gained rapid and widespread international recognition. In addition to her responsibilities as a mother of three, Karman remained firm in her protest activism and celebrated her Nobel Prize in Taghir Square, where she received congratulatory visits in her tent.

Time magazine named her one of history's sixteen most rebellious women, an accolade that attested to her courage and leadership. According to Abubakr Al-Shamahi, a British-Yemeni journalist, Karman was integral to the Yemeni protest movement: "In all honesty, the Yemeni protest movement that we see today would not be the same without Tawakkol Karman. Throughout the nine months of the ongoing Yemeni uprising it has become normal to walk through Change Square and hear her voice over the loudspeaker, leading the youth in chants" (2011, 5).

Karman gained international attention as a result of her activism: she met with former US secretary of state Hillary Clinton and UN secretary-general Ban Ki-Moon and traveled to New York, lobbying various actors to support the uprising. In a message of congratulations for the Nobel Prize from former secretary of state Hillary Clinton, Karman was praised as a shining example of the difference that women can make and the progress they can help achieve. Clinton and First Lady Michelle Obama honored Karman with the International Women of Courage Award. In her meeting with Ki-Moon in October 2011, Karman discussed human rights, the dire situation of Yemenis amidst the uprisings, and how peace and political stability can be achieved. She shared with him her belief that her Nobel peace award would help accelerate the revolution and garner more support and protesters (UN News Centre 2011). Karman was right, as she was celebrated across Yemen and was recognized by prominent celebrities, news anchors, and human rights organizations for her Nobel Prize and for her leadership. By initiating the first protests, leading and mobilizing protests, and using social media to garner support, Karman became one of the most prominent leaders of Yemen's uprisings.

Afrah Nasser: The Journalist and Online Activist

Blogger and freelance journalist Afrah Nasser has been writing about democracy, women's rights, and Yemen's politics since 2010. CNN named her blog one of the Middle East's top ten must-read blogs, which also made the *Monitor*'s top thirty-five Middle East blogs. The International Journalist Network also labeled her one of the most active women journalists on Twitter. She boasted nearly fourteen thousand Twitter followers (@Afrahnasser 2013) and nearly five thousand Facebook followers (Nasser 2014), a significant number considering the low Internet usage rates in Yemen.

Nasser's online activism played a significant role in the protests that erupted in Yemen, as she focused her efforts on uploading videos and photos calling for revolution. She was active in blogging about the uprisings and posting updates of the unfolding events in Taghir Square. She also contributed news and editorial pieces about Yemen through various news outlets, including CNN, Al Jazeera English, the *Huffington Post*, and others. In one of her articles, she describes women's exceptional participation as one of the uprisings' greatest merits, particularly noting the political seminars that were run by women, for women. She argues that women's activism proved that they too are entitled to demand democracy and lifted what she calls "gender apartheid" (Nasser 2011). After receiving threats for her antiregime opinions, in May 2011 Nasser exiled herself to Sweden, where she represented Yemen and Yemeni women's rights through cyberactivism.

Atiaf Alwazir: Researching and Blogging a Revolution

Researcher and blogger Atiaf Alwazir was another key female figure who helped drive the Yemeni uprisings. Alwazir was an active leader in the protests, particularly through social media. According to Yemeni activist Shatha Al-Harazi, Alwazir took an active role in the protests from the beginning by "working as part of a youth group on various events, talking to the media to spread information on the revolution, organizing with women on how to guarantee women's rights in the future government, translating documents, helping with awareness raising events" (Al-Harazi 2011). She used her blog, *A Woman from Yemen*, and her Twitter account to document and share photos, videos, and eyewitness accounts. In her blog, Alwazir argued that the perception of male public dominance in Yemen changed with the uprisings, as thousands of married and single women took to the streets. She claims that "the visibility of these women in the public arena became an iconic symbol of women's empowerment. In comparison to other Arab Spring states, the sheer number of Yemeni women in the streets for a period of 12 months became a point of pride for Yemeni citizens" (Alwazir 2012). The massive number of women protesting in the streets signaled their refusal to take a back seat in the uprisings. It was also an indication of the active participation of women as a collective social group in a country where their public participation is often unwelcome.

Alwazir went beyond organizing and leading protests and, through social media, became an active analyst, public advocate, and citizen journalist. She had over ten thousand Twitter followers (@WomanfromYemen 2013) and received invitations to speak at numerous key conferences, such as the Trust Women Conference, sponsored by the Thomas Reuters Foundation and the International Herald Tribune, and the London Conference on Cyberspace. She has contributed articles to news sites such as Jadaliyya, Open Democracy, *al-Akhbar English*, the Arab Reform Initiative, the *Guardian*, and *Foreign Policy*.

In one of her articles, Alwazir argues that despite the low Internet penetration rate in Yemen, social media cannot be discounted or underestimated as an effective tool, because the majority of Internet users are youth ages fifteen to twenty-four, who constitute about 60 percent of Yemen's population (Alwazir 2011). Media and wi-fi tents were set up during

Figure 8.1. Atiaf Alwazir holding two signs. The first says, "Women Quota," and the second says, "New Right: Yemeni Women are the spirit of the secular state. The Country for all Movement," with a caricature of Saleh pushing a woman to go back to the house. Photo by Atiaf Alwazir (used with permission from activist).

the protests, and those who accessed the Internet throughout the uprisings disseminated the information they acquired through SMS, word of mouth, flyers, and other means. Alwazir asserts that the lack of independent media in Yemen caused Yemenis to turn to alternative media sources such as blogs, Facebook, and Twitter, resulting in a significant increase in citizen journalism ("ISD Interview" 2012, 3:03). While she does not believe that women's activism has granted them greater access to the political sphere, she does argue that their leadership was a primary factor in the uprisings. The active engagement of leaders such as Alwazir increased the exposure of women in the protests and led to a more robust amount of literature and documentation about women in the uprisings.

Rasha Jarhum: Empowering Women and Youth

Rasha Jarhum is yet another female activist who undertook a leading role in Yemen's uprisings by her human rights activism and focus on empowering women and youth. Jarhum began a career in development, coordinating activities on women's empowerment with the Sisters Arab Forum for Human Rights. She acted as a technical support assistant for the Coalition of the International Criminal Court in the region and worked as a communication consultant for UNICEF under the Girls Education and Equality Programme. In response to the hardship and violence Yemenis faced during the uprisings, Jarhum launched Yemeni Youth for Humanitarian Relief (YYHR), a youth-led humanitarian response coalition. The coalition was initially formed to grant support to injured protesters from Aden, but quickly expanded relief efforts to Hasaba and Abyan. She was active in raising much-needed funds for the injured protesters and was among a slew of female citizen journalists who used social media to expose the regime's aggressions. Jarhum had nearly three thousand Twitter followers; while her followers were not as extensive as others', her Twitter account constituted one of the many ways she was active in the uprisings (@RashaJarhum 2013).

Jarhum has been credited with creating a map of military positions in the capital city of Sana'a. The map provided protesters and activists with a blueprint of the locations of shelling, violent clashes, neutral forces, and areas of political stability ("Sana'a Clashes Map" 2013). She has been publicly recognized for her support and has had her calls to protest retweeted by prominent activists (Topsy Pro 2013). While she considers her contribution to be "a fraction" of what others did, her founding of a relief organization and political mapping initiative make her contributions during the protests important (Jarhum 2013). Her most recent assignment was with UNDP/Yemen as a communications and visibility expert for the Joint Electoral Assistance Project. At the core of her campaign was the promotional video "Sawa Nebnehah," a video that received widespread praise when posted by the "Your Vote Protects Yemen" group on Facebook. Through her advocacy for women and youth, promotion of democracy, and citizen journalism, Jarhum became a leading female voice calling for change throughout Yemen's uprisings.

Breaking Boundaries: Revolutionary Activism

Both individually and collectively, Yemeni women pushed the boundaries of women's public participation with their revolutionary activism.

Although they played a driving role in the uprisings, the impact of their participation remains to be determined (Kandar 2013, 96). When asked about the role women played in the protests, Hanaa Saleh, a female Yemeni film director, said that women's contribution was decisive. Saleh stresses that women's activism was effective and that Karman's role is proof of this, as she "ignited the first spark of the Yemeni revolution" (2013). Many other women were leaders, organizers, and media activists who also contributed to the evolution of the protests, such as Bushra Al-Maqtari, Shatha Al Harazi, Ghaida Al Absi, Sarah Ishaq, Sahar Ghanem, Hend Aleryani, Nadia Al-Sakkaf, and Sarah Jamal. In an in-person interview, when praised for her leading role in the uprisings, Karman stressed that the protests would not have succeeded without the influence and leadership of four key female martyrs, among many others, who were killed by government forces in Taiz: Tufaha Al-Antari (also referred to as "Mother of the Revolutionaries"), Aziza Al Muhajiri, Yasmin Al-Asbahi, and Zainab Al-Mikhlafi (Karman 2014). While these female revolutionaries are seldom referenced in international media and scholarship, they have certainly been hailed by Yemeni sources as prominent and courageous activists and martyrs (shuadā' ta'iz 2011). In describing the protests, Al-Shamahi says, "Women are a sizeable part of the protest movement, and are visible throughout the various protest squares around the country, and in marches. Female protesters have stood atop government vehicles during protests, and faced water cannons and bullets. They have kept the field hospitals running around the clock. There was a recent show on Arab satellite television debating the various issues concerning women in the Arab world. A Saudi woman spoke of wanting to drive, a Yemeni woman of overthrowing a dictator" (2011).

In addition to their exemplary courage, the leadership of Yemeni women was in itself perceived as a form of peaceful protest. Scholars have posited that nonviolent collective action can be enhanced by women's participation (Kuhlow 2013, 17). In a country where tribal alliances run deep and with the second highest rate of gun ownership in the world, the Yemeni protests of 2011 remained relatively peaceful. This defining feature of the uprisings can be credited to Yemen's female protesters and activists.

Dr. Fattah asserts, "Yemen's social intifada created a new space for women's empowerment, networks, courage and voices" (2011, 81). Alwazir agrees that the extent of women's activism during the uprisings broke boundaries in Yemen, and says, "The revolution gave women a voice, boosted their self-confidence and made them believe that the impossible is possible" (2012). Without the activism and leadership of women, the Yemeni uprisings would not have begun with such vigor, nor would they have been sustained.

Conclusion

While the Yemeni uprising shares many similarities with the other Arab uprisings, it differs in terms of duration, with Yemen's lasting much longer and, more pertinently, with women playing such an extensive role as drivers. It is important to note that the term "driver" indicates not only that women were supporters, enablers, and sustainers of the protests but that they satisfied three main criteria: they initiated the first protests, led and organized protests throughout the uprisings, and led and managed social media campaigns. Yemeni women pushed, guided, and directed the protests, significantly contributing to their formation and evolution.

This research supports the theory that the more marginalized women are, the more likely they are to adopt prominent roles in protest. This hypothesis offers a new dimension to Arab women and protest that should be further explored. Yemeni women enjoyed the least rights compared to other Arab Spring countries, which may have compelled them to take the risk of political dissent to secure long-term rights and political incentives. Yemen, the country that seemed least likely to produce women drivers, was in fact a country with highly active female leadership. It appears that lower levels of education, economic prosperity, and governmental participation among women may be connected to higher levels of participation in protest. The Yemeni uprising was planned and organized after most of the other Arab uprisings were over. This lack of spontaneity strengthened the ability of Yemeni women to plan and engage more deeply.

The final conclusions of this paper are based on qualitative research; therefore, these findings are subject to further development and can benefit from analyses of quantitative measures such as statistics on women's continued and sustained political activism through civil society, female governmental representation, and postrevolutionary polling data. This study provides a basic framework for further research on Yemeni women's political activism, Arab women and protest, and the sociopolitical status of women in the Arab world in a post–Arab Spring context. The findings of this work will also assist scholars in formulating policies and in developing and refining existing theories about Arab women and protest.

The Arab uprisings and the political dissent of women in the Arab world are ongoing, and while research on the role of women is still preliminary, a substantial amount of scholarly work is still needed to achieve better understanding of why women protested, whether such protest activism differed from general expectations, and how such protest behavior differed from country to country in the Arab uprisings. These questions might include the following: How do the recent Arab uprisings differ from past protests? What makes women as a social group unique and important to the study of protest? And what does this trend in women's protest behavior mean for the social status of Arab women and their role in the future political landscape?

BIBLIOGRAPHY

(@Afrahnasser). 2013. Twitter account, https://twitter.com/afrahnasser (accessed December 20, 2012).

(@RashaJarhum). 2013. Twitter account, https://twitter.com/rrj_934 (accessed December 20, 2012).

(@TawakkolKarman). 2014. Twitter account, https://twitter.com/tawakkolkarman (accessed December 20, 2012).

(@UNDPYEMEN). 2013. Twitter account, Topsy Pro Analytics, https://twitter.com/undpyemen (accessed December 20, 2012).

(@WomanfromYemen). 2013. Twitter account, https://twitter.com/womanfromyemen (accessed December 20, 2012).

Al-Haj, Ahmed, and Sarah El Deeb. 2011. "Nobel Peace Prize Winner Tawakkol Karman Profile." *Huffington Post*, October 7, http://www.huffingtonpost.com (accessed November 23, 2014).

Al-Harazi, Shatha. 2011. "Faces from Yemen's Revolution Atiaf Al-Wazir." *Shaza171's Blog*, July 8, http://shaza171.wordpress.com/2011/07/08/faces-from-yemen%e2%80%99s-revolution-atiaf-al-wazir-by-shatha-al-harazi/ (accessed November 23, 2014).

Al-Shamahi, Abubakr. 2011. "Tawakkol Karman: Nobel Peace Prize Laureate." Al Jazeera English, October 9, http://www.aljazeera.com (accessed November 23, 2014).

Alwazir, Atiaf. 2011. "Social Media in Yemen: Expecting the Unexpected." *Al Akhbar* English, December 30, http://english.al-akhbar.com (accessed November 23, 2014).

———. 2012. "A Long Road Ahead for Yemeni Women." Open Democracy, December 3, http://www.opendemocracy.net (accessed November 23, 2014).

Basha, Amal, Rana Ghanem, and Nabil Abdulhafid. 2005. "Women's Rights in the Middle East and North Africa—Yemen." The UN Refugee Agency, October 14, http://www.refworld.org (accessed January 16, 2016).

Coleman, Isobel. 2011. "Women and the Arab Revolts." Brown Journal of World Affair 18, no. 1: 1–14.

Evens, Chris Baker, Alia Harb, and Hannah Jones. 2012. "Yemenis Oust Saleh Regime (Yemen Revolution), 2011–2012." Global Nonviolent Action Database. Swarthmore College, August 28, http://nvdatabase.swarthmore.edu (accessed November 23, 2014).

Fattah, Khaled. 2011. "Yemen: A Social Intifada in a Republic of Sheikhs." Middle East Policy 18, no. 3: 79–85.

Finn, Tom. 2011. "March of the Yemeni Women." Foreign Policy, April 19, http://www.foreignpolicy.com (accessed November 24, 2014).

Internet World Stats. 2010. "Yemen Internet Usage and Telecommunications Reports," http://www.internetworldstats.com (accessed November 23, 2014).

"ISD Interview with Yemeni Activist Atiaf Alwazir." 2012. YouTube video, 3:03. Posted by "Institute4SD," March 7, http://www.youtube.com/watch?v=jmoMXSCfHos&feature=youtube_gdata_player (accessed November 23, 2014).

Jarhum, Rasha. 2013. Personal interview with author. Doha, April 8.

Karman, Tawakkol. 2011. "Exclusive: Nobel Laureate Tawakkol Karman on the Struggle for Women's Rights, Democracy in Yemen." Democracy Now video, 59:05. October 21, http://www.democracynow.org/ (accessed November 23, 2014).

———. 2014. Personal interview with author. Doha, March 12.

———. 2014. Facebook Page. November 23, http://www.facebook.com (accessed December 20, 2012).

Kuhlow, Sasha J. 2013. The Differential Impact of Women's Participation in the Arab Spring. State College: Pennsylvania State University.

MCC. 2012. "Millenium Development Goals: Republic of Yemen." United Nations Development Programme, http://www.undp.org.ye (accessed July 7, 2012).

Nasser, Afrah. 2011. "Yemen Is Experiencing Two Revolutions, Says Female Activist." CNN, November 17, http://edition.cnn.com (accessed November 23, 2014).

———. 2014. Facebook Page, November 21, https://www.facebook.com (accessed December 20, 2012).

"Profile: Tawakol Karman." 2011. Al Jazeera English, October 7, http://www.aljazeera.com (accessed November 23, 2014).

Saleh, Hanaa. 2013. Personal interview with author. Doha, April 9.

"Sana'a Clashes Map." 2013. Google Maps, https://www.google.com (accessed March 10).

"Sawa Nebnehah with English Subtitle." 2012. Facebook Page, February 3, http://www.facebook.com (accessed November 23, 2014).

Shackle, Samira. 2012. "The Two Revolutions of Yemen's Women." New Statesman, March 26, http://www.newstatesman.com (accessed November 23, 2014).

Shuadā' Ta'iz شهداء تعز. 2011. Facebook post, November 6, https://ar-ar.facebook.com (accessed November 24, 2014).

Soul for Development. 2002. "Institutional Assessment of Women Local Non-Governmental Organizations in Yemen." Soul for Development. Care International—Yemen, November, http://www.soul-yemen.org (accessed November 23, 2014).

SWMENA. 2011. "Voting in Local Council and Presidential Elections." Status of Women in the Middle East and North Africa, http://swmena.org (accessed November 23, 2014).

Taman, Sahar. 2011. "Tawakol Karman, Nobel Peace Prize Laureate, Talks the Talk and Walks the Walk." *Huffington Post*, October 8, http://www.huffingtonpost.com (accessed November 23, 2014).

Topsy Pro Analytics. 2013. https://pro.topsy.com (accessed March 10).

UNDP. 2011. "Human Development Data for the Arab States: GII: Gender Inequality Index." Arab Human Development Reports. United Nations Development Program, http://www.arab-hdr.org (accessed November 23, 2014).

UNICEF. 2012. "At a Glance: Yemen—Promoting Girls' Education in Yemen," May 25, http://www.unicef.org (accessed November 23, 2014).

UN News Centre. 2011. "Ban and Nobel Peace Prize Laureate Discuss Human Rights Situation in Yemen," October 19, http://www.un.org (accessed November 23, 2014).

The World Bank. 2014. "Yemen Overview," October 1, http://www.worldbank.org (accessed November 24, 2014).

———. 2016. "Proportion of Seats Held by Women in National Parliaments (%)," http://data.worldbank.org (accessed January 16, 2016).

PART II

What They Believe

Ideologies and beliefs are among the most important resources that social movement actors can mobilize to move the masses. Motivated by their own convictions of how things should be, or what is fair or equitable, "Movement organizations, opponents, and countermovement organizations try to persuade individuals to see the world as they do."[1] Integral to movements' success is activists' ability to "anchor their views in existing beliefs or identities."[2] This section highlights the beliefs that women shared in their struggles.

Mounira M. Charrad and Amina Zarrugh show how, believing in the power of words, secularists and Islamists debated the terminology used in regard to women in the new Tunisian constitution. Believing in political institutions, Syrian parliamentarian Maria Saadeh takes an embedded approach to fight corruption within the Syrian Parliament. Searching for the roots of political distress, German-Iraqi professor Nadje Al-Ali contextualizes the resentment that Iraqis express against the colonial legacies that have shaped their authoritarian, sectarian, and Islamist regimes. Other regimes have oppressed Islamist movements, such as the two secret Islamist women's groups in Syria, according to Sana Sayed. Applying religiosity and secularism to political activism, Samaa Gamie and former foreign affairs officer and Egyptian native Maro Youssef take opposing stances. Gamie reveals the internalization of feminist ethos through an Islamic lens in her piece on Egyptian online activist Asmaa Mahfouz, while Youssef shows how Algerian feminists consciously supported President Abdel Aziz Bouteflika's political agenda to limit Islamists' power. Intellectual integrity is the topic of Asaad Alsaleh, who criticizes Syrian regime advisor Buthaina Shabaan for compromising her intellectual and moral integrity, whereas Sudanese professor Fatma Osman Ibnouf feels a sense of regional solidarity to stir a call for action for all Arab women's rights.

NOTES

1 P. B. Klandermans, "Linking the 'Old' and 'New': Movement Networks in the Netherlands," in *Challenging the Political Order: New Social and Political Movements in Western Democracies*, ed. Russel J. Dalton and Manfred Kuechler, 122–36 (New York: Oxford University Press, 1990), 93.

2 Klandermans, 93.

9

"Women Are Complete, Not Complements"

Terminology in the Writing of the New Constitution of Tunisia

MOUNIRA M. CHARRAD AND AMINA ZARRUGH

"Women are complete, not complements!" chanted Tunisian women in a September 2012 demonstration concerning a controversial article in a draft of the new Tunisian Constitution, which was vehemently debated following the Arab Spring protests in Tunisia and the collapse of the Zine El Abidine Ben Ali regime (Ghacibeh 2012). The year 2011 witnessed the fall of three regimes in North Africa, the first of which was that of Tunisia during what has been called the "Jasmine Revolution." Since 2011, the Tunisian state has undergone significant changes in leadership through elections, experienced energized debates within a burgeoning and diverse civil society, and undertaken the revision of foundational texts such as the Constitution. Central to each of these changes have been women, who participated in mass protests, won elections, founded rights-based organizations, and mobilized around the writing of the new Constitution.

We show how women have engaged in politics and civil society, which were transformed by Tunisia's Jasmine Revolution. Our examination focuses on heated debates concerning terminology in regard to gender in the first draft of the new Constitution released in August of 2012. The initial draft contained the term "complementary" to refer to women in relation to men, a reference that was later dropped. Debates centered on whether the term "equal" or "complementary" should be used in the text of the Constitution. The draft ignited public protest and the circulation of petitions critical of the draft. Advocates of women's rights essentially argued for "equal," and sympathizers of the Islamist party then in power were in favor of "complementary."

The impassioned discourse of women around the terminology on gender in the new Constitution illustrates a fundamental shift from a "politics from above" prior to the Arab Spring to a new "politics from below" in the history of Tunisia. By "politics from above," we mean that the government makes decisions for the society as a whole, most often with no discussion among proponents of different opinions. In "politics from below," citizens have a voice and find a way to express their demands, even though they may or may not succeed in influencing policy. Among the significant transformations inaugurated by the Arab Spring in Tunisia was the transition from a top-down politics to a bottom-up politics in regard to women's rights.

Emergence of a New Public Sphere and Politics from Below

The postrevolutionary discussions around politics in Tunisia owe their lively character to what could be termed a new form of civil society, one that was brewing before the collapse of the Ben Ali regime but came to a fuller expression with the Jasmine Revolution. Historically, civil society has been understood as a collection of localized and independently organized networks of social interaction that are beyond the direct purview of the state (Cohen and Arato 1992). Putnam, Leonardi, and Nanetti (1994) argue that even nonpolitical organizations are critically important components of civil society. Cohen and Arato (1992) predicate a notion of civil society on the presence of a public sphere. Habermas (1989) details the emergence of a distinctively novel space, the public sphere, in eighteenth-century Europe. The concept of the public sphere as formulated by Habermas provides a useful starting point for our discussion in that it calls attention to the expression of different understandings of politics and the exchange of different views. However, in analyzing debates on gender terminology in the Tunisian Constitution, we are considering a different process from the one referred to by Habermas, who, focusing on the experience of Western Europe, envisaged a gradual emergence of a public sphere outside the control of the state and one focused on communication and media.

In the case of postrevolutionary Tunisia, we witness the sudden eruption of a public sphere to the forefront of politics and one in which associations played a critical role. According to Khosrokhavar (2012), Tunisia exhibited a particularly robust civil society with over one thousand associations and 110 political parties registered less than a year after the regime's collapse. Women's organizations, which historically did not exert significant influence on the state in Tunisia, were exceedingly important to debates about the Constitution. All of a sudden, the writing of the Constitution, one of the most official texts in the country, emerged as an integral part of the new "politics from below" in which different groups expressed their opinion, sometimes vehemently.

In speaking about eruption of the public sphere and "politics from below," we are not saying that every aspect of politics became a bottom-up process. We do argue, however, that the very fact that there were public discussion, popular outcry, and the redrafting of a constitution following a revolution and elections means that this was a process quite different from earlier formulations of legislation in Tunisia. Debates about the writing of the Constitution in 2012 contrast sharply with the writing of previous official texts such as the Code of Personal Status (CPS), which embodied the "politics from above" that prevailed in earlier eras.

The CPS placed Tunisia at the forefront of the Arab world in regard to women's rights by introducing fundamental reforms of the country's family law starting in the 1950s at the end of French colonial rule and continuing until the 2011 Jasmine Revolution (Charrad 2007, 2011a; Charrad and Ha forthcoming). In abolishing polygamy, making access to divorce more equal between husbands and wives, eliminating the role of matrimonial guardians with authority over women, and a number of other reforms, the CPS of 1956 and its subsequent amendments gave Tunisian women a set of rights unparalleled in the Arab world.

The CPS constituted a reform from above, a political choice by the Tunisian leadership in the 1950s as part of an overall strategy of state building that targeted patriarchal networks, clans, tribal groups, and what Charrad refers to more generally as "kin-based solidarities" (Charrad 2001, 2011b). Part of an effort to build a modern centralized state with a new definition of citizenship, it is a perfect example of what we mean by "politics from above." Initiated by the leadership, the CPS came as a reform from the top, rather than as a response to pressures from an organized women's movement (Charrad 2001). It was not until the 1980s that a women's movement developed in earnest and became vocal in national politics in Tunisia. Women activists suffered censure and lacked freedom of expression under the authoritarian Ben Ali regime from 1987 to 2011. The aftermath of the Jasmine Revolution was the first time that they had a chance to express their views openly in a new climate of public debate.

Controversy over Terminology

On August 13, 2011, nearly two months prior to the ascension of the Islamist party Ennahda to political power in the National Constituent Assembly (NCA), more than a thousand women gathered in the streets across the capital city of Tunis to commemorate the fifty-fifth anniversary of the passage of Tunisia's CPS (Ryan 2011). Women such as Ahlem Belhaj, who ran the Association Tunisienne des Femmes Démocrates (ATFD), or Association of Tunisian Women Democrats, were concerned that gender equality after the revolution was, in Belhaj's words, "facing the threat of a loss in the gains" made since the passage of the CPS in 1956 and the reforms related to women's rights it inaugurated (Terry 2011). The apprehension crystallized around wording on gender in Article 28.

Members of the constituent assembly, who were popularly elected in October of 2011, had the mandate to draft a new constitution to replace the former Constitution of 1959. Following the release of the draft of the Constitution on August 13, 2012, women activists and their male allies paid special attention to the article entitled "women's rights" (Article 28), which some regarded as compromising gender equality because the article defined women as "complementary" to men. The article read as follows: "The state shall guarantee the protection of the rights of women and shall support the gains thereof as true partners to men in the building of the nation and as having a role *complementary* thereto within the family. The state shall guarantee the provision of equal opportunities between men and women in the bearing of various responsibilities. The state shall guarantee the elimination of all forms of violence against women" ("Draft of the Constitution" 2012; italics added).

Much of the consternation was situated around contestation of the Arabic term "*yetekaamul*" in Article 28. The term is frequently translated as "complementary." An alternative interpretation, "integrate with one another," points to a sense of fulfillment and unity between men and women. The translation "fulfill one another" conveys a different meaning, one that, as Marks argues (2012), emphasizes the centrality of the two parts (men and women as mutually fulfilling one another) and is situated within an Islamist ethics of collectivism more generally.

The most common translation of the term, however, is "complementary" (or "*complémentaires*" in French). Different organizations, from women's groups to political parties, assumed various positions on the terminology of the article, many viewing it as a contradiction to other components of the draft Constitution that emphasized unequivocal gender equality. The term "equality" (French: "*égaux*" and "*égalité*"; Arabic: "*al-masawa*") was used in multiple contexts in other sections of the draft Constitution.

The absence of the term "equality" from Article 28 (directly concerned with women's rights) was disconcerting to several women's groups, which issued statements and proposed revisions to the draft. The debate surrounding terminology exhibited more broadly the emergence of a "politics from below," as opponents and supporters of "complementarity" confronted each other.

Opponents

Opposition to the notion of "complementarity" surfaced particularly among some women's groups and organizations seeking to promote an expansive and inclusive democracy (Daragahi 2012). Large-scale demonstrations were promptly organized with as many as six thousand women in attendance at a demonstration in the capital city of Tunis on August 13, 2012, the day that the first draft of the Constitution was released and the fifty-sixth anniversary of the promulgation of Tunisia's CPS (Ghanmi 2012). The demonstration was held after evening prayers during the last week of the Muslim holy month of Ramadan and was attended primarily by women and a few men who supported their claims.

Women in attendance were either unaffiliated with any organization or identified with organizations such as L'Association Tunisienne des Femmes Démocrates (ATFD), La Ligue Tunisienne des Droits de l'Homme (LTDH), and Association des Femmes Tunisiennes pour la Recherche sur le Développement (AFTURD). Women held signs including slogans such as "Rise up women for your rights to be enshrined in the constitution" and "There is no Tunisian future without women" (Coleman 2012; Karam 2012). Women, both young and old as well as

Figure 9.1. Cartoon by Nadia Khiari

rural and urban, attended the large-scale protest and held signs that featured French and Arabic.

Many organizations argued for the preservation of Tunisia's past record as an exemplar for women's rights in the region. For example, Amira Yahyaoui, president of Al Bawsala, an organization dedicated to advancing democracy and fostering a robust civil society, regarded Article 28 as an aberration in Tunisia's history: "It [Article 28] was a major scandal. Tunisia has always liked to say it is a leader in women's rights and all of the sudden we find ourselves more backward than other countries. We like to be the first—the first to have a revolution, the first to write a constitution, but also the first to have equality between the sexes. . . . It [Article 28] was a scandal. Many people came out into the streets to protest. And what was especially good was that *we saw that the problem of gender equality is not just a problem that concerns the elite*" (Rowling and Boeglin 2012; italics added).

Yahyaoui's statement illustrates the extent to which Tunisians felt that a broad segment of the population was actively engaging in debates about foundational texts such as the Constitution. This represented a major reorganization of politics in the Tunisian state. Women's rights issues were no longer the purview of closeted conversations between political elites resulting in "politics from above," but had become the topic of dialogue, dissension, and deliberation in the "politics from below" that were part of the new public sphere. The article became a source of jest across Tunisia. An example appears in figure 9.1 by Tunisian cartoonist Nadia Khiari, who developed a series of cartoons called "Willis in Tunis" during and following the Jasmine Revolution.

Representative of a new form of politics in Tunisian society, a petition was created and disseminated by women who were inspired by insider critiques of the article made by Selma Mabrouk, a politician who was elected to the NCA in October of 2011. The online petition— published on August 2, 2012, and entitled "Protégez les droits de citoyenneté de la femme en Tunisie!"—acquired over thirty thousand signatures (Avaaz 2012). An excerpt read as follows: "A woman is a citizen under the same title as that of a man. The state is about to vote on an article (28) of the constitution that limits the citizenship rights of women under the principle of complementarity to men and not under the principle of equality. If this article were to be adopted in the final version of the constitution, it would limit the principle of equality between men and women. A woman is not defined in terms of a man. We demand the repeal of Article 28 from the draft constitution." The petition further asserted the equality of all citizens before the law, regardless of gender.

Supporters

On the other side of the debate on terminology in regard to gender, some women affiliated with the Islamist party Ennahda defended aspects of the article. The presence of what have been termed "Islamist women" in Tunisian politics has complicated understandings of how religion facilitates, rather than undermines, women's mobilization. Among the most popular figures in Islamist women's politics in Tunisia was Ennhada Executive Council member and leader of the constitutional committee in charge of Article 28, Farida Labidi. A lawyer and human rights activist, Labidi was tortured under the Ben Ali regime (Labidi 2012). She fiercely defended Article 28. Among her most circulated statements was her qualification of women's equality: "The rights and gains of women will not be touched. . . . One cannot speak of equality between man and woman in the absolute" (qtd. in Cavaillès 2012).

Labidi also suggested that the average Tunisian woman was less concerned about gender terminology than other matters. She said, "I think the Tunisian woman is rather concerned to guarantee the right to health, to education, to employment, to access positions of decision-making, to dignity, and to ensure life worthy conditions to rural women" (qtd. in Babnet 2012).

Mehrezia Labidi-Maïza, Ennahda member, vice president of the NCA, and member of Parliament, attempted to distinguish the term "complementary" from notions of inequality: "Complementarity does not mean inequality. In complementarity, there is precisely an exchange, a partnership" (qtd. in Byrne 2011). Labidi-Maïza also argued that a misunderstanding of language had fueled the controversy surrounding the article: "Sharing roles between men and women does not at all mean that women are less than men or that the man has a higher position than women as is currently being popularized by some parties" (qtd. in Ben Abdel Adeem 2012).

Another Ennahda Executive Council member, Mounia Brahim, emphasized the diversity and accomplishments of women who compose Ennahda and Islamist politics more generally: "Look at us. We're doctors, teachers, wives, mothers—sometimes our husbands agree with our politics, sometimes they don't. But we're here and we're active" (qtd. in Marks 2011). Rachid Ghannouchi, cofounder and leader of the Ennahda party, declared the party's allegiance to the spirit of the CPS, though he maintained that "complementation [sic] is an authentic concept, meaning that there would be no man without a woman and no woman without a man. This is an additional meaning to the notion of equality" (qtd. in Ghanmi 2012).

While in favor of the term "complementarity," Ennahda council members stated their commitment to preserving Tunisia's history of protecting women's rights and pledged support for the CPS, seen by most Tunisians as an integral part of Tunisian history and culture.

Outcome: Gender in the 2014 Tunisian Constitution

The National Constituent Assembly approved the final version of the Constitution on January 24, 2014. In the final version, the clause of Article 28 that included the term "complementary" and had catalyzed popular protest was omitted. Gender equity is now enshrined in the final 2014 version, in Article 46, entitled "Women's Rights," which explicitly affirms several protections for women: "The state commits to protect women's accrued rights and to work to strengthen and develop these rights. The state guarantees the equality of opportunities between women and men to have access to all levels of responsibility in all domains. The state works to attain parity between women and men in elected Assemblies. The state shall take all necessary measures in order to eradicate violence against women" ("Tunisia" 2014).

In addition to Article 46 on women's rights, another article (no. 21) also addresses women's equality and emphasizes that all citizens regardless of gender have equal rights and duties: "All citizens, male and female, have equal rights and duties, and are equal before the law without any discrimination. The state guarantees freedoms and individual and collective rights to all citizens, and provides all citizens the conditions for a dignified life" ("Tunisia" 2014).

These protections, articulated in the final version of the Constitution, were met with considerable praise by many women in Tunisia as well as with calls to extend their reach and impact.

Conclusion

The debate surrounding the terminology on gender and the omission of the "complementary" clause from the final text of the Constitution highlight the ways by which a new form of Tunisian public sphere and politics from below has emerged. Official and foundational texts that had heretofore been the prerogative of elites and politicians became not only accessible to the general population but also the site of public critique. It is clear from the engagement of women's organizations and women's acquisition of elected positions in the Tunisian National Constituent Assembly since the collapse of the Ben Ali regime that women have been prepared to pursue their interests, which should not be understood as uniform.

The perspectives and positions of women across the political spectrum outlined here illustrate a transition in Tunisia from a "politics from above," in which political elites made decisions regarding gender policy, to a "politics from below," in which individuals organized, associated, and made demands upon the state. The debate over gender terminology in the new Constitution of Tunisia suggests the potential for an active public sphere, the character and course of which could transform gender politics in Tunisia and possibly across the region. No one can predict the future, however, and reversals are conceivable. We must be wary of operating by the clockwork of a set, rigidly defined calendar, with its concomitant temporal expectations about how quickly revolutions should unfold and how democracy should be instituted.

Acknowledgments

This chapter reproduces and updates sections of Mounira M. Charrad and Amina Zarrugh, "Equal or Complementary? Women in the New Tunisian Constitution after the Arab Spring." *Journal of North African Studies* 19, no. 2 (2014).

BIBLIOGRAPHY

Avaaz. 2012. "Protégez les droits de citoyenneté de la femme en Tunisie!" Avaaz.org: Pétitions Citoyennes, August 2, https://secure.avaaz.org (accessed August 12, 2012).

Avant-Projet de la Constitution de la République Tunisienne. 2012. "Article 2, Section 28. Draft of August 13, 2012. Translation (from Arabic) by Democracy Reporting International (DRI)," http://www.fichier-pdf.fr (accessed April 20, 2013).

Babnet. 2012. "Tunisie: La Société Civile Dénonce L'art 28 de La Constitution Comme Une Régression Des Acquis de La Femme." Babnet, August 13, https://www.babnet. net (accessed April 17, 2013).

Ben Abdel Adeem, Maha. 2012. "Calls for a National Celebration of Women in Tunisia amid Fears about the Principle of Equality." France24, August 13. Translated from Arabic by the authors (accessed April 21, 2012).

Ben Hassine, Wafa. 2012. "Tunisia Assembly: It's a Man's World, but Women Can Help!" *Naawat*, August 3, http://nawaat.org (accessed May 15, 2013).

Byrne, Eileen. 2011. "The Women MPs Tipped to Play Leading Roles in Tunisia's New Assembly." *Guardian*, October 28, https://www.theguardian.com (accessed April 30, 2013).

Cavaillès, Thibaut. 2012. "Amertume et Colère des Femmes Tunisiennes." *Figaro*, August 14. http://www.lefigaro.fr (accessed August 28, 2012).

Charrad, Mounira M. 2001. *States and Women's Rights: The Making of Postcolonial Tunisia, Algeria, and Morocco.* Berkeley: University of California Press.

———. 2007. "Tunisia at the Forefront of the Arab World: Two Waves of Gender Legislation." *Washington and Lee Law Review*, no. 64: 1513–27.

———. 2011a. "Gender in the Middle East: Islam, State, Agency." *Annual Review of Sociology*, no. 37: 417–37.

———. 2011b. "Central and Local Patrimonialism: State Building in Kin-Based Societies." In *Patrimonial Power in the Modern World*, the Annals of the American Academy of Political and Social Science Series, ed. Julia P. Adams and Mounira M. Charrad. New York: Sage.

Charrad, Mounira M., and Hyun Jeong Ha. Forthcoming. "Sustained Reforms of Islamic Family Law: Tunisia under Authoritarian Regimes, 1950s to 2010." In *Family Law and Gender in the Modern Middle East*, ed. Adrien Wing and Hisham Kassim. New York: Cambridge University Press.

Cohen, Jean, and Andrew Arato. 1992. *Civil Society and Political Theory*. Cambridge: MIT Press.

Coleman, Isobel. 2012. "Women, Free Speech, and the Tunisian Constitution." Council on Foreign Relations, August 15, http://blogs.cfr.org/coleman/2012/08/15/women-free-speech-and-the-tunisian-constitution (accessed May 23, 2013).

Daragahi, Borzou. 2012. "Term Used for Women in Tunisia's Draft Constitution Ignites Debate, Protests." *Washington Post*, August 16, https://www.washingtonpost.com (accessed May 15, 2013).

"Draft of the Constitution of the Republic of Tunisia. Chapter 2, Article 2.28. Translation (from Arabic) by International IDEA." 2012. Constitutionnet, August 13, http://www.constitutionnet.org (accessed April 20, 2013).

Farrell, Jeremy. 2012. "Tunisian Constitution: Text and Context." Jadaliyya, August 23, http://www.jadaliyya.com (accessed April 13, 2013).

Ghacibeh, Greta. 2012. "Tunisian Town Hall on Women's Rights." American Abroad Media, September 6, http://www.americaabroadmedia.org (accessed July 7, 2018).

Ghanmi, Monia. 2012. "Tunisian Women March for Their Rights." Maghrebia, August 15, https://www.eurasiareview.com (accessed July 5, 2018).

Habermas, Jurgen. 1989. *The Structural Transformation of the Public Sphere*. Cambridge: MIT Press.

Khosrokhavar, Farhad. 2012. *The New Arab Revolutions That Shook the World*. London: Paradigm.

Labidi, Mehrezia. 2012. "Tunisia's Women Are at the Heart of Its Revolution." *Guardian*, March 23, https://www.theguardian.com (accessed May 15, 2013).

Marks, Monica. 2011. "Can Islamism and Feminism Mix?" *New York Times*, October 26, sec. Opinion, https://www.nytimes.com (accessed May 13, 2013).

———. 2012. "'Complementary' Status for Tunisian Women." *Foreign Policy*, August 20, https://foreignpolicy.com (accessed April 15, 2013).

Putnam, Robert, Robert Leonardi, and Raffaella Y. Nanetti. 1994. *Making Democracy Work: Civic Traditions in Modern Italy*. Princeton, NJ: Princeton University Press.

Rowling, Megan, and Claudine Boeglin. 2012. "Video: Tunisian Constitution Must Enshrine Equal Status of Women—Activist." Thomas Reuters Foundation, September 13, http://www.trust.org (accessed April 17, 2013).

Ryan, Yasmine. 2011. "Tunisia: Women's Rights Hang in the Balance." Al Jazeera English, August 20, https://www.aljazeera.com (accessed April 28, 2013).

Terry, Jonathan. 2011. "Tunisian Women Protest to Protect Rights, Equality." bikya masr, August 14, http://bikyamasr.com (accessed October 23, 2011).

"Tunisia. The Constitution of 2014." 2014. Constitutionnet, http://www.constitutionnet.org.

10

A Patriotic Christian Woman in the Syrian Parliament

MARIA SAADEH

Translated by Samyah Alfoory

During the 128th Inter-Parliamentary Union Assembly (March 22–27, 2013) in Ecuador, parliamentarians from around the world stressed the need to include women in politics. Syrian parliamentarian Maria Saadeh contributed to the discussion by explaining her motives to enter politics and her commitment to political reform.

* * *

I would like to share my personal experience as an independent Parliament member, an architect, and a Syrian woman. I decided to run for Parliament during a difficult period of the Syrian crisis because I believed in defending my right and the right of the Syrian people to have freedom of expression and the freedom to determine our destiny. This right has been denied by some countries that claim to speak on behalf of our people without considering the realities on the ground. These countries claim to champion human rights and to support the Syrian people and their freedoms. Instead, they have violated the sovereignty of the Syrian state by manufacturing an external opposition of people who claim to be the only legitimate representative of the Syrian public despite not having lived in Syria for over twenty years. This opposition allegedly wants to overthrow the current secular regime in order to institute democracy. However, freedom and democracy cannot be achieved through arming civilians, using intimidation tactics, dismissing and disregarding the majority's opinion, opening borders to global networks of terrorists, spreading sectarianism, disseminating false propaganda, or changing facts on the ground.

As a patriotic Syrian Christian woman, I felt a strong responsibility to mitigate the crisis in my country, as did many other Syrian women, who have shown great resolve and endurance. Like many, I experienced the widespread corruption in Syria, but I refused to let my emotions determine my reaction to these conditions, as others have, or to ignite a war in my country. Recognizing that the crisis is quintessentially a national issue, I chose the Syrian Parliament as a legitimate platform upon which to advocate for reform, defend the rights of my people, and work for peace and true democracy in my country.

Through this international forum that advocates for democracy worldwide, I stand today, along with every parliamentarian who was elected by the public, to represent the Syrian people. Although the Syrian public did not elect the opposition, Syria's doors are open to the internal and external opposition groups if they wish to participate in its governance. However, they must be elected if they wish to represent the Syrian people. Those who want to change the system, or even the regime, must provide a clear and legitimate proposal for reform that can be supported at the ballot and ensure that it does not advance foreign agendas.

Legitimacy cannot be won through war, killing innocent people, or destroying the state's infrastructure under the pretext of changing the regime or protecting civilians. As a woman parliamentarian, I join you in assuming the responsibility for protecting people's freedom and women's roles in politics and society. I invite you to stand with the Syrian people in order to stop the violence and work for peace in Syria and the Middle East. I reiterate our rejection of any international intervention that ignores our role as legitimately elected women parliamentarians, or that intervenes in our affairs or the sovereignty of any other state.

11

Iraqi Women's Agency

From Political Authoritarianism to Sectarianism and Islamist Militancy

NADJE AL-ALI

Much of what we do and say as scholars positioned in Western societies and working on gender issues in relation to the Middle East is a reaction to the ongoing sweeping generalizations and platitudes, stereotypes, misconceptions, and distortions about Middle Eastern men and women. In this context, it is a huge challenge for those of us who think of ourselves as feminist scholars to juggle between struggling for more equal and fair gender relations and tackling Islamophobia and racism. This dilemma is not new, and I am not the first to mention it, but I think it is worth reminding ourselves of the significance of positionality, which by no means is static, but can be shifting. I am personally painfully aware of this dilemma when talking or writing about Iraqi women, who continue to be represented in a dehumanizing and essentialist manner, often as passive victims of either war or male patriarchal oppression. At the same time, there has been a tendency within Western media and policy circles to dismiss the devastating impact of British and American military and political intervention in Iraq. Instead, they instrumentalize Iraqi women to illustrate military "success" in bringing freedom and democracy to Iraq or to claim that gender-based violence and injustices are inherent parts of Iraqi culture (Al-Ali and Pratt 2009a). My own emphasis shifts depending on my audience, either stressing Iraqi women's agency or stressing the lack thereof.

It is not only my positionality and that of my audiences that might shift, however, as the developments we see unfolding in Iraq are also extremely complex. In the life stories and oral histories I gathered over the past years, from Iraqi women of different generations and ethnic and religious backgrounds, accounts of agency—ranging from political participation, women's rights struggles, welfare provision, and cultural and creative expressions to everyday survival—were narrated to me, alongside the failure of agency—that is, the individual's inability to affect the course of events. While this tension is not unique to Iraq, as it reflects the realities of most people's lives, the extremely debilitating conditions circumscribing Iraqi women's and men's agency cannot be ignored when challenging the narratives and predominant representations of the victimized Iraqi female body (Al-Ali and Pratt 2008).

Clearly, agency and structural constraints exist in a dialectic; and any meaningful analysis will have to engage with both, at the very least to highlight the significance of women's actions, forms of resistance, contributions, involvements, and creative coping mechanisms within, and despite, any historically specific context. However, rather than a simplistic framing of structural constraints in terms of patriarchal culture or imperialism—depending on one's political lens—I argue that an intersectional approach is needed to grasp the changing and interrelated configurations of power and inequality that enable or restrict women's agency. Such intersectional analysis recognizes the link between the struggle for women's rights and the struggle against political authoritarianism, sectarianism, and Islamist militancy. Intersectionality also recognizes that challenges are not merely local and national, but also have regional, transnational, and international dimensions. To do so, I share a few key historical and current instances of Iraqi women's agency in increasingly challenging contexts as linked to revolutionary struggles, dictatorship, economic sanctions, invasion and occupation, widespread militarization, growth in Islamist and sectarian politics, and rampant authoritarianism. My reflections are based on ongoing research on the impact of changing political and economic developments on Iraqi women and on prevailing gender norms and relations, as well as on women's resistance to gender-based inequalities and wider forms of social injustice, violence, and authoritarian politics.

Historical Perspectives

Throughout the 1940s and 1950s, the period leading up to the 1958 revolution that changed Iraq from a monarchy to a republic, Iraqi women were involved in providing humanitarian assistance and welfare work, but they also participated in demonstrations, strikes, sit-ins, and underground political activism. They were active across the political spectrum, attracted to both leftist Iraqi nationalism—in the form of the Communist Party and its associated students' and women's organizations—and different trends within Arab nationalism, including Baathism (Al-Ali 2007). Several of the older women I interviewed over the years were involved in the emergence of Rabitat al-Mara' al-'Iraqiya (the Iraqi Women's League), an active and, at some point, broad-based women's organization that was closely linked with the Iraqi Communist Party.

Dr. Naziha al-Dulaymi's name was often mentioned in connection with the struggle for women's rights and the emergence of the Iraqi Women's League. She was a pioneer in both her professional and her political lives: as a medical doctor, she was instrumental in improving public health in Iraq; as a political activist, particularly a women's rights activist, Dr. al-Dulaymi inspired thousands of young women to join the struggle for advancing women's legal rights. Appointed as the minister of municipalities in 1959, she became the first female minister in the Arab world. But the league was not a one-woman show: by the late 1950s and early 1960s, over forty thousand of its members advocated for women's educational, legal, and political rights (Al-Ali 2007).

Despite widespread opposition and protest by conservative social forces, the revolutionary regime of 'Abd al-Karim Qasim prioritized women's demands for increased legal rights and equality, and passed in 1959 one of the most progressive family laws in the region. Leading activists within the Iraqi Women's League were instrumental in drafting the Personal Status Code that was enshrined in the Iraqi constitution in 1959 after the revolution. Many of the educated, middle-class women of urban background I interviewed, who experienced the political developments and transformations prior to and after the 1958 revolution, talk of a time in which they felt growing opportunities rather than increasing constraints. Young women pushed boundaries and systematically challenged traditions. They entered higher education and a range of professions, socialized outside universities in cafes, frequented galleries, participated in cultural events, and actively took part in Iraq's vibrant social and cultural scene.

Baathi Iraq

A handful of women activists I spoke to admitted having been initially attracted to the Baath Party as part of their Arab nationalist orientation and admiration for the pan-Arab leader Gamal Abdel Nasser.[1] They stressed the difference between pan-Arabism's ideology, which is rooted in tradition and regional solidarity, and the way it was implemented by political leaders like Saddam Hussein when he came to power (Al-Ali 2007). While political agency was severely limited during the Baath era, due to the constraints of an emerging centralized dictatorship, the General Federation of Iraqi Women, the only women's organization allowed during the Baath regime, succeeded in challenging the political leadership on occasion, particularly in the first decade of the regime. The federation became the vehicle for the regime's modernizing project, especially in term of literacy, healthcare, and reproduction (Al-Ali 2007).

The accounts of women who lived through the first decade of the Baath regime are not merely stories of hardship and struggle under dictatorship; they also reflect a nostalgia for what some believe to be the golden age of state building, educational expansion, and women's broader entry into the labor force, as well as increased social spaces for women in terms of dress code, mobility, and gender norms more widely. These went side by side with the refining of the authoritarian state's innovative ways to maim and torture its population, engage in regional expansion and control, and inflict maximum fear on its citizens (Al-Ali 2007).

During the period of the war with Iran (1980–1988), there was a shift in state rhetoric and government policies vis-à-vis women and gender relations. Maybe more so than before, women were needed in the public sphere as thousands of Iraqi men were fighting and dying in what was meant to be a quick war. Instead, years of intense warfare negatively affected not only the Iraqi economy but also the social fabric itself. Most families lost someone to one of Saddam Hussein's many senseless wars. Many women I spoke to talk about the period of the Iran-Iraq war as a time when they carried the burden of becoming the main motors of state bureaucracy and the public sector and the main breadwinners for their families—de facto heads of households—while also remaining the caregivers and mothers.

The severe economic sanctions, imposed on Iraq four days after its invasion of Kuwait on August 2, 1990, disrupted the state's modernizing capabilities and altered the discourse around women and gender. The same regime that had defined the "good Iraqi woman" as an educated working woman in the context of an expanding economy and labor market in the 1970s asked women in the 1990s to return to their traditional roles as mothers and housewives when confronted with the economic crisis, large-scale unemployment, and, most importantly, a large number of disgruntled men who had just returned from the eight-year war with Iran. The elevation and construction of "tradition" in relation to gender roles was clearly a way to appease and bargain with the male population at a time of heightened vulnerability.

Despite the shift towards a social conservatism linked to the changing economic and political reality, Iraqi women were creative in coping with their drastically worsening living conditions. As wages and jobs in the formal labor sector shrank drastically, women began to work informally, starting their own small businesses in catering, sewing, recycling, and repairing household goods. They increasingly started homeschooling children, as many teachers left teaching due to low wages. Most women I talked to remember the sanctions period as extremely challenging in terms of economic hardship, failing infrastructure, widespread poverty, inadequate healthcare, as well as a significant shift towards conservative gender norms and relations. Yet, they also stressed that they were key to the survival of their families and to holding society together in an increasingly volatile and difficult context.

In the "safe haven" established after the post–Gulf War uprisings of 1991 in the north of Iraq, Kurdish women started to challenge tribal and conservative gender norms within their own communities. Their gender-based activism followed decades of women's participation in the Kurdish national struggle and the resistance against Baathi repression, which had culminated in the 1986–1989 genocidal Anfal campaign. In the 1990s, Kurdish women activists started establishing civil society organizations to advocate against gender-based violence, especially honor-based crimes and killings. Kurdish women also began to enter the labor force in greater numbers and become involved in higher education at higher rates. Meanwhile, life for women in central and southern Iraq was severely curtailed and grueling in the general context of lawlessness, a dysfunctional state, and inadequate infrastructure.

Resisting Gender-Based Violence, Sectarianism, and Authoritarianism

Gender-based violence increased all over Iraq amid broader political, sectarian, and criminal violence, as well as the hypermilitarization of society, coupled with mounting sectarian and extremist Islamist politics. During the first years after the invasion in 2003, the picture was mixed, despite the occupation and the Iraqi regime's failure to pursue women's rights or liberation in any meaningful way (Al-Ali and Pratt 2009b). Iraqi women activists saw in the fall of the Baath regime an opportunity to make their mark and take part in reshaping the country.

Without doubt, both the occupation and the new Iraqi government systematically marginalized and sidelined Iraqi women in the official political institutions and processes. Yet, Iraqi women did not merely stand by; instead, they mobilized by engaging in formal civil society organizations and informal community and interest groups. Women activists were at the forefront of a growing political movement for de-mocracy and human rights that, in line with wider political movements and processes in the region, asked for greater transparency and for ending corruption and political authoritarianism. Many Iraqi women's rights activists realized that their struggle for greater gender equality and social justice could not be separated from the struggle against the emerging dictatorship, the remilitarization of society, Islamist militancy, corruption, and nepotism (Al-Ali and Pratt 2009a; Al-Ali 2013).

More specific mobilization around women's rights also mushroomed over the past decade, despite the many challenges and threats to women's rights activists. Women-led NGOs, as well as informal community asso-ciations, campaigned for women's legal rights, especially with reference to the unresolved dispute over the Personal Status Code (Article 39)— the set of laws governing marriage, divorce, child custody, and inheri-tance. This set of laws continues to be fought along sectarian lines as well as conservative versus more progressive interpretations of Islamic law. They also fought to reform criminal laws that do not offer sufficient protection against gender-based violence, particularly honor-based crimes. Given the dire humanitarian situation, most organizations became involved in welfare and charity work, offering income-generating activities and training for women, in addition to providing shelters and advice to victims of domestic violence (Al-Ali and Pratt 2009a; Al-Ali 2013).

During the wave of protests in the region in late 2010 and throughout 2011, Iraqi women demonstrated in Baghdad's Tahrir Square and in the Kurdish region, particularly in Sulimaniya. For many months, groups of students and activists were gathering in the square, demanding political and economic reforms, jobs, electricity, and clean water. Many protesters were brutally beaten and arrested by the police; some disappeared and others were killed, in what activists allege were targeted assassinations ordered by former prime minister Nouri Maliki.

Between February and April 2011, Kurdish female students in Sulimaniya joined the demonstrations against corruption and social injustice and asking the Kurdish Regional Government to step down. Hundreds of demonstrators, including women, were arrested and harassed by the security forces. Yet, protests continued despite the violence, the tear gas, and the security forces' other antiriot tactics. Although no other large Kurdish cities witnessed protests, Kurdish women activists were challenging the Kurdish political elite, particularly in Sulimaniya, both in relation to gender-specific issues and in relation to wider issues pertaining to social justice, corruption, and democracy.

Resisting ISIS and Sectarianism

Context is far from conducive to discussing agency when viewing images. The emergence of the Islamic State in Iraq and Syria (ISIS) in 2014 made thinking about agency even more difficult. Images of Yazidi women fleeing enslavement became too familiar in the media. Many Iraqi Sunnis became internally displaced as they tried to escape Anbar province after it fell under ISIS control. They were equally fearful of the sectarian violence perpetrated by the Shia militia. Kurdish women continued to experience a range of gender-based violence (including female genital mutilation in areas under the control of the Kurdish Regional Government). Survival clearly became the main prerogative of the thousands of internally displaced women and men, as well as those living under the control of ISIS militants. While Iraqi women of all ethnic and religious backgrounds and social classes continue to exert some level of agency within their respective contexts, this is not what I want to stress here.

Iraqi women's rights activists across Iraq have been spearheading calls for solidarity and international assistance in containing and resisting ISIS. On August 23, 2014, the Iraqi Women's Network issued a statement calling on the international community to take action against ISIS. The network consists of over ninety NGOs throughout Iraq, with largely female activists of all ethnic and religious backgrounds involved in humanitarian assistance and lobbying (Al-Ali 2014).

Many Iraqi and Iraqi-Kurdish women activists link gender-based violence to other forms of violence, including sectarian violence. They lobby their respective governments and political parties to take the struggle against gender-based violence seriously and to protect women's legal rights by implementing existing legislation. According to their own lived experiences and those of the women for whom they have been advocating and campaigning, sectarianism and Islamist extremism work hand in hand with political authoritarianism and militarism to severely curtail women's freedom, opportunities, and abilities to live dignified lives.

Iraqi women activists, like their counterparts in other countries in the region, are tremendously challenged when trying to approach women's rights and gender-based justice in contemporary Iraq. What does it mean to resist gender-based violence in a context of occupation, or neoliberal and imperialist encroachment? What and who needs to be resisted when there are multiple overlapping sources of gender-based violence, some linked to structural inequalities and others to Islamist militancy, sectarianism, and authoritarian militarism? As stated above, Iraqi feminists are challenged to pursue an intersectional political struggle that recognizes the multiple and overlapping configurations of power and inequalities impacting on their lives and severely curtailing their spaces for agency. Local and historically specific forms of patriarchy are inextricably linked to political authoritarianism, and, in the case of Iraq, also sectarianism and ethnic struggles between Arabs and Kurds. The challenges for Iraqi feminists are not merely local and national but also have regional, transnational, and international dimensions. Neoliberal economic restructuring and neoconservative policies go hand in hand in reshaping local gender regimes. In this sense, Iraqi women's rights activists have the rather impossible task of reacting to very immediate and short-term emergencies while keeping the bigger picture in mind.

NOTE

1 Gamal Abdel Nasser was president of Egypt from 1956 to 1970. He assumed the presidency after leading a military coup with the Free Officers, a group of Egyptian army officials. Nasser formed the United Arab Republic with Syria in 1958 and led wars against Israel in the 1950s and 1960s.

BIBLIOGRAPHY

Al-Ali, Nadje. 2007. *Iraqi Women: Untold Stories from 1948 to the Present.* New York: Zed.

———. 2013. "Iraq: Gendering Authoritarianism." Open Democray 50.50, July 15, https://www.opendemocracy.net.

———. 2014. "Sexualized Violence in Iraq: How to Understand and Fight It." Open Democracy 50.50, December 3, https://www.opendemocracy.net.

Al-Ali, Nadje, and Nicole Pratt. 2008. "Researching Women in Post-Invasion Iraq: Negotiating 'Truths' and Deconstructing Dominant Discourses." *Bulletin of the Royal Institute for Inter-Faith Studies* 8, nos. 1 and 2: 1–22.

———. 2009a. "The United States, the Iraqi Women's Diaspora, and Women's Empowerment." In *Iraq: Women and War in the Middle East*, 65–98. London: Zed.

———. 2009b. *What Kind of Liberation: Women and the Occupation of Iraq.* Berkeley: University of California Press.

12

Hidden Voices, Hidden Agendas

Qubaysiat Women's Group in Syria

SANA SAYED

Spring is not just a season; it symbolizes rebirth, revival, and reawakening. However, as more years of civil unrest and political protest ensue, there is no other Arab nation where the words "Arab" and "Spring" are more dissonant than in Syria. As the months have progressed and the deaths have multiplied since March 2011, the revolution in Syria has, as of the writing of this chapter, become a path of destruction, bloodshed, civil war, and an Islamic state invasion.

With the countless losses of lives and the refugees becoming a socioeconomic problem in all neighboring countries, Syrian women have taken on important functions on the war front, whether through cooking for fighters, counseling those who lost loved ones, supplying aid to needy families, administering first aid, or acting as mediators between conflicting parties (Zobairi 2012). Yet Syrian women have questioned what their roles will be, if any, in the aftermath of the conflict.

Though the willingness to fight for human and women's rights in Syria is present, a collective consciousness or voice for Syrian women is lacking. Most women are divided between Islamists and secularists and have organized female-led groups such as the secularist Syrian Women Association, the General Union of Syrian Women, and the Free Syrian Women Organization, as well as the Islamist Syrian Sisterhood and al-Qubaysiat. Probably the most notorious and well organized, al-Qubaysiat has become prominent through its apolitical motto and religious ties to Islam.

This chapter seeks to answer the following question: What is the impact of Islamist women's groups in Syria? To answer this question, this chapter gives an overview of women's activism in Syria by (1) identifying female presence during the Syrian revolution; (2) discussing the non-secular female-led groups that exist in Syria and why they are problematic in terms of enacting sociopolitical change; and (3) explaining the implications that women's participation in the revolution have had for women and their rights in Syria if the current government is removed from power. Research for this chapter consists of online news articles, post–Arab Spring book publications, and interviews with people who have lived in Syria.

Female Presence within the Syrian Revolution: "We Can Do It!"

Organizational efforts on behalf of women are not a new phenomenon in Syria. Regan (2012, 243) suggests that the women's movement dates back to 1948 with the formation of the Syrian Women Association, and to 1967 when the General Union of Syrian Women was established. While these groups have been mostly sponsored by the state, many new groups have recently surfaced. When the Arab Spring began in 2011, women were among the first people to demonstrate through peaceful protests against al-Assad's regime when they marched in Daraa and Damascus in 2011 ("Deaths" 2011). Their roles and functions have expanded since then as the conflict developed. They assisted in smuggling cash, medicine, and arms across checkpoints. They also flocked to provide help in hospitals and media centers, and to organize relief efforts. Rana, a Syrian woman who has been actively participating in the protests, describes how Christians, Muslims, liberals, and conservatives were all involved (Sinjab 2012). Irrespective of their socioeconomic status or religious creed, women united to effect change in Syria and were a proactive part of the political dissidence within the country. One of the few positives of the Arab Spring in Syria has been the exchange of ideas and ideologies of people who would have otherwise never interacted with one another (Giglio 2012).

The revolution has also had many drawbacks, and women have borne the cost of conflict. The Syrian Network for Human Rights (2018) estimates that 27,226 women have been killed in the uprisings as of November 2018 and at least 9,906 women have been detained by the regime. Women are exposed to extremely dangerous situations irrespective of the side they represent. Syrian women describe acts of sexual violence and rape, including abductions by all sides to either gain intelligence or barter for prisoners (International Federation for Human Rights 2013). Fighting for a particular cause renders women easy, vulnerable targets.

Despite their significant participation in protest, women's representation in the governance of secular or religious opposition groups remains meager. Even in opposition areas, women were underrepresented in oppositional councils both inside and outside of Syria (Damon 2013). While women formed a delegation during the 2014 United Nations Conference on Syria in Geneva, their concerns were neither incorporated nor heard.

In an atmosphere where authoritarian regimes reign supreme, women face a challenge in finding their "place" within the larger leadership to express their voices and address their concerns. Only one woman was placed as vice president to the body of forty-one members of the opposition coalition in the 2012 Syrian National Council conference that took place in Doha, Qatar (Laub 2012). Though al-Assad has appointed a female vice president and female cabinet ministers and lawmakers, one potential consequence to his toppling is that women will have to start all over to find their place within the political sphere.

The Rise of Religious Women's Groups in Syria

The Qubaysiat is one of the most popular Islamic revivalist groups in Syria. Founded by Sheykha Munira al-Qubaysi in the 1960s, this group's membership is restricted only to women and has its stronghold in Damascus. As a former teacher who worked in many different schools, Munira al-Qubaysi used her profession to preach the Islamic teachings she had learned under Syrian grand mufti Shaykh Ahmad Kuftaro. The organization's main goal is to focus on Islamic teachings of the Quran and Hadith, with the belief that society benefits when ethics and morals are rooted in faith. One of the reasons why the movement attracted so many followers is that it does not identify itself with a specific Sunni sect of Islam.

Members of the Qubaysiat are organized in hierarchical ranks and can be identified by the color of their hijab. All wear dark blue overcoats and a hijab with a distinctive knot below their chins. New members, or those with nominal participation, wear white hijabs. Women in the middle rank wear light blue hijabs. Their primary functions are to recruit new members, execute organizational tasks, and disseminate religious education to younger followers of the group. Senior members demarcate themselves by donning dark blue hijabs or entirely black attire. These women are responsible for explicating complex concepts such as Islamic law and jurisprudence. Irrespective of rank, al-Qubaysiat women do not wear *niqab* (Islamic face covering). The reason the Qubaysiat embraces the color blue is that its members believe blue is the color of the place between heaven and earth, which is also the figurative location where they spiritually exist ("Al-Qubaysiat" 2006).

Another defining attribute of the Qubaysiat is its secrecy. It is a tightly knit group that exerts a lot of control, especially over its younger members. Former Qubaysiat members say that they are indoctrinated to revere Munira al-Qubaysi more than their own family members and are supposed to establish close relationships with the Shaykhahs, higher-ranking Qubaysiat women. They are encouraged to report all of their personal information to the Shaykhah, and oftentimes marry and divorce based on the Shaykhah's encouragement (Sarkis 2006). To maintain their secrecy, the organization prohibits regular women from attending Qubaysiat meetings without prior appointments and approvals. Munira al-Qubaysi's location is also guarded; she is believed to be living in a heritage area of Damascus ("100 Most Powerful" 2011). Some believe that the regime is completely aware of the Qubaysiat's activities considering the government's iron-fist control (Sarkis 2006). Whether this is true or not, the fact remains that the Qubaysiat flourishes in all parts of Syria and is the largest Islamist group that is exclusive to women.

The Qubaysiat has retained its popularity with and without government support. For example, after the 1982 Hama massacre, in which the Syrian Arab Army and the Defense Companies crushed antigovernment sentiments led by Sunni Muslim groups, al-Qubaysiat members met secretly within mosques and *madrasas* despite having nothing to do with the 1982 uprisings. These clandestine and undisclosed meetings are the reason why it was estimated that by the end of 2000, half of the religious schools designated for women in Damascus were controlled by the Qubaysiat (Lefèvre 2013).

Syria's political climate in the earlier part of the twenty-first century solidified the organization's presence through government support.

Bashar al-Assad, still in the early years of his rule, faced foreign pressure because of the US-Israeli axis and the ongoing Lebanese crisis (Pierret 2013, 94). To generate domestic support and conscious of his nation's growing religious fervor, al-Assad relaxed laws and regulations that had previously been implemented by his father, Hafez al-Assad. Clerical salaries increased, girls were allowed to wear hijab to public schools, and the Qubaysiat were permitted to publicly organize. To further legitimize his intentions and broker goodwill, al-Assad established ties with religious factions. By appointing Muhammad al-Sayyid as the minister of religious affairs in 2007, al-Assad accomplished two tasks: he further reestablished state authority and unified the content of al-Qubaysiat's religious teachings (Pierret 2013, 98).

The Qubaysiat's founder, Munira al-Qubaysi, publicly supported the regime. In a speech delivered in 2014, a spokesperson for the Qubaysiat stated that its movement had stayed strong because of the support it received from the Ministry of Religious Affairs, and because in 2008 the government officially moved the organization to mosques so that members no longer had to organize privately in homes ("Al-Qubaysiyat" 2014). Currently, the Qubaysiat has the largest number of official schools in Damascus, Aleppo, Homs, Hama, and Deir ez-Zor. Their most popular and well-established schools are Dar Al Naeem and Dar Al Falah in Damascus. Although primarily established in Syria, the Qubaysiat are also now located and organized in Vienna, Paris, and various parts of the United States (Landis 2006). From remote areas of Syria to major international cities, it is clear that the revolution has not curbed the Qubaysiat's activities.

Some people believe that the Qubaysiat's apolitical stance has been threatened by the ongoing civil war in Syria. The movement's primary aim continues to be focusing on teaching its followers the Quran and Hadith, neither of which are followed by the regime. In interviews, al-Qubaysiat women admit to being taught how to influence male family members so that their husbands, fathers, and brothers demonstrate a greater public manifestation of Islam (Zoepf 2006). The group is also known to draw support from women of high rank, i.e., women who are daughters, wives, and sisters of people who are in politically, socially, and financially viable positions. While the organization's founder, Munira al-Qubaysi, continues her movement rooted in faith, she was also

Figure 12.1. Qubaysiat

recognized as the twenty-fourth most influential Muslim in the world by the Royal Islamic Strategic Studies Centre in 2011. Divisions have arisen within the Qubaysiat because it certainly has the power to enact change; however, whether or not it will take action remains a contentious issue.

Many Qubaysiats believe that Islam needs to expand on national and global fronts. They believe that Islam's foundational beliefs, such as Sharia law, are ultimately ideologies that oppose al-Assad's ruling minority. Though the official stance of the Qubaysiat is apolitical in nature and does not support the revolution, a small but increasing number of the Qubaysiat have left the movement to join the revolution or the Syrian Sisterhood (Lefèvre 2013). Other members acknowledge that al-Assad's regime conflicts with their Islamic teachings, but they remain silent out of fear. Women who have left the Qubaysiat believe that the organization's ongoing support for the government only makes it more difficult to call out al-Assad's dictatorial regime. As long as the Qubaysiat continues to exclude itself from politics, it will not reconcile with other secular or nonsecular women's groups in Syria.

The Syrian Sisterhood

Like the Qubaysiat, the Syrian Sisterhood is also an Islamist movement. Its history can be traced back to the 1950s when its creator, Amina Sheikha, was influenced by Mustafa al-Sib'ai, cofounder of Syria's Muslim Brotherhood. While they have always been active organizers with strong influences over leaders of the Muslim Brotherhood, the Syrian Sisterhood (along with the Muslim Brotherhood) was crushed after the 1982 Hama massacre and membership in the organization became illegal. Similarly to the Qubaysiat, their activities had to be carried out in secret. Eventually, key leaders who were not imprisoned found refuge abroad, and the movement continues to operate primarily in networks outside of Syria.

As Syria's Muslim Brotherhood gained ground abroad, so did the Sisterhood. By providing services to exiled Syrians within Jordan after the Arab Spring, the Syrian Sisterhood achieved greater recognition and prominence through its philanthropic efforts (Lefèvre 2013). It enhanced the Brotherhood's image among antigovernment supporters and their own within the organization. They elected leadership positions and are part of the Brotherhood's consultative body. The Syrian Sisterhood also has a small yet integral role in the Muslim Brotherhood's youth division. When the youth branch organized a meeting in Istanbul in December 2012, the Sisterhood proposed offering financial assistance to small businesses located in rebel areas and formulated solutions to help sexually abused women reintegrate into society (Lefèvre 2013).

Despite its independent positive efforts, the Sisterhood is essentially under the umbrella of Syria's Muslim Brotherhood. Accordingly, it actively opposes al-Assad's regime. The Brotherhood preaches democratic ideals for Syria once al-Assad is relieved of governmental control. The Muslim Brotherhood released a statement in October 2012, defining its vision for Syria, which is very inclusive of women. According to its list of guiding principles, Syria's Muslim Brotherhood asserts women's equal rights to education, employment, and politics; it believes in "safeguarding women's gains and enhancing their role in various fields so they can contribute to the advancement of society" (Carnegie Endowment for International Peace 2013). With its promise of democracy and autonomy for women, the Syrian Muslim Brotherhood garners tremendous support among its Sisterhood wing. The Syrian Sisterhood is further witnessing an increase of members as oppositional support mounts.

Female-led movements such as the Qubaysiat and the Syrian Sisterhood are a primary means through which women organize and have a collective voice. They gain rights, freedoms, and greater mobility through unifying and aligning themselves with such groups. However, since the Qubaysiat is politically impartial and the Syrian Sisterhood is politically involved, two of the most popular women-led Islamist groups in Syria are dissident with one another. Unable to coalesce, they continue to work on independent fronts.

Women's Rights in a Postwar Future

The current landscape of Syria has become more complex considering the existence of Islamist women and men. While the Syrian Sisterhood is an example of Islamist women who are politicized, the Qubaysiat consists of Islamist women who mostly keep to themselves and do not take sides in the conflict. The myriad of movements within Syria with their own ideologies and goals is an inherent outcome since oppositional thoughts and principles stem from discordant discourses between state and civil society.

A challenge will remain as to how to reconcile the conflicting ideologies of Islamists and secularists under one nation. As one activist states, "For many, the biggest challenge now faced by women is that of claiming 'their place' in the Arab Spring as traditional ideas and practices, as well as Islamist beliefs and interests reassert themselves" (Regan 2012, 248). The civil war is ongoing in Syria because there are so many rival ideological groups vying for power. They have their own followers and established power centers depending on the region of Syria where they are well-liked and prevalent. If al-Assad's regime is toppled by an extremist group, women's participation in the revolution will be in vain. Islamist women's groups in Syria will have to resolve their differences with one another and with secularists for a constructive postwar future.

BIBLIOGRAPHY

"Al-Qubaysiat: A Mysterious Islamic Female Movement with more than 70 Thousand Members; Started in Syria, Dressed in Dark Blue Hijab." 2006. Al Arabiya, May 3, http://www.alarabiya.net (accessed October 24, 2019).

"Al-Qubaysiyat and the Syrian Regime: The Jurisprudence of the Conflict." 2014. You-Tube video, 4:06. Posted by "Munshaqat from Qubaysiiat," April 18, https://www.youtube.com/watch?v=JpYos_IC-_k (accessed February 6, 2019).

Carnegie Endowment for International Peace. 2013. "Building the Syrian State: A Plan by the Syrian Muslim Brotherhood." January 17, http://carnegieendowment.org (accessed February 6, 2019).

Damon, Arwa. 2013. "Syria's Women: Fighting a War on Two Fronts." CNN, March 7, http://edition.cnn.com (accessed February 6, 2019).

"Deaths as Syrian Forces Fire on Protestors." 2011. Al Jazeera, March 7. https://www.aljazeera.com.

Giglio, Mike. 2012. "Syria's Women of the Revolution Indispensable to Rebel Fight." *Newsweek*, October 1, https://www.newsweek.com (accessed February 6, 2019).

International Federation for Human Rights. 2013. "Violence against Women in Syria: Breaking the Silence." April 9, http://www.fidh.org (accessed February 6, 2019).

Landis, Joshua. 2006. "The Qubaysi Women's Islamic Movement by Ibrahim Hamidi." *SyriaComment.com*, May 16, http://joshualandis.oucreate.com/syriablog/2006/05/qubaysi-womens-islamic-movement-by.htm (accessed February 17, 2019).

Laub, Karin. 2012. "Women Shut Out of Syria's Oppositional Leadership." *USA Today*, November 8, http://www.usatoday.com (accessed February 6, 2019).

Lefèvre, Raphaël. 2013. "The Rise of the Syrian Sisterhood." Carnegie Endowment for International Peace, April 25, https://carnegieendowment.org (accessed February 6, 2019).

"100 Most Powerful Arab Women 2011: Sheikha Munira Qubeysi." 2011. *Arabian Business*, https://www.arabianbusiness.com (accessed February 6, 2019).

Pierret, Thomas. 2013. "The State Management of Religion in Syria: The End of 'Indirect Rule'?" In *Middle East Authoritarianisms: Governance, Contestation, and Regime Resilience in Syria and Iran*, ed. Steven Heydemann and Reinoud Leenders, 83–106. Stanford, CA: Stanford University Press.

Regan, Colm. 2012. "Women, Citizenship, and Change: The Role of the Women's Movement in the Arab World." In *Change and Opportunities in the Emerging Mediterranean*, ed. Stephen Calleya and Monika Wohlfeld, 234–51. Malta: Gutenberg Press.

Sarkis, Mona. 2006. "Al-Qubaysiyat Work to Penetrate Decision-Making Circles." Qantara.de, October 9, http://ar.qantara.de (accessed February 6, 2019).

Sinjab, Lina. 2012. "Women Play Central Role in Syria Uprising." BBC News Middle East, May 13, http://www.bbc.co.uk (accessed February 6, 2019).

Syrian Network for Human Rights. 2018. "A Suffering Syrian Woman Is a Recipe for a Torn Country and Displaced Society." November 25, http://sn4hr.org (accessed February 6, 2019).

Zobairi, Ambar. 2012. "Using Research on the Status of Women to Improve Public Policies in the Middle East and North Africa." International Foundation for Electoral Systems, October 23, https://www.ifes.org.

Zoepf, Katherine. 2006. "Islamic Revival in Syria Is Led by Women." *New York Times*, August 29, http://www.nytimes.com (accessed February 6, 2019).

13

The Egyptian Revolution and the Feminist Divide

SAMAA GAMIE

Asmaa Mahfouz was one of the influential women figures of the Egyptian revolution, a twenty-eight-year-old Egyptian woman who had gained fame for being one of the founders of the April 6th movement (one of the Egyptian youth movements that played a central part in propelling the revolution) and a prominent member of Egypt's Coalition of the Youth of the Revolution. Mahfouz's January 18 video log, which was posted one week before the start of the 2011 Egyptian revolution, is credited by many for igniting the first spark of the mass Egyptian uprising. The pro-Mubarak regime and its successive military establishment used counterrevolutionary cyber pockets and the media to discredit and vilify Asmaa Mahfouz along with most revolutionary and activist figures of the April 6th movement. They framed her winning the Shakarov Prize for Freedom of Thought in 2011 (an international human rights prize honoring activists who fight against intolerance, fanaticism, and oppression)[1] as a reward for conspiring with the West against Egypt. These claims fueled rumors such as her receiving millions of dollars from foreign financiers, being arrested for espionage, or being an undercover Islamist and Muslim Brotherhood (MB) supporter.[2] Circulated on Facebook pages and state-controlled media sources, these rumors triggered massive backlash against her and other revolutionary figures. In her January 18 and 24, 2011, video logs (vlogs) on YouTube,[3] Asmaa Mahfouz laid out her argument for participating in the January 25, 2011, demonstrations in Egypt, by utilizing both secular and Islamic feminism.

Deploying secular feminism, her rhetoric evoked the discourses of Western humanism, democracy, and Arab nationalism as she defied the culturally sanctioned concept of male guardianship over the female body, whose freedom of movement is restricted in public spaces.

Figure 13.1. Asmaa Mahfouz

Mahfouz's January 18 vlog referenced the four Egyptians who lit them-selves on fire to protest poverty, hunger, and government corruption. She presented these Egyptians' self-immolation act as symbolic of their sacrifices and their hope that Egyptians would replicate the Tunisian revolution and reclaim their human rights, freedoms, and dignity.

Asmaa Mahfouz also employed Islamic feminism and used an Islamic framework to articulate and legitimate her call for action and construct her Islamic feminist ethos. With her multiple references to "Allah," her use of Quranic verses, and her evoking the fear of God, she made the argument for political activism as a religious obligation to end injustice and corruption, asserting the following: "You have to fear God. God says that he does not change the conditions of a people until they change themselves." She merged her feminist standpoint and ethos, and fluctu-ated between secularism and Islamic feminism. This strategic fluctua-tion allowed her to construct a liberating discourse that transcended the delimiting powers of patriarchal hegemony, and critiqued the political and religious patriarchal discourses that had long oppressed the Egyp-tian people and rendered them powerless in the face of a corrupt police state that had long acted with impunity. Her strategic deployment of traditional Islamic symbols softened the violent backlash of religious conservatism and its vigilantes in cyber- and real spaces who consistently admonish Muslim women's visibility in public spaces.

In deconstructing and rhetorically analyzing the cyber feminist discourses of Asmaa Mahfouz, I examine the ways in which her activism critiqued hegemonic discourses (Hekman 1997), defied patriarchy, and reinstated the authority of experience in her discourses as a woman. Undeniably, her "multiple consciousness" (McClish and Bacon 2002, 33), which often characterizes the rhetoric of the marginalized, shaped her antihegemonic and innovative discourse. Mahfouz represented the "privileged" standpoint of the subjugated, whose voices "are privileged because they seem to promise more adequate, sustained, objective, transforming accounts of the world" (Haraway 1988, 584). In this analysis, I explore how the construction of ethos in these discourses becomes inseparable from one's gendered and racialized experiences, paying particular attention to the dynamics of constructing one's real and virtual self/selves in interactions with others and with/in digital media.

In this essay, and as part of my analysis of the feminist ethos in revolutionary digital pockets, I explore whether the Internet propagates genuinely new, nonracist, and nonsexist, but intersubjective, ways of identity construction that effectually critique hegemony. I also ask whether cyberspace becomes merely a tool of reenactment and reproduction of the dominant culture and discourses at large, where the minority and dominated subjects reenact the narratives they seek to resist (Nakamura 2008). Finally, I ask Judith Butler's question: What makes certain nonconformist discursive and rhetorical repetitions "become domesticated and recirculated as instruments of cultural hegemony" (1990, 139) and thus unable to carry within them the potential and possibility for social transformation?

In digital communications, ethos emerges as a central component, whether we view ethos as one's credibility displayed by one's good or moral character (Plato 2001), an element of style (Quintilian 2001), a "dwelling place" (Hyde 2004), a network of communal discursive practices that is ideally "multi-voiced and authentic" (Brooke 1991), negotiated with social institutions, or situated in "one's locatedness in various social and cultural 'spaces'" (Reynolds 1993, 325–38). The rich discourses on ethos stem from the central role feminism plays and has played in challenging and redefining the traditional conception of ethos, which was conventionally seen as singular, emphasizing the conventional and the public rather than the private and idiosyncratic. Thus, ethos emerges as a central element for carving a space for untraditional voices and instating authority in conventionally unauthoritative spaces, discourses, and experiences, while articulating one's subject position, one's "limited location," and one's "situated" and "embodied knowledges" (Haraway 1988, 583).

Furthermore, the conception of ethos among Middle Eastern feminists asserts that their modes of articulation of womanhood depart from the Western construction. These Middle Eastern feminists claim their agency and political maturity as subjects (Zine 2004, 168) who are capable of defining and articulating their own legitimate mode of feminism within the sign systems they already inhabit. Hence, secular feminism and Islamic feminism emerge as the two dominant feminist paradigms in the Middle East. Secular feminists offer a progressive, antipatriarchal, reformist, "Islamist," humanistic discourse (Badran 2005) that is antiracist and antisexist, while Islamic feminists advocate a new understanding of gender justice and reform in Islam within the parameters of Islamic tradition (Zine 2004, 176), without, however, disavowing or challenging patriarchal theocracy. However dominant these two feminist paradigms are in the discourses of Arab women, they do not exclude the emergence of other hybrid feminist paradigms that are influenced by Western secularism and liberalism.

I explore here the complexity of ethos construction in Asmaa Mahfouz and her revolutionary digital feminist discourses by analyzing the visual and textual elements employed in her political activism and revolutionary work. I further examine the challenges posed to her ethos in these virtual discourses, including the mechanism of silencing the female other and discrediting the feminist ethos. Finally, I reflect upon the means that Mahfouz used to subvert these challenges through the re-deconstruction, re-definition, and re-imagination of feminist ethos in cyber spaces.

Asmaa Mahfouz's Feminist Ethos

Mahfouz employed both secular and Islamic feminism to construct her feminist ethos. By framing her revolutionary and activist discourse within the parameters of secular Western humanistic values, she referenced "fundamental human rights," "dignity," "freedom," and "humanity" and impressed upon Egyptians the necessity "to go down on January 25 . . . and demand our rights, our fundamental rights as human beings." Her activist rhetoric and her evocation of the values of universal humanism, democracy, and human rights for all presented the crux of her argument for political activism and framed her revolutionary feminist ethos and standpoint. Mahfouz also employed Islamic feminism and used an Islamic framework to articulate and legitimate her call for action. Her consistent use of traditional Islamic references and symbols, evident in the Islamic headscarf, to discursively and visually frame her discourses and ethos were attempts to validate her revolutionary discourses and avoid the violent backlash of religious conservatives who consistently admonish women's visibility in public (cyber and physical) spaces.

In her January 24 vlog, Mahfouz articulated the belief that the collective will and action of the people, both men and women, Muslim and Christian, would bring about political change and end injustice. These beliefs laid the groundwork for her appeals to people to join the demonstrations. Mahfouz emphasized the Arab dream for unity, freedom, and democracy and voiced her hopes for a nonsectarian Egypt, as she stated, "I want to buy, with all the money I have, roses and to go to all the Christians in Egypt and give each a rose and tell them, it is my duty to protect you. This is our country and you are our brothers and sisters." Thus, in these calls, Mahfouz transcended religious boundaries between Christians and Muslims and fused her discourse with Islamic modernism and the emergent postsectarian Egyptian nationalism.

On her Facebook page, Mahfouz called for Egyptians to keep up the fight following the Egyptian revolution, and she attacked the old, undemocratic tactics used by the military establishment, which took over after Mubarak's ousting, its mishandling of political and economic reforms, and the power assigned by the military to remnants of the old regime in postrevolutionary Egypt.

In her September 28, 2011, note titled "A Revolution to Reclaim a Revolution," Mahfouz listed the policy and security failures of the Supreme Military Council that had been ruling Egypt since Mubarak's ousting. She reminded Egyptians that they were the ones who made possible the greatest revolution in history but that revolution was being ravaged and plundered by what she perceived to be the "incompetence" of the military regime. Instead of accepting the new status quo, Mahfouz presented an alternative national plan of action to redirect the revolution to its perceived correct path of reform by calling for a civil state to replace the military in overseeing the post-Mubarak transitional period. Mahfouz's activist posts framed her feminist ethos and gave credence to her calls for a more just and free Egypt within a secular feminist framework.

The feminist standpoint Mahfouz articulated on her pages presented her defiance of the discourse of political patriarchy. She asserted that it was the power and will of the people that had ignited the revolution, rather than those in power, who only sought to maintain the status quo. She also expressed her defiance of the injustices perpetrated by the military, security forces, and the political elite in violating the rights of Egyptian citizens. In her Facebook posts, through claiming her standpoint as an Egyptian revolutionary and activist, she was able to present her dual perspective and analysis of the state of affairs in Egypt. Mahfouz unabashedly criticized what she saw as the undemocratic practices of the military while laying out an alternative route for the liberation of her people.

Challenges to Her Activism

In an attempt to halt the revolution and maintain the status quo in Egypt, the state-sponsored media intensified the defamatory campaign against Asmaa Mahfouz. She was accused of being an Islamist, a Masonic, a Zionist, a Western agent, and even a traitor. Some claimed that she "has sunk our country and left it" to continue her work for the foreign organizations that had sponsored her. Anti-Islamists, pro-Mubarak, and pro-military vigilantes also used gender bashing and personal attacks that carried within them overtly misogynistic and graphic sexual references. Such verbal attacks represented the patriarchal mechanism for silencing, shaming, and discrediting the female "Other." Mahfouz shared her frustration with the derogatory comments and insults on her page in two posts on October 8, 2012. She contemplated whether she should allow people to post again on her Facebook page or restrict the page.

By canceling the comment option, Mahfouz illustrated that in online spaces, the need arises to silence radical dissenting voices. In this space, however, silencing and ostracism are exercised in order to maintain the integrity of activist and revolutionary discourses against the systematic, vehement cyber attacks that are constantly deployed to discredit these activists and muffle their voices.

When a widely supported military coup reinstated the power of the military under General Abd El Fattah El Sissy in July 2013,[4] Asmaa Mahfouz expressed her defiance of the military rule. On October 22, 2013, she shared a letter to the then minister of defense, General El Sissy, calling him the "actual President" of Egypt and discrediting the authority of the civil government that he had appointed. She criticized the curfew and the reinstated emergency laws, arguing that they failed to improve security conditions as people continued to feel unsafe and terrorist attacks continued to increase every day. Mahfouz was unphased by the violent backlash against her, and her public defiance of the military at the height of its popularity underscores her feminist ethos and her standpoint that rejects the silencing of revolutionary voices through the paternalistic rhetoric of the military. Mahfouz's defiant rhetoric and fearless criticism of the government, combined with her calls for the freedom of all political prisoners, were amplified on Facebook. In the cover picture of her page, she featured Mahienour ElMassry, a young woman activist who was sentenced to three years in prison for participating in one of the 2011 demonstrations against police brutality. The cover picture makes a profound statement attesting to the atmosphere of fear that has become pervasive among many activists in Egypt. This fear has resulted from the recently-passed law that criminalizes demonstrations and unauthorized public gatherings. The pictures and stories she posted of Mahienour and others expressed her defiance of the forgotten and untold stories of all political prisoners.

Mahfouz's feminist ethos was also constructed throughout the page with posts about her husband, her one-year-old daughter, and her family. Her personal story was intermixed with her political activism. Through her posts, she expressed a profound articulation of womanhood as a form of revolution. Revolution was no longer just the real and virtual banners carried in demonstrations but also the deployment of the female body in public spaces. By posting her wedding pictures and her pictures with her daughter, she created a profound narrative of visibility of womanhood that challenged the physical limitations placed on the female body. She also defied the conservative patriarchal religious discourse that constantly polices the female body and calls for its invisibility and exclusion from public spaces. In foregrounding her defiant feminist narrative, Mahfouz wrote on June 5, 2014, "The more ruthless the prison guard is, the more scared he is of my voice." By situating her fight for justice and freedom in her right to speak, she was able to tell her story and affirm her own subjectivity, while shedding light on the oppressive material, political, and social conditions that perpetuate oppression and women's silencing in her society.

Mahfouz's deployment of the female body is also evident in her posts on June 8 on the gang raping of a young mother in Tahrir Square on the night of the national celebrations of the inauguration of President El Sissy on June 8, 2014. She condemned the society's denial of women's humanity and rights and its objectification of women's bodies, which she said are only seen as "shameful" and treated as "sources of male pleasure." She blamed Egyptian men for habitually turning a blind eye on sexual harassment and for shamelessly blaming the rape victim. Her frustration with the violation of the female body by men, who feel entitled to grope or violate it whenever they wish, was amplified when she wrote, "Have Mercy! Have Mercy! The Egyptian woman has been screaming for years and everyone turns a blind eye." Her posts gave voice to the women who had been sexually and verbally harassed on the streets of Egypt, and who were made to feel ashamed of their bodies and to hate that they were ever born in a society they felt had little regard for women, while simultaneously condemning the culture of male entitlement and patriarchal impunity in her society.

Through the discursive and visual representations of protest, Asmaa Mahfouz used her digital discourses to successfully construct a coherent racialized and gendered digital ethos that assimilated this digital medium by bringing voice to the silenced and erased struggles of the marginalized in her community. Undoubtedly, the intensification of the public attacks on Mahfouz raises many questions about the challenges facing activists in revolutionary and nonconformist cyber pockets where one's ethos can be easily discredited. In this revolutionary cyber pocket, cyberspace no longer became a tool of reenactment and reproduction of the dominant culture and discourses or a venue for the tacking together of identity from stereotypical cultural narratives in media sources and in dominant discourses. Instead, it was transformed to become a means of subverting political erasure, patriarchy, male entitlement, and oppressive gender power relations for the purpose of creating a space for liberation.

Conclusion

Asmaa Mahfouz's emergent ethos, from the onset, combined both an Islamic and a secular feminist ethos that was visually and discursively constructed through her utilization of Islamic symbols and references and her use of the body with its Islamic symbol of the headscarf as the signifier of the Islamic nation and its desire for liberation, as well as of the values of democracy, universal humanism, Islamic modernism, and postsectarian Egyptian nationalism. Her hybrid Islamic and secular feminist ethos framed her civic and political activism and gave credence to her calls for all Egyptians to demand a more just and free Egypt. The feminist standpoint Mahfouz articulated in her vlogs and on her Facebook pages presented her defiance of the discourses of political and military patriarchal entitlements, as she asserted the power and will of all the people who had ignited the revolution, and presented her defiance of the injustices perpetrated by the military. The misogynistic and patriarchal backlash against Mahfouz for her defiance of the Mubarak regime, the Supreme Military Council, and, later, President El Sissy presented a snapshot of the mechanisms of silencing and discrediting the female Other. It also embodied the challenges facing Arab and Muslim women who traverse the virtual domain and tread the masculine political sphere in their patriarchal and conservative societies, hence violating the code of silence and invisibility that confines women within the private domain of domesticity.

The feminist ethos Mahfouz constructed in articulating her central feminist standpoint created a powerful activist and revolutionary discourse that did not subscribe to the normative representations of Arab women in Western or Arab contexts. Undeniably, in the context of the Egyptian revolution, Mahfouz's feminist digital discourses facilitated the construction of empowered digital identities and the emergence of substantial opportunities for shifts in gender power relations that enabled the partial subversion of normative gender performatives, illustrating how in rare revolutionary times substantial opportunities for shifts in gender power relations emerge that enable the subversion of gender performatives and gendered identities. However, these shifts were on a small scale and did not produce the massive or lasting transformation hoped for by this woman activist. These transformative feminist discourses were constricted by the power of patriarchy and its discourses of religious and political propriety, which did not allow for the widespread exposure of these liberatory discourses. Eventually, these dissident discourses were dismissed, effectually hindering the transformative powers of these discourses to change these oppressive norms and practices and realize women's liberation.

The mechanism used for silencing the female Other, discrediting the feminist ethos in cyberspace, and policing feminist spaces replicated the challenges facing women and minorities in real spaces as the same forms of cyber shaming, harassment, and misogyny are replicated in these virtual antipatriarchal spaces. As evident from these activist discourses, the Internet is a powerful medium with a tremendous potential to disseminate activist and revolutionary discourses and challenge patriarchy, oppression, and the concentration of power in real and virtual spaces. However, that narrative does not account for limited access for minorities, including the socially, culturally, and economically disadvantaged, and the marginalized in Third World communities whose stories are left untold. It also does not question the relevance of cyberspace as a means of disseminating activist discourses and messages to dismantle the dynamics of silencing and erasure of the marginalized, nor does it account for the oppressive structures that limit the transformative powers of these discourses.

The above analysis of this activist's virtual space revealed an undeniable fact that revolutionary times carry within them the potential for creating fluid social spaces that allow for social change through shifts in gender power relations and normative gender performatives. The in-between space women activists occupy between identification and dis-identification within the web of normative gender and cultural performances that define womanhood allows for the production of a counterhegemonic discourse that could become an instrument of cultural awareness and political change. Thus, the need arises to examine how the digital medium can promote and sustain revolutionary and activist discourses and to examine the means of subverting the limitations of the virtual domain and of escaping the stronghold of patriarchal, conformist, and normative discourses and spaces.

NOTES

1 For more about the Shakarov Prize for Freedom of Thought, see "About Parliament," European Parliament, http://www.europarl.europa.eu.

2 The MB had been vilified by media sources ever since it rose to power following the first democratic elections in Egypt in 2012.

3 "Meet Asmaa Mahfouz and the Vlog That Helped Spark the Revolution." YouTube, January 18, 2011, http://www.youtube.com/watch?v=SgjIgMdsEuk.

4 General Abdel Fattah El Sissy was formerly a member of the Supreme Military Council (SCAF) during Mubarak's rule. He was later appointed as the head of the Supreme Military Council by the former president, Mohammed Morsi, who was later ousted by SCAF in July 2013. General El Sissy was elected as president in June 2014.

BIBLIOGRAPHY

Badran, Margot. 2005. "Between Secular and Islamic Feminism/s: Reflections on the Middle East and Beyond." *Journal of Middle East Women's Studies* 1, no. 1: 6–28.

Brooke, Robert E. 1991. *Writing and Sense of Self: Identity Negotiation in Writing Workshops.* Urbana, IL: NCTE.

Butler, Judith. 1990. *Gender Trouble: Feminism and the Subversion of Identity.* New York: Routledge.

Haraway, Donna. 1988. "Situated Knowledges: The Science Question in Feminism and the Privilege of Partial Perspective." *Feminist Studies* 14, no. 3: 575–99.

Hekman, Susan. 1997. "Truth and Method: Feminist Standpoint Theory Revisited." *Signs* 22, no. 2: 341–65.

Hyde, Michael J., ed. 2004. *The Ethos of Rhetoric.* Columbia: University of South Carolina Press, 2004.

McClish, Glenn, and Jacqueline Bacon. 2002. "'Telling the Story Her Own Way': The Role of Feminist Standpoint Theory in Rhetorical Studies." *RSQ* 32, no. 2: 27–55.

Nakamura, Lisa. 2008. *Digitizing Race: Visual Cultures of the Internet.* Minneapolis: University of Minnesota Press.

Plato. "Gorgias." 2001. In *The Rhetorical Tradition: Readings from Classical Times to the Present.* 2nd ed., ed. Patricia Bizzell and Bruce Herzberg, 87–138. Boston: Bedford/St Martins, 2001.

Quintilian. 2001. "Institutes of Oratory." In *The Rhetorical Tradition: Readings from Classical Times to the Present.* 2nd ed., ed. Patricia Bizzell and Bruce Herzberg, 364–428. Boston: Bedford/St. Martins, 2001.

Reynolds, Nedra. 1993. "Ethos as Location: New Sites for Understanding Discursive Authority." *Rhetoric Review* 11, no. 2: 325–38.

Zine, Jasmin. 2004. "Creating a Critical Faith-Centered Space for Antiracist Feminism: Reflections of a Muslim Scholar-Activist." *Journal of Feminist Studies in Religion* 20, no. 2: 167–87.

14

Algerian Feminists Navigate Authoritarianism

MARO YOUSSEF

Starting in the 1990s, Algerian feminists, who were committed to human rights and women's rights, oddly supported the authoritarian rule of President Abdel Aziz Bouteflika and viewed him as the best option available to women, until his ouster from power in 2019. Their support was founded on their fear of the Islamists and on their beliefs that Bouteflika was capable of preventing Islamists from regaining power. By aligning their efforts with him, women believed that they could stop Islamists from reversing the rights that women had already achieved by imposing their conservative version of Islam on Algerian society. During the Algerian Civil War, Islamists used extreme violence and brutality against civilians and women. After the devastation of the Algerian Civil War, women formed a "patriarchal bargain" (Kandiyoti 1988) with the Bouteflika regime wherein they provided their political support in exchange for protection from Islamists and the preservation of women's rights. Feminists I interviewed in 2013 saw this alliance as a partnership for gender equality in Algeria.

Algerian women, similarly to other Middle Eastern and Muslim women, strike a bargain in patriarchal settings based on strategizing "within a set of concrete constraints" (Kandiyoti 1988, 275). Secular elite women often offer their support and allegiance to the state in exchange for security, economic incentives, and liberal gender policies. Given the trauma of war and disappearances, women in particular, especially elite women, felt vulnerable and in need of stability. However, these women's alignment with Bouteflika's National Liberation Front party (FLN) was not surprising, as it reflected their secular beliefs and privileged economic status.

This study draws on interviews conducted in Algiers and Oran, Algeria, in 2013, as well as on consultations with Algerian and Western media sources, US and UN annual reports, and academic scholarship on Algeria. I conducted nine semistructured in-person interviews in Arabic, English, and French with women from diverse professional and ideological backgrounds. I identified highly educated elites known in diplomatic and international nongovernmental organization (NGO) circles, including two human-rights and family lawyers (Karima and Samia), a physician (Yasmine), a scientist/engineer (Amina), an entrepreneur (Hoda), a journalist (Lina), a women's rights activists (Nour), the director of a women's organization (Sherifa), and a member of Parliament (Nawal). They identified as Islamists, nationalists, moderates, and socialists, all along the ideological spectrum. I interviewed Amina, Sherifa, and Hoda in Oran, Algeria, on September 5, 2013, and I interviewed Lina, Samia, Nour, Yasmine, Nawal, and Karima in Algiers between September 1 and September 10, 2013. I have substituted my interviewees' actual names with pseudonyms to protect their identities.

Bouteflika: A "Champion for Women"

When Bouteflika came to power in 1999, he imposed an authoritarian political system that, despite its many flaws, demonstrated a strong commitment to women's rights. Although many Algerians who had economic grievances challenged the authoritarian regime, many did not want to see his regime overthrown. They considered his secular policies a bulwark against Islamism and a guarantor of women's rights (Karima). Activists expressed their conviction that the gender gap is indeed diminishing in Algeria's labor market and political landscape. They pointed to their own successes as testament to their claims (Nawal, Amina, Hoda). Older feminists were proud of their generation's achievements, which enabled women to enter positions that were traditionally dominated by men—such as journalism, law, the military, and law enforcement (Lowe 2009). Nour, a renowned journalist, activist, and former FLN member, described Bouteflika as the "champion for women" for his ability to restore some of women's rights that had previously been denied. She admired Bouteflika for pushing for women's reforms despite Parliament's opposition on several occasions, by issuing presidential ordinances while Parliament was on recess.

The Algerian state has used legislation in an effort to consolidate support and establish its legitimacy. The Bouteflika government introduced new legislation to foster more equality within the family and raise women's social and economic status, including amendments to the Algerian Family and Nationality Codes. In 2005, Bouteflika amended the Family Code, which strengthened women's right to divorce, to gain custody of their children, and to restrict polygamy. He also amended the Nationality Code, allowing women to pass down on their nationality to their children.

The Islamists passed a series of repressive laws during the 1980s that limited women's rights. In 1981, conservative Islamists backed a family code that permitted married women to work outside the home only if specified in the marriage contract or allowed by their husbands. The code imposed some restrictions on polygamy and offered six grounds for women to divorce their husbands (Charrad 2001). Many feminists protested the law, arguing that these reforms were insufficient (Salhi 2003). In 1984, the National People's Assembly (APN) hastily passed a more restrictive family code that "imposed many serious limitations on women's rights, including the right to equality before the law and the right of self-determination" (Kelly and Breslin 2010). The new law weakened women's right to divorce and permitted polygamy. Again, many women protested the law, but to no avail. Some activists even referred to the 1984 Family Code as "the Code of Shame."

During his second term's presidential campaign in 2004, Bouteflika vowed to abolish the 1984 Family Code and bolster women's rights (Karima, Samia). He proposed a presidential "ordinance" to amend the Family Code in 2005, which the Parliament later approved (Mammeri 2008). The revised law strengthened women's right to divorce, improved their ability to gain custody of their children, and provided financial security for them in the case of divorce; it also specified marriage rights and imposed stricter laws on polygamy (Kelly and Breslin 2010; Karima). Moreover, women gained parental authority over their children once they obtained custody (Samia, Karima), unless they remarried. The 2005 code permitted polygamy but required the husband to obtain the permission of the first wife, the proposed wives, and the Family Court, which provides the final ruling (Kelly and Breslin 2010).

Bouteflika increased women's citizenship rights in other ways beyond the Family Code. In 2005, he also amended the 1970 Nationality Code in favor of women (UNHCR 1970). Under Article 6, Algerian women gained the right to pass their nationality to children whose father is not Algerian. The original language stated that Algerian women had the right to pass down their nationality if the non-Algerian father was unknown or was stateless (including Palestinians and Saharawis) (United Nations Division for the Enhancement of Women 2003). Several feminists used the amended Nationality Code as an example of Bouteflika's commitment to gender equality, which extended beyond that of any of his predecessors. They also cited how, in 2004, Bouteflika supported Article 341 of the Penal Code, which criminalized sexual harassment. In fact, he vowed to implement a law that increases the penalty for sexual harassment up to five-year prison terms (Kelly and Breslin 2010; Howam 2014). In 2014, he presented Parliament with legislation to establish funds for widows in order to provide for their children (FIDH 2013). This further depicted Bouteflika as a protector of and ally for women.

Top-Down Reforms Necessary but Not Enough

While recognizing Bouteflika's top-down legal reforms, respondents engaged in grassroots activism in an effort to pressure the regime to do more and to remind Bouteflika of their bargain (Sherifa, Nour, Lina, Yasmin). For example, despite the advances made in the 2005 Family Code amendment, some women's rights groups voiced concerns about the lack of its implementation (Mammeri 2008). They argued that Algerian women are generally unaware of their rights under the amended law while judges often ignore its stipulations. They cited cases in which women are legally permitted to use the marriage contract as a negotiation tool to secure greater rights within the marriage. However, undereducated women who have a lower socioeconomic status were never made aware of their rights to amend their marriage contract (Raghaven and Levine 2012; Samia and Karima). Three respondents—two lawyers and a UN consultant—work on marriage contracts with an international nongovernmental organization focused on strengthening civil society and democracy (Samia and Karima). They train judges and lawyers at the city council level to increase women's awareness of their legal rights before they sign marriage contracts.

Samia, Karima, Yasmine, and Nour raised concerns about gender-based violence and insufficient institutional support for victims. The closure of Gender-Based-Violence (GBV) shelters due to lack of governmental financial support and the absence of protection for women was a central issue. Yasmine, a physician, viewed GBV as a public health issue. She conducted an in-depth study over a ten-year period on violence against women and presented it to the government. She found that health institutions were unable to deal with GBV cases. They often hid the identity of the abuser by failing to document it on medical reports. She concluded that the physical and psychological harm caused by GBV has a major impact on Algerian society as a whole.

Activism for women's rights under Bouteflika continued despite having a symbiotic relationship between state-sponsored legal reforms and grassroots activism. My respondents believed that their continued activism at the grassroots level towards gender equality is what drove the government to reform laws that previously prevented women from enjoying rights available to their male counterparts. They believe that without Bouteflika's backing, reform would have been slow, if not impossible, and in fact some of the minimum rights they have gained could be at risk. This, after all, is what preserved the alliance between feminists and the four-term president.

Up until his ouster from power in 2019, women's groups and many ordinary women continued to characterize Bouteflika as the champion of women's rights in Algeria. The Algerian president's use of feminist rhetoric and his execution of some legal reforms bolstering women's rights, especially the amendment of the Family Code, the amendment of the Nationality Code, and increased financial support for widows, enabled him to secure many women's votes and maintain their support over twenty years. His rigid views on the separation of state and religion, and his support of women's rights, together with the repressive measures exercised against Islamists, allowed Bouteflika to remain in power until 2019. Algerian feminists were among those who abandoned Bouteflika after a series of sustained popular protests that led to his resignation on April 2, 2019.

BIBLIOGRAPHY

Charrad, Mounira M. 2001. *States and Women's Rights: The Making of Postcolonial Tunisia, Algeria, and Morocco.* Berkeley: University of California Press.

FIDH (International Federation for Human Rights). 2013. "Women and the Arab Spring: Taking Their Place." https://www.fidh.org.

Howam, Belkassem. 2014. "Imprisonment for Five Years for Any Man Who Sexually Harasses Women." *Jawahar Al Shorouk*, March 10, http://jawahir.echoroukonline.com.

Kandiyoti, Deniz. 1988. "Bargaining with Patriarchy." *Gender and Society* 2 (3): 274–90. doi: 10.1177/089124388002003004.

Kelly, Sanja, and Julia Breslin. 2010. *Women's Rights in the Middle East and North Africa: Progress amid Resistance*. Lanham, MD: Rowman & Littlefield.

Lowe, Christian. 2009. "Algeria's Women Police Defy Danger and Stereotypes." Reuters, August 6, https://www.reuters.com.

Mammeri, Achira. 2008. "Algerian Women Cite Problems with Implementation of New Family Code."

Magharebia. Last modified February 15, 2008. http://magharebia.com.

Marzouki, Nadia. 2010. "Algeria." In *Women's Rights in the Middle East and North Africa: Progress amid Resistance*, ed. Sanja Kelly and Julia Breslin. New York: Freedom House.

Raghaven, Chitra, and James P. Levine. 2012. *Self-Determination and Women's Rights in Muslim Societies*. Waltham, MA: Brandeis University Press.

Salhi, Zahia Smail. 2003. "Algerian Women, Citizenship, and the Family Code." *Gender & Development* 11, no. 3 (November): 27–35.

United Nations Division for the Advancement of Women Department of Economic and Social Affairs. 2003. "Women, Nationality, and Citizenship." Women 2000 and Beyond, June, http://www.un.org.

United Nations High Commission for Refugees (UNHCR). 1970. "Law No. 1970–86, Nationality Law." Refworld, December 5, http://www.refworld.org.

15

Failing the Masses in Syria

Buthaina Shabaan and the Public Intellectual Crisis

ASAAD ALSALEH

Each generation must out of relative obscurity discover its
mission, fulfill it, or betray it.
—Frantz Fanon, *The Wretched of the Earth*

Buthaina Shabaan was born in 1953 outside Homs, one of the Syrian
revolution's birthplaces. Having graduated as the top student in Homs,
and fourth in Syria in 1971, she was awarded a scholarship and recognition by President Hafez Assad. Despite his strictness, Buthaina's father
allowed her to study at Damascus University; she was the first girl to
leave her town unaccompanied by a male relative. She was also the first
female student to major in English, and she received a fellowship to continue her studies in Britain. At Warwick University, she earned a master's
degree and PhD in English. Shabaan's academic achievements and early
commitment to the Baath Social Party's ideology attracted President
Assad's attention. She became his personal translator and accompanied
him on negotiations with foreign counterparts ("Nuqtat Tahawal" 2010).
Her work with President Assad became a source of unmatched social
power. Shabaan used her career alongside Assad to build a burgeoning
professional profile as a politician and a public intellectual ("Buthaina
Shaban" 2008).

As a graduate student of English literature at the University of Damascus, I was able to take a class offered by Professor Shabaan before the
revolution. Despite tiring overseas trips and a busy work schedule, Shabaan would come to class in high spirits, eager to listen to her students'
opinions on the readings she had carefully chosen. Shabaan openly criticized Arab societies' reluctance to grant women full recognition and

rights. As students, we were impressed by such an open-minded professor who was working for the Syrian government—someone whose character defied public perceptions of Syrian officials. Commonly perceived as inaccessible and inefficient, officials tended to disdain those unconnected to the government and relentlessly praise the regime to keep their positions or jockey for higher ones. Shabaan, on the other hand, not only broke this image but also voiced dissatisfaction with regime-sponsored discourses, as in its "obscure socialist education textbooks" (as she described them, referring to the textbooks that used to teach the party ideology)—an especially daring comment considering that Shabaan herself held a leading role as a member of the Baath Central Committee.

It has been difficult to watch someone who celebrated women's resistance of colonization abandon women at such a key moment in Syrian history. Her writing about (and celebration of) the political role of women—while not participating in the calls for regime reform—has come to seem like a position she only held hypothetically. More than any other Syrian, Shabaan presents the regime to the world as a reform-oriented establishment. She worked to sustain its survival as one of its trusted messengers, particularly between 2011 and 2012. While her role in the Syrian government before the revolution painted her as a great role model for Syrian women, her role during the revolution has undermined this image. Her legacy has been further marred by the perceived illegitimacy of the regime in the eyes of many Syrians.

In this chapter I discuss the problematic and double-sided role of the public intellectual in the Syrian revolution. I trace the case of Buthaina Shabaan (b. 1953), a writer, a professor, and an advocate of the Syrian regime. While spurring the populace to embrace the possibility of democratic reform, this female intellectual has accepted—even embraced—the political control employed by an authoritarian one-party regime, which uses her as a representative of their supposed progressive and women's liberation agendas. Shabaan has been playing a significant role in supporting and ultimately sustaining a totalitarian regime, compromising in the process the interests of women and even children, for whose cause she has long claimed to be a champion and a spokesperson. The shift of Shabaan from being a feminist to serving the propaganda of the regime has damaged her integrity as an intellectual. This shift requires not only a revisionary approach to the Western reception of her but also an analysis of the way the Syrian people have perceived her role in undermining the revolution.

Shabaan and the Arab Spring

Before the Syrian revolution, Shabaan was widely considered a respected public intellectual who set an example by fighting for the causes she had long claimed as her own. Since the 1980s, Shabaan has ceaselessly demonstrated two intellectual activities in her scholarly and journalistic writings as well as in her public lectures. The first is denouncing and exposing the practices that devalue women and pose an existential threat to their lives and human rights. For example, in her first book, *Both Right and Left Handed: Arab Women Talk about Their Lives* (2009), she graphically describes, probably with damning intent, an honor killing that took place in her home town when she was a young child. The second is criticizing the West for failing to efficiently react to human rights abuses when it comes to the treatment of Palestinians, Iraqis, or the Lebanese in times of war. As a supporter of the Syrian regime, she is certainly not blameless of complicity when the same power structures violate human rights at home. Shabaan condemned the Mubarak regime's brutal response to the 2011 uprisings in Egypt but kept silent when those uprisings metastasized into Syria.

On January 31, 2011, in the wake of the Tunisian and Egyptian revolutions, and just two weeks before Syrians started their own, Buthaina Shabaan wrote an op-ed in the London-based Arabic newspaper *al-Sharq al-Awsat* that praised the Arab masses for creating "a new epoch" and paving the way for "freedom." Under the title "The Voice of the Masses" (2011), Shabaan presented herself as an overjoyed intellectual hailing Egypt's newly gained freedom from Mubarak's corrupt rule. Imploring the Arab masses "not to forget or neglect" the leaders who failed them, approving the revolutionaries who "overcame their leaders," and failing to foresee that the Syrian regime would face a massive uprising the like of which toppled Hosni Mubarak and Ben Ali, Shabaan asks, "Has the moment come when Arab masses take to the streets to force their will on their governments, the governments which for decades have imposed their will, slogans, failures . . . and disagreements over millions of them and without achieving their hopes and aspirations?" While it is true that chronological gaps existed between Arab Spring uprisings, it is hard to see how Shabaan could mistake this dormancy for Syrian content. She endorsed non-Syrian revolutions before the Syrian people would revolt, as well, and would be chanting, "The people want to overthrow the regime."

Shabaan, however, adopted a different rhetoric to deal with the fact that Syrians could indeed manage a revolt. There is no doubt that had she known that Syria itself would face the same uprisings, she would not have responded in the same manner, reflecting the regime's long-standing underestimation of Syrians—the same regime that had been working for decades to stifle any potential uprisings, accumulating loyalists in the country's infrastructure and making Syria a security state, where it became almost impossible to do anything without government clearance.

Shabaan's name became repeatedly intoned in the Syrian demonstrations immediately following a conference on March 24, 2011, where she announced that the government was considering ending emergency rule, allowing more political freedom, and raising salaries. This marked the first official response to the Syrian uprisings, which started in the southwestern city of Daraa, where some children were imprisoned and tortured for antiregime graffiti. The regime's reaction to the uprisings left many people dead; demonstrators chanted slogans indicating that it was not food they wanted, but freedom and dignity. Some of the popular slogans were, "Ya Buthaina ya Shabaan, al-sha'b al-Suri mish jou'aan" (Oh Buthaina Shabaan, the Syrian people are not hungry) and "Ya Buthiana ya Shabaan, al-sha'b al-Suri ma biyinhaan" (Oh Buthaina Shabaan, the Syrian people will not be humiliated). These slogans confirmed popular speculations made well prior to the revolution that it would be not hunger but national pride that would motivate a Syrian revolt against the regime.

Shabaan: The Public Intellectual

Shabaan has assumed the regime's habit of blaming outsiders and armed gangs for the unrest, which continues to dominate the official Syrian rhetorical response to the uprisings. This response might be accurate in the latter years of the Syrian war, but the regime has been among the criminal actors even in this latter phase. Yet, she did not even recognize the first peaceful period of the Syrian revolution. Shabaan's relationship to the regime is typical of that of many intellectuals who sell their souls to authoritarian dictatorships, eventually losing any respect gained for voicing commitments to values that they do not commit to in times of trial. Though she allied herself with intellectuals who take on the burdens of humanity, when such responsibilities became urgent in her own country, she relinquished the opportunity to take a stand against the regime. Her relentless defense of Palestinian rights and her legacy as an activist and defender of women's rights cannot stand up to scrutiny. When Bashar Assad revealed his true face, following the steps of the other power systems she constantly criticized, such as the Israeli government and its treatment of civilians in Gaza or Lebanon, Shabaan stood by the regime, ignoring its violations of human rights and blaming the situation on extremists, which is exactly how Israel regularly justifies its retaliatory actions against Palestinians.

While not the first untrustworthy intellectual, Shabaan is the most recent within the Arab Spring. But it seems that the term "public intellectual" hangs on vague definitions and assumes unspecified values. The definition and role of the intellectual have been the subject of extensive studies, mostly addressing the intellectual in a Western context. According to Helen Small (2002), although issues related to the public intellectual do not pertain to the American culture exclusively, the term gained currency in the United States one decade before the turn of the twenty-first century, and was used in Britain ten years later with little treatment given to it in other European countries. Small's claim that public intellectuals are declining certainly rings true in Syria and other Arab countries, particularly given the challenges modern cultures face, with "increased power of the media . . . greater state regulation of the universities and, simultaneously, their penetration by commercial and corporate interests" (2002, 2). Likewise, Richard Posner (2003, 170)—who defines the public intellectual as "a person who, drawing on his intellectual resources, addresses a broad though educated public on issues with a political or ideological dimension"—laments public intellectuals' lack of expertise or experience. Posner's concerns fit Shabaan, especially in his depiction of the way some intellectuals establish a legacy of public authority about certain issues though they lack the integrity to stand by them.

Whether it is a positive or negative one, the intellectual has played a significant role since antiquity. Gramsci contrasts the traditional intellectual, "whose position in the interstices of society has a certain inter-class aura about it but derives ultimately from past and present class relations and conceals an attachment to various historical class formations," with the organic intellectual, or "the thinking and organizing element of a particular fundamental-social class" (Hoare and Smith 1971, 2), arguing that intellectuals should raise the consciousness of the masses and point to manipulation exercised by various kinds of power. Influenced by Gramsci, Edward Said (1994) argues that the intellectual should publicly "raise embarrassing questions . . . confront orthodoxy and dogma (rather than . . . produce them). . . . [and] be someone who cannot easily be co-opted by governments or corporations and whose raison d'être is to represent all of those people and issues that are routinely forgotten" (9). Even though Said's definition reduces the responsibility of the intellectual to that of opposing only political and corporate hegemony, his definition nevertheless shows the influence of such powers to control, mislead, and abuse the public.

Many Western (particularly European) intellectuals have failed at this expected and often simple task, even while they have enjoyed democratic systems and little fear of persecution. In this regard, Mark Lilla in *The Reckless Mind* (2001) poses the disturbing question, "What is it about the human mind that made the intellectual defense of tyranny possible in the 20th century?" (198). Lilla's treatment of certain European intellectuals and their irrational approach to politics is meant, he suggests, to be a companion to Czesław Miłosz's 1981 *The Captive Mind*, a classical work of anti-Stalinism written the same year that Miłosz defected to France, losing a prestigious government position in Poland as the cultural attaché. In this book, the Nobel laureate of literature examines the "vulnerability of the twentieth-century mind to seduction by sociopolitical doctrines and its readiness to accept totalitarian terror for the sake of a hypothetical future" (Miłosz 1981, vii). As a public intellectual, Shabaan is susceptible to the critique leveled by these authors against those whose relationship to political power endangers their responsibility: intellectuals whose role merits reevaluation as they serve the power system that crushes the masses. Shabaan has long enjoyed speaking in the name of the masses, yet in the shadow of the thuggish Syrian regime she stands tongue-tied.

The dual positionality of public intellectuals becomes more troubling when one realizes that Shabaan, while applying universal values to condemn a country like Israel or the United States, does not apply these values against an aggressive regime fighting its own people to stay in power. If this is due to lack of courage, then one is pained to understand why Shabaan always praised those courageous writers and activists who tell the truth and resist silence when facing abusive power structures. For example, in "What We Have in Common with Stanley McCrystal" (2010), Shabaan accuses the US administration of turning a deaf ear to the voices of its own military experts, specifically those who advocated for leaving Afghanistan. She wonders why someone like General Mc-Crystal, who has a "courageous, praiseworthy, and honorable history," as she puts it, "cannot convince his superiors of the validity of his anti-war views." She has a clear sense of the distinction between governments that almost exclusively dictate the way power is used or abused and a truth-telling citizen rejecting such a dictatorship, but she totally denies the fact that her regime unquestionably exploits power.

In so many ways, Buthaina Shaban has failed the masses in Syria. One may wonder whether she has, instead of honoring her intellectual responsibility, internalized the culture of subordination by following a path of either supporting the regime or remaining silent about its crimes. The position she has taken dashed the hopes of many Syrians, who wished that she would join other intellectuals in support of their cause. Instead, she has empowered the regime, allowing it to continue its killing of dissenting civilians.

Acknowledgments

With some modifications, this chapter is based on Asaad Alsaleh, "Failing the Masses: Buthaina Shabaan and the Public Intellectual Crisis." *Journal of International Women's Studies* 13, no. 5 (2012): 195–211, available at http://vc.bridgew.edu. Reprinted with permission.

BIBLIOGRAPHY
"Buthaina Shaban Presidential Advisor Minister." 2008. *Al-Sharq al-Awasat*, July 31, http://www.aawsat.com.
Fanon, Frantz. 1963. *The Wretched of the Earth*. Trans. Constance Farrington. New York: Grove.

Hoare, Quentin, and Geoffrey Nowel Smith, eds. 1971. "Introduction." *Selections from the Prison Notebooks*. New York: International Publishers.

Lilla, Mark. 2001. *The Reckless Mind*. New York: New York Review of Books.

Miłosz, Czesław. 1981. *The Captive Mind*. New York: Octagon.

"Nuqtat Tahawal." 2010. *Turning Point* on MBC (Middle East Broadcasting Center). New York, March 31, www.mbc.net.

Posner, Richard A. 2003. *Public Intellectuals: A Study of Decline*. Cambridge, MA: Harvard University Press.

Said, Edward W. 1994. *Representations of the Intellectual: The 1993 Reith Lectures*. London: Vintage.

Shabaan, Buthaina. 2009. *Both Right and Left Handed: Arab Women Talk about Their Lives*. Indianapolis: Indiana University Press.

———. 2010. "What We Have in Common with Stanley McCrystal." *Asharq Al-Awsat*, 28 June, http://www.aawsat.com.

———. 2011. "Voice of the Masses." *Asharq Al-Awsat*, 31 January, http://aawsat.com.

Small, Helen. 2002. *The Public Intellectual*. Oxford: Blackwell.

16

Time to Seize the Opportunity

A Call for Action from Sudan

FATMA OSMAN IBNOUF

Women's involvement in transitional processes represents a window of opportunity for women to challenge the policies and laws that violate their rights. It also offers the possibility of challenging gender discrimination and gender stereotyping, which oppress women and continue to reinforce their subordinate position. Further, there is the potential to challenge entrenched gendered practices, those deep-rooted structures that are not easily changed. Despite real and significant needs, the realization of women's rights has not been made a benchmark of success in the transitions taking place in the Arab world. Attainment of the basic rights of women politically, socially, and economically is of paramount importance to the future security and development of the Arab world. Women at all levels must therefore collaborate and organize to secure a critical mass capable of influencing decision-making processes.

Women need to preserve the gains they have made thus far, and they should continue to refuse to be sidelined and marginalized in the aftermath of the Arab uprisings. Significant changes must be made in order for gender equality to be brought closer to reality in this climate of change. Laws addressing violence against women need to be enacted, many family laws need to be modified, gender equality needs to be made the norm in policies and legislations at all levels, gender-responsive budgeting needs to be adopted, and the number of women in elected bodies needs to be increased. There is also an urgent need to adopt laws prohibiting marriage before the age of maturity and to criminalize female genital mutilation. Women's involvement in these processes is essential for lobbying to establish institutions, such as women's affairs ministries, that address women's direct concerns. Transition phases offer a unique opportunity for making these sorts of transformational changes. Therefore, women's involvement in transitional processes is essential to dealing with issues of oppression and exploitation.

While it is necessary to establish legal equality between women and men, equality must also be achieved in economic participation, education levels, political representation, and social norms. This must be achieved not just for the sake of women themselves but also to achieve development goals for these societies as a whole. Gender inequality does not just exist at the legal and political levels, and it does not affect women alone. Gender inequality at an economic level remains an impediment to overall development in the Arab world in general, and the "Arab Spring" states in particular.

While male allies are critical to effecting lasting change for gender equality, women must be the primary agents for transformation and empowerment in the transitional process underway in the Arab world. To that end, they must cooperate and coordinate their activities with each other and with men, regardless of their divergent interests, ideologies, and political affiliations. Although there are several specific ways in which women may accomplish this, one way forward could be the formation of political parties by women. These parties would lead to a gradual but continuous change, address women's direct concerns, and contribute to female representation in legislative and decision-making bodies. Even at this preliminary stage, such political parties would promote avenues for increased female participation in the political process. Another way in which women can act as agents of change is through civil society organizations. There are already a number of women's rights organizations, activists, advocate groups, and even individuals working on women's issues in Arab countries attempting the transition to democracy. A broad coalition that unites a variety of different women and women's groups needs to be established to ensure success in this transitional phase. Such united fronts have much better chances of success in achieving gender equality.

The rest of the world can learn from the experiences of women in the Arab uprisings. Arab women must seize the opportunities offered to them in the aftermath of these revolutions, or else they will lose a golden opportunity for empowerment and increased participation. Previously,

Arab women participated actively in their nations' struggle against colonialism, but in the transition from colonialism to postcolonialism in the Arab world, women were marginalized. In the current transitional phase, there is a new opportunity to bring women's concerns to the forefront of society. It is only by doing so that we can ensure that history does not repeat itself.

PART III

How They Express Agency

In *The Art of Moral Protest*, James Jasper posits, "The view of social life as artful, in which people play on cultural meanings and strategic expectations in a variety of ways, allows us to see many benefits of moral protest. . . . Much like artists, [protesters] are at the cutting edge of society's understandings of itself as it changes."[1] Arab women applied creative means and cultural nuances to advocate for social change and make their claim to social and politics rights.

Rita Stephan takes us back to the emergence of Arab women's activism in cyberspace in 1999, though social media became a major venue for activism during the Arab Spring, when stories of activists' campaigns, such as Karina Eileraas Karakuş' Aliaa Elmahdy and Michela Cerruti's 50% Syrian, became common. Andy Young describes how Bahia Shehab raised women's awareness to fight corruption and oppression through graffiti while Nisrine Chaer examines protest soundscapes and the auditory sensations in Lebanese queer protest. Women adopted historicization as a way to express their agency, and used films, literature, and photographs to document that agency. Nurulsyahirah Taha discusses a film that captures the activism of a Quranic school founder in Syria whereas Nicole Khoury traces the way *Al-Raida*'s founding editor redefined international discourse on gender issues in a Lebanese context, and finally, Kevin Davis introduces us to Um Sahar, who has collected photographs documenting protests since the early 2000s in Yemen.

NOTE

1 James Jasper, *The Art of Moral Protest* (Chicago: University of Chicago Press, 1997), 13.

———

17

Long before the Arab Spring

Arab Women's Cyberactivism through AWSA United

RITA STEPHAN

The Arab Women Solidarity Association United (AWSA United) emerged as an outlet for Arab women in the diaspora to express solidarity and support for women in the Arab world. It pioneered transnational Arab women's groups that connected Arab women in all six continents, especially those in the United States. Between 1999 and 2011, AWSA United's activists, who felt restricted by cultural apathy and ideological irrelevance in the West, and by unfavorable governmental policies, oppressive patriarchal systems, and rigid religious doctrines in the Arab world, used cyberspace to express dissatisfaction with their sociocultural fetters and create solidarity among like-minded activists.

As a member of AWSA United, I was curious to know what exactly AWSA United provided for this ideologically and politically marginalized group of women activists. I found that Arab women used AWSA United to foster their collective identity, strengthen their connectivity, and increase their activism. By analyzing electronic archival documents and conducting an online survey, I provide a historical perspective on Arab women's cyberfeminism and an overview of the development of AWSA from its birthplace in Egypt in 1982 through its migration to cyberspace in 1999. I then explain how Arab women activists used AWSA United to participate in collective action, solidify their individual and collective activist identities, and strengthen their relations with each other.

Arab Women's Cyberfeminism

Cyberspace gave women access to the public sphere and an opportunity to advocate for women's rights (through blogging, joining listservs, and creating websites). As early as 1999, scholars started documenting Arab and Middle Eastern women's use of cyberspace to create "alternative discursive spaces where it is possible to redefine patriarchal gender roles while questioning the sociocultural, economical, political, and legal institutions constraining them" (Skalli 2006, 36–37). Using the Internet, Arab women discussed women's issues, engaged in grassroots mobilization for improving women's conditions, and published research on social and gender inequalities.

The Internet was instrumental in empowering women in regional and transnational settings as well. For instance, it fostered the emergence of an Iranian blog community known as "Weblogistan"—a group of young professional women (university students, journalists, activists, literary and social critics) who used the Internet to discuss feminism and social equality (Nouraie-Simone 2005). Also, cyberspace allowed Kurdish women living in Europe and North America to establish the International Kurdish Women's Studies Network in 1996 as "a forum for the exchange of experience and knowledge among those who are interested in and work for improving the lives of Kurdish women" (Mojab 2001). In today's international system, in which Kurdistan does not exist as a sovereign state, cyberspace offers its women "the opportunity . . . to resist and reform [the] masculine, patriarchal-feudal-religious [process of state formation]" (Mojab and Gorman 2007, 66). Likewise, AWSA United members used cyberspace to launch a transnational virtual forum and support one another in their commitment to Arab women's rights.

From AWSA International to AWSA United

Until losing momentum in 2011, AWSA stood alone for almost thirty years to link Arab women everywhere. The Arab Women's Solidarity Association International (AWSA International) was founded in Egypt in 1982 by 120 women under the leadership of the feminist Dr. Nawal El Saadawi. Its aim was to link the Arab struggle for freedom and reform with the advancement of women's rights. AWSA International was the first pan-Arab women's organization to be accorded international status by the United Nations and to have representation of both sexes. By 1985, it had three thousand members worldwide and was granted consultative status with the Economic and Social Council of the United

Nations. Between 1982 and 1991, AWSA International organized several international conferences, developed income-generating projects for economically underprivileged women, produced films about Arab women's lives, and published books and literary magazines. In 1991, AWSA International took a stance against the Gulf War and demanded that the United Nations take a firm position against the war. This action provoked the Egyptian government to close down the association until 1996; during this period AWSA International's headquarters moved to Algeria.

In the United States, an AWSA chapter was first established in Seattle, Washington, in 1994, and remained active until 1996. The AWSA-Seattle American chapter held a benefit event for the victims of the Hebron massacre in 1994 and developed coalition-building projects with other women activist groups. It also organized a delegation of Arab women for the International Conference on Population and Development in Cairo in 1994 and the International Conference on Women in Beijing in 1995.

A second chapter was established in San Francisco, California, in 1995 and was active until 2002 under the name of AWSA–North America (AWSA-NA) as a nonprofit, nonsectarian 501(c)(3) organization. Members organized a fundraiser for women victims of war, a protest against the racist portrayal of Arab women in Israeli arts, a workshop on racist media images of Arab women and men, and empowerment-based events for Arab women and their communities (Stephan 2007). In 1997, AWSA-NA participated in sponsoring an annual Arab film festival and published a training guide entitled "The Forgotten '-ism': An Arab American Women's Perspective on Zionism, Racism, and Sexism."[1]

In 1999, members of the AWSA-NA chapter established Cyber-AWSA, which later became known as AWSA United. As stated in its mandate, AWSA United was distinct institutionally and logistically from other AWSA chapters. The website and e-mail listserv were launched by the San Francisco members "as a springboard for activism related to Arab women's issues" and to provide "a space for Arab women and their allies to share information and discuss issues relevant to Arab women's lives and experiences." The majority of members used the listserv as an informational medium without actively engaging in dialogue. Although the listserv membership was free, access was highly restricted. Shortly after its foundation, internal conflicts arose over how much conservatism could be tolerated on the listserv. Several founding members left the listserv and launched other organizations, while the few who stayed carried on its mission.[2] The listserv evolved with new members and remained active until 2011, when all physical chapters in North America had folded.

AWSA United kept its focus on women's rights in the Arab world while branching out its attention and membership to other areas in the world. By 2011, the membership of AWSA United was about 206 members; about half lived in the United States, many in Egypt, and the rest were scattered in several countries worldwide, ranging from Jordan, Lebanon, and Saudi Arabia to Belgium, Norway, Kosovo, and even Iran. While a transnational feminist vision inspired Arab feminists "to imagine a world without oppression and think about alternatives to exclusionary heteromasculinist and xenophobic politics" (Abdulhadi, Alsultany, and Naber 2011, xxxv), AWSA United allowed Arab feminists in all six continents to express solidarity with other groups and assert their relevance to the feminist movement.

Joining and Studying AWSA United

When I joined the listserv in 2003, I found in AWSA United the intellectual refuge that I had been seeking. A year later, I conducted an online questionnaire to learn about its members' social and ideological characteristics. The thirty-four responses I collected revealed aspects of AWSA United members' shared identity and factors that influenced them to join the listserv. It also measured AWSA United members' affinity with other members, and whether they considered them as part of their social networks. Finally, it explored AWSA United's contribution to furthering its members' virtual and physical activism.

Collective Identity

Through AWSA United, members felt empowered to construct their collective identity. They described the listserv as "a progressive organization which advocates for the empowerment of Arab women against all forms of oppression." They claimed, "We maintain an international activism and discussion list for Arab women and their allies, providing

a progressive space for debate, networking, and organizing in an atmosphere that values sexual, religious, and racial diversity." To examine
how AWSA United fostered its members' collective identity, I sought
answers to two questions: How did individual members identify themselves? And how did they define the parameters of their self-selected
grouping?

As a group, AWSA United consisted of mostly educated women
ranging in age between their twenties and fifties. In the questionnaire,
sixteen members identified themselves as scholars and eleven said they
were activists; eleven members held a bachelor's degree and ten had a
graduate degree, whereas eight had postgraduate education. Members'
fields of work ranged among the social sciences, the natural sciences,
and the arts (biologist, chemist, computer engineer, environmentalist,
nurse, journalist, professor, artist, and students).

In examining the basis upon which AWSA United members constructed their personal identities, I sought to unveil the difficult position that transnational Arab women occupied vis-à-vis other feminists.
My findings suggest that respondents who lived outside the Arab world
were more likely to embrace a feminist identity than those living in Arab
countries. Generally, a feminist identity in the Middle East carried the
negative connotation of embracing Western imperialism and cultural
colonialism.

Although feminist identity was the overwhelming collective identity
among members, an overwhelming majority expressed a strong ethnic identity as Arabs or hyphenated-Arabs (twenty-two members). It
is noteworthy that the majority of the respondents (twenty-four members) lived in the United States and the rest in Australia, Canada, Egypt,
Iraq, England, Palestine, Lebanon, and Saudi Arabia. Most members
designated Algeria, Egypt, Iraq, Jordan, Lebanon, Libya, Morocco, Palestine, Saudi Arabia, and Yemen as their countries of origin, and their
nationality as Australian, Canadian, German, and even Filipina. Some
declined to identify themselves along the categories I specified and instead claimed to be "queer," "liberal," "pacifist," or "white American."
One respondent described AWSA United as a forum that encompasses
Arab women's activism internationally: "Cyber AWSA is much more an
Arab American listserv than an Arab one, so because I live in the Arab
world it was mostly helpful in terms of information provided about the

organizations and activities of Arab American feminists. [It] provided a productive framework through which to see my own local activism as part of a more international struggle."

In interrogating whether religion conflicted with activism or feminism in terms of identity construction, Miriam Cooke (2000) claims that Arab women activists gain legitimacy for their struggle in their sociopolitical environments by socially capitalizing on their Muslim identity in a modern Arabic sociopolitical context and creating harmony between religion and rights. These strategies include associating with other disadvantaged women in patriarchal societies, linking themselves with Muslim men who were victimized by colonial policies, and increasing their political activism. My questionnaire revealed that religious identification was strong among AWSA members, as half of the respondents listed religion as a part of their identity. While this questionnaire shows that religious affiliation was not a divisive factor among Muslims and Christians, it also shows that half of AWSA members did not find it contradictory to identify as both religious and feminist/liberal.

Next, I was curious to know whether the group experienced a shared identity as "AWSAn." Collectively, AWSA United members identified themselves as feminists who were committed to advancing Arab women's rights. Hence, members reported their views of AWSA United as "a group of Arab and non-Arab individuals dedicated to Arab women's causes and issues"; a forum that "allows members all over the world to share their concerns"; "a group of Arab women and their allies"; "Arab ladies"; "active Arab women"; "liberals"; "feminists"; and "intellectual Arab feminists." One respondent described the group as "an online group of transnationally based Arab women, mostly living in the West and united by the struggle for women's rights in the Arab world, for Arab rights in the West, and for freedom and democracy in the Arab regions."

In a nutshell, AWSA United members felt safe and free to proclaim and embrace their individual controversial identities as "queer," "liberal," "pacifist," and "progressive," and their collective oppositional identity as educated feminists who are united in the fight for Arab women's rights.

Connectivity

AWSA members recognized the significance of connecting in a spatial context. One respondent acknowledged that there "may be a downside to the interconnectedness so often prevalent in the dynamics of the group," yet she found that AWSA United members were able to connect with each other "because of their transnationality." Despite the high concentration of members in the United States, women joined AWSA from all over the world. AWSA United members also felt connected by their Arab heritage, gender identities, and the intersection between gender and culture in what came to define them as transnational Arab feminists. This transnationality was also felt in the adoption of the feminist stance to which members subscribed. Members viewed AWSA United as a safe forum to discuss issues related to "culture and politics, especially those that affect women," as well as other subjects such as peace, social justice, human rights, women's liberation, and collaboration in cyberspace.

Words like "solidarity," "support," and "networking" were often used by respondents to describe their connectivity through AWSA United. The most common bond that AWSA United members shared was their interest in advancing the rights of Arab women. Members believed that their listserv was mostly successful in promoting knowledge of Arab women and building solidarity among them, as the following discussion reveals.

The goals that AWSA United had the most trouble achieving were the "idealistic" ones. Over half of the members did not see it as being within AWSA United's capability to increase women's active participation in public life or to infiltrate the Western feminist movement. However, members saw potential in goals such as promoting knowledge concerning Arab women and their movements. In general, the majority of the respondents (twenty-five members) felt that AWSA United had succeeded in strengthening their sense of solidarity, and over half the respondents were satisfied with AWSA United's role in encouraging cooperation among Arab women in the diaspora and the homeland. Members also expressed a sense of satisfaction with AWSA United's efforts to promote and sustain a positive image of Arab culture and Arab women in North America.

In response to the negative portrayal of Arab women in the media, public discussions, governmental policies, and even academia, members found relief in this e-community. AWSA United showed an alternative image of Arab women as rational, strong, and civically engaged. One person stressed the role that AWSA United played in creating a safe haven in a politically uncertain environment: "I joined AWSA after 9/11 in need to [experience] solidarity with other Arab women. Since then, I have met many women from the email list and have collaborated with them in a variety of ways—through conference panels and writing. I have been less active on the AWSA list after the many disagreements among members." So what connected these women was their resistance to the ethnic and gender-based injustices they experienced despite their diverse places of residence.

Cyberactivism

The case of AWSA United showed that online chatting in 2004 was already a legitimate form of activism. To AWSA United members, this forum was a part of their activism in the local and national politics of their countries of residence and the international politics that affect their countries of origin. Many indicated that their online activism had increased as a result of their membership in AWSA United, as the following discussion reveals.

The highest number of respondents asserted that AWSA United helped them become more informed, while a significant number considered it a medium through which to express their opinions by writing e-mails to appropriate parties, signing petitions, or taking polls. Others found in AWSA an opportunity to network and learn about calls for actions, through the e-mails that were posted regularly on the listserv. One respondent stressed that AWSA United helped in "validating my viewpoints and giving me confidence to voice them in other settings," and another explained how "hearing other views from women around the world has helped me round out my own perspectives." Others also felt the need to validate their viewpoints and "round out" their perspectives.

Promoting knowledge and awareness seems to be a major theme that reoccurs in members' descriptions of the listserv's utility. Contextualizing their activism is another service that this entity provided, offering "a productive framework" to help members understand their own local activism and relate it to global struggles. In fact, between 2000 and 2001, AWSA United members led a campaign against honor killings and organized efforts to lend solidarity to regional and local groups and individuals taking a stand against this traditional practice (Stephan 2007).

As the founders had hoped to make AWSA United a protected forum in cyberspace, they also wanted to develop it as a tool for civic activism and political participation. AWSA was imbued with a spirit of activism and progressiveness, evident in most of the discussions and information disseminated on the listserv. Calls for action were regular postings to which several members responded: they called Congress, e-mailed foreign authorities, and signed petitions.

Members' opinions of the effectiveness of AWSA United were divided. Some viewed AWSA United as a unique outlet for information and an "objective gate" for Arab women. A respondent called it "a phenomenal place to meet others and get more informed about issues at the center stage of the Arab World." Another contrasted AWSA United with the *New York Times*, stating that from AWSA United, "I get articles and stories that I wouldn't naturally get otherwise and also get a sense of the opinions and thoughts of a group of women who I much respect but who aren't reflected in mainstream media. . . . I look to the listserv to give me a better sense of what a diverse group of people (more diverse than the NY Times op-ed page) thinks about it."

Others were unhappy with the low utility of the listserv and the ideological conflicts that occurred occasionally. They felt that AWSA United fell short of meeting their expectations for progressive activism. A few respondents expressed the opinion that the lack of "passion and activism" on AWSA United was a sign of apathy, as was its use by those who saw it as a means "simply to pass on information and articles." Another group said that AWSA United was a "hostile environment" that sometimes "can be easily hijacked by loud and empty mouths." One respondent described AWSA as "very political and extremely partisan and intolerant on some issues." These descriptions offer a vivid picture of the dynamic on the listserv, which varies among being conflictual, merry, and calm. However, the listserv remained at all times unmoderated (i.e., messages were not monitored or blocked) and open for all members to communicate freely.

The third group yearned for greater participation of all members, especially "older members who could enrich conversations on the listserv." They expressed a strong desire to be involved in more discussions and to increase their civic engagement, and wished for a greater role for the listserv, especially its steering committee, in guiding the members in that direction. One respondent expressed her aspiration for the development of AWSA United globally: "I think it is a worthwhile endeavor—I have learned a lot from this group. I think it should expand even further worldwide—perhaps it can get promoted even more to English-speaking Arab women around the world."

Indeed, cyberspace has made it possible for AWSA United members in the West to wage their ideological struggles for existence, especially after September 11, 2001, when their mere Arab identities became a threat. Similarly, the Internet allowed Arab women in the homeland to escape patriarchal control over their quest for rights and to construct for themselves new definitions of their identities. The Internet opened a gate to women, even in strict Saudi Arabia, to interact with other Arab women and exchange experiences. Through the transnational setting of AWSA United, women offered each other support, shared information, expanded their networks, and validated the formation of their gendered and ethnic identities.

Conclusion

After 2004, when this study was conducted, activities on the listserv started decreasing in 2007 and stopped totally in April 2011. These dates coincide with two global events. The first event marks the rise in Facebook popularity in 2007, and the second event is associated with the intensifying of the Egyptian revolution and the Arab Spring. This decline could have resulted from (a) an increase in alternative nodes launched on other social media outlets such as Facebook and Twitter, and (b) the fever of the Arab Spring that diverted people's attention from women's rights to promoting democracy and political reforms.

Nonetheless, a number of projects spun off from this listserv, including a collaborative British play highlighting women's role in the Arab Spring, a book project on the veil, announcements for conferences, a call for support of the Global Coalition for Egyptian Women Unions, a petition to the Arab League to impose sanctions on Syria, and calls for papers and contributions to special issues on Arab feminism. Unfortunately, as a collective, members of AWSA United did not take a stance nor did they become collectively involved in any activities associated with the various uprisings of the Arab Spring.

AWSA United's contributions to Arab women's cyberactivism and cyberfeminism are noteworthy. It paved the way for others to create an alternative process of dissidence in three ways. First, AWSA United was a safe space for women to claim their individual and collective Arab feminist identities. Second, it connected them with other Arab feminists and activists around the world. Third, it provided them with a means to disseminate information and cultivate collaborative efforts. By fostering networks, relationships, and recognitions, AWSA United provided its members with solidarity and camaraderie.

In terms of identity, activists were able to construct and express their collective identity as Arabs and feminists. Despite cultural and gender homogeneity, diversity was evident in members' nationalities, religions, sexualities, educational backgrounds, and political views. AWSA United brought together people from varied paths into a forum to share issues relevant to their lives without the censorship of any authority. Members maintained their association with this listserv because it was one of the very few places where they felt safe to be women, Arabs, intellectuals, queers, feminists, Americans, pro-Palestinians, pacifists, and everything else.

Finally, this study affirms the presence of cyberfeminism long before the Arab Spring, as an alternative expression of power struggle. In cyberspace, AWSA United members were empowered to share their feminism, network with one another, and expand their activism, not only locally or nationally but also transnationally. As a cyberfeminist e-community, AWSA United was a geographically dispersed women's advocacy group that strengthened connectivity among Arab feminists around the world. It was transnational in its scope, plural in its governance, and progressive in its politics.

Acknowledgments

An earlier and more thorough version of this piece was published as "Arab Women's Solidarity Association–United and Cyberfeminism." *Journal of Middle Eastern Women Studies* 9, no. 1 (2013): 81–109. The views expressed here are the author's and should not be attributed to the US Department of State.

NOTES

1 Nadine Naber, Eman Desouky, and Lina Baroudi, "The Forgotten '-ism': An Arab American Women's Perspective on Zionism, Racism, and Sexism," Arab Women' Solidarity Association, San Francisco Chapter, 2001, https://globalfeminisms. umich.edu.

2 Causes and consequences of the conflict are beyond the scope of this study.

BIBLIOGRAPHY

Abdulhadi, Rabab, Evelyn Alsultany, and Nadine Naber, eds. 2011. *Arab and Arab American Feminisms: Gender, Violence, and Belonging.* Syracuse, NY: Syracuse University Press, 2011.

Cooke, Miriam. 2000. *Women Claim Islam: Creating Islamic Feminism through Literature.* London: Routledge.

Mojab, Shahrzad. 2001. "The Politics of 'Cyberfeminism' in the Middle East: The Case of Kurdish Women." *Race, Gender, and Class* 8, no. 4 (October): 42–61.

Mojab, Shahrzad, and Rachel Gorman. 2007. "Dispersed Nationalism: War, Diaspora, and Kurdish Women's Organizing." *Journal of Middle East Women's Studies* 3, no. 1 (Winter): 58–85.

Nouraie-Simone, Fereshteh, ed. 2005. *On Shifting Ground: Muslim Women in the Global Era.* New York: Feminist Press.

Skalli, Loubna. 2006. "Communicating Gender in the Public Sphere: Women and Information Technologies in the MENA." *Journal of Middle East Women's Studies* 2, no. 2 (Spring): 35–59.

Stephan, Rita. 2007. "Arab Women Cyberfeminism." *Al-Raida*, no. 110: 116–17.

18

Aliaa Elmahdy, Nude Protest, & Transnational Feminist Body Politics

KARINA EILERAAS KARAKUŞ

My message is gender equality and my body is no sin.
—Aliaa Magda Elmahdy, Femen protest, Stockholm,
July 1, 2013

Freedom does not come from me or from you; it happens as
a relation between us, or indeed among us.
—Judith Butler, *Bodies in Alliance and the Politics of the Street*

On October 23, 2011, Aliaa Elmahdy, a middle-class Egyptian art student at the American University of Cairo, posted a nude selfie to her blog, *A Rebel's Diary*, alongside a manifesto indicting the suppression of female sexuality and free speech in Egypt.[1] She launched her nude body into the blogosphere to mark the Arab revolutions as a highly sexualized topography. By elevating gender and sexuality to the forefront of local and global geopolitical conversation, Elmahdy brought sex to Tahrir Square, or underscored its primacy there.

Given its emergence as a radically different form of protest at that historical moment—especially its clash with contemporary cultural and religious taboos against female nudity outside of the commercial domain—Elmahdy's image went viral. In the week following her post, Elmahdy received over 1.5 million hits to her blog. Much more than an erotic object of contemplation, Elmahdy's body incited discourse and rage. The Egyptian public as well as her online audience greeted her selfie with an ambivalent mix of pride, solidarity, outrage, and shame. After receiving a barrage of rape and death threats, in 2013 Elmahdy fled to Sweden, where she was granted political asylum. Because exile separated Elmahdy from her local political community of Arab feminists, transnational and online organizing has become a vital resource for her activism.

After Elmahdy arrived in Sweden, she briefly collaborated in live nude protest actions with global feminist organization Femen. This alliance revealed points of tension with her virtual re-visionings of the body politic when joined with a neocolonial, Islamophobic feminist agenda on the streets. Yet both phases of Elmahdy's activism enlisted her body where least expected to challenge the patriarchal cartography of Tahrir Square and the gendering of national space, and to "re-member" the global feminist public square.[2]

By exploring the social protest of Elmahdy, aka "the nude Egyptian blogger," this chapter reflects on the "pause" that naked bodies insert in civic life and evaluates nudity as a means of protest in Egyptian as well as transnational feminist politics. Elmahdy's nude protest offers a compelling invitation to map out sites of sexual and political provocation that challenge dualisms of secular and religious, erotic and sacred, real and virtual.[3] By "making visible what had no business being seen" (Ranciere 1989, 674), Elmahdy's nude body reconfigures the body politic and reimagines the theater of the "political." This chapter asks whether Elmahdy's campaigns of oppositional nakedness online and in the streets reinforce or contest conventional understandings of female sexuality and "empowerment" that travel between East and West. By positioning her body at the heart of transnational feminist praxis, Elmahdy raises key questions about whether and in which contexts the female nude may be appropriated as a site of feminist resistance.

The Geopolitics of Vulnerability: Bodies in "Improper" Places

Our bodies inhabit the borderlands of the natural and the constructed, the marvelous and the mundane. Neither biological givens nor passive sites of inscription, they represent stunning political interventions, living canvases, and endlessly fascinating achievements in time and space (Foucault 1995; Weiss 1999; Grosz 1994). When bodies hit the streets en masse to oppose the status quo, their power can appear either so infinitesimal or so spectacular as to arrest onlookers in their tracks.

Bodies on the street "redeploy [public] space in order to contest and negate the existing forms of political legitimacy" (Butler 2011). Bodily protest raises the question of how diverse lives are valued, and whose experiences are officially named, celebrated, or repressed within collective memory. When protesters lie down before tanks in Tiananmen Square, light themselves afire like Mohamed Bouazizi, the Tunisian street vendor credited with igniting the "Arab Spring," go on hunger strikes, fashion themselves into human missives or missiles, occupy Wall Street or Tahrir Square, disrobe in the name of animal rights, or inhabit a tree to challenge multinational corporations, they pose a fundamental metaphysical, socioeconomic, ontological, and geopolitical question: "What is my body—my life—worth to you?"

Because they violate sacrosanct dichotomies of public/private and visible/hidden, naked bodies constitute a uniquely explosive site of protest. Nude protest has a special capacity to reconfigure the body politic by framing vulnerability as a basis for exchange and staging intimate zones of disruption and dis-identification.[4] As Hamid Dabashi (2012) writes, "The deliberate stripping of clothing . . . is an act of staged formal destruction that disrupts the normality of socializing norms for a deliberate pause. It is the staging of the body for a momentary reflection."

Online and on the streets, gendered bodies signify differently. Their mutable meanings confirm the tense negotiations that accompany any dreaming of the "body politic." If, as Ernst Renan has theorized, the nation is forged through collective forgetting of the violence at the origins of state formation, amnesia also haunts the "imagined community" of global feminism, whose foundational violence often involves Islamophobic and Orientalist cultural mythology, Western rescue narratives, and "discursive colonization" of Third World women (Anderson 1983; Jarmakani 2008; Said 1979; Abu-Lughod 2002; Mohanty 1988).

If, as Claude Guillon suggests, the most pressing question of our time is whether the human body has a future, it is equally vital to imagine what lies ahead for feminist body politics. Contemporary feminist activists work at the interface between the traditional "public square" and the expansive frontiers of cyberspace. If the public square is a "space of appearance" wherein people and ideas express solidarity through concerted action, this space is multiplied online, where wireless networks and real-time uploads on YouTube and social media reach global audiences in a frenzy of accelerated circulation (Arendt 1958; Fiske 1989; Baty 1995). Although the digital era offers expanded platforms for surveillance and monetization, it also invites plural nodes for dissent. By tactically deploying critical media literacy and social networking savvy in this liminal space, a new generation of feminist makers, influencers, and activists is engaging in resistant tactics of *la perruque* to upend traditional distinctions between production and consumption, public and private (Certeau 1984; Fiske 1989). In this new geopolitical theater, young feminists negotiate between image and identity in endlessly fascinating ways to enact new bodily imaginaries and forms of belonging.

The creative, political deployment of Elmahdy's body in cyberspace and on the streets activates new bodily imaginaries, or symbolic spaces in which to reimagine corporeal vulnerability as impetus for solidarity and social change. The bodily imaginary set in motion by Elmahdy simultaneously provides common ground for, troubles, and rewires the "body" of transnational feminist praxis. By sex(t)ing revolution—or attending to the sexual and digital politics of revolution in Egypt—and deploying her body as living tableau, Elmahdy challenges conventional paradigms of political engagement, and enacts productive—if occasionally problematic—spaces of disturbance that suggest new horizons for transnational feminist solidarity *a venir*, still to come.

Sex(t)ing the Revolution: A Rebel's Diary

On October 23, 2011, Aliaa Magda Elmahdy sparked a sexual and political revolution by launching her naked body into cyberspace. By uploading a series of nude photos to her blog, she staged a virtual coup within contemporary Egyptian society in which female modesty on the streets collides with hypersexualized images of women on billboards and social media. Her most popular image—a full-frontal nude selfie—features Elmahdy in black, patterned stockings and red flats with a red flower arranged playfully in her hair. Her image conveys an insouciant sexiness that can be read as bold, erotic, vulgar, or seductive. Elmahdy's direct stare communicates the most daring aspect of her protest: to *own* her naked body and sexuality with pride and provocation, sans the shame that so often circumscribes the expression of female sexuality in Egypt and around the globe.

Alongside her photos, Elmahdy published a manifesto asserting freedom of expression: "Put on trial the artists' models who posed nude for art schools until the early 70s, hide the art books and destroy the nude statues of antiquity, then undress and stand before a mirror and burn your bodies that you despise to forever rid yourselves of your sexual hang-ups before you direct your humiliation and chauvinism and dare to try to deny me my freedom of expression" (Elmahdy 2011).

How might one read Elmahdy's effort to "re-vamp" the female nude—a loaded signifier with a complex history in diverse national and cultural contexts and genres, ranging from classical painting to comic books, porn, and popular culture—in cyberspace? What are the promises and perils of resurrecting the naked female body as vehicle of protest? For critics, Elmahdy erroneously equates nudity with "liberation"; violates modest religious codes of dress; reinforces pernicious toxic Western aesthetic codes of man as surveyor/subject and woman as surveyed/object of the gaze; and mirrors philosophical conceptions of the value of the "feminine" as primarily sexual, decorative, and ornamental.[5] On the other hand, fans celebrate Elmahdy's protest as a feminist effort to reclaim her body and sexuality from heterosexual circuits of desire, looking, entitlement, fetishistic objectification, and voyeuristic titillation.

Elmahdy's self-portrait starkly contrasts Orientalist odalisques, or paintings of nude women reclining in the domestic interior of the harem. The odalisque reclines passively, staring into the distance and presumably waiting for a man to enter the space. Most striking about the odalisque are her languor and passivity, which make it impossible to regard her as a "subject" of history in her own right. She is reduced to passive object, waiting for space to be filled and history to be shaped by others.

Conversely, Elmahdy stands upright with one leg resting casually on a stool. She faces the camera head-on, directly confronting it with her potent gaze. Defying expectations of female modesty, Elmahdy boldly opens her legs to expose her genitals. Elmahdy's choice to adorn her naked body with stockings, a red flower, and red flats instantly sexualizes the image. Her portrait is iconic: arresting in its simplicity and insistent in its determination to put sexuality in conversation with revolution.

Elmahdy wrests the female nude from the realm of passive aesthetics, investing it instead with sexual and political agency. She stares back at the photographic lens with a defiant, "oppositional" look (hooks 1992,

115–31). Restaging an encounter between camera and naked woman that has historically functioned as voyeuristic (especially in Orientalist *odalisque* paintings, often framed as if seen through a keyhole), Elmahdy orchestrates a virtual confrontation that affirms her body's right to occupy an erotically charged space; fuses the private zone of the *boudoir* with the revolutionary public square; and transforms the photographic field into a space of possibility wherein she writes herself into history as artistic, political, and sexual subject.

Elmahdy deploys the female nude to suggest its disruptive, militant potentials. By enlisting visual culture and social media in sexual and revolutionary praxis, she troubles the borders and redoubles the force of conventional organizing. She also locates the material body within the "body politic" as the creative and political agent best suited to challenge structural inequality. Positioning her body as canvas, Elmahdy performatively expands the public square into a virtual community for those living in diaspora.

As Cynthia Enloe notes, "not now, later" echoes within nationalist revolutionary movements that ask women to put feminist aspirations aside in favor of issues deemed more pressing to the body politic. Feminist aspirations have alternately been construed as antithetical to or constitutive of Egyptian national identity. Leila Ahmed (1982b) describes a history of state feminism in Egypt, most notably the unveiling campaign initiated by British colonial administrator Lord Cromer, which identified unveiling women as integral to the "modernization" of Egypt. Against this backdrop, women's bodies have constituted a battlefield— alternately framed as icons of oppression or as symbols of national, cultural, and religious "tradition" and identity deployed to oppose colonial encroachment and "modernization." Elmahdy extracts her body from this tangled symbolic web to reconfigure it as a malleable geopolitical signifier. By so doing, she transmutes the tension of sexual and colonial symbolic politics into a representational strategy of subversion. Like many feminist activists in the MENA, Elmahdy deploys social media to reclaim bodily agency and create a safe space, or digital *umma* ("community" in Arabic) (Barlas 2005, 95), through which to challenge gender inequality and sexual marginalization. Elmahdy and other warrior-activists, or "netizens," "forge an 'other space'—akin to Foucault's 'heterotopias'—to engage in frank discussions about sexuality and the female body; contest and redefine gendered views of honor and shame; and collectively imagine Egypt free of gender inequality and sexual violence" (Galán 2012).

Elmahdy's refusal to postpone issues of gender and sexuality sent an explosive message within revolutionary Egypt's milieu of sexual harassment, gang rape, forced virginity testing, and public shaming of women occupying Tahrir Square alongside men. Her nude photos challenged longstanding cultural taboos by forcing the public to acknowledge sex and gender as critical components of revolution. In this sense, her message resonates with feminist visual activism throughout the region, including a billboard campaign that has become a cornerstone of women's protest in the Arab revolutions, especially in Tunisia and Lebanon. This campaign—"I am with the Arab women's uprising because . . ."—asks supporters to finish the sentence. Elmahdy's audacious cyber campaign echoes one woman's assertion: "I am with the Arab women's uprising because I *am* a revolution, not a shameful private part" (Weirich 2013).

Re-membering the Transnational Feminist Public Square: On the Streets with Femen

While I have argued that Elmahdy's naked body circulates online with significant transnational feminist potential, I am less convinced of the emancipatory possibilities of her nude protest on the streets in association with global feminist organization Femen. Her alliance with Femen raises troubling questions about the limits of nudity as vehicle of feminist solidarity, and about the "emancipatory" potentials of appropriating the female nude as cultural symbol.

Femen represents a lightning rod in debates over how to craft global feminist solidarity, and a litmus test for the claim that nudity portends "liberation." Famous for its "noticeably erotic rallies" (Greenhouse 2013), Femen was formed in the Ukraine in 2008 as a reading group to address gender inequality within socialist movements. The group initially staged public rallies wearing pink uniforms, but soon found that they attracted more media attention through topless protests. While critics chide the organization's homogenous "army" of thin, young, white, supermodel-like volunteers, Femen leaders emphasize the group's diversity, but claim that the media affords more visibility to members who align with Western beauty norms. Now based in Paris, Femen's "topless warriors" use their naked bodies as sites of protest, appearing topless on the streets with provocative slogans scrawled on their flesh. Savvy readers of mainstream media, Femen activists are well versed in guerrilla performance tactics. Through its signature brand of topless theatrics, Femen uses antireligious, often distinctly Islamophobic rhetoric to advance Western humanist ideals of "liberation" and "freedom." Founders brand the group as a proponent of a "new feminism" that celebrates sexual difference and deploys breasts as sexy yet militant symbols of femininity (Reinbold 2013).

Until recently, Femen was presumed to have been women-organized and -led. A recent documentary identifies political scientist Victor Svyatski as the "male mastermind" behind the organization, raising questions about possible cooptation of Femen's goals, tactics, and sources of funding.[6] Although details of Svyatski's involvement are inconclusive, critics contend that his alleged involvement undermines Femen's feminist credibility and forces a radical reexamination of its politics.

In December 2012, Elmahdy joined Femen outside the Egyptian Embassy in Stockholm to protest Egypt's draft constitution (figure 18.1). Her street protest with Femen marked a shift from the use of her body as artistic canvas to its deployment as megaphone (Dunn 2012). It also relocated Elmahdy's nude protest from cyberspace to the streets. Elmahdy's alliance with Femen sparked controversy among liberals in Egypt, many of whom blamed her actions for igniting conservative backlash that paved the way for the victory of President Morsi and the Muslim Brotherhood in Egypt's constitutional referendum. Others suggest that Elmahdy's work with Femen problematically aligned her with Islamophobic, neocolonial Western feminism. On April 4, 2013, Elmahdy intensified global feminist debate by joining Femen's "International Topless Jihad Day" (ITJD). Femen leader Inna Schevchenko described the event—which targeted mosques and Tunisian embassies throughout Europe—as a protest against "Islamism" and "Sharia," vaguely construed. In response, Muslim women critics staged "Muslimah Pride Day" online "to show the world that we oppose Femen and their use of Muslim women to reinforce Western imperialism."[7] Thousands of Muslim

Figure 18.1. Aliaa Elmahdy protests with Femen in Stockholm, 2013.

women posted selfies on Twitter and Facebook in which they wore the hijab and held signs directed to Femen such as, "Nudity does not liberate me—and I do not need 'saving.' You do not represent me!"[8] The scandal of ITJD recalls how acts of "solidarity" authored by naked female bodies in the West often may serve to oppress and marginalize rather than to "empower" all women.

Elmahdy's alliance with the Islamophobic rhetoric of Femen also erases the re-visioning of religious identity associated with contemporary Islamic feminist movements that question the binary "Islamist-secularist" divide by which Western media often view Elmahdy's protest.[9] This stance ignores an entire spectrum of Islamic feminist praxis that seeks to integrate religious and feminist identities. By allying with Femen, an organization that uniformly equates nudity with empowerment and hijab with oppression, Elmahdy short-circuits the complexities of her political message. Her liaison with Femen invites us to reflect on the dangers of neocolonial feminism and the limits of transnational feminist solidarity if premised on Western feminist paradigms of "liberation."[10]

Conclusion

As they circulate in public space, female bodies mark vital sites of friction, empowerment, and "occupation" that rewire the body politic; re-vision the interface between sexuality and liberation; and re-member revolution from feminist perspectives. At stake in their provocations is the ability not only to forge counternarratives of the Arab revolutions but to multiply future possibilities of transnational feminist praxis. In this sense the re-vamped female nude at the heart of Elmahdy's protest does more than create "safe space" for women protesters. It invites us to imagine the body politic and feminist "solidarity" in relation to myriad sites of disloyalty, fracture, and dis-identification, in a time and space still to come.

NOTES

1 See "Nude Art نف يراع," *Aliaa Elmahdy, A Rebel's Diary*, October 23, 2011, http://arebelsdiary.blogspot.com/search?updated-min=2011-01-01T00:00:00%2B02:00&updated-max=2012-01-01T00:00:00%2B02:00&max-results=7.

2 In the sense described in Homi Bhabha (1986): "Remembering is never a quiet act of introspection or retrospection. It is a painful re-membering, a putting together of the dismembered past to make sense of the trauma of the present."

3 See also Asma Barla 2005; Nouraie-Simone 2005; Lazreg 2011; Al-Ali 2012; Mejias 2012; and Morozov 2011.

4 As theorized in terms of performative spaces of disjuncture and disidentification in Butler and Athanasiou 2013.

5 As articulated for example in Jean Jacques Rousseau 1979 and Kant 2004.

6 Eichhofer and Schepp 2013; Green 2013.

7 See "Muslim Women Decry Topless Gender Protests" 2013.

8 "Muslim Women Decry Topless Gender Protests" 2013.

9 For a useful introduction to the origins and practices of "Islamic feminism" see Margot Badran 1999.

10 Abu-Lughod 2002; Ahmed 1982a.

BIBLIOGRAPHY

Abu-Lughod, Lila. 2002. "Do Muslim Women Really Need Saving? Anthropological Reflections on Cultural Relativism and Its Others." *American Anthropologist* 104, no. 3 (September): 783–90.

Ahmed, Leila. 1982a. "Western Ethnocentrism and Perceptions of the Harem." *Feminist Studies* 8, no. 3 (Autumn): 521–34.

———. 1982b. *Women and Gender in Islam*. New Haven, CT: Yale University Press.

Al-Ali, Nadje. 2012. "Gendering in the Arab Spring." *Middle East Journal of Culture and Communications* 5, no. 1: 26–31.

Anderson, Benedict. 1983. *Imagined Communities*. London: Verso.

Arendt, Hannah. 1958. *The Human Condition*. Chicago: University of Chicago Press.

Badran, Margot.1999. "Towards Islamic Feminisms: A Look at the Middle East." In *In Hermeneutics and Honor*, ed. Asma Afsaruddin, 159–88. Cambridge, MA: Harvard University Press.

Barlas, Asma. 2005. "Globalizing Equality: Muslim Women, Theology, and Feminism." In *On Shifting Ground: Muslim Women in the Global Era*, ed. Fereshteh Nouraie-Simone, 91–109. New York: Feminist Press.

Baty, Paige S. 1995. *American Monroe: The Making of a Body Politic*. Berkeley: University of California Press.

Berger, John. 1990. *Ways of Seeing*. New York: Penguin.

Bhabha, Homi. 1986. "Foreword: Remembering Fanon." In *Black Skin, White Mask*, Franz Fanon, vii–xxvi. London: Pluto Press.

Butler, Judith. 2004. *Precarious Life: The Powers of Mourning and Violence*. New York: Verso.

———. 2011. "Bodies in Alliance and the Politics of the Street." European Institute for Progressive Cultural Policies. Transversal, September, http://eipcp.net (accessed September 19, 2012).

Butler, Judith, and Athena Athanasiou. 2013. *Dispossession: The Performative in the Political*. Cambridge, UK: Polity.

Certeau, Michel. 1984. *The Practice of Everyday Life*. Translated by Steven Rendell. Berkeley: University of California Press.

Dabashi, Hamid. 2012. "La Vita Nuda: Baring Bodies, Bearing Witness." Al Jazeera, January 23, http://www.aljazeera.com (accessed January 13, 2013).

Dunn, Michael Collins. 2012. "Aliaa Elmahdy Revisited: 'The First Time as Tragedy, the Second as Farce?'" *Middle East Institute Editor's Blog*. Middle East Institute, December 27, http://mideasti.blogspot.com/2012/12/aliaa-Elmahdy-revisited-first-time-as.html (accessed January 13, 2013).

Eichhofer, Andre, and Matthias Schepp. 2013. "Femen's Male Mastermind: 'I Am No Tyrant.'" *Spiegel Online International*, September 26, http://www.spiegel.de (accessed September 30, 2013).

Elmahdy, Aliaa. 2011. "Nude Art." *A Rebel's Diary*, October 1, http://arebelsdiary.blogspot.com/2011_10_01_archive.html (accessed October 23, 2011).

Fiske, John. 1989. *Understanding Popular Culture*. Boston: Unwin Hyman.

Foucault, Michel. 1995. *Discipline and Punish: The Birth of the Modern Prison*. Translated by Alan Sheridan. New York: Vintage.

Galán Susan. 2012. "'Today I Have Seen Angels in the Shape of Humans': An Emotional History of the Egyptian Revolution through the Narratives of Female Personal Bloggers." *Journal of International Women's Studies* 13, no. 5: 19.

Green, Kitty, dir. 2013. *Ukraine Is Not a Brothel*, https://www.youtube.com/watch?v=OHyPSREmeRA.

Greenhouse, Emily. 2013. "How to Provoke National Unrest with a Facebook Photo." *New Yorker*, April 8, http://www.newyorker.com/online/blogs/elements/2013/04/amina-tyler-topless-photos-tuni (accessed April 21, 2013).

Grosz, Elizabeth. 1994. *Volatile Bodies: Toward a Corporeal Feminism*. Bloomington: Indiana University Press.

Jarmakani, Amira. 2008. *Imagining Arab Womanhood: The Cultural Mythology of Veils, Harems, and Belly Dancers in the US*. New York: Palgrave MacMillan.

Kant, Immanuel. 2004. *Observations on the Feeling of the Beautiful and the Sublime*. 2nd edition, translated by John Goldthwait. Berkeley: University of California Press.

Kennedy, Marwan. 2012. "The Revolutionary Body Politic: Preliminary Thoughts on a Neglected Medium in the Arab Uprisings." *Middle East Journal of Culture and Communications*, no. 5: 66–74.

Lazreg, Marnia. 2011. "What Do We Call Them? The Arab People's Movements and the Language of the Media." Muftah, March 4, http://muftah.org (accessed March 24, 2011).

Mejias, Ulises A. 2012. "Liberation Technology and the Arab Spring: From Utopia to Atopia and Beyond." *Fibreculture Journal* 147, no. 20.

Mernissi, Fatima. 2011. *Scheherazade Goes West: Different Cultures, Different Harems*. New York: Washington Square Press.

Mohanty, Chandra. 1988. "Under Western Eyes: Feminist Scholarship and Colonial Discourses." *Feminist Review*, no. 30: 61–88.

Morozov, Evgeny. 2011. *The Net Delusion: The Dark Side of Internet Freedom*. New York: Public Affairs.

Mulvey, Laura. 2009. *Visual and Other Pleasures*. 2nd edition. New York: Palgrave MacMillan.

"Muslim Women Decry Topless Gender Protests." 2013. Al Jazeera, April 5, http://www.aljazeera.com.

Nouraie-Simone, Fereshteh. 2005. "Wings of Freedom: Iranian Women, Identity, and Cyberspace." In *On Shifting Ground: Muslim Women in the Global Era*, ed. Fereshteh Nouraie-Simone, 124–44. New York: Feminist Press.

Ranciere, Jacques. 1989. *The Nights of Labor: The Workers' Dream in Nineteenth-Century France*. Philadelphia: Temple University Press.

Reinbold, Fabian. 2013. "Male Mastermind: Was the Femen Scandal a Publicity Stunt?" *Der Spiegel Online*, September 6, http://m.spiegel.de (accessed December 2, 2013).

Rousseau, Jean Jacques. 1979. *Emile; or, On Education*. New York: Basic Books.

Said, Edward. 1979. *Orientalism*. New York: Vintage.

Weirich, Sarah. 2013. "From the Sacred to the State: Memory, Women's Human Rights, and the Tunisian Revolution." Unpublished paper presented at the Journal of Middle East Women's Studies 2013 Distinguished Lecture and Research Workshop, New Haven, CT, Yale University.

Weiss, Gail. 1999. *Body Images: Embodiment as Intercorporeality*. London: Routledge.

19

Sensing Queer Activism in Beirut

Protest Soundscapes as Political Dissent

NISRINE CHAER

The codification of homophobia in Lebanon is embedded in article 534 of the penal code, which criminalizes "sexual acts against nature." Together with social discourses, the state-sponsored legal imperative—which actually originates in a colonial intervention during the French Mandate—shapes the current realities of queer subjects who struggle with homophobia (Gagné 2012). Homophobia in Lebanon cannot be separated from the patriarchal, capitalist, racial, and sectarian nature of the state, especially in the ambiguous and discriminatory manner by which article 543 targets marginalized queers exclusively (Mikdashi and Puar 2016).

In response to legal and social discrimination, the LGBT movement started organizing in 1990 after the end of the civil war. Helem,[1] the first officially registered, "above-ground" LGBT organization in the MENA region, was founded in 2004. Three years later, Meem[2] brought together more than four hundred lesbian, bisexual, queer, transwomen, and transpeople to give them a safe space and adopt a less visible approach and flatter organizational strategies than Helem had done. From 2007 to 2014, Meem focused on building a community based on strategies grounded in feminist politics (Moussawi 2015) and emphasized the importance of member confidentiality, which explains why the community house of Meem (or the House) remained underground for that period. Meem constituted a community in the form of an "organized" support group until it folded in 2014. Since then, an aggregation of former members constitutes an informal and undefined queer activist community/network in Beirut, and is engaged in diverse activist projects and forms of "alignment" (Ahmed 2004). Therefore, the narratives below are not representative of the group at large, given its diverse and fragmented nature.

Mapping Meem's MENA-Situated Queer Politics

The scholarly debate over LGBT activism in the Middle East and North Africa region (MENA) has largely revolved around addressing the colonial histories of queer geopolitics and the unequal flow of meanings from West to East. Such scholarship has problematized the adoption of universal identities of sexuality—called "the Gay International"—arguing that these categories are constructed through Western imperialist discourses on sexuality (Massad 2007). Yet, by exclusively subscribing to discursive frameworks of representation, these approaches reinforce the position of the periphery for queer Arab bodies. They do so by insisting on excluding the lived experiences and sensorium of Arab subjectivity and signaling the modes of complicity with the West (El-Ariss 2013; Sabry 2012).

Refusing to subscribe to such narratives, Meem members express their sexuality in relation to gender identity, "coming out," relationships, discrimination, family, religion, class, community, activism, and emigration (Meem 2009). I attempt to map Meem's activism vis-à-vis this debate through combining findings from interviews with Meem members with its two publications: the online magazine *Bekhsoos*[3] and the autobiographical collection of stories by queer women and transpeople from Meem, *Bareed Mista3jil: True Stories* (2009), the first part of the title translating as "Express Mail."

In challenging the "Gay International" concept, Meem members shift the meaning of queerness to include the heterosexual women who challenge normative taboos or conservative women who do not wear the hijab, as described by my respondent Edi: "We need to also challenge the symbolism of the closet as being only an attribute of queer people. I think everyone has a closet. . . . For example, in the south [of Lebanon], the closet is about not wanting to wear the hijab and being obliged to because this is the norm. We should not use the closet as something that is only for Western lesbian and gay sexualities. We should think of it in a larger way, in relation to oppression and phallic morality" (Edi 2015).

Members also problematize the metaphor of the closet and the rigid meaning of queerness to highlight the commonality in practicing a form of "politics of difference" based on multiplying possibilities and understanding the bodily experiences of "Others" in their locations and backgrounds. The following quotation is illustrative of their approach: "Heterosexual bodies can also be very queer. It depends when and in which society we are speaking. . . . For instance, when a girl in Lebanon fucks a guy, that's considered queer because that's not normative at all" (Shant 2016).

When I asked activists about coming out and the tension between identity politics and queer politics, one respondent, Shant, asserted that the concept of "coming out" is situational and does not have to be worn on one's sleeves: "I don't care about this. If the person doesn't want to come out, let them not come out. If the person believes that homosexuality doesn't exist because it is an epistemic issue, then they should not come out . [L]et them call themselves 'Batrik' [penguin]. You are not constantly out. You might be out to your friends, but not to your co-workers, and not to the supermarket dude downstairs. And it's not like you are driving your car and every time you see someone, you park and scream at them, 'hiiiiiii I am gaaaaaaaay!'" (Shant 2016).

Edi agrees that queer politics should not subscribe to the binary logic in identity politics: "I don't want to drown in identity politics without challenging it and I don't want to melt in queer politics either. They have both become like a binary. . . . We should not reproduce it. There are lots of alternatives and forms of activism that are between them and outside them" (Edi 2015). In fact, Edi locates her theorization of power in the sociopolitical context of Lebanon. She further criticizes Islamic feminism and the articulations of the "Gay International" for being detached from context, her notion of queerness and activism being framed by her geopolitical location:

My position is unapologetic towards political Islam, but it doesn't come from my hatred to Islam. . . . [I]t is with the academically produced knowledge about our region emerging from positions of center about the peripheries, like Islamic feminism, or the "Gay International," who have completely different contexts. Here, Islam is the powerful and the woman with the hijab is the strong one that is oppressing me, and this woman is different from the veiled woman in Paris who is oppressed because of her hijab. Here in Beirut, in Dahieh,[4] I am the oppressed because I have no hijab and I have short hair and piercings. (Edi 2015)

As these quotations show, Meem members find their queer identity representative of their dissent vis-à-vis their position in their Middle

Eastern society, which experiences some unique and some universal geopolitical challenges. To capture the political dissent of the MENA-situated and nonidentitarian queerness of the Meem community, I proceed by moving away from the discursive field of politics. I ask, How could investigating the sonic realm of protest help us understand the nature of political activism and its relationship to public space?

Drawing on an ethnographic study I conducted in Beirut between August 2015 and April 2016 in the Meem space(s) (Chaer 2016), I take up "sensation" (Panagia 2009) as a geographically layered analysis to configure how the invisibility of queer bodies has a political life. Then, through looking at the sensual dimensions of activism in space within the embodied practices of protesting, I capture the political dissent in which this MENA-situated and nonfixed queerness is engaged. In particular, I focus on the sensations in embodied encounters within the spaces of the You Stink protest that have emerged in the wake of the garbage crisis in Lebanon in 2015—which focused on the corruption of the ruling class—and in the feminist march Take Back the Night in 2016.

Sensing Activism in Urban Spaces: Protesting

Meem's activism can be characterized as multiplying difference and rupturing identity politics. It is grounded in its local geopolitical context and escapes uniformity and binaries such as West/East, visibility/invisibility, and outness/closetedness. In taking up sensation as a methodological grounding for my fieldwork, I conduct a geographically layered analysis that allows me to configure how the invisibility of queer bodies is deflected through enacting destabilizations to the political order. I look at the interruptive force of sensation and the ways in which the interruption of dominant regimes of perception destabilize (or reinforce) the gendered, classed, and heteronormative political order.

Investigating how bodies *feel* and experience sensations in social space—with the aim of reconceptualizing agency and political life more generally (Hayes-Conroy and Hayes-Conroy 2010; Munt 2015; Sweet and Escalante 2014; Waitt 2014)—is about mobilizing frameworks that *sense* the political by way of disrupting the "sensible." By "sensible" I mean both "what makes sense" and "what can be sensed" (Panagia 2009, 3). Addressing the "political life of sensation" is useful to conceptualizing the notion of the political emerging from the queer community of Meem. I am not suggesting that queer bodies are subversive merely because of the non-normative homoerotic sensation they embody, but rather that this sensation of nonnormative sexual/gendered desire unlocks the potentials of reshaping the political in the particular spatio-temporal context of the queer community in Beirut.

Nonnormative sexual/gendered sensation is transgressive, not because it is antiheteronormative/anticisnormative but because it nurtures a collective sensory disposition among marginalized, nonnormative bodies. These dispositions orient queer bodies towards other queer bodies and put them in a form of contact not shaped by past histories of compulsory heterosexual or normative contact (Ahmed 2004, 165). I flesh out this transgression in which the queer community in Beirut is engaging, by gathering in protest spaces—which I conceptualize as a "political dissent."

Acoustic Affects: Protest Soundscapes as Political Dissent

In the following I analyze the street protests that started in Beirut in August 2015 in response to the garbage crisis and the accumulation of waste on the streets, and later turned into a popular anticorruption movement. The government's contract with the waste collection company Sukleen ended in July after being continually renewed since the 1990s. Sukleen is considered to be a model for the privatization of the waste management sector, in which political allegiances, corruption, and the robbery of public funds are administered by the ruling class who control state institutions. The protests were initiated by the You Stink campaign, made up of a group of civil society and social media activists. The campaign later reached out to a larger public, and various other civil organizations joined, including student groups, leftist, antisectarian, and feminist collectives, and people from the queer community.

The second case I investigate is Take Back the Night, a march in which I participated on International Women's Day in 2016 and which was organized globally as a protest against sexual harassment and violence against women. Although Meem activists have organized Take Back the Night several times since 2010, this year the American University of Beirut's leftist club led the effort. The protest took place on the

Corniche of Beirut seashore, where people walk, jog, wander along the wide pavement, fish, sit on the benches, rent a bicycle, or smoke a *shisha*.

One way to unpack the relationship among the senses, space, and politics is to examine the embodiment of songs and dances in political demonstrations, which offers an insight into how protests involve a shared sensory disposition among marginalized communities (Jolaosho 2015). Instead of focusing on the politics of protest, I analyze the aesthetic embodiment of collective protest singing as a site of transgression (Jolaosho 2015, 2) and regard the performance of chanting in the Beirut protests as a "dissent from inequality and an insensibility" (i.e., an inability to be sensed, noticed, or accounted for) (Jolaosho 2015, 2). In other words, I explore how activists used songs to counter the invisibility and the inaudibility that the oppressive patriarchal system imposes on their marginalized communities.

In grappling with the auditory potentials of chanting, I argue that the realm of the visible—of what we *see*—is centered on analyzing political forces in the landscape of the protest. However, the sense of sound is a central apparatus through which protest is experienced. For instance, the human microphone in the Occupy movement is a model of how the human amplification of sound is a technology used in political organizing (Protevi 2015, 32). The power of sound stems from the difficulty of keeping it at bay since it hits us and pours into our interior with no possibility of distancing ourselves or stopping our exposure to it (Dolar 2006, 78–79). In the space of urban protest, the sensory apparatus is a way of experiencing activist engagement through chanting, yelling, rhythmic clapping, and drumming.

The embodied sense of rhythm can also be used to help us understand togetherness given that the responses to rhythm contribute to the marking out of spaces of communal identity and notions of belonging (Reyskens and Vandenabeele 2016, 649). The shared experience of protest—in particular the sensation of being moved by rhythm—has a potentially disruptive effect of suspending the social order, and the way people relate to each other and to space (Panagia 2009). The auditory features of protests thus have the capacity to suspend the normative social order.

During the protests of the You Stink campaign, a feminist-leftist alliance called Al-Shae'b Yourid (The People Want) was formed, and I took part in it, along with a number of queer activists from the Meem community. The Feminist Bloc also emerged during the protests as a platform, offering a safe space for women and queers in the urban and digital space of the protests and creating a practice of feminist solidarity (Nayel and Moghnieh 2015). In these protest encounters, the visible and the audible composed my sensorial embodied experience, in addition to the olfactory. My senses were saturated with sounds of loud chanting (and music), explosives, and the echoes of the riot police shooting and evicting the protesters, sounds of hands clapping, of harmonious drumming, and the speeches of You Stink activists. I saw aggregated bodies in different circles of activists confronting police violence, and I smelled tear gas.

The repetition of the chants amplified the energy in the crowd. The performance of rage through songs, rioting, and confronting police violence was cultivated as dissent, and bodies were used to channel "sensations and embodied experiences about violence and in the process transformed spaces" (Sweet and Escalante 2014, 14). In many of the You Stink protests in August, the feminists grouped in The Feminist Bloc and shouted, "We want to dance, we want to sing and we want to topple the regime"; "Remove the rapists and release the prisoners"; "Down with Solidere";[5] "We belong to the streets"; "Feminist revolution until freedom"; "Shame on the state"; "Salute to the revolution in Syria, Egypt, Yemen . . ."; "Solidarity with the migrant worker against racism"; "Solidarity with the sex worker"; "Solidarity with the lesbian"; and "Down with the military rule." By chanting feminist slogans, protesters embodied sensations of rage and happiness, enacting transgressive possibilities for living in oppressive spaces such as the sexist and privatized space of Downtown.

The following excerpts are selected phonetic chants from the protests in Beirut during September and October 2015, which serve to capture the role of sound in politics as a technology of protest:

[monotonous, solemn, triumphant with drums beats and clapping, slow, sustained, and even tempo]

Ma men reedo ma men reedo (We don't want it, we don't want it)

Ma men reedo ma men reedo (We don't want it, we don't want it)

El nizam el abaweh badna nbeedo (The patriarchal system we will abolish)

El nizam el abaweh badna nbeedo (The patriarchal system we will abolish)[6]

[synchronized and amplified with clapping and drums, marching and even tempo, marked with emphasis]
Ta-harrosh, 'onf, 'on-so-riyyeh . . . (Sexual harassment, violence, racism . . .)
Kella, sifat, el-'a-ba-wiyyeh (All are patriarchal traits)[7]

[fast tempo, continuous, no drums, with constant clapping, ascending in amplitude, volume, and tempo when repeated, vibrant and lively]
Badna nor'os badna nghanneh w badna nsa'it el nizam (We want to dance, we want to sing, and bring down the regime)[8]

[chants and joyful shouts in a riot, shouts with clapping, *Derbakki* drum playing, sounds of water cannons and splashing of water]
Yasqot yasqot hokm el Az'ar (Down with the regime of the corrupted)[9]
[In this chant, the protesters were rhythmically dancing and parading, epitomizing the synchronization of the rhythmic effect of sound with the performative practices of bodily movement. As a result, the protest here was "a visible and audible practice of material and bodily interactions constituted in movements, gestures, sounds, clothes and objects" (Reyskens and Vandenabeele 2016, 657) and captured a sense of urban political togetherness.]

[movement, lively and gradually going faster/forward tempo]
Ya nizam w ya zbeileh, todrab enta w hal shkeileh, el-sha'ab tmarrad 'al hikkeim w yalla enzal 'al share' (Oh regime of garbage, damn you and your look, the people have revolted against the ruling elites, so come down to the street)
Yalla inzal 'al share' (Come down to the street)
Akhado el baher w jarafo el tal w lal zeileh ma 'endon hal, w lal zbeileh ma 'endon hal, w yalla inzal 'al share' (They took the sea and bulldozed the mountains and they don't want to find solutions for the garbage crisis, so come on down to the streets)
Yalla enzal 'al share' (Come down to the street)[10]

In light of this reflection, I want to turn to the sound of the female voice as a technology that *queers* space. In the early stages of the protests—at times when it was not so common for women to take over the megaphone and lead chants—I recall many instances when the crowd did not fully respond or became agitated when a woman chanted on the megaphone, especially if the woman had a high-pitched voice. Therefore, this gendered texture of the vocal chords manifests how the voice is a technology of disrupting the heterosexist space. This account of urban protest reminds us how the human microphone at the Occupy movement shaped the protest as "not quite a choir, but . . . a chorus, and so the bodies of the chanters (their chests, guts, throats, eardrums) would be vibrating at something close to the same frequency, something close to being in phase" (Protevi 2015, 91).

Taking the affective technologies of the body into consideration, it becomes clear that, based on the narratives and descriptions of sounds in the protests, the cacophony of noises filling the streets of Downtown and Corniche intermix different rhythms of chants, drumming, clapping, moments of silence, screaming, sounds of water cannons showering protesters, and seawater splashing on rocks. The protest and the togetherness interact not only with the surrounding urban space but also with spectators—for instance on the Corniche—who either observe in shock or take pictures. The appropriation of space happens side by side with the disruption of the spectators' experience of dominant social order. To be precise, this disruption occurs at the site of the relationality among people, objects, and places (Panagia 2009).

In the same manner, by occupying the soundscape of the Corniche, the feminist protesters of Take Back the Night seized ownership of the physical public space from which women and gender-nonconforming people are excluded. In fact, the practice of collectively making noise—regardless of what the lyrics of the chants actually say—pierces the ears of the perplexed dwellers, and enacts a political transformation of the sexist space. Being noisy occupies the physical space. The performance of protesting is a claim to the city that operates with the sensation of ephemeral public conviviality that could not be experienced elsewhere. The marchers in Take Back the Night practiced dissent against forms of misogyny and exclusion. It was an ephemeral suspension of the dominant—heteronormative and sexist—social order.

Conclusion

In this exploration of the senses in the political sphere, I framed two cases of protests in Beirut as a way of crystallizing the multiplicities and intersectionalities of queer activism. Political dissent in the case of Meem embodies a political practice that recognizes the gendered, racialized, sectarian, and classed forms of oppression alongside the sexualized.

Attending to the senses of queer marginalized bodies has the potential to disrupt the common sense that gives traditional meaning to spaces and objects. While these experiences are not entirely narratable because of their complexities and their paradoxical natures, they direct us towards engaging with the power of the relationships that control the creation of the aesthetic space. In light of this investigation of the auditory affects of protest, it becomes clear that using rhythm in chants is not only representative; it particularly produces an experience of community through shared acousmatic sound and embodied senses of rhythm.

NOTES

1 An acronym of the Arabic Himaya Lubnaniya lil Mithliyyeen (Lebanese Protection for LGBTs), it also means "dream."

2 "MEEM" is an acronym for Majmou'at Mou'azara lil Mar'a al Mithliya (a support group for the lesbian woman). The word "Meem" is also the phonetic pronunciation of the letter "m" in Arabic, which usually symbolizes women.

3 *"Bekhsoos"* translates as "concerning," which implies subcultural LGBT terms used in Lebanon, such as the verb *"bi khoss"* or *"bit khoss"* (to be concerned), which means "to be gay/lesbian." See www.bekhsoos.com.

4 Dahieh is the suburb of Beirut.

5 A private company that owns the Downtown of Beirut, Solidere leads the reconstruction of the center of Beirut in the post–civil war period as a luxury enclave designed to cater to tourists from the Gulf. See Samir Kassir (2010).

6 Untitled Video, Sawt Al Niswa, September 22, 2015, 00:08–00:17, https://www.facebook.com/Sawtalniswa/videos/1043503179023303/.

7 Untitled Video, Sawt Al Niswa, September 22, 2015. See 00:17–00:24, https://www.facebook.com/Sawtalniswa/videos/1043503179023303/.

8 Untitled Video, Sawt Al Niswa, September 22, 2015. See 00:47–00:59, https://www.facebook.com/Sawtalniswa/videos/1043503179023303/.

9 The audio captures the soundscape of the protest with sounds of the chants saying, *"Asha'ab Yourid Isqat Annizam"* (The people want to bring down the regime), *"Yasqot yasqot hokm el Az'ar"* (Down with the regime of the corrupted),

the drums, and the water cannons. The chant is inspired by the Egyptian chant against the military regime of el-Sisi: "*Yasqot yasqot hokm el 3askar*" (Down with the regime of the military), see Untitled Video, October 8, 2015, https://www.facebook.com/alshaabyoureed/videos/vb.1592127394382725/1603721553223309/?type=2andtheater.

10 See Untitled Video, August 28, 2015, https://www.facebook.com/alshaabyoureed/videos/vb.1592127394382725/1592555934339871/?type=2andtheater.

BIBLIOGRAPHY

Ahmed, Sara. 2004. *The Cultural Politics of Emotion*. Edinburgh: Edinburgh University Press.

Chaer, Nisrine. 2016. "Sensing Meem Space(s): Queer Activism in Beirut and the Potentials of Affect." Master's thesis, University of Utrecht.

Dolar, Mladen. 2006. *A Voice and Nothing More*. Cambridge. MA: MIT Press.

Edi. 2016. Interview with author, Beirut, Lebanon, April 2.

El-Ariss, Tarek. 2013. *Trials of Arab Modernity: Literary Affects and the New Political*. Bronx, NY: Fordham University Press.

Gagné, Mathew. 2012. "Queer Beirut Online: The Participation of Men in Gayromeo.com." *Journal of Middle East Women's Studies* 8, no. 3: 113–37.

Hayes-Conroy, Jessica, and Allison Hayes-Conroy. 2010. "Visceral Geographies: Mattering, Relating, and Defying." *Geography Compass* 4, no. 9: 1273–83.

Jolaosho, Omotayo. 2015. "Political Aesthetics and Embodiment: Sung Protest in Post-Apartheid South Africa." *Journal of Material Culture* 20, no. 3: 443–58.

Kassir, Samir. 2010. *Beirut*. Berkeley: University of California Press.

Massad, Joseph. 2007. *Desiring Arabs*. Chicago: University of Chicago Press.

Meem, ed. 2009. *Bareed Mista3jil: True Stories*. Beirut: Meem.

Mikdashi, Maya, and Jasbir Puar. 2016. "Queer Theory and Permanent War." *GLQ: A Journal of Lesbian and Gay Studies* 22, no. 2: 215–22.

Moussawi, Ghassan. 2015. "(Un)critically Queer Organizing: Towards a More Complex Analysis of LGBTQ Organizing in Lebanon." *Sexualities* 18, nos. 5–6: 593–617.

Munt, Sally. 2015. "Sensory Geographies and Defamiliarisation: Migrant Women Encounter Brighton Beach." *Gender, Place, and Culture*, no. 8: 1093–1106.

Nayel, Moe Ali, and Lamia Moghnieh. 2015, November 7. "The Protests in Lebanon Three Months After: A Reading of Police Coercive Strategies, Emerging Social Movements, and Achievements." *New Politics*. Retrieved from http://newpol.org.

Panagia, David. 2009. *The Political Life of Sensation*. Durham, NC: Duke University Press.

Protevi, John. 2015. "Semantic, Pragmatic, and Affective Enactment at Ows." In *Occupy: A People Yet to Come*, ed. Andrew Conio, 88–96. London: Open Humanities Press.

Reyskens, Peter, and Joke Vandenabeele. 2016. "Parading Urban Togetherness: A Video Record of Brussels' Zinneke Parade." *Social and Cultural Geography* 17, no. 5: 1–21.

Sabry, Tarik. 2012. *Arab Cultural Studies: Mapping the Field*. London: Tauris.

Shant. 2016. Interview with author, Beirut, Lebanon, March 31.

Sweet, Elizabeth, and Ortiz Escalante. 2014. "Bringing Bodies into Planning: Visceral Methods, Fear, and Gender Violence." *Urban Studies* 52, no. 10: 1826–45.

Waitt, Gordon. 2014. "Bodies That Sweat: The Affective Responses of Young Women in Wollongong, New South Wales, Australia." *Gender, Place, and Culture*, no. 21: 666–82.

20

On the Contrary

Negation as Resistance and Reimagining
in the Work of Bahia Shehab

ANDY YOUNG

In 1158 BC, ancient Egyptians organized the first strike in recorded history and documented their activism in sketches and literature (El Shazly 2014, 8). By 2011, street art emerging from Egypt's revolution became a visual revolution that reflected, perhaps more than any other medium, the nature of opposition in Egypt, which draws on its past and of which women are a vital part. "It is graffiti artists who successfully fused aesthetics and politics (as well as theory and practice) in their work, emerging as one of the most powerful creators of *revolutionary culture*" (Elias 2014; emphasis added). In an effort to explore this "revolutionary culture," I look at Egyptian street artists' resistance since early 2011 through the work of one street artist, Bahia Shehab, TED global fellow and Islamic art historian. Shehab's work is an example of some larger dynamics in Egypt's street art movement, which has resisted, to date, four regimes and counting. I focus particularly on how her work negates dominant narratives, giving voice to resistance and reimaging the realities of revolutionary Egypt.

Going to Egypt

As part of a half-Egyptian family, my life changed in early 2011 when the Egyptian revolution began. For Khaled, my Egyptian husband, and I, living in New Orleans, the historic events unfolding in Tahrir Square were more than news; they held tangible repercussions for our friends and family. We had made our first journey to Egypt together in 2005, spending our time in Upper Egypt and Alexandria with friends and family, all of whom were artists and activists. We waited impatiently to hear if we recognized any of the names of those who died when police sprayed protesters with water cannons on Kasr El-Nil Bridge on January 28, 2011, the Friday of Anger, or when protesters were attacked on February 2, 2011, during the "Camel Battle." We organized a march in downtown New Orleans to question US support for Mubarak, and we shared the jubilation when the indelible announcement came from then Egyptian vice president Omar Suleiman announcing that Mubarak would step down. Khaled's Egyptian retail shop became a hub for local media who came to get the angle from a local Egyptian.

In 2012, I was thrilled to accept an offer to teach at the American University in Cairo. We saw this opportunity as the realization of a lifelong dream to bring our children closer to our family, immersing them in their second tongue and culture at a historic and intoxicating moment. Mohamed Mahmoud Street, which leads to Tahrir Square, was top on our agenda of places to visit and witness the graffiti murals we had been following on social media. This street serves as a "barometer" of the revolution, according to Professor Mona Abaza (Shehab 2012). It is a living monument to many protests against the abuses of Mubarak's government.

The Graffiti Revolution

It was not long before the euphoria of the eighteen days of early 2011 had faded as violence and suppression reemerged under the rule of the Supreme Council of Armed Forces (SCAF). Protesters stormed state buildings and torture centers to prevent the SCAF from destroying evidence of the crimes of the past. The abuses of SCAF continued to escalate, as did the protests. All-out battles were held on Mohamed Mahmoud Street, where many protesters were killed with live ammunition, or maimed when they had their eyes deliberately shot out. All of these events were depicted visually in the work of graffiti artists on Mohamed Mahmoud Street, particularly in elaborate murals of the dead. Since Mubarak's stepping down, the graffiti, like the mood of the country, has changed from hopeful, in its defiance, to stark and damning. The graffiti of Mohamed Mahmoud Street offered an alternate, emotional documentation of many of the salient events that took place between Mubarak's fall and the ascendency of Mohamed Morsi to the role of president, a moment concurrent with when we came to Egypt in the summer of 2012. I would continue to come to the wall on Mohamed Mahmoud as events unfolded in the following months, contrasting mainstream "news" with the revolution's iterations as seen in paint. Throughout 2012 and into 2013, the polarization and the level of violence in the streets escalated, and we all seemed to grow less and less surprised by it. Like many, I wanted to resist getting used to it and to continue life as if it were normal; but I had to teach and care for my two small kids who went to school, played in the park, and needed dinner each night. There was a certain necessity in continuing life as normal. Following and documenting street art reminded me that the resistance was alive, if not always well, even as life went on.

Bahia Shehab

Bahia Shehab was my colleague at the American University of Cairo. She was selected in 2013 by BBC as one of the one hundred women who speak for the world, for having responded through street art to the various iterations of power after she began working on the street in late 2011. In her essay for *Walls of Freedom*, she describes spraying her first graffito in November 2011 under SCAF rule: "All I had was one small stencil and four spray cans." Her stencil read "'No to military rule.' The lam-alif [referring to the letter "la," which means "no" in Arabic] letter I took off an eighth-century tombstone from the Islamic museum in Cairo. I have seen so much death circulating that only a letter off a tombstone would work" (Shehab 2014b, 119). The choice of font is emblematic of her work as it pulls from the past while speaking to the present.

Bahia was nervous, hoping she would be lost in the crowd of millions. She could get a variety of reactions, many of which could be dangerous. "I will ignore them and spray quickly," she thought, "because anyone can turn violent even with a million people around" (Shehab 2014b, 119). Then she was encouraged when she noticed another group of graffiti artists "scurrying like rats." Watching the crowd, she realized she was not alone. "It is good to feel like you are part of a bigger whole," she concluded (Shehab 2014b, 119). Years later, she still has not met most of the other graffiti artists in person, though she takes heart in their solidarity as well as their diversity. "Our worries and concerns are one, but the ways we express these concerns are completely different. This is what's beautiful," she contemplates.

The work Shehab is perhaps best known for is a series of visual "no's" about which she gave a 2012 TED talk, "A Thousand Times No." This work punctuates Cairo's dusty, chaotic streets in small iterations that interact with some of the murals and with other decorated and undecorated surfaces. From bridges, utility poles, and walls leading into Tahrir, her chorus of negation shouts "la, la, la" ("no, no, no"), each "la" pronounced with a glottal stop at the end like the "uh" in "uh-oh."

Living in Cairo during the era of Mohamed Morsi's presidency and in the aftermath of his removal, I would find the word strangely affirming. There was, and is, so much to say "no" to. As the "no's" pop out from stoops and pipes and the metal coverings of light boxes, "no" affirms the path to the iconic Square, the alpha and omega of Egyptian resistance. Like most of the street art in Egypt, the work negates not only those in power but also their ownership of the revolution's narrative. The negation gives voice to opposition and affirms its existence.

Figure 20.1. "No to Military Rule." Photo by Andy Young.

Figure 20.2. The word "no" printed over the face of former Egyptian President Morsi. Photo by Andy Young.

Figure 20.1 shows one of Shehab's thousand "no's" that fashions the letters of the Arabic word for "no," لا, *Laam Aleph,* into interlinked crescents. Figure 20.2 features the "no" as wide, angular blocks. The flexibility of Arabic script is such that the letters, even if they are intimately known, can look entirely different in different fonts. Her work exploits this flexibility, and the result is a lingering on the word itself.

Shehab's project "A Thousand Times No" evolved from her being commissioned to do a museum piece that involved Arabic font into her spray-painting graffiti that put her work in dialogue with the Egyptian revolution. Her project took one thousand versions of the Arabic script for "no" from various sources of Islamic influence throughout the last thousand years. The exhibit was displayed in a museum in Munich but more widely on the walls of Cairo's streets. Shehab described her beginnings as a graffiti artist: "The no campaign was my induction to the street, and it is ongoing. . . . It is a beautiful bank of visual ammunition."[1] She did not think the "no" project would continue after the first democratic presidential elections in 2012, but with the election of Morsi, she felt the urge to express how "Morsi lost the sympathy and support of the Egyptian people in November of 2012," as she noted in the TED blog (2013).

On November 22, Morsi issued a mandate that put him above judicial oversight. He then used that power to draft, and pass, a constitution that, among other flaws, did not protect the rights of women or religious minorities. During the short and contentious period between the drafting of, and the public referendum on, Morsi's constitution, a countrywide campaign resounded Shehab's no. Amidst many inconsistencies and boycotts, the referendum was said to have officially passed. Signs, stickers, posters, and "No, No, No" chants everywhere joined Shehab in chorus: "His actions made me go down again to Tahrir to paint the following message on the road leading up to the square: *We are back. No to a new Pharaoh. No to Morsi*" (Shehab 2013).

When I asked Shehab in a 2012 interview whether the "no" campaign was, itself, a confrontational message, she responded, fittingly: "No, on the contrary." To her, saying "yes" indicated compliance and acceptance that "the conversation is over." Alternatively, when one says "no," one opens a dialogue. To Shehab the "no's" suggest, "I don't agree with what you are doing. I don't agree with your ideas. Can we have a conversation? It's not a blunt 'no' that rejects the other; it's a 'no' that's asking for dialogue, for solutions." The Thousand Times No project allowed her to express that "I'm asking for a thousand solutions, that's all" (Shehab 2014c).

One of my favorite versions of Shehab's images was taken from a mausoleum in 1384 CE, Cairo. Spray painted around the "no" is part of a quotation that reads, "You can crush the flowers, but you cannot delay spring." The quotation was found scribbled on a scrap of paper in a field hospital in Tahrir. The "no" in that quotation (translated from Spanish into Arabic, the "not" from "cannot stop the spring") balances in the middle, the central figure of an ultimately affirming message despite

Figure 20.3. "No" as a flower with Arabic calligraphy surrounding it

its reminder of crushed flowers. I had that design tattooed on my arm, relieved when Shehab said she loved the idea and glad to have a visible sign of, a way of being marked by, the revolution when I leave Egypt. "No," it says, but it also says you cannot stop a force of change that is larger than the pettiness of power.

Commemorating All Martyrs

Everyday discourse in Egypt includes regular reference to the "martyrs" of the revolution. People have died, are dying, and will continue to die in the struggle for change. Another of Shehab's projects commemorates martyrs whose identities have been lost in the power struggles of recent times. A series of her murals commemorates the lives of fifty-one kindergarten-aged children killed in late 2012 when a train in the southern city of Assuit hit their school bus. Despite the Minister of Transportation's resignation, there was a wide public outcry over the disaster—the result of corruption and years of

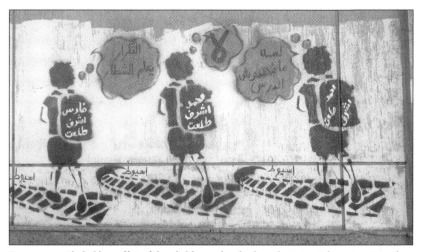

Figure 20.4. Shehab's graffiti of the children who died on the train ride to Assuit with each of their names on their silhouette with the letter signifying "No" in between them. Photo by Andy Young.

neglect of the railway system. The amount of money that was given to these children's families as compensation was less than the cost of an iPhone, as Shehab points out. Further, President Morsi's response, or lack of it, seemed to relegate the memory of the doomed children to another headline soon to be subsumed by the next one. "I wanted to bring the children back to life," she declared (Shihab 2013). Shehab painted the children of the accident as silhouettes all over the streets of Cairo. Each child is painted in black, with their names written on their backpacks, shown standing on train tracks, facing away from the viewer. Their hopes and dreams for Egypt's future are written in color in speech bubbles.

The morning of the accident, I was with my family in Upper Egypt, in the province of Sohag, adjacent to Assuit. The trains were becoming less predictable and even dangerous, sometimes breaking down and sometimes blocked due to protests. We were on the train behind the one that crashed, though we did not know it at the time ours ground to a halt. There was no explanation or rerouting. We simply sat for hours before giving up and taking a minivan that, ten hours later, got us to Cairo. We did not realize until later that our train was sitting behind so many lost lives just a year older than our oldest child.

The silhouettes of the train victims began to appear downtown, staring into the burnt remains of the National Democratic Headquarters, on bridges, and on the cinderblocks in front of the Ministry of Interior. The very presence of the children is defiant; remembering them is an act of resistance in itself. "We started a revolution so that accidents like this would not happen again," wrote Shehab (2013). But accidents still happen, as well as abuses of power. Morsi is gone now, but military rule and the deeply reviled state security apparatus have remained largely unchanged from Mubarak's time and, with the emergence of support for current president Abd Fattah el-Sissy, the country seems doomed, at least for now, to being a fascistic state. Her work, like that of so many artists, continues, in dialogue with the street, and keeps hope alive that it will not always be this way.

These images keep the children from being quickly absorbed into the fast-moving relentlessness of history, event, or "the past." Among the faces, the "no's" stand to signal not only defiance but mourning. They also command the viewer to condemn and to witness. Different in presentation and message, the "no's" negate the proliferation of these faces, the number of dead that builds into a blur. They negate our ability to see the dead as just another item we minimize on our screens and forget.

Resisting Sexual Aggression

The Shehab work that hit the biggest nerve, not only among the "Powers" but also among the common people's "powers," is her *Tamaradi ya Otta*, or *Rebel Cat*, which aims "to feminize" the act of rebellion. While she was spraying it, three men came by and erased it. "It was the fastest time I ever had anything erased with my own spray can!" (Shehab 2013). Shehab had to drive around for half an hour waiting for them to leave before she could go down and spray again.

The piece was a response to the sexual aggression that had become more present in the years since Mubarak's fall. Mob sexual assaults on women in Tahrir became common under Morsi's rule on any given protest night. I was on my way into the square one night when a stampede came thundering out. My friend and I were warned of men attacking women with machetes. The attacks were invariably orchestrated, frightening group acts, dozens of men surrounding the woman as if in a cir-

Figure 20.5. *Rebel Cat*

cular swarm, methodically attacking her. The way the mob attacked made it nearly impermeable to anyone who tried to help. Most activists believed these were politically motivated acts. Shehab thinks that the attackers were "employed by the followers of the Muslim Brotherhood to intimidate the women of Egypt from going down to protest in the Squares" (Shehab 2013).

"[*The Rebel Cat*] was a call to women to join the revolution," wrote Shehab (2013). "I feminized the verb 'to rebel,' so more women could relate to it, and I added the word 'cat,' a harassment howl that men sometimes call to women on the street." Women, after all, are "half the revolution." Feminizing the verb "*tamarod*" included women, but by adding "*ya otta*," she argued that "it becomes a very funny pun because 'ya otta' is a degrading term, a domestic animal, something that men yell at women on the street." The term was originally inspired by the Egyptian "Tamarod movement," which gathered a reported twenty-two million signatures to attest to a lack of confidence in Morsi. Shehab posits that the initial movement had started as "grassroots but was appropriated later on by other factions" (Shehab 2014c).

"*Tamarodi Ya Otta*" has a double meaning, explains Shehab, in that the word "tamarod" comes not only from the verb that means "to rebel" but also from the word "*mared*," which is a giant or genie. "So it does not only mean rebel, but it also means [to] become big, to change things." The image of the cat also evokes Bastet, a protective goddess of ancient Egypt. So with "*Tamarodi Ya Otta*," Shehab is transforming the meaning to indicate that "you are asking a domestic animal to become a pharaonic god again." The phrase resonates, then, "in the Arabic culture, in the Pharaonic culture, and in feminist discourse," she explained. "To me these three words were really important because they built on many aspects calling on women to rebel but also calling on women to change things" (Shehab 2014c).

The rebel cat, as well as its quick erasure, is an illustrative example of some of the larger movements in street art: connecting the ancient to the present, subverting the dominant message of who has, and is allowed to have, agency in the evolving landscape of politics in Egypt, and inventing and reinventing the voices of resistance. Years out from the revolution's beginning, resistance is under more pressure than ever before to present these voices effectively, and many, including Shehab, are reassessing the best methods.

Conclusion

Shehab views graffiti as "anti-system" by nature, and she will always interact with the "city as canvas" and the "street as a museum." But she has shifted her interest to finding new approaches to changing things, not least because street actions and direct, vocal opposition are resulting, especially since the enactment of the protest law, in widespread incarceration and worse. To Shehab, the important thing now is to find a way to reach her goals of changing society while seeing people enjoy basic freedoms such as clean water, clean streets, and good education. "Being imprisoned and being shot on the street will not get me there, so it's just a matter of being intelligent about it," she says.

In addition to avoiding possible repercussions, Shehab thinks evolving methods of resistance are the necessary next stage of creating a new country. "What's the point of going to the street and screaming over and over again?" she asks. "I've been doing that for three years because I consider my painting on the street a form of screaming." Instead, Shehab wants those who, like her, want social change to find ways to "become the system." The youth of the country should be allowed to run it because "they have solutions." Recently invited to give a keynote speech in Berlin, she was inspired by meeting street artists who were now leading major cultural institutions. "It's not a dream," she exclaimed. "This is real politics. How do you convince the other of the validity of your argument and get what you want?" (Shehab 2013c).

Another of Shehab's projects presents twenty minarets from the Arab world as part of the Louisiana Museum of Modern Art's "Arab Contemporary" exhibit in Denmark. As part of that project, she commissioned Mai Kamal, a young mezzo soprano from the Cairo Opera House, to record the *adhan*, the call to prayer. "For the past 1400 years only men have been raising the calls for prayer all over the Arab world; I felt that it was time for the feminine to raise their voices with the same chant calling for people 'to hasten to worship and to hasten to success' using Mai's melodious young strong voice" (Shehab 2014a).

During the height of the sexual violence against female protesters, I participated in a women's march through downtown Cairo. "The voice of women is not a shame; the voice of women is the revolution" was a chant that many repeated. This was one of the most powerful chants, especially because it rhymes in Arabic. Also, its meaning countered the Islamic conservatives' notion that women's voices should not be heard. It was in that atmosphere that hearing a woman chanting the Islamic call to prayer was so moving, reminding me of Shehab's question, "How different would people be if this is the voice they heard all the time?" (2014c).

The feminized call to prayer played during the recent exhibit, surrounding museum-goers with a new way of not only seeing, but hearing, the world. Egypt's street art has been re-visioning the official narratives of the country, linking the past to the present and giving power and voice to a resistance not represented there. As Shehab's work shows, negating the dominant narratives invites a dialogue of imagination and a way for people to envision the world they want or, as she articulated it, "The revolution is an awakening, a chance for us to rethink our present and try to change it" (Shehab 2014c).

NOTE

1 Bahia Shehab, e-mail message to author, September 20, 2013. Shared with permission.

BIBLIOGRAPHY

Abaza, Mona. 2012. "The Revolution's Barometer." Jadaliyya, http://www.jadaliyya.com.

Elias, Chad. 2014. "Graffiti, Social Media, and the Public Life of Images in the Egyptian Revolution." In *Walls of Freedom: Street Art and the Egyptian Revolution*, ed. Basma Hamdy, Karl Don Stone, and Mona Eltahawy 89–91. Berlin: From Here to Fame.

El Shazly, Yasmin. 2014. "The Origins of the Rebellious Personality." In *Walls of Freedom: Street Art and the Egyptian Revolution*, ed. Basma Hamdy, Karl Don Stone, and Mona Eltahawy, 6–9. Berlin: From Here to Fame.

Shehab, Bahia. 2012. "A Thousand Times No." *TED Blog*, http://www.ted.com/talks/bahia_shehab_a_thousand_times_no.

———. 2013. "The New Revolution in Egypt and Why I Wanted to Feminize It." *TED Blog*, July 5, http://blog.ted.com/2013/07/05/the-new-revolution-in-egypt-and-why-i-wanted-to-feminize-it-an-essay/.

———. 2014a. "Landscape/Soundscape: 20 Minarets from the Arab World." Arab Contemporary Louisiana Museum of Modern Art, May 10, http://www.worldarchitecture.org.

———. 2014b. "Spraying NO." In *Walls of Freedom: Street Art and the Egyptian Revolution*, ed. Basma Hamdy, Karl Don Stone, and Mona Eltahawy, 117–19. Berlin: From Here to Fame.

———. 2014c. Personal Interview. Cairo, Egypt, May 27.

21

Half Syrian Sufi Blogger

Faith and Activism in the Virtual Public Space

MICHELA CERRUTI

[M]y blog, I started it after I felt I needed a place to "grow" spiritually by expressing my experience as an Arab woman who does not believe in conventional Arab traditions that restrict our thinking and movement. I have been a rebel all of my life, and probably that is what attracted me into delving more into Sufism.

—Half Syrian, Interview, July 2010

Since the early 2000s, Syrian secular and religious female bloggers have created unique forms of engaged online visibility. Although the Syrian blogosphere is still primarily a male-dominated realm, female participation in it grew exponentially between 2004 and 2011. From the privacy of their rooms, or the exposed confidentiality of an Internet café, a generation of female bloggers evaded the confines of their country while renegotiating the boundaries of their traditional society. Secular activists (such as Dania, blogger of *My Chaos*) and religious ones (such as the author of *Damascus Dreams*) raised awareness of their beliefs and struggles. Whether looking for a space to freely preach their faith or seeking a tool to spread their modernizing, secular, feminist ideals, Syrian women showed equal determination to advocate for women's agency.

This chapter analyzes the life story narrated by a blogger based in Damascus in the pre–Arab Spring Syria. It examines her use of the virtual public space to promote Sufi tradition and to support gender equality. This study is based on substantial nonparticipant observation and textual analysis of the weblog maintained by the author Half Syrian (also referred to as "50%" or "%") between January 2008 and June 2010.

Using an interpretative approach to the entries posted on 50%'s weblog, I explore how this Sufi woman creates a dynamically meaningful public space online by expressing her beliefs and her opinions. In particular, I examine how Half Syrian shapes an alternative space to narrate her individualized religious experience and to express a Sufi morality that may enrich the Syrian religious debate.

In 2008, while observing and analyzing the blogs belonging to the so-called Levantine English Cluster (Etling, Kelly, Faris, and Palfrey 2009, 3), a group of well-educated, upper- and middle-class Syrian women were actively involved in shaping the virtual public space. These bloggers opted to communicate mainly in English in an effort to send their messages beyond the Arab blogosphere. They expressed their pride in their Arabic culture and Syrian nationality and simultaneously explored their multidimensional identities. Half Syrian was among the bloggers who captured a lot of attention for the way she described her multilayered identity in her posts on "About being 50%": "Identity is a matter of choice at the end of the day. It's about self-image. . . . What really matters is 'Heart.' Where does your heart find itself? My heart is half Syrian, has always been like that, since my mother is from a Syrian Family. This half is more important to me than the 'other half,' which I consider to be a vague mishmash of identities that I don't like to venture into (it includes identity crisis inherited from my ancestors, society and the role the media plays in shaping what we believe . . . we are)" (2008).

Half Syrian stresses her love for Damascus. Being Sufi in Damascus is optimal. In fact, her personal religious roots have been shaped by the city's Sufi soul; coherent with Sufi belief, she considers Damascus the focal spiritual center of the world: "Damascus is the spiritual center of the world. Here, great Sufis were initiated into their spiritual trusts. Prophet Mohammad (*SAL*) said that during the end-of-time, Sham (Damascus) will be the safest place on earth for believers to find refuge" (2008).

Indeed, her Sufi identity is at the base of her activism. Sufi values are widely evident throughout her blog. In a post entitled "Why There Are So Many 'Atheists/Skeptics' These Days," she reiterates her resentment against clerical men who, she believes, destroy the profound meaning of Islam. In her view, these ideologues discourage people from following the religious path with their followers: "Allah is beautiful, Sayyidna Prophet Mohammad is beautiful; they have nothing to do with today's 'ulama' (religious leaders). Those are polluted spirits that roam the earth. May Allah rid us of all shapes of hypocritical religion" (2011b).

In an online interview, she confirms her rejection of "official" Islam for being dogmatic *Salafi* (a revivalist movement within the Sunni Islamic religion), "mutated" from its original profound meaning and focused on "terrorizing people into religious dogmas" (2010b). In contrast, she expresses a strong empathy towards what she considers moderate Islam by quoting Syria's grand mufti, Sheikh Ahmad Hassoun, whom she met in 2010. Hassoun's wisdom touched Half Syrian, as she emphasizes in her posts: "'Don't force your children to perform prayers,' [Hassoun] told us. 'Don't even tell them to go to the mosque to pray. Just let them watch you do it and they'll pick it up, but don't terrorize them into religion.' He recounted several stories of his days as a child—when their school master used to beat them up if he caught his friends laughing during prayer time. 'What kind of a generation are we raising if we tell them "believe in God or else!"'" (2010b).

To her, Sufi Islam considers love as the deeper meaning of religion. The theme of true love, according to a Sufi perspective, is quite recurrent in this activist's observations. She uses her blog as a platform to give voice to the spiritual dimension of her faith. In a post of October 2010 dedicated to the inner sense of love, she comments,

> A common saying in Syria, and some parts of the Arab World, is: "Love is from God." This is to explain the unexplainable motives of love of one person to another, or love of a certain ritual, place, theme, concept, way, etc. Commonly it is believed that our hearts are steered by another force, by a higher truth that drops in it the love of someone we might rarely see or meet, but feel great joy at their presence. This is a Sufi (*i.e.* Mystic Islam) concept discussed and affirmed by a host of Sufi scholars in different centuries (among them Ibn Arabi in "The Meccan Revelations"). . . . According to Mystics, the heart is the dwelling place of Allah. (2010c)

Half Syrian expresses that the heart is the center of the highest spirituality, and her choice of blogging comes as a spiritual expression: "I write my blog posts following intuition. My heart connects to my Sheikh's heart and words come out of me" (2010b). She clarifies this correlation, adding that she has learned to let her intellect follow her heart (at the base of all knowledge). In fact, she believes that the people who follow the blog are in search of the truth: "Deep down inside we all want to reach happiness, we all want to end our own inner suffering, or state of loss. Some people choose to camouflage that by creating false things around them, like status, power, image, etc. But this never quenches the thirst of the heart waiting to unravel the truth behind our existence" (2010c).

Half Syrian's unique form of online visibility does not only promote Sufism but also gives voice to women. The relationship between body and soul is paramount in her online activism. Her idea of female agency transcends the modernist, Western ideals of secular feminism. Through her negotiation between women's rights and religious values, she embodies a non-Western form of modernity (Göle 1999, 40) that seeks to offer an alternative path to secular female activism. A March 2011 post entitled "How Different Are Liberals from Religious Fundamentalists" exemplifies where she stands in the dichotomous conflict between the secular and religious views of gender equality: "By the looks of it, liberals stand on one end of the spectrum, while religious fundamentalists are on the other. But I believe both are fundamentalists in their own ways. Both are control freaks, and both exercise discrimination and oppressive behavior against 'the other.' Both want to clone people so they would become just like them to fit into either one of their camps" (2011a).

She compares the difficulties encountered by a hypothetical veiled woman in a secular society to the ones faced by a nonveiled one in a "fundamentalist" religious society. She claims that in both cases, women would be targeted because they represent the "otherness" in each society:

> But my heart aches when I meet people who think they can put *hijab* on a woman's head, or remove *hijab* from her head: People who think they can terrorize her so she can fit in, who think they have a rule and a power on this earth to reject or accept her based on her looks. Who think they can take away from her humanity just because they do not agree with her, who back-stab her, speak ill of her, exercise all kinds of bad manners against her, just because she does not resemble their clothing, she doesn't mirror their ideals, and she does not cherish their little gods. It's her head, she does what she wants with it. Leave her alone! (2011a)

In general, the topic of women's right to express their femininity be-yond the constraints imposed by their society is a frequent and poignant theme of her blog. In November 2010 she invited women to say "no" to visual discrimination: "Don't be a prisoner to narrow cultural defini-tions. That's what I learned from extensive traveling. In one culture you might be the coolest looking young lady, when in another you might simply don't fit into their definition of what is beautiful or fashionable" (2010d).

Half Syrian's posts provide direct insight into how a Syrian female Sufi activist did dynamically contribute to the modification of the Syrian virtual social imaginary. She uses her narrative as a series of snapshots of social reality, fragments of everyday life, to help the reader focus on the corporeal and gendered aspects of the traditional Syrian society. She aims to change the public sphere not through a political or ideologi-cal confrontation but rather through the creation of spaces where spiri-tual practices would shape the Syrian public space (Pinto 2006, 2). Her outlook on the question of gender offers an opportunity to read female agency from a Sufi perspective.

BIBLIOGRAPHY

Elting, Bruce, John Kelly, Robert Faris, and John Palfrey. 2009. "Mapping the Arabic Blogosphere: Politics, Culture, and Dissent." In Internet & Democracy Case Study Series. The Berkman Center for Internet & Society at Harvard University, http://cyber.law.harvard.edu.

Göle, Nilüfer. 1999. "Global Expectations, Local Experiences, Non Western Moderni-ties." In Through a Glass, Darkly: Blurred Images of Cultural Tradition and Moder-nity over Distance and Time, ed. Wilhelmus Antonius Arts, 40–55. Leiden: Brill.

Half Syrian. 2008. "About Being 50%." Half Syrian. Syria's Nooks and Crannies . . . from Everything Hidden: Sufism, Corporate Culture, and Stories from Within, November, https://halfsyrian.wordpress.com/about.

———. 2010a. "I Met the Grand Mufti of Syria, and I Like Him." Half Syr-ian. Syria's Nooks and Crannies . . . from Everything Hidden: Sufism, Corpo-rate Culture, and Stories from Within, June 12, https://halfsyrian.wordpress.com/2010/06/12/i-met-the-grand-mufti-of-syria-and-i-like-him.

———. 2010b. Interview with author, July 14.

———. 2010c. "Perspectives on 'Love' from an Inner Point of View." Half Syrian. Syria's Nooks and Crannies . . . from Everything Hidden: Sufism, Corporate Culture, and Stories from Within, October 9, https://halfsyrian.wordpress.com/2010/10/09/perspectives-on-love-from-an-inner-point-of-view.

———. 2010d. "Say NO to Visual Discrimination: You Are Beautiful." *Half Syrian. Syria's Nooks and Crannies . . . from Everything Hidden: Sufism, Corporate Culture, and Stories from Within*, November 3, https://halfsyrian.wordpress.com/2010/11/03/say-no-to-visual-discrimination-you-are-beautiful.

———. 2011a. "How Different Are Liberals from Religious Fundamentalists." *Half Syrian. Syria's Nooks and Crannies . . . from Everything Hidden: Sufism, Corporate Culture, and Stories from Within*, March 4, https://halfsyrian.wordpress.com/2011/03/04/how-different-are-liberals-really-from-religious-fundamentalists.

———. 2011b. "Why There Are so Many 'Atheists/Skeptics' These Days." *Half Syrian. Syria's Nooks and Crannies . . . from Everything Hidden: Sufism, Corporate Culture, and Stories from Within*, April 3, https://halfsyrian.wordpress.com/2011/04/03/why-there-are-so-many-athiestsskeptics-these-days.

Pinto, Paulo G. 2006. "Sufism, Moral Performance, and the Public Sphere in Syria." *Revue des mondes musulmans et de la Méditerranée*, December, http://remmm.revues.org/3026 (accessed February 27, 2015).

22

The Light in Her Eyes

A Woman Is a School. Teach Her and You Teach a Generation:
An Interview with Filmmakers Julia Meltzer and Laura Nix

NURULSYAHIRAH TAHA

Houda al-Habash, a conservative Muslim preacher, founded
a Qur'an school for girls in Damascus 30 years ago. Every
summer, her female students immerse themselves in a rig-
orous study of Islam. . . . Shot right before the uprising in
Syria erupted, *The Light in Her Eyes* offers an extraordinary
portrait of a leader who challenges the women of her community to live according to Islam, without giving up their
dreams.
—*The Light in Her Eyes* website, 2015

I interviewed filmmakers Julia Meltzer and Laura Nix in November 2011
after the world premiere screening of their film was sold out at the International Documentary Film Festival Amsterdam. As Julia and Laura
spent time in Houda's mosque, they saw many parallels between their
own religions and the program Houda was directing, as they explained
in the following interview:

NURULSYAHIRAH TAHA: What does your film tell us about the posi-
    tion of Muslim women in Syria?
LAURA NIX: The women in Houda's mosque are educated women,
    and they consider themselves modern women; and they are
    modern women! I think one of the things that it teaches us is that
    there's a potential for religious education to be a liberating force for
    women. In the West, most people think that an Islamic religious
    education must be oppressive, and in fact we find something quite

Figure 22.1. A scene from *The Light in Her Eyes.*

different. Houda teaches women that education is a form of worship and that in pursuing their education they are worshipping. Allowing them to become educated and to get jobs, and to choose a public life if they want to—this is something she encourages, and this is not a message most people would think you would find in a religious school.

NURULSYAHIRAH: How do you think Houda affirms Western feminism and also departs from it?

JULIA: I think that in a way, a lot of the challenges that Houda faces are really similar to the challenges that women in the West face. Women in the West are trying to balance a career with having a family, and Houda's living that life too. There are maybe more concrete, inflexible expectations on Houda—that she needs to be there for her kids first, and that she needs to serve her husband. But if you think about that a little bit farther, women in the West are doing that too. They're not abandoning their families, their husband, or their children. So, I think that in a way, we find a lot of our values as Western feminists and our ideals confirmed and affirmed and reflected back to us in what Houda is struggling with as well.

LAURA: But I think one of the things that was, to me, the most interesting thing about Houda and spending time around her and her school is how much it made me reflect on my own definition about what feminism means. I think in the West we can sometimes make that definition too narrow and it can become rigid. Houda would never describe herself as a feminist. This is a word and a theory that she rejects completely. But at the same time I do see feminist principles in what Houda is doing. And I also am inspired by her as a feminist in a way that might seem contrary.

NURULSYAHIRAH: Why does Houda call women to be involved without neglecting their family duties?

JULIA: Houda is part of a movement, there are women doing things exactly similar to what she's doing all across the Middle East.

LAURA: And this movement is not necessarily organized or centralized in a way, it's essentially a grassroots movement. Some people have said that this growing—some people call it the women's mosque movement or the piety movement—and some people have said that second to the Arab Spring, it's the most important social movement happening in the Middle East today. Because of the way it's changing the culture and how it can potentially change the face of Islam.

NURULSYAHIRAH: What would you want viewers to take away from the film?

JULIA: We want people to be able to have a connection and to be able to feel and see what it's like in the women's side of the mosque, and to understand that through these characters. These are their lives. This is the life they are living. And I think that by showing it through their eyes and their experiences in a deliberately nonjudgmental way, people can be open to understanding that perspective. And I hope that that happens. I hope that if people see the film and then they're walking down the street and they see a woman wearing hijab, and if their proclivity or their general stereotype before watching the film would be "Why is that woman doing that?" or "Was she forced to do that?" that it might just open people's eyes to the complexity that goes into the decision makers to wear hijab, to practice Islam in a more open way. And that it might deepen their understanding of that.

* * *

As of 2012, Houda and her family have left the school and Syria to live in the Arabian Peninsula. Her daughter, Enas, contemplates, "A light has gone out in our community," because it is no longer safe to go to the mosque since the uprising against President Bashar al-Assad's regime. While it is impossible to know what will eventually happen to her school in Syria, one can only hope that the firm foundations that Houda has given her students will help them rise to any challenges they face (Meltzer and Nix 2012).

BIBLIOGRAPHY

Meltzer, Julia, and Laura Nix. 2012. "An Islamic School for Girls." *New York Times*, July 16, http://www.nytimes.com (accessed October 15, 2015).

23

Writing Lebanese Feminist History

Rose Ghurayyib's Editorial Letters in
Al-Raida *Journal from 1976 to 1985*

NICOLE KHOURY

The Lebanese feminist journal *Al-Raida* of the Institute for Women's Studies in the Arab World (IWSAW, now known as the Arab Institute for Women) at the Lebanese American University first appeared in 1976—one year after the Lebanese civil war erupted. Though it began as a newsletter sharing information on regional conferences and studies on Arab women, its archives are rich historical accounts of women's activism, coalition building, and feminist arguments for equality, revealing a history of women's movements in Lebanon that has shaped the discourse on gender across the Middle East.

A prominent figure in the early issues of *Al-Raida* was its first editor, Rose Ghurayyib, a contributing writer to *Sawt al-Mar'ah* (The Woman's Voice) and author of *Aesthetic Criticism in Arabic Literature* (1952), a study of Gibran's works (1969), and *Introduction to Modern Literary Criticism* (1971). In 1976, Rose was displaced from her home in Dammour, a city south of Beirut, and came to live on the university campus. Julinda Abu Nasr, the director of the institute, knew Rose as a well-known literary author and invited her to join *Al-Raida* as its editor. Since Rose was free to make editorial decisions independent of the institute, she raised bold questions on taboo issues, including family planning and contraception; and her contributions to *Al-Raida* reflected the larger regional conversations on gender issues. This chapter explores *Al-Raida's* archive for historical accounts of activism and feminist writing, and looks specifically at Rose's editorials from 1976 to 1985, during the civil war years, as it is a period of Lebanese feminist activism that is often overlooked.

IWSAW History and Background

Established in 1973 at the Beirut University College (BUC), which became known as Lebanese American University as of 1994, with a grant from the Ford Foundation (Ghurayyib 1980b, 10), IWSAW prioritized the documentation of research on Arab women, the funding of emerging research on Arab women, communication between the institute and the journal's readership, and the development of educational projects for women in rural areas. IWSAW began publishing student newsletters providing information with a focus on the role of women in national, rural, and industrial development; women's position in the labor force; women's social and legal status, living conditions, contributions to academic fields, and self-concept; the development of women's organizations, education and vocational training, and health services; the abolition of illiteracy in rural areas; and addressing population growth through family planning services ("Areas of Research" 1976, 9).

Al-Raida was a direct response to the First World Conference on Women held in Mexico in 1975, in which participants adopted a World Plan of Action for women's equality, with statements on health, political participation, education, paid work, peace, the environment, and violence against women. As a result, "Almost all development agencies—international, regional, national, and UN specialized agencies—had to engage with the woman question. This system-wide mandate created enormous demands for information, which produced an explosion of knowledge" (Jain 2005, 64).

Al-Raida began as a newsletter focusing on raising consciousness about women's issues and educating readers about their history and rights. Julinda Abu Nasr explains, "[Women] have rights that their religion gives them, Islam and Christianity. [We focused on] things they should know about their body, how to raise children, laws from their government to protect them. And we wanted them to know about the women who came before them and how they reached this development" (2011). Rose's editorials are a testament to the feminist work undertaken by activists who lived through the civil war, as they continued writing, teaching, and publishing.

Al-Raida published a range of genres, including reports, studies, conference proceedings, summaries of research subsidized by IWSAW, and information on training programs and women's studies courses. Additionally, prolific in Arabic, English, and French, Rose translated newspaper and magazine articles from local newspapers and literature by Arab authors, including twentieth-century fiction writer May Ziadah. She wrote biographies of pioneers, such as Salwa Nassar—former president of BUC and the first Lebanese to receive a PhD in nuclear physics. In her editorials, Rose draws connections between current issues of women and gender and historical works and biographies to provide readers with a nuanced perspective and understanding of the local conversation on gender.

Rose's Feminist Editorials

When Rose was appointed editor for *Al-Raida*, her perception of the status of women initially was limited because she attempted to "enlighten" Lebanese women by encouraging them to emulate Western feminist movements. Her early editorials obscure the differences between women of different ethnic, social, economic, political, cultural, and educational backgrounds in Lebanon.

Betty Freidan and Simone de Beauvoir are two feminist thinkers who strongly influenced Rose Ghurayyib's initial approach to women's issues and whose works she heavily cited. For example, Rose's first editorials compared Lebanese women with "Western women" using de Beauvoir's feminist existentialist philosophy in *The Second Sex* (1953). This seminal text posits that women's bodies restricted them to certain roles in society and in labor, and that women's identity as "other" is a result of their reproductive capacity. De Beauvoir considers woman's subordinate position to be a result of the continued division of labor associated with their reproductive capacities, which restrict them to the "other" status. De Beauvoir also explains that women have a choice to reject femininity in order to be liberated from their subordinate status, and defines "woman" as a social construct. Similarly, Betty Friedan's *Feminine Mystique* (1963) traces media representations of women in postwar America and the construction of the "Happy Housewife Heroine" who has a "problem with no name." Friedan calls for liberation from oppressive practices that exclude women from public participation.

Beauvoir and Friedan's approach to defining "woman" as a social construct appealed to Rose. She drew parallels to definitions of gender in the Lebanese social context—making direct comparisons in several editorials between "women's roles" in Lebanon and in the United States. Using these feminist texts, she articulated the unique challenges in Lebanese society.

In 1978, Rose's editorial titled "Will to Power" emphasizes concepts such as individuality and self-actualization, identifying an individual's will power as the solution to complex issues. American women are more liberated in their approach to marriage, she argues, in comparison with Lebanese women, who are "born for marriage" (1978a, 1). She maintains that Lebanese women are given two options by their families: to get married or "to live like an outcast and to work as a servant in her brother's house or at some other relative's" (1978a, 1). Whereas Lebanese women are being forced into marriage, she writes, women in the West are marrying for love. However, neither being persuaded into marriage nor marrying for love is making women happy, she observes. Marriage, she writes, is not where women find happiness.

She also states how May Jumblatt, the former wife of Lebanese political leader Kamal Jumblatt, married for love but was now divorced. In comparison, Ann and Charles Lindbergh—who were not married—are an example of a successful relationship, as "[Ann] rejects the mystic notion of complete union between lovers, and insists on self-realization, with or without marriage" (1978a, 1). According to Rose, Ann managed to "have her own existence and realize her own creative activity" (1978a, 1), an indication to Rose that American women are liberated from social constructionist notions of marriage and gender roles whereas May Jumblatt was not.

Rose's writing emphasizes autonomy, urges Lebanese women to reject the social practice of marriage, and describes married women as those who "chose lives of leisure" but who lead lives of illusion. She insists that individual education, will power, and self-awareness are essential to overcoming oppressive social practices. This emphasis on autonomy is further illustrated in her narrative of her former classmate who was never satisfied with anything in life and had "the germ," which she defines as a bitterness created by an "unquenchable lust for importance" and a "mad thirst for domination" (1980a, 1). Defining "the germ" as a biological disease that can be cured by the exercise of will power places the responsibility for resisting oppressive structures on the reader and urges her to rebel against institutional social concepts. Ghurayyib describes Western women as having made the crucial step in self-awareness and rejection of social norms, and her editorials attempt to instigate a similar women's liberation movement in Lebanon.

While she compared marriage practices and labor practices in the United States to those in Lebanon, her editorials initially neglected to identify socioeconomic conditions under which women marry and work. Her solution includes education and will power, but little else. Consequently, Rose's editorials illustrate an attempt to instigate a gender revolution eschewing marriage practices in the upper echelons of educated Lebanese society through sheer will power, a feminist philosophy she strongly espoused. As a result, she directed her editorials towards an upper-middle-class audience.

She makes a statement in her seventh-issue editorial that in developed countries, a person has "an unprecedented freedom to choose his work and to indulge in activities that will transcend the bare necessities" (1978a, 1), addressing an elite group of Lebanese women, which ultimately obscures the socioeconomic arrangements shaping women's lives. This reflects scholarly and activist criticism of the Lebanese women's movement as obscuring class consciousness in a fragmented fight for women's rights, as activists working in organizations are unable to enact lasting social transformation.

Women, Work, and Class

Rose further engaged with issues of labor when she responded to challenges to women's participation in the labor force, and returned to the argument on the division of labor in the editorial "Women and Work." She begins this editorial by citing Arab reformer Abdel-Rahman el Kawakabi's 1905 argument blaming women for the division of labor: women have created an unjust division of labor based on the pretext of their weakness (1979, 1). Rose challenges this statement, meant to inspire women to join the work force by affording women agency, saying it is "a sweeping statement which may apply to a minimum number of rich women, who live in luxury and lead a lazy parasitic life" (1979, 1). Arguments such as el Kawakabi's, she claims, do not apply to rural women who "carry a full time work-load in endless housekeeping tasks, requiring skill in many fields and forming a basic element in the life of the family" (1979, 1). Here she addresses for the first time how class intersects with labor in Lebanon, and further points to the class division between women and the effect it has on both labor and national development: "Women who work at the same time in and outside the home perform a double task. If women have until now carried out these functions without any return except maintenance, this does not reduce the value of their achievement because it has a basic importance in the building of the family and of society" (1979, 1). Women's participation in the labor force and women's access to education were the two main issues considered integral to the development and modernization of the nation-state, but by highlighting the difference shaping women's lives, Rose challenges the assumption that women have the autonomy to choose work.

In the late '70s and early '80s, IWSAW collaborated with the Lebanese Family Planning Association to raise awareness of rural women's need for healthcare and access to contraceptives, which were illegal until 1983. IWSAW also designed and implemented development programs: basic living skills program, a literacy initiative, and rehabilitation and vocational programs for women in prison. These programs were often framed as national development projects for women's advancement in society. This effort revealed discrepancies between the international development and modernizing programs, on the one hand, and the lives of women across class, religious, ethnic, and social lines, on the other. By calling attention to the conditions of women's work in rural areas in her writing, Rose emphasized women's participation in and integration into development and job training programs implemented by IWSAW and other national and international organizations.

Rethinking Autonomy

Rose challenged the assumptions of autonomy in international feminist arguments as a result of the prolonged civil war after the 1982 Israeli invasion of Beirut and the subsequent international feminist movement's call for disarmament; Rose's discourse on autonomy shifts, marking an intersectional understanding of hierarchical social structures, particularly class divisions, and how they shape the discourse on women's issues. Israel invaded Lebanon in 1979 and seized the capital in 1982, marking a pivotal event during the civil war, as indicated by the responses of France, the United States, Saudi Arabia, and Iran, and leading to a multifaceted conflict. A close reading of Rose's editorials suggests that women's activism was significantly shaped by this event in two ways. First, the women's International League for Peace and Freedom organized the Stop the Arms Race (STAR) campaign, which *Al-Raida* responded to by calling for the universalization of the campaign. Second, the realization that foreign involvement implied international and foreign culpability in the violence that tore Lebanon apart challenged the assumptions that Western women were self-aware, autonomous individuals to be emulated, concepts on which Rose's feminist arguments for equality were grounded.

In 1982, Rose's editorials began employing a feminist theory centered on difference, arguing that both women and men were victims of patriarchal social structures and neoliberal imperialist forces. For example, Rose's editorials draw from Nawal El Saadawi's writings and her strategy for women's participation in the Arab Unity Movement, which also appear frequently in *Al-Raida*, arguing for a radical upheaval of the patriarchal capitalist system oppressing the Middle Eastern region. Rose's editorials articulate an understanding of the ways women are marginalized by patriarchal capitalist structures and also by Western imperialist forces, revealing a notable influence of postcolonial feminist theory. Employing human rights discourse to address the increasing complexities facing women, Rose wrote, "Respect for human dignity, recognition of the other person's rights, regardless of his appearance, color, age, sex, race or rank, is the primary requirement of civic education and the first mark of development" (1981, 1).

The violence during the civil war halted all activist movements working towards women's progress as it became necessary to focus on the immediate needs of the people, including the most immediate need—survival. On February 14, 1982, Wajiha Wazzan, wife of Prime Minister Shafiq Wazzan, held a panel at the Makassed School for Girls condemning violence, including family violence, and urged Lebanese mothers to join the international campaign for peace (1983a, 10). Rose, and many others, took up nonviolent peace work on the ground, an approach taken up once again years later by women's movements during the 2006 war (Stephan and Khoury 2015).

Identifying Structural Challenges

Rose's final editorial before stepping down, "You Cannot Set the Clock Back" (1983b), identifies challenges for women's advancement in Lebanon: the secularization of the political sphere and the personal status laws. Activism had long been hindered by the fragmented confessional political system, which weakened the government's legal decisions by relegating personal status and family laws to religious courts representing the sixteen different confessional groups. In response to this systemic injustice, Rose cited increasing gains France had made for women's rights, specifically legislation on abortion, protection against sexual assault, and laws ensuring the right to work. "In Lebanon," she maintains, "which may be taken as a specimen of Third World developing countries, women's problems are much more complicated when compared with those of the First World" (1983b, 1).

The structural oppression inherent in Lebanon's government and legal system remains the largest obstacle to women's rights. Rose ended her editorial positively, expressing solidarity across international movements: "The achievements realized by [the Western feminist movement] within the last 15 years serve as encouragement and spur [global women's groups] to walk in their sisters' steps" (1983a, 1). Her editorial marks increased attention to complex oppressive hierarchical structures, shaping current discourse on women's issues in Lebanon, and articulating structural challenges we continue to face today.

Critics of the Lebanese women's movement argue that there is no real united feminist movement with a common strategy. While it may seem that there is a pluralistic approach to addressing issues of gender, closer attention to the archives of *Al-Raida* during the civil war years reveals that Rose's writing—her editorials in particular—are an example of the kind of civic work writers, scholars, and activists have taken up to address inequalities, ultimately contributing to regional discourses on gender. This writing-as-activism approach, before digital distribution and online community building, reminds us of the history of dedicated feminist interlocutors who have helped shape the discourse on gender and laid the groundwork for current activism through their writing and teaching, a history we have yet to fully recover.

BIBLIOGRAPHY

Abu Nasr, Julinda. 2011. Personal interview, 5 August.

"Areas of Research." 1976. *Al-Raida* 1, no. 1: 9.

de Beauvoir, Simone. 1953. *The Second Sex*. New York: Knopf.

Friedan, Betty. *The Feminine Mystique*. New York: Norton, 1963.

Ghurayyib, Rose. 1978a. "Will to Power." *Al-Raida* 2, no. 7: 1.

———. 1978b. "Woman between Reality and Illusion." *Al-Raida* 1, no. 5: 1.

———. 1979. "Women and Work." *Al-Raida* 2, no. 9: 1.

———. 1980a. "The Germ." *Al-Raida* 3, no. 13: 1.

———. 1980b. "A Survey of the Asian Women Institute's Activities in 1979." *Al-Raida* 3, no. 12: 10–11.

———. 1981. "1981, the Year of the Handicapped." *Al-Raida* 4, no. 15: 1.

———. 1982. "Women and Old Age." *Al-Raida* 5, no. 20: 1.

———. 1983a. "Women and Peace." *Al-Raida* 6, no. 24: 9–10.

———. 1983b. "You Cannot Set the Clock Back." *Al-Raida* 6, no. 23: 1.

Ismail, Ghena. 1997. "Rose Ghurayyib." *Al-Raida* 14, no. 78: 42–44.

Jain, Devaki. 2005. *Women, Development, and the UN: A Sixty-Year Quest for Equality and Justice*. Bloomington: Indiana University Press.

Stephan, Rita, and Nicole Khoury. 2015. "Lebanese Women's Nonviolence: Action and Discourse." In *Women, War, and Violence: Topography, Resistance, and Hope*, ed. Mariam M. Kurtz and Lester Kurtz, 279–98. Santa Barbara, CA: Praeger.

24

Um Sahar, the Adeni Woman Leader in al-Hirak Southern Independence Movement in Yemen

KEVIN A. DAVIS

For what seemed like an eternity, I waited in the front seat of my friend and guide Saheb's old Toyota on a dark cul-de-sac for the short ring of Saheb's cell phone, signaling the "all-clear." I was about to sit down in the bustling center of the city of Aden in southern Yemen, with Um Sahar, the female leader of the Adeni women's chapter of the Southern Peaceful Movement's women's chapter, or al-Hirak. This movement had been the central organized resistance that had been demanding independence for the Yemeni south since 2006. Its members had resisted the systematic political and economic deprivation of the south by the northern-dominated government since the unification of north and south Yemen in 1990, in which the south was systematically disadvantaged by the northern-dominated government, both politically and economically. Though I had met many other women involved in the movement briefly and encountered them in daily protests and strikes, my public interactions had been limited. Finally, I was escorted to the door of the apartment building down the quiet street.

After the quick introductions, Saheb departed and I was left with Um Sahar, her daughter (an English teacher in her early twenties), and her son (a high school student). Um Sahar was the mother of three children and the coordinator of the women's chapter of al-Hirak in Aden under the loose leadership of Ali Salim al-Beid, the former and now exiled president of South Yemen. Not only was she active in organizing women and participating in protests and other community-based action; she was also a self-appointed historian of the struggle for independence.

In this chapter, I explore the role of women in the Adeni nationalist movement through the work of Um Sahar.[1] While in Yemen in 2013, I conducted interviews and spent time with twelve different activists, focusing on their work in al-Hirak. Um Sahar was the only female activist I was able to speak to. I found that as active agents in the formative process of southern nationalism, women draw upon romantic, nostalgic memories of Aden's colonial and socialist past to highlight how they enjoyed equal citizenship rights in preunification South Yemen. Such notions give a sense of urgency in calls for independence, and make women symbolic of Aden's cosmopolitan character. For parallel reasons, these women are specially targeted by the conservative northern system. While they carry a special burden of being national symbols, they must straddle the realities of everyday life where their manners, dress, and aspirations are constricted by contemporary northern hegemony.

My findings, based on Partha Chatterjee's scholarship (1989, 1993), reveal how, just as it is in India, nationalist discourse in other postcolonial countries is deeply gendered. Every mention of women, especially in ethnographies of the Middle East, tended to "over-embody" women and to equate them "with body, nature, passion, secrecy, shame, and the private domain" (Ghannam 2013, 4). The intense focus on the hijab and body appearances epitomized this over-embodiment, and many discussions of women and nationalism have continued this pattern. Here I capture local discourses around Yemeni women in the nationalist movement, which have the same over-embodying tendency.

After discussing the history of al-Hirak and the failure of the 1990 unification, Um Sahar invited me to look through a few of the records she kept, which included hundreds of newspaper articles documenting protests since the early 2000s, mainly from *al-Ayyam*, the most well-known southern newspaper, as well as photographs and reports on every known martyr of the movement. Since the Southern Uprising began in 2006, many protests have been met with overzealous resistance from central government forces, which are dominated by soldiers of northern descent.

Um Sahar pointed to a newspaper clipping from 2007, when al-Hirak was officially formed. The article documented a large protest in Khor Maksar, a neighborhood of Aden, where dozens of protesters had been killed after a violent response from central government forces. After going through pages and pages of martyr profiles, she showed me digital records and videos of many martyrs. The disturbing collection of photos contains both images of martyrs when they were alive and photographic evidence of their deaths. Most victims were males between the ages of twelve and twenty-five, although there were also pictures of infants and children. Um Sahar knew many of the martyrs and remembered especially rallies that had high death tolls. "How can I not sympathize with this?" she asked, tearing up at the sight of the corpse of a close friend's four-year-old daughter.[2]

Saheb had referred to Um Sahar as the "mother" of the movement. Indeed, her own endeavor in documenting the killings of southern Yemenis and her role as one of the most prominent women in the movement gave her a symbolic position that connected her womanhood to her role as a national protector. Much as with Chatterjee's Indian woman as the mother of the nation, the very foundation and organization of the nationalist movement adopted gendered notions that were both practical and symbolic.

Um Sahar's prominent position in the movement was also indicative of the way that southern nationalists are making a concerted effort to frame their demands for independence in terms of an international human rights discourse by highlighting the status of women. By using words such as "civil," "modern," and "progressive," they not only appeal to the international community for recognition but also frame a national image that incorporates the cosmopolitan ideal of the southern past. Within this human rights discourse, the role of women is often highlighted by Adenis as indicative of southern identity. Especially in the south, nationalists' own language adopts over-embodying tendencies, focusing especially on the fact that before unification, women often did not veil, and rarely wore the *abaya* and *niqab*.

Photographs of the British and socialist eras often depict scenes of uncovered women, serving as reminders of past social norms. Most southerners lament the shift in gender norms since unification as part of the cultural homogenization project of the north, where such customs of dress, at least in Sana'a, are the norm. Discourse that focuses heavily on women serves to both resonate with international rights groups and typify the southern identity as distinct and progressive vis-à-vis the north. It was not just Um Sahar's role as a female that symbolized her safeguarding of the nation, but specifically her status as a liberal, well-educated woman who could speak both as a mother and as a marginalized southerner.

In the context of south Yemen, the prominence of discussion surrounding women's dress is indicative of how the spiritual realm of south Yemeni nationalism becomes a space for rejecting certain clothing traditions such as *niqab* and focusing on women as progressive, rather than a space for reasserting cultural norms imposed from the northern occupation. Within this space, women and their involvement in the struggle are utilized to assert a symbolic southern identity in opposition to the north. This discourse emphasizes northern women as voiceless, powerless, and subject to northern patriarchal structures such as tribalism and religion. Alternatively, it puts the south's socialist past, a time when women like Um Sahar were educated and active in political life, in sharp contrast with the time period since unification, when women have been reduced to a subjugated position.

This discourse of women's emancipation is taking place in a social environment where unification is the reality, and often women are caught between their symbolic role in nationalist discourse and their lived realities under the current northern-dominated government. Despite the assertion that improving the material conditions in which women live and their legal status is part of the anticolonial and nationalist struggle against northern hegemony, the contemporary social reality is dominated by northern-imposed conservative social norms. Likewise, despite the ideals of femininity in the south, women are still held to standards of behavior, dress, and movement that reflect norms of the more conservative north. While Um Sahar actively rejected northern styles of dress and behavior, her visible dissent made it difficult for her to be mobile and instilled fear in her of backlashes and harassment from the military apparatus stationed in Aden, which remains composed almost entirely of northern employees. Furthermore, southern women have been increasingly subject to criticism from a growing northern conservatism that rejects a public role for women.

The role for women like Um Sahar in the popular southern uprisings, centered in Aden, is also critical on the national level. Despite the role of women in the uprisings, their activism puts them in specific danger of persecution by the northern-dominated military tasked with countering protests and southern dissent. Like members of nationalist movements across the globe, southern Yemenis continue to rely heavily on women to express their sense of identity and national culture. At the time of writing, as the current war between the Houthis in the north and southern militias rages on, women have continued to take on critical noncombat roles in Aden such as feeding and housing soldiers, further cementing their roles as caretakers of the Southern Movement and symbols of South Yemen. The future of an independent South Yemeni state remains unclear, but women will surely continue to be pivotal in the nationalist imagination.

NOTES

1 "Um Sahar" is a pseudonym that she publicly employs for her activism work.
2 Um Sahar, interview, June 22, 2013.

BIBLIOGRAPHY

Chatterjee, Partha. 1989. "Colonialism, Nationalism, and Colonialized Women: The Contest in India." *American Ethnologist* 16, no. 4: 622–33.

———. 1993. *The Nation and Its Fragments: Colonial and Postcolonial Histories.* Princeton, NJ: Princeton University Press.

Ghannam, Farha. 2013. *Live and Die like a Man: Gender Dynamics in Urban Egypt.* Palo Alto, CA: Stanford University Press.

PART IV

How They Use Space to Mobilize

Tiananmen Square is remembered as a space that was transformed in the 1989 uprisings from a monument and a space of representation to a representational space of political discourse.[1] Scholars have long discussed "free spaces" as a way to understand the dynamics of minority mobilization.[2] To Polletta,[3] "free spaces" provide the powerless people an alternative space to that of the dominant group and a safe haven in which to articulate grievances against those in power. Arab women navigated alternative spaces to make their claim and build their movements.

This section takes us away from power centers to interesting peripheral places. Margot Badran's journal features a space, Tahrir Square, that has represented freedom over time by comparing the 2011 revolution with protests during the 1919 and 1952 revolutions. Alternatively, Amina Zarrugh takes us to Libyan prisons, where she traces women's collective defiance of the Qaddafi regime regarding the fate of their missing relatives. Defiance is also evident in Theresa Hunt's piece, which highlights the way HarassMap became a tool to geo-tag sexual harassment locations in Egypt, and writing from Australia, Nelia Hyndman-Rizk traces the extension of women's rights activism in Lebanon from on the ground to cyberspace. Manal Jamal takes us back to 1988 in her Palestinian village where she and her peers turned a modest march for International Women's Day into an intifada by claiming free public spaces. Iraqi-British student Zahra Ali returns home to share with Iraqi women their celebration of Women's Day in the dangerous streets of Baghdad. Transforming these spaces, Soumia Bardhan and Karen Foss roam the streets of Cairo to analyze the strategic positioning of the graffiti's gaze, whereas Lorenzo Kamel and Maha Ezzat Elkholy go to rural Egypt, where women waited to participate in the revolution.

NOTES

1 Craig Calhoun, "Revolution and Repression in Tiananmen Square," *Society* 26, no. 6 (Fall 1989): 21–38, 57.

2 Charles Tilly, "Spaces of Contention," *Mobilization: An International Quarterly* 5, no. 2 (September 2000): 135–59.

3 Francesca Polletta, "'Free Spaces' in Collective Action," *Theory and Society* 28, no. 1 (February 1999): 1–38, 14.

25

Marching with Revolutionary Women in Egypt

A Participatory Journal

MARGOT BADRAN

I was in Egypt from the start of the 2011 revolution through its militant stage of two and a half years, taking part in events and interviewing revolutionaries, and have remained ever since while the ongoing revolution (*al-thawra al-mustamira*, as many call it) persists, in other forms. As a young scholar in the making back in the 1960s and 1970s, I interviewed women who had experienced the 1919 revolution in Egypt and pioneered a feminist movement in its aftermath. I published *Feminists, Islam, and Nation: Gender and the Making of Modern Egypt* (in English and later in Arabic), capturing their experience. During the 2011 revolution I kept a journal, which I am using to write a book on women, gender, and the changing fate of the revolution. I share below a few pages from my journal during the first year of the revolution, together with a brief note on the eve of the fourth anniversary of the revolution in 2015. I end with a reflection on women and gender in the 1919 revolution and the 2011 revolution.

March 8, 2011

On International Women's Day, March 8, revolutionary women went out on the first women's demonstration since the deposing of Mubarak on February 11, 2011. As I joined those who had begun to gather around midday among the tents in the center of Tahrir Square, I remembered the very first demonstration Egyptian women held on March 16 at the start of the 1919 revolution in protest against British colonial rule. I remembered Hilana Sidarus telling me back in the 1970s how she and Gamila Atiya had distributed revolutionary leaflets at the Saniyya School for Girls in 1919.[1] In 2011, I found myself among the protesters distributing placards. We were exhilarated in anticipation of the start-up of the demonstration reconfirming women's revolutionary commitment and protesting their exclusion from the constitutional committee appointed at the behest of the Supreme Council of the Armed Forces (SCAF) to propose amendments to the constitution prior to parliamentary elections. Scores of workers and professional groups had publicly agitated for their rights since the fall of Mubarak, but women were the first group in Egypt to take SCAF head on.

While in the square, I noticed a dark look come across the face of one of the young men who had just heard ominous threats coming from what might have been thugs. I thought it was just swagger and paid no attention. I left the square early to pack to fly to Istanbul the following day en route back to Washington. On the flight, I learned that the women's demonstration had turned ugly and that women had been verbally and physically assaulted. It was the first clear public sign since the euphoria of the initial eighteen days and early aftermath that all was not well. The new revolution was being attacked through women by thugs, and their paymasters were presumed to be *felool*, or remnants of the old regime. The following day, young women protesting the abuse were themselves assaulted by men in military uniform and subjected to virginity tests. All of this revealed a more complex and troubling picture.

* * *

Throughout the summer and fall women continued defending the revolutionary ideals of dignity, freedom, and social justice, making sure that all segments of society were included in the making of the new democratic order. Women remained in the forefront of fighting the counterrevolutionaries, and tyrannical authoritarianism and patriarchal atavism in whatever clothes and guises. In December, following the recent parliamentary elections, repression of demonstrators from all walks of life turned violent as the world witnessed another bout of attacks by men in uniforms and plainclothes. Women, as usual, were on the front line. The assault of a young woman protester who was stripped of her black abaya (an all-enveloping cloak) and knocked to the ground in front of the cabinet building by uniformed men was captured in a picture. It showed one of the soldiers with his boot raised above her stomach. The image of "the woman in the blue bra" went viral, bringing thousands of women out into a demonstration on December 20th.

December 20, 2011

On this Tuesday afternoon, as the conference on "Islam, Citizenship, and the New Media in Pre- and Post-Revolutionary Egypt," organized by the Netherlands-Flemish Institute in Cairo, was winding down, news came through to us on cell phones that a women's march was assembling in Tahrir Square. A few of us drove immediately across the Nile to Tahrir Square. As we walked toward the marchers assembling, I saw a huge banner flying high carrying the name of the Coptic martyr Mina Daniel, who had been mowed down in the recent Maspero massacre. We would soon see banners with crescents and crosses entwined, reminiscent of the iconography of the 1919 revolution. We circled once around Tahrir Square and then headed toward the center of town. I was in this teeming stream when I felt a flicker of fear. I felt as though I was on a train and I could not get off. The unease lasted only a brief moment, for I soon felt part of a powerful, defiant mass united in a common cause. The march was in protest against the continued physical and sexual abuse of women by the military and police as a weapon of intimidation. We all felt the violation of women very viscerally.

The women marchers, it seemed, were mainly in their twenties and thirties. However, there were many middle-aged and older women as well. I met one middle-aged woman who said her four daughters were marching. There were a few mothers with infants. Most of the women seemed to be of ordinary circumstances, while some were of more privileged backgrounds. On either side of the women—we were between fifteen and twenty abreast—were lines of men moving in single file and often holding hands, acting as protective cordons. This reminded me of the pictures I had seen of male students who formed lines on either side of the women protesters in 1919. The men alongside us were mainly of modest background. Near me was a man in a hard hat, a peasant with a wool scarf wrapped around his head like a turban, a man with bandages on head wounds, and a wizened elder. Women protesters held up the front page of newspapers with the picture of "the blue bra woman" and posters saying "women are the red line." As we went along, men in the lines on the side shouted in rhyme, "*Wahid itnayn! Ragula rah fain?*" (One, two! Where has your manhood gone?).

Figure 25.1. Margot Badran

As we marched down Talaat Harb Street, crowds appeared on balconies of apartments and offices high above, looking down at us and cheering us on. Some of the women shouted up to them, "Come down and join us, look what they are doing to your daughters." When we looped toward Ramsis Street, we found people lined up shoulder to shoulder on the overpass. The sun was going down as we headed toward the Journalists' Syndicate, where we stopped to greet the throngs standing on the steps. We then continued on toward the center of town. By this time, it was dark, but the hundreds of tiny lights from flashing cell phones and cameras lit up the night, giving it a festive air.

December 23, 2012

The following Friday, a common day for protests ever since the very first Friday protest on January 28, known as "the day of rage," I participated in another women's demonstration condemning orchestrated violence against women and other revolutionaries. We gathered in front of Al Azhar mosque, where we joined forces with other groups. As we were amassing, I cast my eye at an Al Azhar building across the square, where I used to go for lessons as a young student in the late 1960s. After Friday prayer, we headed in a huge phalanx toward Tahrir Square, marching up on the flyovers high above the city. People were decrying the recent shooting at close range of Shaikh Emad Iffat, who was a leading light at the Dar al-Ifta' (the government department that issues *fatwas*, religious rulings) and an immensely popular and inspirational revolutionary. I carried two posters back to back: one with white letters against a red background saying "women are the red line" and the other with a picture of Shaikh Imad.

In the heaving mass, I got separated from my two women companions with whom I had been marching. A scary moment occurred when something sounding like gunshots went off and I saw birds dart up into the sky. But I did not see anyone else paying any attention. When a man noticed my apprehension, he said in words that took a minute to decipher that the explosions were firecrackers. It was an amazing sight as we walked miles above the city looking down on tiny figures below going about their everyday business. After about four hours we made it to Tahrir Square.

* * *

More than three years have passed since these events. During these years, I went out on other demonstrations. Every year, on January 25, I joined the massive crowds gathering in Cairo's streets rallying for the ongoing revolution, chanting *"al-thawra al-mustamira"* while those holding the reins of power and supporters celebrated the revolution as a fait accompli. In the fall of 2014, the interim government that took over following the deposing of President Muhammad Morsi issued a decree banning all public demonstrations. Permission might be granted upon request to hold public gatherings, only under strict conditions. Following the ascendancy of Abd al-Fattah al-Sissy to the presidency in November 2014, security was declared the number one concern of the government. There have been some displays of free public expression, but they were swiftly dealt with and people paid the price with incarceration or with their lives.

January 24, 2015

On Saturday, January 24, a group of women and men gathered just off
Talaat Harb Square with banners and wreaths of flowers that they were
preparing to take to Tahrir Square, just meters away, to commemorate
the thousands of martyrs who had given their lives in revolutionary
struggle. It was a crisp winter's day. I see the tableau before my eyes
from footage on the Internet of a horizontal line of women and men and
the wire hoop of a floral wreath; it reminded me of a halo. Suddenly I
heard the shattering sounds of gunshots crackling from my computer. I
saw men in uniform with lethal weapons running toward the line with
the hoop of flowers. I saw people scattering in all directions. I saw the
slumped body of a young woman. Then I saw a young man holding
her. I saw another young man scooping her up in his arms and rushing
toward a vehicle. I saw the blood pouring from the woman's mouth.
The woman was Shaimaa Al-Sabagh. This young poet and human rights
activist steadfastly dedicated to the ideals of the revolution was dying in
front of us. The wreath that Shaimaa had held to take to commemorate
the martyrs of the revolution became a wreath for herself as she now
merged with them.

January 25, 2015

It was a quiet day. It was a sad day. The streets were empty. I stayed
home. If January 25 was the official "revolution day," this year it started
tragically on January 24. It is a day that will not just go down in infamy
but will be imprinted in Egyptian hearts and psyches. Around midday on Sunday, January 25, I went to run errands nearby and to check
things out. The streets were silent. The two shops I went to were nearly
empty. Despite being stunned, I could see people beginning to process
what happened as I talked with some of them. Terrible sadness. Who
did it? Why? Who could not have done it? Why? It is the Ministry of
Interior—the police? It is not them. It is the Muslim Brothers? It is not
them. Is it other forces? We will know. We will never know. If Shaimaa
was slaughtered to scare revolutionaries, to scare "the revolution" and its
memories, it did just the opposite. It could be seen in the huge numbers
who accompanied her coffin in Alexandria. Funerals are public events

that cannot be interdicted. Several mosques, however, were reported to have turned down requests to receive condolences and give prayers. But Shaimaa was on everyone's lips. Shaimaa, a young woman in her early thirties, became the icon of January 25, 2015.

The *Longue Durée* of Revolution: 1919 to 2011 and Beyond

Women and men rose up against tyranny in 1919, initiating a tradition of revolutionary protest that would find echoes in 2011. It was on the fiery stage of nationalist militancy that women made their public debut as political actors. During the 1919 revolution, upper-class women organized, on March 16, their first of many demonstrations against the persistence of unjust, oppressive colonial rule. In the words of Huda Shaarawi, they rose up "to protest the repressive acts and intimidation practice by the British authority," which tried to suppress nationalist uprisings that were intensifying following the end of the First World War when the nation demanded its independence (Shaarawi 1987, 112). Women among the poor surged forth spontaneously alongside men in their families and neighborhoods in defiant anticolonial protest. It was women from among the poor, like the young Shafiqa bint Muhammad, who became the first revolutionary martyrs. Her funeral procession became the first massive demonstration of women and men of all classes. Women and men, kept apart by social convention (expressed differently across the classes), came together in revolutionary protest. Egyptians of different religions rose up together in defiance of the British practice of "divide and rule." "The British," Shaarawi wrote in her memoirs, "claimed our national movement was a revolt of the Muslim majority against the religious minorities. . . . Egyptians showed their solidarity by meeting in mosques, churches, and synagogues. Shaikhs walked arm in arm with priests and rabbis" (Shaarawi 1987, 119). The 1919 revolution displayed the trope of the unity of gender, class, and religion that would reappear with the outbreak of the 2011 revolution.

In 2011, Asma Mahfouz was famously hailed for issuing the clarion call via the Internet for the nation to rise up against homegrown tyranny and despotism. The national uprisings, which began in a massive march to Tahrir Square on January 25, sparked off what would become the legendary eighteen days of revolutionary solidarity. Women and men rose up in equal numbers. Most were young, but not all, as Egyptians of different ages rapidly swelled the ranks. There was an electric spontaneity. The numbers were monumental. Lines of demonstrators poured into Tahrir Square from districts all over Cairo and environs, bringing the prosperous and poor alike. During the first eighteen days, when protesters remained in Tahrir Square until the goal of ousting the despotic ruler was achieved, the unity of gender, class, and religion that was seen in 1919 was repeated. Banners with the same configuration of crescents and crosses on view in 1919 were carried aloft in 2011 in a scene of eerie déjà vu. The demonstrations, sit-ins, and marches were gender-mixed. The demonstrations of women on March 8 and December 2011 were major exceptions to the rule of gender-united marches. After the first eighteen days, centrifugal forces set in with counterrevolutionary elements at work, contending forces within the insurrectionary ranks, and atavistic cultural pulls. Now in 2015, the time of free revolutionary activism has ended following the imposition of the antiprotest law of 2014 and subsequent arrest and jailing of many who defied orders. But the revolution, in its gender and culture dimensions, persists as part of the ongoing *longue durée*.

Acknowledgments

This is a revised and extended version of a piece that was published in the spring 2012 issue of *Trinity Magazine* and has been reprinted in this form with permission from the author and *Trinity Magazine*.

NOTE

1 Hilana Sidarus became one of the first women doctors in Egypt. Gamila ʿAtiya became an educator and was a founding member of the Egyptian Feminist Union, established in 1923.

BIBLIOGRAPHY

Shaarawi, Huda. 1987. *Harem Years: The Memoirs of an Egyptian Feminist, 1879–1947.* Translated and introduced by Margot Badran. New York: Feminist Press.

26

Memories of Martyrs

Disappearance and Women's Claims against State Violence in Libya

AMINA ZARRUGH

Stories of resilience saturate Libyan history, from the resistance to violent Italian colonial conquest to the revolution against the brutal repression of Moammar Gaddafi's forty-two-year dictatorship. One particular case of resilience, however, remains overlooked in Libya's national collective memory: the family-based protests against the Abu Salim Prison killing. In this essay, I investigate the legacy of family-based mobilizations on behalf of forcibly disappeared relatives from the unique vantage point of several interviews with Maryam Shkiwa,[1] the sister to one of the prison killing's victims, Rafiq Shkiwa. Through Maryam's narrative, I investigate how the family relived the moment of Rafiq's disappearance for many years. Her story reveals the significant impact the loss of Rafiq had on the family and how the Shkiwa family's persistent efforts to learn of his whereabouts constituted a significant form of resistance to the state. This type of resistance is subtler, quieter, and more circumspect than demonstrations and public campaigns but is nevertheless an important form of social action that illustrates the limits of the Libyan regime's power. I contextualize Maryam's story within Libyan history by highlighting the climate of repression in Libya and the targeting of movements mobilizing under the rubric of Islam in the 1980s, as well as the resistance movement composed of families who sought answers about their loved ones' disappearances and deaths. Thus, this essay connects the persistence of families in remembering and commemorating the loss of loved ones in the Abu Salim Prison killing to the emerging resistance to the Gaddafi regime in the years before its fall in 2011.

Abu Salim Prison Killing

Maryam's brother Rafiq disappeared and subsequently died in Abu Salim Prison. The prison, located in Tripoli, primarily incarcerated disappeared persons and prisoners of conscience, including a number of men believed to be active in religious movements. Known as a "massacre" among many Libyans, the event occurred on June 29, 1996, after a prison guard was held hostage by a handful of prisoners. Upon freeing themselves, inmates facilitated the escape of others from their cell blocks. Several prisoners were shot to quell the uprising, and Libyan intelligence officials met with prisoner representatives to discuss their demands. The representatives made several requests, which included rights to visitation with family, clean clothes, better medical care, and occasional access to the outdoors (Human Rights Watch 2006). According to percipient witness reports, the next morning, just before dawn, an explosion detonated in the vicinity of a courtyard occupied by political prisoners. Six khaki-uniformed men, who stood along the perimeter roof of the courtyard, rained bullets upon the prisoners from above. The estimated number of prisoners killed was 1,269 (Human Rights Watch 2006; Amnesty International 2010). The Libyan government did not acknowledge these deaths for nearly a decade; and families continued to visit the prison to deliver packages for their loved ones, not knowing that they had been killed years earlier. The bodies remain missing, though several mass graves continue to be excavated throughout Libya (Franklin 2011). The absence of the prisoners' bodies continues to compel many families to demand further investigation into the incident and the disappearances of their relatives.

This event is remembered with melancholy in Libya, especially among families whose encounter with the regime's violence began with their relatives' disappearances over thirty years ago. The collective uprisings against the regime in 2011 also claimed many more lives, sometimes among the same families affected by the Abu Salim Prison killing. This was the case for Maryam, who lost another brother, Adel, to fighting in 2011. For many families, the regime's violence is not acknowledged in a single past incident but culminates in a series of losses and absences that constitute the present.

Persistence as Resistance

Among these hundreds of stories of disappearance in Libya, Maryam's story is not exceptional. However, her reflections exhibit how resistance to oppression, including more grandiose moments of resistance in the form of organized opposition, are born of daily, small-scale moments of persistence. Of particular significance is the relationship between the persistence of loss on the part of the Shkiwa family, as experienced through Rafiq's disappearance, and the persistence of the family in seeking knowledge of his whereabouts. I argue that these forms of persistence are intertwined and constitute an important form of resistance to the Libyan state's oppression.

The study of resistance has been conducted since roughly the 1980s in a range of disciplines to question the relationship between power structures and individual or collective agency (Bourdieu 1998). In numerous studies, resistance is defined first and foremost as a form of action undertaken by individuals or groups in opposition to specific persons, places, or institutions (Hollander and Einwohner 2004). Whether these actions must be "intended" by the actors or "recognized" by the power holders remains disputed in studies of resistance. Intentional and legible actions are frequently accorded greater attention in the study of collective action and social movements; however, scholars have also emphasized the significance of small-scale, less overt forms of resistance (Scott 1985). At the interactional level, forms of resistance against repression may be constituted through questioning what is regarded as unquestionable or employing new vocabularies that undermine the state's conception of reality. These discrete forms of resistance may be especially significant in contexts of extreme political repression where overt acts of defiance to the state are prohibited by law or elicit strong sanctions.

In the case of Maryam, her mother's incessant inquiries about her son's whereabouts at security police stations and Maryam's childhood trips to the prison to leave boxes of clothing and homemade sweets constituted a refusal to allow Rafiq, and his memory, to be erased by the state. The persistence of the loss of Rafiq meant that, long after his disappearance, he figured into every choice the family made in their lives. In some ways, it was as if the teenager had never been taken from the family home—clothes were still bought on his behalf and his share of the homemade treats was set aside. For Maryam, Rafiq was present despite his absence. Amid the government's attempts to disappear Rafiq and, by extension, his memory, Maryam's family's persistent inquiries and belief that Rafiq lived on are themselves important gestures in resisting the state's violence.

It is this persistence of loss that motivates, in many ways, the persistence of families to seek answers about their relatives. Maryam's story and her family's travails illustrate the multiple ways by which violence permeates the everyday even when the eventful momentary violence has passed. As Das contends, not only is the event attached to the everyday but "the everyday is eventful" (2007, 8). Violence and the development of individual subjectivities are intimately related long after specific deaths or traumas are inflicted by a given event, raising questions about what it means to live during and after loss: "What is it to bear witness to the criminality of the societal rule that consigns the uniqueness of being to eternal forgetfulness through a descent in everyday life—not simply to articulate loss through a dramatic gesture of defiance but to inhabit the world, or inhabit it *again*, in a gesture of mourning?" (Das 2007, 62).

In this way, Maryam's family contends not only with Rafiq's forced disappearance by secret security forces of the Libyan regime but also with inhabiting the world in his absence and preserving his memory as a "martyr" despite the state's attempted erasure of his existence. In the Shkiwa family, Rafiq is deemed a martyr, or "*shaheed*" in Arabic.[2] In the Libyan context, the honor of martyr is bestowed upon individuals who have actively fought on behalf of social justice or have died as a result of unjust acts of violence. Families that bestow the term "martyr" upon their disappeared and deceased relatives are themselves enacting a form of resistance vis-à-vis the state, which deliberately sought to efface their lives.

Repression of Religiosity in Libya

Maryam's family originates from a small town called Mizdah in the area known as the Jabal al Gharbi, or Western Mountains, three hours south of Tripoli. Her father was in the army for several years, and shortly after his eldest children were born, he and the family moved to Tripoli, where he purchased a small tract of land and began building their family home with "his own hands," as she emphasized in our conversation.

The death of Maryam's father in 1979, at which time Maryam's mother was pregnant with her last of eight children, was a traumatizing and transformative moment for the Shkiwa family. At the time of his father's death, Rafiq, who would die years later at Abu Salim Prison, was only eleven years old. To cope with the death, Rafiq would frequently spend his time going out with his friends in the neighborhood, and at the age of eighteen, Rafiq took a growing interest in attending his local mosque to perform most of his prayers, including the *fajr*,[3] or early dawn prayer. Rafiq's attendance at the dawn prayer, which is often prayed at home given the early morning hour, was a significant expression of piety that signaled to others his religiosity and dedication to his faith. Rafiq's commitment to prayer at his local mosque continued throughout his adolescence. "Then came 1989," Maryam told me in an ominous tone.

The most repressive policies towards social mobilization and all forms of political opposition to Gaddafi's regime were pursued in the 1980s, almost a decade after he led a military coup against the monarchy that ruled in Libya's postcolonial period. Following the 1976 publication of Gaddafi's self-authored political treatise, *The Green Book*, the former monarchical legal system was suspended and new governing institutions were formed. Among these new organizations were the "popular committees," a collective of citizens modeled after the Chinese Red Guards (Kawczynski 2010). These groups, which numbered in the thousands, were responsible for ensuring that the principles of Gaddafi's revolution were implemented in Libyan society. The parameters of their duties were fluid—from encouraging and mobilizing revolutionary fervor to suppressing perceived critics of the regime. These committees ultimately became an armed security and surveillance force that was eventually incorporated into the regular military (Anderson 1987).

Among the movements Gaddafi feared most were those associated with Islam. He explicitly prohibited religious authorities in the country from commenting on political affairs, and in the late 1980s, the state criminalized and imprisoned, without due process, individuals suspected of belonging to Islamic movements (Kawczynski 2010; Vandewalle 2006). Criminalization and suppression of those feared to be part of Islamic movements resulted in the policing of expressions of piety, particularly among men and especially so for those who performed regular prayers at a local mosque.

It was in this political context that Maryam forebodingly casts 1989 as a turning point not only in her family's life but also in Libya more generally. In Rafiq's case, intimidation by the regime began with threatening phone calls that culminated in his disappearance before an afternoon prayer. According to Maryam,

> [Rafiq] did the ritual cleansing to pray and he left outside. He went outside [voice strains]. . . . and he found the group of security forces standing in front of the house. We did not get a look at them. They took him and [pause] and they went away with him. We didn't see them. They were spotted by no one [in the family]. They were spotted by no one. The neighbors saw them. . . . [T]hey said "you know, your son, he was taken by a red car, they veiled his face and his mouth and took him forcibly."

Maryam emphasizes that no one in her family witnessed the abduction of her brother, which attests to the ambiguity and uncertainty that would later compel her family to seek answers regarding his whereabouts. Rafiq's disappearance to an unknown location set in motion the beginning of the family's regular visits to security offices, where they persistently sought answers about Rafiq despite the state's multiple denials of information.

Searches, Rumors, and Visits

Following Rafiq's disappearance, Maryam's mother pursued every lead possible to track down her son's whereabouts. She made multiple visits to the offices of the security forces. A child at the time, Maryam recounts one interaction in which her mother directly confronted a security officer. Her mother boldly argued that one of the security force's vehicles had been used to kidnap Rafiq, despite denials on the part of the security personnel: "He said to us, 'It wasn't us.' I remember it, there was one man who was an administrator in the security forces there, he had his leg one over the other as he sat. He was resting this way. My mother said to him, 'It was you all who held my son.' . . . She left, she returned here [home] and was crying for a long while and . . . she went through a lot, my mother." What Maryam finds memorable in this interaction is not only her mother's defiance but also her persistence in confronting men

Figure 26.1. The gates of Abu Salim Prison in Tripoli, Libya. Photo taken on February 2, 2014. Courtesy of Amina Zarrugh.

who, though undeniably complicit in the regime's repressive policies, coolly and calmly denied their involvement.

After a full year of silence concerning Rafiq's whereabouts despite regular inquiries, Maryam says the family began hearing rumors from other people that the military police might have answers about Rafiq's whereabouts. Upon visiting a military police station, the family was informed that Rafiq was in military police custody at Abu Salim Prison, and the family was asked to bring him food. For years, the Shkiwa family prepared packages for Rafiq: "Food, drinks, clothing. . . . and the clothing was not just one thing, I mean. No, no, no, no. Not just a tank top, not just one. A stack of them. The juice wasn't just one box. No, it was a box or two. . . . Whenever we felt like making bread at home or making cakes or making pastries at home, all of it would go. The extras, extras, extras, all would go to him."

On specific days each month, families were allowed to come to Abu Salim Prison, where many believed that their sons, brothers, husbands, and fathers were held. Families waited for hours outside the prison walls to load some of the food, clothing, and mementos they had collected for their loved ones onto a designated truck. However, the families rarely saw or were able to visit the imprisoned family member. Many traveled as far as the eastern city of Benghazi, a journey of over a thousand kilometers. The families' persistence in visiting month after month and year after year amid a range of obstacles, including geographic distance, bureaucratic indifference, and deliberate government circulation of misinformation, was a challenge to the government in and of itself. Their visits constituted a refusal to accept the state's attempt to disappear their relatives and was a form of resistance against the state's concerted effort to impede their quest for information.

Government Denials and Family Appeals

Despite being denied visitation with Rafiq, Maryam's family, like so many others, continued their monthly journeys to Abu Salim Prison. Visits continued long after 1996, the year of the prison killing, and their packages were still accepted by the prison under the pretense that their relatives were alive. In 2001, some families began to be notified that their relatives had died; they were sent death certificates with dates that did not correspond to June 1996 or indicate the cause of death. Finally, in April 2004, Gaddafi formally acknowledged that killings took place at Abu Salim Prison (Human Rights Watch 2006).

Maryam's family received belated news of Rafiq's death, though, compared to other families, they considered themselves among the earlier recipients of the news: "We found out in 2002. We were some of the first bunch to learn along with some people in our neighborhood," stated Maryam. The news of Rafiq's death had come eight years after the prison killing at Abu Salim Prison—Maryam and her family had continued to deliver care packages during this time, long after Rafiq had died. As more death certificates were issued to families, suspicions of foul play grew.

Increasing pressure from dissident groups and Libyan lawyers led to action on behalf of the Gaddafi International Charity and Development Foundation (GDF), an organization managed by Gaddafi's son Saif al-Islam. The organization permitted international access to detention facilities and pressured authorities to offer families reparations amounting to two hundred thousand Libyan dinars (approximately US $158,000 at the time of the offer) for married men who had been killed (Amnesty International 2010). This offer was contingent upon a family's agreement that they would desist from filing any more complaints concerning their loved ones' whereabouts (Human Rights Watch 2009).

In response to the circulation of false information and the lack of forthright acknowledgment of the deaths of their loved ones, in 2008 families of the victims formed the Association of the Families of the Martyrs of the Abu Salim Prison Massacre. Led by lawyer Fethi Terbil, who had lost a brother in the prison killing, the association demanded specific answers about Abu Salim Prison, visual evidence of the purported killings, judicial accountability for those deemed responsible, and the return of any existing remains to family members. The organization made legal claims against the Libyan government and urged families to stage weekly demonstrations outside the People's Leadership Building in Benghazi. Their mobilization was unprecedented in Libya, where surveillance and suppression of civil society activity was among the worst in the world.

Many in Tripoli learned of these bold and defiant demonstrations in the eastern city of Benghazi but could not themselves organize their own protests because the regime's security forces and surveillance apparatus were stronger and more entrenched in the capital. After the 2011 uprisings, a branch of the association was formally organized in Tripoli, where Maryam is currently the secretary.

The association, which consists of many women who lost family members in the massacre, continues to pursue remuneration for families of the victims, working closely with the newly established Ministry of Martyrs and Missing Persons' Families' Affairs. Disappearance as a protracted and ongoing form of violence is underscored in the work of the association, which arranges official divorces for women whose husbands were killed but who do not possess death certificates and collects paperwork to document government inconsistencies in the issuance of death certificates to families. The association also organizes demonstrations, often using banners featuring the images of a number of the men believed to have died at Abu Salim Prison, to advocate for the arrests of former regime personnel responsible for orchestrating the prison killing and other human rights abuses (see figure 26.2).

The creation of a formal organization by the families of disappeared men and women illustrates how "covert" forms of resistance, such as the persistence of family inquiries about loved ones' whereabouts exemplified in Maryam's story, can pave the way for more "overt" and collective forms of resistance (Hollander and Einwohner 2004). An important

Figure 26.2. A poster of several of the men believed to have been killed on June 26, 1996, at Abu Salim Prison. Photo taken February 2, 2014. Courtesy of Amina Zarrugh.

consequence of family persistence since the 1980s was to keep alive the memory of the disappeared. Just as Gaddafi's security regime pitted Libyan against Libyan, an unintended consequence of the repression was that it also opened the possibility for networks of families to develop, united by the common experience of losing a relative through disappearance. These existing networks, facilitated by both the persistence of loss that characterized their everyday lives and their persistence in seeking knowledge of their loved ones, were an important precursor to the formation of the association years later.

Conclusion

The story of Rafiq's disappearance and the responses of the Shkiwa family offer vivid and intimate illustrations of the ways by which families remained resilient in the face of Gaddafi's security and surveillance apparatus. Maryam's narration of her family's experience—in addition to the continuing work of Association of the Families of the Martyrs of the

Abu Salim Prison Massacre—illuminate how state violence is seldom momentary or fleeting.

As recently as June 2014, weeks prior to the annual commemoration of the prison killing, posters of the victims displayed in the central Martyr's Square in Tripoli were violently torn down by crowds that deemed them "terrorists." The stigma of Islamic extremism still haunts many of these families in contemporary Libya, where armed insurrection by some organizations who mobilize in the name of religion, such as Ansar al-Shari'a, continues to threaten the country's political stability. Reverberations of the regime's demonization and incarceration of hundreds of young men across Libya, many of whom had no connection to Islamic fundamentalism, continue beyond the tenure of the Gaddafi regime. Violence persists in the everyday for the families impacted and challenges them to "inhabit the same space now marked as a space of destruction" (Das 2007, 62). Resisting the regime's legacies, therefore, remains a day-to-day struggle for families and the association.

Maryam's story highlights how resistance to repression developed from two related aspects of persistence: the persistence of loss in light of the disappearance of a loved one and the persistence to keep memories alive through concrete actions taken on behalf of families in search of their relatives. It was in the persistence of these everyday actions, trips, packages, and inquiries that families resisted state violence in Libya in a way that challenged the regime's repressive power. This case illustrates how men and women were integral to keeping alive the memories of the disappeared and how, in the process, their persistence set the stage for the formation of a family association that would come to challenge the state in unprecedented ways.

NOTES

1   This chapter is part of a larger project on the family association in Libya and is based on fieldwork conducted in Tripoli, Libya, in the spring of 2014. The project includes interviews, conversations, and correspondence with over twenty women and men members of the family association in both Tripoli and Benghazi. All quotations that appear here are drawn from an interview and ongoing conversations, conducted by the author in Arabic and later transcribed and translated into English, with Maryam Shkiwa, since February 2014.

2   The term "martyr" means "witness" in both Arabic and Latin and derives its meaning from Greek. "Martyr" is frequently invoked in discussions of the Abu

Salim Prison killing to ascribe a special status to its victims. The status of martyr, which dates to the Hellenistic period, is conferred upon individuals under different paradigms (Cook 2007).

3 *"Fajr"* refers to the early dawn prayer, the first of five daily prayers observed by Muslims.

BIBLIOGRAPHY

Amnesty International. 2010. "Libya of Tomorrow: What Hope for Human Rights?" London: Amnesty International Publications, June 23, https://www.amnesty.org.

Anderson, Lisa. 1987. "Libya's Qaddafi: Still in Command." *Current History* 86, no. 517 (August): 65–87.

Bourdieu, Pierre. 1998. *Acts of Resistance: Against the New Myths of Our Time.* Cambridge, UK: Polity.

Cook, David. 2007. *Martyrdom in Islam.* Cambridge: Cambridge University Press.

Das, Veena. 2007 *Life and Words: Violence and the Descent into the Ordinary.* Berkeley: University of California Press.

Franklin, Stuart. 2011. "Abu Salim: Walls That Talk." *Guardian*, September 30, http://www.guardian.co.uk.

Hollander, Jocelyn A., and Rachel L. Einwohner. 2004. "Conceptualizing Resistance." *Sociological Forum* 19, no. 4 (December): 533–54. https://doi.org/10.1007/s11206-004-0694-5.

Human Rights Watch. 2006. "Libya: June 1996 Killings at Abu Salim Prison. Report." June 27, https://www.hrw.org.

———. 2009. "Truth and Justice Can't Wait: Human Rights Developments in Libya amid Institutional Obstacles," December 12, http://www.hrw.org.

Kawczynski, Daniel. 2010. *Seeking Gaddafi.* London: Dialogue.

Scott, James C. 1985. *Weapons of the Weak: Everyday Forms of Peasant Resistance.* New Haven, CT: Yale University Press.

Vandewalle, Dirk. 2006. *A History of Modern Libya.* Cambridge: Cambridge University Press.

27

Mapping the Egyptian Women's Anti–Sexual Harassment Campaigns

THERESA HUNT

As revolutionary fervor swept through Egypt in 2011, scholars and journalists began to look closely at the actors involved. Images of young, tech-savvy revolutionaries flooded the media, their actions suggesting that small groups are capable of deposing an authoritarian regime. Narratives about youth and the catalyzing impact of Western social media brands were constructed; it was indeed difficult to find coverage of the revolution in mainstream media that did not feature stories of young activist men drawing on the power afforded them by American companies such as Facebook and Twitter. The attention paid to women activists in this context reflected these dominant narratives of social networking online and "cyberactivism." Stories of Asmaa Mahfouz's January 18, 2011, YouTube video urging fellow citizens to join her in mobilizing on Tahrir Square proliferated, as did a focus on Esraa Abdel Fattah's role in creating the April 6th Movement, a group that used Facebook to support striking factory workers and spread revolutionary messages through the country. This attention is justified and can serve the purpose of upending dominant assumptions that "revolutionaries" are young men (Winegar 2012) and that technology, in terms of both innovation and use, is inherently masculine (Wajcman 1991). However, the focus on women engaged in these spectacular forms of protest immediately before or in the earliest days of the revolution obscures some of the decades-long efforts of organized women's movements before the revolution. I argue in this chapter that many women's movements in fact worked to engender the kinds of proactive, community-based, and even technology-facilitated activism that has come to be associated with the 2011 revolution.

While not necessarily presenting themselves as "anti-state," many women's organizations nevertheless worked in more mundane contexts to subvert the limitations placed on their rights by Egypt's authoritarian regime. Women's movements often pointed to their government's failings, at times in very public campaigns, and created community-based solutions to issues they had little faith would be addressed by the state. Here I examine one such case: Egypt's anti–sexual harassment movement in the last decade. I make an effort to avoid treating the antiharassment movement reductively, as indeed its participants have as much variance in their philosophies and tactics as they do in their definitions of "harassment." Nevertheless, I do argue that particular actors within the movement embodied the kinds of actions associated with the 2011 revolution, long before it began. Women have worked subversively to gather and publish data about widespread, "epidemic" (Hassan, Komsan, and Shoukry 2008) sexual harassment occurring in public places, such as streets and public transportation, despite the fact that doing so undermines the state's efforts to appear progressive in maintaining and supporting women's rights (Rizzo, Price, and Meyer 2012, 459). They have launched local and global media campaigns highlighting the state's failure to study and report on harassment and gender-based violence, and in some cases underscored governmental complicity in or responsibility for propagating it. Women within this movement have also produced and launched their own social media and crowd-sourcing technology to confront the epidemic at the community level since, as one young Cairo-based activist named Marwa explained in a 2010 interview, "The government has no interest in [doing so]."[1]

In the following sections, I introduce organizations active in the antiharassment movement: the Egyptian Center for Women's Rights (ECWR), the antitorture organization El Nadim, and a small collective of activists working on a digital mapping project called "HarassMap." I focus on the aspects of their work that have come to be affiliated with the 2011 revolution, including open and widespread criticism of the authoritarian regime, advancement of civil society–based solutions, and the subversive use of technology to disseminate information and mobilize the public. The stories that emerge from these sources demonstrate that Egyptian women activists are not simply spectators caught up in the 2011 revolution; rather, they had a hand in catalyzing it.

Egypt's Anti–Sexual Harassment Movement

Scholarly examinations of sexual and gender-based harassment in Egypt often highlight the complexity of efforts to define the term in the absence of any official or legal definition. While women's organizations in Egypt have certainly made efforts to target workplace, home-based, and prison-based harassment in anti–sexual harassment campaigns, "street harassment" emerged as a common focus because this is the form most frequently reported to organizations such as the Egyptian Center for Women's Rights (ECWR) (Rizzo, Price, and Meyer 2012, 460). The ECWR in particular worked from anecdotal evidence to conduct more thorough and nuanced investigations into the systematic and widespread nature of sexual harassment, and to mobilize clarified definitions of "street harassment," including "unwanted sexual conduct," expressed physically or verbally, "resulting in sexual, physical or psychological abuse of the victim" (Hassan, Komsan, and Shoukry 2008, 13). Subsequently, empirical, scholarly studies, such as Ilahi's (2009) and Rizzo, Price, and Meyer's (2012), focus on such organizations targeting *street harassment*, or that which happens in public spaces. Because of the ways in which this reduces women's mobility and "ghettoizes" women into "private spheres" (Ilahi 2009, 58), women's organizations often focus on this form of harassment, framing it as a serious challenge to the procurement of women's political and civic rights.

Paul Amar's comparison of antiharassment campaigns (2011) highlights the work of women activists who, in rejecting statist cooptation of their efforts, focus directly on community. Amar's discussion of the El-Nadim Center for Rehabilitation of Victims of Violence, founded in 1993 with a primary aim to provide "psychological management and rehabilitation" to "victims of torture" (El Nadim 2013), provides a window into one such progressive campaign, as does the center's own extensive documentation of its activities over the last two decades. Interviews from a 2010–2011 study on young women's activism in the MENA, which I initiated prior to the revolution, are also rife with examples of women participating in campaigns actively seeking to subvert and criticize governmental neglect of and involvement with harassment of women. It is the founders and facilitators of a Cairo-based, crowd-sourcing, and social-media project called HarassMap who perhaps best embodied this approach. HarassMap interviewees stressed their independence from local, government-sanctioned NGOs and international feminist campaigns. They repeatedly identified themselves as a group of "volunteers" whose primary focus is "the community." Interviewees frequently contrasted their work with that of organizations who "[bother to] work with the law," as research manager Rasha explained. "What we do is completely different," she added, emphasizing that their interest in working directly and peaceably with people to "change practices and attitudes" was different from compelling change by force or punishment. Finally, while distinct from these because of its efforts to work though state channels with a mission to address women's civic rights, the Egyptian Center for Women's Rights nevertheless faced "a risky, neopatriarchal environment" when making efforts to call for reform (Rizzo, Price, and Meyer 2012) and pressed on.

The Egyptian Center for Women's Rights (ECWR)

During the first day of the Eid holiday in 2006, a large number of men in Cairo turned their frustration at a movie theater's lack of available tickets towards women in the crowd. Men began "ripping off [women's] clothes" and very publicly attempted to "assault them" (Abdelhadi 2006). Local bloggers recorded and published images and videos of women being swarmed and violently groped, underscoring that police were present but simply looked on, neglecting to intervene.[2] The mass assault was underreported by various presses (Rizzo, Price, and Meyer 2012, 464) until media personality Mona Al Shazly, who hosted a television talk show on Egypt's Dream network, investigated the claims several days later and collected eyewitness accounts. Al Shazly attempted to get statements from the Ministry of Interior about the incident, offering the corroboration she had gathered, but the state officially "denied that anything had taken place" (Al-Malky 2007).

A year prior to the Eid incident, the ECWR began a multifaceted campaign framing sexual harassment as a public safety issue (Hassan, Komsan, and Shoukry 2008). This campaign also highlighted state failure to address and respond to widespread occurrences of harassment, and reported on women being victimized by police. Founded in 1996 by six women lawyers in the Dar el Salaam neighborhood of Cairo, the

ECWR was originally intended to provide legal aid and education directly to poor women in the community. Working with its ties to the Egyptian Organization for Human Rights, the ECWR expanded its mission to more broadly secure women's civic rights and political representation, often citing the state's failure to uphold its pledged commitment to enforcing international gender-equality agreements (ECWR 2012). Under the directorship of founding member Nehad Abul Komsan, the ECWR successfully changed legislation related to labor and personal status policies, and more recently the organization began to focus on epidemic levels of sexual harassment.

Since the ECWR had already established itself as a leading organization on the issue of harassment, "with [formal] goals and programs" (Rizzo, Price, and Meyer 2012, 465), it was sought out as a resource by both local and international media after the Eid incident. This furthered the organization's credibility and public trust, as well as its leverage: "Such media attention served to protect ECWR against harsh sanctions by the government" (Rizzo, Price, and Meyer 2012, 465). Members of the ECWR and other antiharassment activists indeed recount efforts to conduct focus groups and hold workshops in the interest of data gathering in earlier iterations of their antiharassment campaigns, only to have them consistently shut down by the state.[3] "Authorities are able to disrupt [our meetings] without sufficient time warning, and with little room for compromise," Komsan wrote in a 2006 newsletter, detailing the stalled progress of the ECWR's 2004 Safer Streets for Everyone campaign. By Komsan's own explanation in the introduction to the 2008 summary report *"Clouds in Egypt's Sky,"* which surveyed over two thousand men and women about harassment experiences, the ECWR was able to successfully complete the fieldwork detailed in the study in part because it had more access and reach than it had had in the years prior.

With this attention and access, the ECWR publicly highlighted the lack of legal channels women had for responding to experiences of harassment. Hassan, Komsan, and Shoukry point out that the lack of official data on the prevalence of harassment, along with the apparent pervasiveness of it, can be linked to the fact that "no attention has been paid" to the problem in Egypt's Penal Code (2008, 7). To this end, ECWR's survey data reports on women's experiences in attempting to "officially" report experiences of harassment: "We found that some [police] officers mock . . . women [attempting to report harassment] or harass them as well. The vast majority of women [surveyed for the 2008 study] did not seek police assistance because they didn't think it was important or because no one would help them" (Hassan, Komsan, and Shoukry 2008, 16–17).

The ECWR made a specific decision to focus on sexual harassment in public spaces because complaints they received from women most often detailed what occurred on the street and on public transportation, and included grabbing, verbal harassment, indecent exposure, and public masturbation (Rizzo, Price, and Meyer 2012, 460). That police were not only onlookers but also perpetrators of this type of harassment disrupted women's daily lives even more, the ECWR claimed, and constituted a major threat against their security and access to civil rights.

Antiharassment activist Rasha, who worked on producing *"Clouds in Egypt's Sky"* and now works with HarassMap, explains that "few numbers existed in any way that [clearly] showed the problem." Where data did exist, Rasha continues, it was piecemeal, anecdotal, and generated by civil society organizations that found it nearly impossible to conduct formal research on the issue involving a large sample of participants. The ECWR's capability to leverage its publicity in an effort to gather and publish this data is indeed remarkable. Such effort is also reflected in the work of the El Nadim Center, which in addition underscores the importance of "including women's perspectives" (El Nadim 2009) on experiences of harassment taking place within homes, on the street, and during incarceration.

El Nadim Center

At its inception in August 1993, the El Nadim Center, a Cairo-based antitorture organization founded by a team of four doctors, focused its efforts on "the psychological rehabilitation" of people experiencing torture, particularly those detained under the provisions of Egypt's Emergency Law. As explained in the center's literature, however, administrators quickly realized "that working with torture cannot be complete without making the issue public," particularly through "publishing" to reveal that "[the] practice . . . has gone completely out of hand over the past two decades" (El Nadim 2013). Human rights activist Dr. Magda

Adly explains that her role in helping to found El Nadim alongside Suzan Fayaad, Aida Seif El-Dawla, and Abdullah Mansour was tied to her own experiences with having been incarcerated for participating in anti-state demonstrations in 1977. But the more pressing motivation, she explains, was related to the utter lack of healthcare available to people who had experienced violence—including women victims of torture, domestic violence, and rape (Borg and Mayo 2007, 54).

During its first years, El Nadim "found great difficulty" in understanding the scope of torture, as information from "official medical institutions, [universities,] and government hospitals" was nonexistent. El Nadim thus sought to make such information public, an approach it continues contemporarily (El Nadim 2013). The center's *Diaries of Torture*, for example, featured on its website, details the stories of "women and men, youth, [the] elderly and children" experiencing "human rights violations" in the form of torture perpetrated by state agents who "continue to [be] protected" by "the Emergency state" (El Nadim 2013). As the center began developing programs specifically addressing abuses of women, it continued to "adhere to this approach" (El Nadim 2013), publishing detailed testimonies of women's experiences with violence and harassment.

Adly explains that one such study consisted of assessing the prevalence and forms of violence women were experiencing in Egypt through surveys; it also investigated the perceptions and attitudes women had toward the violence they and others were experiencing (El Nadim 2009; Borg and Mayo 2007, 54). As one of the first of its kind, the study was utilized as the basis for follow-up investigations that would comprise "shadow report" data prepared for United Nations monitoring committees. While the report presented data quantitatively, it also underscored the importance of including *women's perceptions* of gender violence and harassment, including "attitudes [women have] toward . . . [their experiences]" (El Nadim 2009). Later reports generated by expanded research in 2007 suggested that participants were skeptical about the state's interest in protecting women from violence and harassment through the provision of law, and especially through police enforcement. Nevertheless, they still "objected to" violence or harassment happening to them; they did *not* consider it a "natural or private component" of their personal lives and would speak out against violence in the context of their own families and communities (El Nadim 2009). Women who reported that they would not be likely to use legal protections afforded to them by a change in state law still made clear to researchers that "they wished [legal antiviolence protection] would be there for their daughters in the future" (El Nadim 2009).

Like the women activists and professionals founding El Nadim, younger generations of antiharassment activists made efforts to disseminate information about Egyptian women's experiences of violence. They sought to clarify the problem a bit differently, making use of newer technologies in their efforts to circumvent the limitations and failings of the state.

Turning to Technology

When in 2009 a group of young Cairo-based women founded HarassMap—a technology-based project that draws on and maps crowd-sourced reports of sexual harassment—they wanted to gather data. In fact, they were interested specifically in creating community-based solutions that would not be subjected to or limited by state intervention. The result, according to HarassMap cofounder Engy Ghozlan, is a system that provides women an "alternative" place to "report" and "speak out." Engy explains that her mission for the project is to "help . . . women have [a] voice" and to "use [technology] to tell the world what actually happens [to them]."[4]

For several years prior to starting the project, Engy, like her cofounders, had been working on several antiharassment campaigns, including the ECWR's Safer Streets for All campaign. Working with "officially registered" NGOs was a frustrating process, explains cofounder Rebecca Chiao, as their primary "focus on the state" and "the law" was doing little to "change realities on the ground." Both Rebecca and Engy articulate a strong belief that sexual harassment is not "inherent" in Cairo's culture, and is not simply "characteristic" of life for Egyptian women.

This sentiment is precisely what motivated Engy, Rebecca, and fellow cofounders Amal Fahmy and Sawsan Gad to seek out radically different solutions they felt would be both more accessible and more productive. They purposefully work not as an NGO but rather as an "all-volunteer team," to circumvent what Rebecca calls the "awful bureaucratic mess"

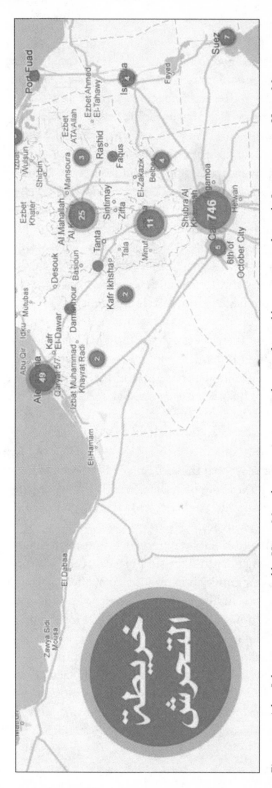

Figure 27.1. A late July 2013 map generated by HarassMap, documenting reported cases of sexual harassment and assault. Image courtesy HarassMap, 2013.

of "officially" registering with the state. The HarassMap system uses a combination of technology-based and on-the-ground methods to target harassment. The online component draws on crowd-sourcing technology as well as principles of geographic information systems (GIS) to produce a reporting and data-collecting mechanism, the results of which are published on the HarassMap website.

Women experiencing sexual harassment can report it for free to the system using text messaging, voicemail, or e-mail. The reported incident, complete with a description and location, will appear on a live, digital map of Cairo as a clickable red dot. The dots link to full reports provided by individual victims, which are classified according to "category." Categories include "Catcalls, Indecent Exposure, Stalking or Following, Sexual Invites and Touching" (HarassMap n.d.).

As the mobile phone penetration rate in Egypt was over 97 percent in 2009 when the project began, the cofounders felt confident it would become the only routinely accessible method for women to report on what was happening to them. The interactive platform served a dual purpose: women could "find a space to vent their frustration" and "alleviate their sense of helplessness" immediately after experiencing harassment, explains Engy. Egyptian women reporting to HarassMap also actively contribute to data collection, and so aid in the team's efforts to make "epidemic levels" of harassment "globally visible."[5] But Rebecca is also quick to underscore that the tool remains a service to the community, and to the empowerment of local women: "[This is about renewing] a sense of communal pride [and restoring] the Egyptian people's tradition of standing up for justice."

Women reporting to HarassMap receive information that reinforces a community-based effort to offer support, recovery, and protection: lists of NGOs and community organizations that offer legal and psychological counseling—including El Nadim—are provided to women who probably "did not know such things even existed for them,"[6] explains Engy. In addition, HarassMap community outreach volunteers are going into their own neighborhoods monthly, armed with printouts of HarassMap's data and what Rebecca terms "respectful and factual" answers to anticipated questions. The target of these efforts is mostly "people who have a presence" in a local area: shop owners, doormen, "the guys that are standing there parking cars," or "the people watching the neighborhoods," explains Rebecca. "These are the people [who] have the ability to change the atmosphere in their own streets."

Rebecca feels that these teams have been marginally successful, in particular with shop owners, who receive a "safe zone" sticker for their door and promotion on HarassMap's website if they agree to intervene in and report on sexual harassment. It is Engy who clarified in a 2011 interview with Egyptian journalist Marwa Rakha that part of the project's raison d'être is to empower people, women in particular, to be proactive in developing their own solutions to national problems:

In Egypt, there is no [longer] a belief that anything can be effective. Most of the time people are very depressed . . . and I can understand why—you are not seeing anything progressing, or anything moving forward. So [HarassMap, like] any initiative is usually faced [with] this rush of negativity, like "what are you going to change?" . . . We . . . lost hope in governments, we lost hope in authority doing something. And that's the goal of the project: to actually empower people, to take ownership of the problem and ownership of their communities, and do something and be part of this solution [to] this issue they are experiencing every day. So we try to [be part of that] answer.

HarassMap's cofounders were engaged in this direct-action community response prior to the 2011 Egyptian revolution, having begun their project early in 2009. Like their colleagues in Egypt's anti–sexual harassment movement, including those in the long-standing organizations ECWR and El Nadim, these women undertook the effort to publicly denounce the failures of the state, and to galvanize and mobilize a public response to circumvent such failures. The story of HarassMap ultimately involves a group of young women developing their own social media–based technology several years earlier, as the result of two pressing issues: first, their desire to mobilize the public around a social issue despite the seeming impossibility of doing so in a repressive regime; and second, their disbelief in the state's interest in offering and its ability to offer any kind of solution. Therefore, having been active in cyberspace at least two years before the revolution, their work poses a challenge to narratives focusing exclusively on the pairing of foreign social media brands and technologies and the facilitation of revolutionary action in Egypt. The American social networking services Facebook and Twitter are routinely credited with circumventing governmental efforts to obstruct protest and facilitating the widespread recruitment of movement participants (Lim 2012). Countless stories of the Egyptian revolution locate its "start" with a June 2010 Facebook page created by Google executive Wael Ghonim, or indeed with the January 2011 video posted to Facebook by April 6 movement cofounder Asmaa Mahfouz. But the story behind HarassMap—how it developed, and especially how it evolved to rely on community-centered notions of justice and people-powered change—suggests that the origins of revolutionary fervor characterizing the 2011 revolution may lie elsewhere.

While HarassMap might not necessarily be viewed as a direct catalyst to the January 25 revolution itself, the team's work certainly demonstrates that such efforts were already underway, and were led by young women using non-Western mechanisms to adopt available technologies and media. HarassMap's cofounders drew from the innovation of two systems developed in Africa to create the application: the Ushahidi crowd-sourcing platform, developed by Kenyan bloggers to report on the 2008 postelection violence occurring in Nairobi, and the Frontline SMS communication system, developed by technology and social justice activists to aid communications for communities living in South Africa. The origins and ongoing efforts of HarassMap can add much-needed empirical evidence to arguments disputing the central role American social media services played in "catalyzing" Egypt's social and political change, including those offered by Lim (2012).

Conclusion

Under former president Hosni Mubarak's authoritarian leadership, engaging in protest almost certainly meant risking personal safety. The publishing of data about women's experiences with harassment and violence, particularly that which is perpetrated by state officials, can therefore certainly be considered remarkable. So, too, can the subsequent "survival" of organizations that endeavor to expose and challenge the failings of the state (Rizzo, Price, and Meyer 2012, 459).

As Amar has argued, local antiharassment campaigns advancing "new kinds of assertive women's subjectivities" demonstrate exactly the sort of "ingenuity" that cultivated the "progressive achievements" of the 2011 revolution (2012, 301). And yet, where media attention to women's issues and sexual harassment in the context of revolution has surfaced, the stories usually feature women as victims. While staggering statistics about rape and violence committed against women at the hands of both civilians and military during periods of unrest understandably command outrage and attention, a focus only on this representation of women undermines their agency and capability for self-reliance, survival, and leadership. Perhaps more tragically, it limits public exposure to examples of women who are the forerunners of change and the engines of revolution, and not simply "victimized" by it. The stories featured in this chapter show that Egyptian women are indeed catalysts. They show that besides surviving what some scholars have called an authoritarian, neopatriarchal state staunchly opposed to any oppositional voices (Rizzo, Price, and Meyer 2012), women in fact have thrived in their efforts to subversively enact change.

NOTES

1 All interviews were conducted in English, with English responses provided by interview participants.

2 See, for example, Radwa Osama's October 26, 2006, blog post reflecting on the incident and providing details. "استمرار ثورة الجيايع لليوم الثاني علي التوالي," http:// hakazaana.blogspot.com/2006/10/blog-post_26.html.

3 Rizzo, Price, and Meyer (2012, 463) explain that under the provisions of Egypt's "Emergency Law," protest and communication are suspended.

4 "Engy Ghozlan on the Power of Harassmap," Ushahidi, YouTube, March 15, 2012, http://ushahidi.mirocommunity.org/video/55/engy-ghozlan-on-the-power-of-h.

5 "Harassmap—Being Positive about Sexual Harassment in Egypt," Marwa Rakha for Think Africa Press, January 2011, http://marwarakha.com.

6 "Harassmap—Being Positive about Sexual Harassment in Egypt," Marwa Rakha for Think Africa Press, January 2011, http://marwarakha.com.

BIBLIOGRAPHY

Abdelhadi, Magdi. 2006. "Cairo Street Crowds Target Women." *BBC News*, November 1, http://news.bbc.co.uk (accessed October 13, 2013).

Al-Malky, Raina. 2007. "Blogging for Reform: The Case of Egypt." *Arab Media and Society* 1, no. 1: 1–31.

Amar, Paul. 2011. "Turning the Gendered Politics of the Security State Inside Out? Charging the Police with Sexual Harassment in Egypt." *International Feminist Journal of Politics* 13, no. 3: 299–328.

Borg, Carmel, and Peter Mayo. 2007. *Public Intellectuals, Radical Democracy, and Social Movements: A Book of Interviews.* New York: Peter Lang.

ECWR (Egyptian Center for Women's Rights). 2012. "A Series of Trainings for Teachers under the Framework of the 'Safe Streets for Everyone' Campaign," September 23, http://ecwronline.org (accessed December 9, 2012).

El Nadim. 2009. "Once Again, Women Speak Out: Results of a Field Research on Violence against Women in Egypt," http://alnadeem.org (accessed May 19, 2013).

———. 2013. "El Nadim Center for Rehabilitation of Victims of Violence," https://alnadeem.org (accessed May 15, 2013).

HarassMap. N.d. "What We Do: The Map," http://harassmap.org (accessed October 13, 2013).

Hassan, Rasha, Nehad Abu Komsan, and Alyiaa Shoukry. 2008. *"Clouds in Egypt's Sky": Sexual Harassment from Verbal Harassment to Rape.* Cairo: Egyptian Center for Women's Rights, http://egypt.unfpa.org (accessed October 13, 2013).

Ilahi, Nadia. 2009. "Gendered Contestations: An Analysis of Street Harassment in Cairo and Its Implications for Women's Access to Public Spaces." *Surfacing: An Interdisciplinary Journal for Gender in the Global South* 2, no. 1: 56–69.

Lim, Merlyna. 2012. "Clicks, Cabs, and Coffee Houses: Social Media and Oppositional Movements in Egypt, 2004–2011." *Journal of Communication* 62, no. 2: 231–48.

Rakha, Marwa. 2011. "Being Positive about Sexual Harassment in Egypt." Retrieved 20 November 20, 2019, from http://marwarakha.com.

Rizzo, H., A. Price, and K. Meyer. 2012. "The Anti–Sexual Harassment Campaign in Egypt." *Mobilization* 17, no. 4: 457–75.

Wajcman, Judy. 1991. *Feminism Confronts Technology.* University Park: Pennsylvania State University Press.

Winegar, Jessica. 2012. "The Privilege of Revolution: Gender, Class, Space, and Affect in Egypt." *American Ethnologist* 39, no. 1: 67–70.

28

A Village Rises in the First Intifada

International Women's Day, March 8, 1988

MANAL A. JAMAL

Since the start of the "Arab Spring," much of the discussion on the circumstances of Arab women has been ahistorical—yet again addressing
the plight of this disempowered, abused collective. Despite the serious
challenges that Arab women face today and the legitimate grievances
raised by many, it is crucial at this critical juncture not to ahistoricize
Arab women and their experiences, their challenges, and their victories.
Hence, it is vital to draw on past experiences of women during different periods of upheaval to ensure that these issues are presented with
the multilayered complexities they embody. Unlike much of the discussion on the plight of Arab women today, the scholarship on Palestinian
women during the first Intifada is significant in the extent to which it
captured women's nuanced experiences—as agents of change confronting the multiple challenges of gender relations in their society. Presented
here, however, is only one of millions of stories of daily battles.

An Idea Is Born

Determined to have the name of Deir Dibwan broadcast on the pirated
Intifada radio station in 1988, a group of young women—four high
school students and one university student from Deir Dibwan—decided
to organize the first protest in the village to mark International Women's
Day. What was supposed to be a modest women's march turned into
a protest of over five hundred people. Shocked that a group of young
women would organize a protest without consulting them, the men
furiously rushed to take over the protest to ensure that the women did
not get credit. Realizing the stakes at hand, Fateh and the Islamist men

activists, including the village sheikh, united and joined forces to put the women in their place. Thinking that our parents and the village elders would support them, they informed us that the following day there would be conditions that we would have to abide by if we wanted to participate in "their protest." By the second day, a full-blown battle of the sexes had ensued. As we furiously fought to assert our positions, by the end of the week Deir Dibwan had probably received one short announcement on the pirated Intifada radio station. Unbeknownst to us at that time, however, the protest unleashed the political spirit of the village.

It was initially Yasmine's idea. At the time, Yasmine was a university student at Bethlehem University. She found women her age to be boring, since they often had men and marriage on their mind. Instead, and sometimes to her mother's dismay, she hung out with me, my cousin Zakira, our friend Nadia, and her neighbor Mahira; we were all high school students then. During the initial months of the Intifada, we had quite a bit of free time on our hands, since the Israeli military closed down all educational institutions and outlawed all forms of organized education. My mother's intent was that Zakira and I should return to the United States to finish high school, but we felt that we would be selling out and abandoning Palestine in its moment of need. Plus, Zakira, then aka *Hassan Sabi* (tomboy in Arabic), had established a reputation as one of the best woman "rock throwers" in Ramallah, and she felt that the Intifada needed her unique skills. My father left the decision to us. He rationalized that if teenagers are bound to rebel and get themselves in trouble, they might as well do so for a good cause.

By May of that year, the Israeli military allowed educational institutions to reopen briefly for about three weeks. It became clear that the schools needed to plan for the indefinite long haul, and many schools became more systematic in organizing alternative "underground" education. In some locations, the popular neighborhood committees organized classes in different homes. In other locations, they organized classes in churches, mosques, or community centers. In our case, the Friends Girls' School relocated the secondary classes to the basement of the Jerusalem YMCA, since our principal's husband was its director. Until our classes resumed in the dark basements, however, we spent a lot of time ruminating on how to cope with the general strike, school closures, and daily events and protests. We ended up becoming experts at playing *hand*—a Palestinian card game. Some of our teachers organized reading groups for the students, and Sherron, an American teacher at Friends Girls' School, stood out in particular. She kept us busy with long reading lists, discussion sessions, and superb breakfasts. As leaders in the student council and members in various coordinating committees, we also organized an array of underground discussion groups.

Like many others in our generation, we also became authorities in identifying the most politically active villages, counting protests and casualties, and reflecting on the most effective forms of protest and civil disobedience. Although we were aware of the historical weight of that period, only in hindsight did we fully appreciate the significance of coming into political age during that period and the consequences of every daily decision—small and large.

Putting Our Village on the Map

As the West Bank and Gaza Strip protests raged, the name of our village, Deir Dibwan, was absent from any news broadcasts, both the pirated Intifada radio station and mainstream media alike. What initially was a popular joke about Deir Dibwan being the liberated American zone, where outlawed Palestinian flags hung freely, turned to a source of embarrassment. The inhabitants of Deir Dibwan were about 50 percent US citizens, and that was the likely reason, we thought, that the military avoided the village altogether, maybe as a way not to provoke any confrontations that might result in American ire.

On the morning of March 8, 1988, International Women's Day, Yasmine and Mahira showed up at our house unexpectedly. Yasmine was adamant that we needed to organize a women's march. We called our friend Nadia, who quickly joined us. The plan was simple: we would split into two teams and go door to door asking women to meet us at noon in front of our house. We were already a group of five, and we calculated that if only twenty-five more women joined us, our march of thirty was bound to draw some attention. To our surprise, the numbers surpassed our expectations. By noon hundreds of women of all ages amassed in front of our house. Our first worry was our lack of preparation, and our second was my mother screaming and falling apart in the kitchen. Given the randomness of military occupation policies, it was not uncommon for Israel to demolish the homes of activists. She had had it with us, and resolved that she was going to forcefully send me and Zakira to the United States and enroll us in private Catholic schools since our Quaker school had failed to discipline us or teach us how to respect authority.

We proceeded with the march as planned. Chanting the standard Intifada chants, we planned to walk two rounds around the village, and then meet to discuss how we would move forward. Shortly, our emerging adversaries, men in the village confronted us. They wanted to join the protest. We marched onward, ignoring their dismay. We were informed that we were not being inclusive; yes, we were not, but that was not our plan or objective. Although the young men tried to lead, our voices were too loud. They decided that the march should be divided, with the men leading up front. We let them. They did not want the sexes to mix during the protest. We complied. In controlled disarray, we proceeded with our march, exchanging dirty looks along the way.

We felt protected and supported as the older women of the village joined us, especially when Yasmine's mother showed up. Although I cannot remember whether she initially supported us, she eventually did when she knew we were under attack. One did not mess with Umm Mohammed, who knew how to stand her ground. She was one of seven daughters (no sons), and as usually happens in such cases, Umm Mohammed and her sisters were raised to think of themselves as honorary males. With her cigarette in hand and no-nonsense attitude, she stood by our side. My aunts also joined, and they wanted to make sure that no one upset us. Meanwhile, my mother cried in the kitchen.

Without further incident, we marched around the village two times, and ended the protest in front of our house. Everyone was so pleased with the showing and solidarity, we decided to reconvene for another protest the following day, and the purpose would be to voice Deir Dibwan's unwavering solidarity with the Intifada. Our male adversaries—members of Fateh and Islamist activists who put their differences aside in the interest of patriarchy—announced that if we liked, we should meet to discuss the next day's arrangements. They felt that a protest that included everyone, males and females, would be more effective. On that point, we agreed. We met at the house of a neutral party. The men laid out a number of conditions by which we had to abide: they would lead the protest and select the chants, make it mandatory that we cover our hair and wear loose jeans, and require that our chants not be as loud as theirs. Of course, we disagreed. They had one determining advantage over us: keys to the door that would lead to the speakers of the village mosque's minaret. Their plan was to announce the protest after the noon call to prayer, and to ask everyone in the village to meet in front of the mosque. They rationalized that the numbers would be far larger than we could reach if we had gone door to door, and they were correct. So, if we wanted to be part of what promised to be a successful protest and a historic moment of Deir Dibwan's largest protest to date, we had to abide by their conditions. They also had two bullhorns that would help make the protest a success. We agreed to join them in front of the mosque the following day.

We were outraged by how they took the reins from our hands. Suddenly, we were no longer the organizers, and we were following their directions. A complete random coincidence worked to our advantage: my father unexpectedly arrived that evening for his spring visit. He was excited to hear our stories but had one question for us: Why would you follow their orders if you disagree? Yasmine's mother shared the same sentiment.

We deliberated well into the evening and decided that we would follow our adversaries' general guidelines, but only to a point. We would allow the male part of the protest to march ahead of us, but we would ask the older women to march in front of the young women, creating a demarcation barrier between the men and the women, and hence making clear that we still were leading our protest. Although we would be part of the same march, we would carry on as if the women's protest was separate. We decided to prepare our own slogans, and we would only chant their slogans if we agreed with the contents. We would throw the *kuffiyeh* on our heads, but not cover our hair entirely, making clear that this was a nationalist marker and not an Islamist one. Then, most importantly, we would surprise them with the final blow to their plan—a bullhorn of our own that was superior to the one they had. The bullhorn was a dated relic from Nadia's father's days as a police officer in Oakland, California, during the 1970s, but it still worked perfectly.

The protest announcement echoed throughout the village, and before we knew it, hundreds were assembling in front of the mosque. It soon appeared as if the entire village was on the streets. Even my mother joined. Our adversaries kept looking at us suspiciously, trying to understand why we were suddenly friendlier and more agreeable. We asked the older women to assemble between the two parts of the march, and they agreed. Although the males were distrustful and worried about our motives, they silently obliged out of respect for and deference to their elders.

Then the march began. It stretched endlessly—no one person could see the start and the end of it simultaneously. The men started with the standard Intifada chants, but before we knew it, the content degenerated and the protest turned to an endorsement of Fateh and the Islamists. We then began with our own chants. They gave us dirty looks, but we pretended not to notice. The village's sheikh then took us aside and asked us to behave. At that point, outraged, we decided our chants should attack all reactionary forces, including them. Yasmine came up with the defining slogan of the day: "'al makshouf wa al' makshouf, al-rajieh ma bidna inshoof! 'al makshouf wa'al makshouf, ikhwanjieh ma bidna inshoof! Bil toul, bil ard, Fateh taht al-ard" (Let us be clear, we are fed up with backwardness! Let us be clear, we are fed up with fundamentalism! No matter where it goes, Fateh's fate is doomed!).

We deliberated among ourselves whether such a move would divide our ranks. At that point, we were passing our house, and my father, who was too jet lagged to join us, was smoking his argileh and watching the protest. I worried that if we proceeded with our plan, my father might be disappointed. But again, he always came around. Comfortable with the familiarity of our surroundings at that point, Nadia pulled the bullhorn out of the bag and handed it to me, and we began our anti–reactionary forces chant. Hundreds repeated it, and suddenly our march was louder than the males' march. To say that the sheikh was furious is an understatement. All the male organizers started walking towards us. By then, my mother had turned purple and was about to start crying. I looked up at our balcony only to see my father laughing. It was then that I knew everything would be fine. We felt emboldened by his support and continued chanting. We exchanged a few terse words with our adversaries, but continued focused on the march.

Like that, the protest ended on a high note. We cooperated, yet stood our ground, and we made clear that we had little tolerance for reactionary politics. Everyone in the village was proud of the amazing showing. A few people mentioned our radical slogans, but definitely, this theme did not dominate the conversations of the day. Deir Dibwan was mentioned on the pirated Intifada radio station, although most people did not notice.

The Aftermath

Skirmishes with the military became more common as a result. A month later, the military made one of their treks through the village, and young boys began confronting them with a barrage of stones. Worried that the military would catch them, Samia, a nineteen-year-old woman, grabbed a slab of brick and hurled it in the direction of the soldiers to disorient them. Though she managed to distract the soldiers from the boys, she did not notice the other soldiers, taking cover on the other side of the street, who then grabbed and beat her, and then arrested her. This is how Samia became the first female political prisoner from Deir Dibwan. Everyone in the village was outraged. We quickly organized to collect donations to help her family hire a lawyer who would facilitate a visit to see her, and to pay for other legal fees. Given the overwhelming generosity of everyone in the village, we collected far more money than was required, and initially did not know what to do with the extra money. This actually was not surprising given the generosity of many of the people of Deir Dibwan—a characteristic of which they are very proud.

We subsequently created a women's popular committee to decide how to use the donations, including the creation of new initiatives that we thought were needed. The women's committee also became responsible for organizing alternative education for children when they were not officially in school. Deir Dibwan became more visibly integrated in terms of the Intifada's overall organization and activism. Samia was released from prison after four months.

Things, however, did not end well. The Israeli military summarily rounded up and imprisoned many of our comrades, our former adversaries, and all would serve heavy prison sentences, the least being two years, while others were held indefinitely under administrative detention. As for us girls, we graduated from our underground high school the following year and eventually moved to the United States to study.

Some of the activists in the solidarity movement were eager to explain the shortcomings of the Intifada to us, including those that were gender related. When we were very appreciative of everything they were teaching us, we would even be included in their gatherings and organizing meetings.

"Hassan Sabi" had an arranged marriage, complied with her husband's request to wear hijab, and severed all ties to her once-rebellious past. My mother eased up and became an accidental organizer involved in breaking the siege on Jerusalem. Since Israel no longer permitted Palestinians to enter Jerusalem without special permits, she and other women from Deir Dibwan would organize weekly trips for Friday prayer during Ramadan. Since the women did not have the necessary permits, Israeli authorities regarded them as entering Jerusalem illegally. Every year, my mother and her friends became more committed to their mission. A little more than three years after the events of that far-away March day, my father died. For young women who dared to move against the current, the loss of a supportive father is nothing short of a personal tsunami.

How wrong we were about the Israeli military avoiding our village for fear of American disapproval. Ironically, as Israeli military infringements on the village increased, including the Israeli military killing of an American-born teenager, American authorities continued to turn a blind eye.

29

Revolutionary Graffiti and Cairene Women

Performing Agency through Gaze Aversion

SOUMIA BARDHAN AND KAREN A. FOSS

Through an unparalleled explosion of street art and graffiti campaigns during and after the January 25, 2011, revolution, many public spaces in Cairo, Egypt, became symbols of people's revolt against the state. Graffiti, which used to be "fleet, anonymous, contextual and irreverent—has emerged as the signature art form of the [Egyptian] revolution," having become "all at once, an act of defiance, an appropriation of public space and a running political counter-narrative" (Lindsey 2012). These spaces resemble open-air galleries showcasing street art on a wide range of social issues, including graffiti that encourage women to resist societal pressures and daily humiliation, to reclaim public spaces, and to confront existing power and gender dynamics.

Graffiti artists such as Aya Tarek, Hend Kheera, Hanaa El Degham, Bahia Shehab, Laila Magued, Mira Shihadeh, and Ammar Abo Bakr have made noteworthy contributions to the revolution in general and to encouraging women's resistance in particular. They have sparked a "revolution through art" and so have numerous campaigns representing women's voices, like Noon El-Neswa (Her) and Women on Walls (Suzeeinthecity 2014a, 2014b). In this essay, we perform a rhetorical analysis of the female-centered graffiti displayed in Cairo's public spaces in post-Mubarak Egypt. We analyze street art and graffiti by prominent graffiti artists, significant graffiti campaigns, and our own photographs of graffiti taken at the sites. We are interested in the various possibilities of the "gaze" the graffiti texts construct, each of which has a bearing on the subject position of the women depicted in the texts and on those doing the viewing (Foss and Foss 1994).

These graffiti show Egyptian women performing agency as they create their own depiction of the role of women in post-Mubarak Cairo. We argue that this perspective challenges the impression outsiders have of Arab/Egyptian women and allows them, as spectators, to comprehend women's dynamics in Cairene society as agents rather than victims: graffiti, the language of art, facilitates comprehension and constructs a position the spectator must occupy. By looking at the rhetorical possibilities of the spectator position in Cairene women's revolutionary graffiti, we seek to offer a new way of viewing women's agency in contemporary Cairo.

The Importance of Studying Graffiti: A Background

The scholarly study of graffiti is hardly a novel endeavor. As early as 1953, Littman and Meredith focused on numerous unpublished Nabataean graffiti/inscriptions. In the decades following them, scholars have analyzed graffiti from archeological, historical, and gender/cultural perspectives. Naveh (1979) examined Hebrew, Phoenician, Aramaic, Thamudic, and Safaic graffiti/inscriptions to make the claim that dedicatory/votive inscriptions and graffiti have numerous commonalities. Studies examining restroom graffiti, using either semiotic approaches or content analysis (Matthews, Speers, and Ball 2012), have suggested that there are fundamental differences in the ways males and females communicate through this art form. Chaffee's (1993) comparative analysis of graffiti in Spain, the Basque country, Argentina, and Brazil demonstrates how street art is a useful indicator of popular conflicts and sentiments across the political spectrum. These studies established graffiti as a cultural and political medium in a communicative process.

Many scholarly endeavors highlighted the phenomenal rise of graffiti as a form of popular political and social/cultural expression following the January 2011 revolution in Egypt. Grondahl (2013) and Hamdy, Karl, and Eltahawy (2013) documented the constantly and rapidly changing graffiti art of today's Egypt and thus depicted the volatile political situation in the country. Khatib (2012) analyzed the politics of imagery, while Abaza (2012) emphasized issues of power, resistance, and identity construction. Khatib contends that visuals encompass "physical, electronic, non-electronic virtual and embodied spaces" (2012, 7); she uses the term "image politics" to describe the various ways in which visuals can be politically important. Studies such as Badran (2014) have paid attention to gender dynamics and creative political activism in contemporary Egypt.

This overview explicates the cultural and political potential of graffiti and street art. The works reviewed suggest that understanding the role of graffiti as a tool for propaganda in specific cultural contexts can illuminate basic societal processes, from gender inequality to public literary practice to identity construction and nonviolent resistance. Specifically, in the context of contemporary Egypt, studies have emphasized the phenomenal rise of graffiti as a form of political activism and the significance of such creative endeavors in revolutionizing gender discourses in post-Mubarak Egypt.

In this study, we build on these claims about graffiti and gender in the contemporary Egyptian context. We argue that revolutionary graffiti in Egypt not only constitute art as a form of political engagement and a medium of communication but also signal Cairene women's sense of agency, evident in the relationship between the women in the graffiti images and the spectators of the graffiti. Through a rhetorical examination of women's agency as demonstrated through the way gaze functions in the graffiti to construct a particular spectator position, we hope to understand how revolutionary graffiti depict the role of women in post-Mubarak Cairo.

Examining Artifacts

For this analysis, we chose seven graffiti images from public spaces in Cairo created during and after the January 2011 revolution, for several reasons. First, all include prominent images of women, and even when men are depicted, the woman or women in the images remain dominant—they are in color and hence stand out, while the men do not; they are positioned above the men; or they are larger than the men. Furthermore, they represent some of the first and/or most popular graffiti pieces to emerge from the revolution, and the renderings address major issues related to Cairene women raised by artists' and activists' campaigns during the revolution. While many of these graffiti images have been erased or modified and no longer exist on the walls around Cairo, they have been immortalized in pictures and videos due to their iconic status. Our access to these images, then, was through several sources.

We photographed some of these graffiti ourselves during a visit to Cairo in March 2013; the remaining images were retrieved from various visual media.

Because we are communication scholars, our method of analysis for these graffiti is rhetorical criticism, a research method designed for the systematic investigation and explanation of symbolic acts and artifacts for the purpose of understanding rhetorical processes. Understanding the nature, functions, and impact of rhetoric—the human use of symbols to communicate—is the purpose of rhetorical criticism. Ultimately, the rhetorical critic hopes to contribute to the kinds of worlds constructed by symbols, the meanings attributed to those symbols, and the communication practices that follow from a greater understanding of rhetorical acts (Foss 2009).

In employing rhetorical criticism to examine graffiti about and/or by women in Cairo, we offer a way to understand women's agency in postrevolution Egypt. We are concerned with ways these graffiti might challenge an ideology of domination and provide avenues for, and the capacity for, agency among Cairene women. At the core of feminist perspectives is challenging oppressive structures that narrowly prescribe women's social roles and choices so women can create their own lives. Agency or self-determination, then, is a hallmark of feminist theorizing—"that women can negotiate social constraints to make the best choices for that particular moment, recognizing the contingencies of their historical contexts and material worlds as limitations but looking for ways to subvert those limitations if possible" (Renegar and Sowards 2009, 9).

Our analysis used frequency and intensity as primary criteria. Frequency represents something that repeatedly appeared in the images—the color red or black, for instance—while intensity represents an aspect of an image that was particularly striking or unusual—a blue bra or an image of Queen Nefertiti. Eye contact of the individuals depicted in the graffiti and the spatial orientation of those depicted in relation to the audience emerged as salient elements across all images. Using these elements as core to our analysis, we examined the interplay among these factors to understand the images in terms of the spectator position created by the revolutionary graffiti and its implications for women's agency in contemporary Egyptian society.

What Do the Images Reveal?

The interplay of eye contact and spatial orientation coalesced around the concept of "aversion." "Averting" literally means to turn away or aside in avoidance; thus it is an action that includes both eye contact and body position. Averting the eyes is a nonverbal sign of submission, appeasement, and deference—qualities often associated with proper feminine comportment (Guerrero and Floyd 2006). Yet in cultures in which eye contact is not valued, aversion carries connotations of respect as well: to avert the eyes acknowledges the esteem or honor in which the other is held (Foss, Domenico, and Foss 2013). Aversion also occurs when one is in a difficult cognitive situation—remembering information, thinking about how to respond to a difficult question, or planning what to say (Doherty-Sneddon and Phelps 2005). Gaze aversion, then, accomplishes several purposes, all of which allow the individual to manage a situation in which there is a power differential or a difficult cognitive task.

But there is another meaning of "avert" as well, and that is to see something coming and ward it off or to prevent something from happening by taking action in advance. The definition of "avert" as fending off suggests behaviors in which an individual deliberately employs strategies to keep something from happening. Both definitions of "avert," then, refer to the strategic management of circumstances through the gaze. Accompanied by a certain body position and augmented at times by color, the graffiti offer an assertion of agency. The interplay of these two logics of "aversion" informs our analysis of the gaze that these pieces of graffiti construct.

When the Supreme Council of the Armed Forces (SCAF) took over in February 2011, following Hosni Mubarak's overthrow, sexual harassment became a means to intimidate and publicly humiliate women protesters on the streets of Cairo. In March 2011, military personnel began to perform "virginity tests" on female protesters. Army spokesmen justified these tests by stating that these protected the military from false claims of rape. One of the victims, Egyptian activist Samira Ibrahim, filed a case against an army medic, Ahmed Adel El-Mogy, who performed the test on her. He was acquitted, like the majority of police officers involved. The graffiti analyzed in figure 29.1 was created on the Friday following El-Mogy's acquittal.

Figure 29.1. *Samira Ibrahim* (Philiptchenko 2012)

This image depicts Samira Ibrahim's face above an army battalion, every member of which is Ahmed Adel El-Mogy. She is looking away from the army, giving a semblance of submission, appeasement, and deference. But her gaze is not submissive when viewed in context: she is in a position of dominance by virtue of her scarved head situated above the army. This stance is augmented by the red color of Samira's scarf. Red, according to ancient Egyptian symbolism, is the color of destructive fire and fury (Nyamache and Nyambura 2012), and in the context of Samira's gaze in this graffiti, manifests a nonsubmissive and silent self-determination that could be destructive towards her perpetrators. In addition, absence of eye contact with the audience implies that the spectator appears to be none of her concern.

Figure 29.2. *Red Dress with Spray Can* (suzeeinthecity 2014a)

Figure 29.2 portrays a woman in heels, using mace against her male attackers. Although her conspicuous body curves, high heels, and provocative dress connote femininity, her stance is strong and so is the text, which is written mostly in striking red paint. It reads "No to sexual harassment." None of the men before her can withstand her mace or her gaze. Although she is partially turned so that she has her spectators in view, her gaze clearly is focused on her aggressors as she wards off an attack with her spray can. She clearly is not in need of outside intervention, and it is as if she is looking at her audience only to make sure they know how capable and confident she is in taking on this task alone. Her power is reinforced by the striking color of her red dress, which communicates both strength and rage (Nyamache and Nyambura 2012).

Figure 29.3. *Woman Rescuing Man.* Photo by Soumia Bardhan, March 2012.

Figure 29.3, on the wall of the Greek campus of American University on Mohammed Mahmud Street, depicts a woman rescuing and protecting a man. This graffiti image is a testimony to women's fierceness in Cairo's protests. The woman's gaze is directly focused on the man, and the text reads, "During battles, I will be behind you, protecting you." Her audience watches as though the scene is playing out on a television screen, thus putting them at a distance from the action. There is no supplication on her part to her audience. The tiny splashes of red and gold on her side of the mural signal her rage, power, and invincibility, with red traditionally associated with rage, and gold traditionally associated with invincibility in Egyptian color symbolism (Nyamache and Nyambura 2012). This image suggests that a woman can perform acts of protection traditionally associated with men, strongly emphasizing female agency in revolutionary activity.

Figure 29.4. *Queen Nefertiti with Gas Mask.*
Photo by Soumia Bardhan, March 2012.

Figure 29.4 depicts the ancient Egyptian Queen Nefertiti wearing a gas mask. Historians consider Nefertiti to have been one of the most powerful and influential queens of Egypt. Tear gas is associated with protest because police frequently used it to break up demonstrations during the January 25 revolution. A traditionally feminine gaze is the foundation for this image. A classic in fashion photography, the woman with her head lowered but her eyes directed upward comes off as coy and flirtatious. Nefertiti's scowl, however, communicates judgment rather than flirtation. The use of a gas mask indicates that she is capable of protecting herself. This image of Nefertiti is entirely in black, a color that may connote death to its audience (Nyamache and Nyambura 2012), and underneath it is a line of dripping red paint, suggesting the feminization of rage. The combination of the gas mask, the judgmental scowl, the connotation of death, Nefertiti's royal status, and the red paint signals to spectators women's power and capabilities in the context of this revolution. An otherwise feminine gaze functions as a sign to spectators to keep their distance.

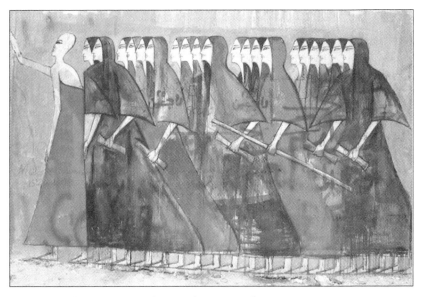

Figure 29.5. *Pharaonic Women* (suzeeinthecity 2014a)

The Pharaonic women figures depicted in figure 29.5 represent royal Egyptian women who were involved in military leadership in Pharaonic times (Carney 2001). In this piece, the marching Pharaonic women depict royalty and leadership, both qualities that place them in a dominant position. That these women carry objects—perhaps staffs and scrolls— signals their willingness to fight, defend, and educate, which is a depiction of courage and self-determination. As with the other images, the women are not concerned with those viewing them; they are looking away, all gazing in one direction, focused intently on the destination toward which they are marching. The colors of the garments, primarily red and blue, suggest power and prestige and contribute to a sense of self-determination, and the nobility of their cause. The combination of stance, focus, and color conveys a sense of strong determination about their task.

Figure 29.6. Gas Canisters (Grondahl 2013)

Named the *Pyramid of Crisis*, figure 29.6 literally depicts women in a very passive moment in the revolution—standing in long lines to fill their gas canisters for cooking but not standing in line to vote. When it can be discerned at all, the gaze of the women is downward and averted; most of the faces are blurred and covered so there is no sense of any external engagement. The lack of gaze combined with the women holding the canisters up with both hands creates a closed loop, seemingly impenetrable by the outside world. But the word "change," written on one canister, offers a possibility of hope and self-reflexivity within the loop; the fact that the word is written in red reinforces this as, according to Nyamache and Nyambura, "this most potent of all colours in Ancient Egypt, was also a colour of life" (Nyamache and Nyambura 2012, 55). Thus, the women themselves are not just constrained in the loops made by the canisters and their arms, but they can subvert their limitations by controlling the loops; this depicts that they will figure out how to bring a change/transformation they can manage, and they will decide how and when to change/transform. The spectator remains outside the image. There is nowhere the spectator can enter the closed loops created between the women's arms and the gas canisters. It is not the spectator's task to interfere.

Figure 29.7. *Protesters Shot in the Eyes* (Van Leuven 2013)

Egyptian women were among the numerous protesters shot in the eyes by central security forces during street clashes in Mohammed Mahmud Street in late 2011. Figure 29.7 depicts some of these victims—one female and two males. For these three individuals, one eye is necessarily averted because it is bandaged. For the male victims, however, the remaining eye looks directly at viewers in a beseeching way, establishing a connection with them. This is not the case for the female victim, however. While her head is tilted, which might give a semblance of submission, she does not look at the audience as the men do. Rather, she is simply offering evidence of what happened to her, and she does not seem to need to reveal anything to the audience. She remains apart from the viewers and her male comrades as well, in a self-contained state. The white color of her bandage, signifying victory (Nyamache and Nyambura 2012), connotes that despite this physical setback, she will be victorious.

Egyptian Women as Agents

We argue that the women depicted in the graffiti analyzed perform agency by simultaneously managing the situation at hand and preventing the observer from intervening on their behalf. Women are seen as engaging in what might initially be considered gaze aversion for purposes of feminine submission. Yet when placed in the context of the image's color, its spatial orientation, and, most importantly, its depiction of eye contact, the interplay of the gaze of the women in the graffiti and the audience of the graffiti creates a powerful sense of Cairene women's agency.

The seven graffiti images reveal that Cairene women are powerful, independent, agentic figures; their aversion communicates tradition and revolution simultaneously. By using the traditionally submissive nonverbal act of gaze aversion, the graffiti artists acknowledge traditional roles and images of women. But the juxtaposition of the traditional averted gaze with the kind of aversion that signals warding off someone/something produces an image that transcends tradition. Women use the traditional gaze not simply to look away from the audience in expected ways but to deflect the audience's attention, intervention, and assistance. When they do look at the audience, the blankness of the stare negates any connection between individual and audience, suggesting again that outside help is unnecessary. This assertion of agency and rejection of outside interference may have a simple explanation that can fit neatly within observers' assumptions: it could be that these depictions of women indicate Cairene women's rejection of the intervention of (male) family members, an authoritarian state, and a conservative society.

The audience viewing the graffiti takes on the passive, second-hand witness role as those who were "not there on the spot" but have "seen or 'remembered' events nonetheless, either through listening to others' testimonies, or by seeing representations of those events" (Bernard-Donals 2007, 340). And although the second-hand witness does not have a personal or sensory experience of an event, the knowledge of its occurrence, as provided through the eyewitness, commits the viewer to engage in the events depicted in some larger way. As Levine notes, the second-hand witness "implicitly commits himself [herself] to the task of assuming co-responsibility for an intolerable burden, for an overwhelming charge" (2006, 7).

Cairene women, as eyewitnesses, are the medium through which women's experiences during and after the January 2011 revolution are supplied to outsiders. In this role they have chosen for themselves, these women exert agency by precluding others from intervening agentically on their behalf but at the same time entrusting them with responsibilities—outsiders cannot interfere, but neither can they look away, ignore, forget, or remain passive to women's revolutionary efforts in contemporary Cairo.

Conclusion

"Agential capacity is entailed in the multiple ways in which individuals inhabit norms" (Foss, Waters, and Armada 2007, 225). In the case of Cairene women in contemporary Egypt, their testimony against injustice, the agency they hold in calling this injustice to attention through revolutionary graffiti, and the relationship they establish with the viewers of these graffiti through aversion suggest an intensely conspicuous and unique sense of agency. Cairene women's agency manifests in revolutionary acts, in choosing to create graffiti—the language of images—to communicate with the world, in making their own agentic choice of the way they interact with the spectator of the graffiti, and in their insistence that their stories be known and remembered. The viewer, they insist, must recognize Cairene women's actions (Peters 2001). By employing this kind of graffiti, Cairene women ask the world to understand that revolutions that lead to the transformation of societies find their vitality in the personal and subjective experiences of individuals and groups—Cairene women in this case—who use creative ways to gain salience, resist, and reform. In the performance of this agency, achieved through creative acts of aversion, Cairene women assert themselves, initiate change, and transform their societies while barring outsiders from defining and designing their destiny.

Cairene women also create a dynamic of "interhuman responsive action responsible for the Other" (Arnett 2003, 39). Both the Cairene women and their spectator are bound to each other. By exercising agency, each responds to a call of responsibility—the Cairene women to break stereotypes about themselves and show the watching world the reality of their existence, and the watching world as second-hand eye-witness responsible for documenting Cairene women's revolutionary struggles. Spectators are not asked to be saviors or to intervene, but to document on terms dictated by Cairene women themselves—terms that insist Cairene women's revolutionary struggles be known, understood, and remembered.

Acknowledgement

This work was supported by a Research Faculty Improvement Grant awarded by the Office of Research and Sponsored Programs at St. Cloud University.

BIBLIOGRAPHY

Abaza, Mona. 2012. "The Revolution's Barometer." *Jadaliyya*, http://www.jadaliyya.com (accessed August 13, 2013).

Arnett, Ronald C. 2003. "The Responsive 'I': Levinas's Derivative Argument." *Argumentation and Advocacy* 40, no. 1: 39–50.

Badran, Margot. 2014. "Dis/playing Power and the Politics of Patriarchy in Revolutionary Egypt: The Creative Activism of Huda Lutfi." *Postcolonial Studies* 17, no. 1: 47–62.

Bernard-Donals, Michael F. 2007. Review of "The Belated Witness: Literature, Testimony, and the Question of Holocaust Survival" and "Testimony after Catastrophe: Narrating Traumas of Political Violence." *Comparative Literature Studies* 44, no. 3: 340–45.

Carney, Elizabeth. 2001. "Women and Military Leadership in Pharaonic Egypt." *Greek, Roman, and Byzantine Studies* 42, no. 1: 25–41.

Chaffee, Lyman. 1993. *Political Protest and Street Art: Popular Tools for Democratization in Hispanic Countries.* Westport, CT: Greenwood.

Doherty-Sneddon, Gwyneth, and Fiona G. Phelps. 2005. "Gaze Aversion: A Response to Cognitive or Social Difficulty?" *Memory & Cognition* 33, no. 4: 727–33.

Foss, Sonja K. 2009. *Rhetorical Criticism: Exploration and Practice.* 3rd edition. Long Grove, IL: Waveland.

Foss, Sonja K., Mary E. Domenico, and Karen A. Foss. 2013. *Gender Stories: Negotiating Identity in a Binary World.* Long Grove, IL: Waveland.

Foss, Sonja K., and Karen A. Foss. 1994. "The Construction of Feminine Spectatorship in Garrison Keillor's Radio Monologues." *Quarterly Journal of Speech* 80, no. 4: 410–26.

Foss, Sonja K., William J. C. Waters, and Bernard J. Armada. 2007. "Toward a Theory of Agentic Orientation: Rhetoric and Agency in *Run Lola Run*." *Communication Theory* 17, no. 3: 205–30.

Grondahl, Mia. 2013. *Revolution Graffiti: Street Art of the New Egypt.* Cairo: American University in Cairo Press.

Guerrero, Laura K., and Kory Floyd. 2006. *Nonverbal Communication in Close Relationships.* Mahwah, NJ: Erlbaum.

Hamdy, Basma, Don Stone Karl, and Mona Eltahawy. 2013. *Walls of Freedom: Street Art of the Egyptian Revolution.* Berlin: From Here to Fame.

Khatib, Lina. 2012. *Image Politics in the Middle East: The Role of the Visual in Political Struggle.* London: Taurus.

Levine, Michael. 2006. *The Belated Witness: Literature, Testimony, and the Question of Holocaust Survival.* Stanford, CA: Stanford University Press.

Lindsey, Ursula. 2012. "Art in Egypt's Revolutionary Square." *Middle East Research and Information Project,* January, http://www.merip.org (accessed October 9, 2013).

Littman, Enno, and David Meredith. 1953. "Nabataean Inscriptions from Egypt." *Bulletin of the School of Oriental and African Studies* 15: 1–28.

Matthews, Nicholas, Laura Speers, and James Ball. 2012. "Bathroom Banter: Sex, Love, and the Bathroom Wall." *Electronic Journal of Human Sexuality* 15, http://www.ejhs.org.

Naveh, Joseph. 1979. "Graffiti and Dedications." *Bulletin of the School of Oriental and African Studies* 235: 27–30.

Nyamache, Tom, and Ruth Nyambura. 2012. "Colour Symbolism in Africa: A Historical Perspective." *Asian Journal of Research in Business Economics and Management* 2: 50–56.

Palmer, Rodney. 2008. *Street Art Chile.* Berkeley, CA: Gingko Press.

Peters, John Durham. 2001. "Witnessing." *Media, Culture, and Society* 23, no. 6: 707–23.

Philiptchenko, Tatiana. 2012. "The Graffiti Battle in Cairo." *Egyptian Women of the Revolution,* http://www.egyptianwomen.info (accessed December 19, 2012).

Renegar, Valerie R., and Stacy K. Sowards. 2009. "Contradiction as Agency: Self-Determination, Transcendence, and Counter-Imagination in Third Wave Feminism." *Hypatia* 24, no. 2: 1–20.

Suzeeinthecity. 2014a. "Women in Graffiti: A Tribute to the Women of Egypt." *Art on the Streets of Cairo,* January 7, http://suzeeinthecity.wordpress.com/2013/01/07/women-in-graffiti-a-tribute-to-the-women-of-egypt/ (accessed August 12, 2013).

———. 2014b. "Ode to Alexandria—Where it All Began." *Art on the Streets of Cairo,* February 21, http://suzeeinthecity.wordpress.com/2014/02/21/ode-to-alexandria-where-it-all-began (accessed August 12, 2013).

Van Leuven, Dallin. 2013. "Colourful Challenges: Street Art from the Middle East." *InPEC Magazine,* October, https://inpec.wordpress.com (accessed December 10, 2013).

30

Celebrating Women's Day in Baghdad, the City of Men

ZAHRA ALI

I belong to an Iraqi family exiled in France since the early 1980s when my parents escaped the Ba'th dictatorship. In October 2010, at the age of twenty-four, I moved to Baghdad for the first time in my life to conduct fieldwork for my PhD dissertation on gender and women's political activism in post-invasion Iraq. For two years I lived in my grandmother's house in the al-Kazmyah area in Baghdad. During this time, I conducted semistructured interviews and participant observations among groups, organizations, and networks dedicated to defending women's rights, especially after the fall of the Ba'th regime in 2003. For two years, I accompanied Iraqi women's rights activists and participated in their activities, initiatives, and campaigns. I lived and shared their everyday life, moments of hope, difficulties, and challenges, as well as their many instances of loss and sadness.

Women's rights have been central to many debates among the new Iraqi elites that came to power after the invasion and occupation by the US-led forces. They are also central to the post-invasion Iraqi political scene, which is dominated by conservative Islamist parties who advance their own gender rhetoric of women as bearers of the "New Iraq." I argue that the "New Iraq" construct, in which the Sunni-Shi'a conflict has shaped the social and political spheres, enforces conservative gender rhetoric through institutionalized sectarianism. The sectarianization of gender issues in post-invasion Iraq is visible in the proposition made by the Shi'a Islamist parties in power to adopt a sectarian-based Personal Status Code, breaking with the unified and quite progressive law formulated in 1959. Proposed in the form of Decree 137 during a meeting of the Iraqi Governing Council in December 2003 by Abdel Aziz al-Hakim, head of the Supreme Islamic Council of Iraq (one of the main Shi'a Islamist parties in power since 2003), the proposition was not im-

Figure 30.1. Al-Rashid Street, central Baghdad, November 2011

mediately adopted. The decree states that the personal status laws of 1959 would be abolished and replaced by Sharia, administered by religious clerics according to the sect to which the relevant parties belonged. It is noteworthy that this decree was reformulated in the shape of Article 41 of the 2005 Iraqi Constitution under the banner "freedom of belief," which determined that "Iraqis are free in their commitment to their personal status according to their religions, sects, beliefs, or choices, and this shall be regulated by law" (Iraqi Constitution 2014). Moreover, the post-invasion context is characterized by the weakness of the new Iraqi state and its inability to provide basic services (water, electricity, and housing) for most Iraqis, and it is marked by generalized sectarian violence. In such a context, Iraqi women's rights activists are facing struggles on many fronts: dealing with the chaotic and violent everyday life, contending with the lack of basic services, and contesting the conservative and sectarian questioning of the unified Personal Status Code.

In this chapter, I present a short ethnographic account of the 2012 Women's Day celebration in Baghdad, held by a longstanding leftist women's rights organization, Rabitat al-Mara' al-'Iraqiah, and the Iraqi Women's League (IWL), which re-formed in 2003 after it was banned by the Ba'th regime for two decades. By providing this brief account, I seek to highlight the context, content, and political significance of the mobilization around women and gender issues in post-invasion Iraq.

Living in Baghdad in 2012 is itself a challenge. Since the invasion of Iraq by the US-led forces, everyday life is marked by violence, political chaos, and a lack of basic services. The difficulty, sometimes the impossibility, of moving around the city severely hinders mobilization efforts. Baghdad is fragmented by checkpoints and sectarian segregation. Concrete T-walls are manned at every corner by male soldiers who randomly stop and scrutinize the population. The capital's outdoor spaces are occupied by men, and armed male soldiers and police officers constitute the main figures of public space in the capital. The city is divided according to class, sect, and political affiliation; the Green Zone is for the nouveau riche political elite and the public is scattered into ethno-sectarian pockets of Sunnis, Shi'a, Kurds, and Christians. The fear of getting kidnapped, shot, or killed by explosions is constant. Public figures and well-known activists are prime targets of the armed gangs that have proliferated since the fall of the Ba'th regime. The political chaos is provoked by the institutionalization of sectarianism by the new political elite and its failure to build a government that provides basic services and assures security to its population. Baghdad has collapsed as a city, with destruction everywhere: no public maintenance, limited electricity and running water, and degraded public supplies. With chaos, disorder, and violence normalized, civil society activities become both a crucial necessity and an act of courage.

Women driving in the capital must pass through dozens of checkpoints every day to go to work. Each time, at every single checkpoint crossing, they have to lower their windows and salute the male soldiers before being allowed to pass. As many women activists have been the targets of violence, assassinations, or explosions, many organizations do not publicize the location of their offices or hang signs outside their doors. An activist from a well-known women's organization in Baghdad told me that she debated with herself every morning whether or not to hang a sign above the organization's new office. She finally decided against it after receiving death threats during the sectarian battle of 2006–2007. Many Iraqi women activists expressed feelings of being "stuck" in and "suffocated" by a city of walls, separations, and checkpoints in which armed men dominate the public sphere.

In March 2012, the Iraqi Parliament organized a meeting with representatives of various women's organizations. Among the guests was one of Iraq's leading figures, Hanaa Edwar, of the Iraqi Women Network (al-Shabaka), who spoke about the difficulties that women face in post-2003 Iraq. While this meeting took place in Baghdad's Green Zone, the Iraqi Women's League organized a gathering at Ferdaws Square, in the city center, for the public. I decided to attend the event at Ferdaws Square. Reaching the square was unusually easy. Attending an event in central Baghdad, as with Tahrir, Ferdaws, or Kerhamana Square, is often accompanied by fear of explosions or attacks. In fact, many Iraqi women activists told me that they had each passed through a place in which an explosion detonated minutes later. At Ferdaws Square that day, at least a hundred people gathered, surrounded by the Iraqi army and a tank that was posted at the entrance of the square. The police were managing traffic, stopping and checking everyone entering the square: men's bodies and pockets, and women's handbags. Soldiers were standing, acting as bodyguards to the speakers. Their presence decorated the square with their green, black, and brown uniforms, and appeared completely normal. It was a reminder that this moment of hope, emotion, and joy was temporary, and that, despite our endeavor to fully enjoy that moment, violence still surrounded us.

White plastic chairs were dispensed for the audience, facing the small podium where the speakers and performers would stand, just behind the middle of the square where Saddam's statue had been overturned nine years earlier. To our left was the beautiful 14-Ramadhan mosque with its blue mosaic dome. Its afternoon prayer calling imposed a moment of silence on the event, where women's rights activists, unionists, parliamentarians, and poets followed one another in delivering speeches. Intermission included Iraqi *'ahazich* performance by middle-aged ladies, wearing the traditional black *abaya* and singing such slogans as, "Let her practice her rights" or "Where is our portion of the oil? Listen oh Hajji." We laughed, sang with the performers, and cried at the beautiful poetry commemorating Baghdad's glory and the unity of Iraqis.

Figure 30.2. Gathering of the Iraqi Women's League in Ferdaws Square to celebrate Women's Day, March 2012

I joined the Iraqi Women's League (IWL) activists in distributing "Social Justice" flyers, water, and sweets and got seated next to an elegant woman in her late thirties. From her, I learned how the IWL had stepped up to help her when she lost her husband in 2006 due to sectarian violence. She had been surviving, just barely, on the 150,000 Iraqi dinars (less than a hundred dollars) monthly pension she received from the state because of her status as a widow. An unemployed mother of three, she said, "Really the government is doing nothing for women like me, for millions of Iraqi women like me. But today, we came to celebrate Iraqi women, all Iraqi women."

Although I was not in Baghdad in 2015 to celebrate and observe Women's Day with the activists of the IWL, I often think of their gathering in Kerhmanah Square, holding signs demanding a civil and unified Personal Status Code, the preservation of the progressive gains of the past, and the abolition of discriminatory laws. More recently, in the context of parliamentary elections, the Iraqi justice minister, Hassan al-Shammari, a member of Ayatollah Muhammed al-Ya'qoobi's al-Fazila

Party, declared that he is preparing a Sharia-based Personal Status Code, the Jaafari Law. Again, the main argument for this change revolves around "freedom of belief." The race for power between the different Shi'a political parties is being played out in gender and family matters, as it is clear that al-Fazila wants to put its mark on Iraqi political life and establish itself as a Shi'a *mazhabi* party. For the Shi'a Islamist political leadership, the Personal Status Code is certainly an opportunity to demonstrate revival and strength, as well as affirm power for Shi'a Islam, whose communities had been viewed with suspicion and distrust over the preceding decades. For Shi'a Islamists, Article 41 formally sanctions their beliefs, marking the end of the era of repression and hidden practice.

Several civil society networks composed of many Iraqi women activists launched a campaign of public intellectuals, activists, representatives of nonsectarian political parties, and religious figures. The campaign against the sectarian Personal Status Code criticized the sectarian dimension of this proposed law, pointing out how it attempts to reinstitute Decree 137 and Article 41 of the constitution, which was introduced by Shi'a Islamists in 2003 and 2005. These proposals were already contested by opponents of sectarianism. Women's rights activists tried to raise awareness both inside and outside the country, engaging international NGOs and media, and focusing on how marriage age (*Sin al-balagha*) is determined by the Jaafari Law that would have allowed girls as young as nine to get married. Such a law would have been a significant setback to the current legislation, which, although not perfect, was progressive in regards to women's rights.

While it is difficult to mobilize as Baghdad is burning again under the recurring sectarian crisis, activists are not giving up. They persevere in a city where public and private spheres are divided according to sectarian affiliations, and leaving the safety of the home has become difficult for women, as they have to endure the gaze of male military control at every corner. Given that basic human needs such as access to running water, electricity, proper housing, and security are not fulfilled, fighting for the preservation of a unified Personal Status Code is important to these women.

Increased conservatism driven by sectarian Islamist parties brought to power by the US-led military invasion and occupation, alongside the militarization of the society with its celebration of the figure of armed men, heavily impacts gender issues and the concrete reality of women's political activism. Sectarianism does not only affect statehood and nationhood; it is also in such a context deeply gendered. With the invasion of the Islamic State in the north of Iraq in June 2014, which threw the country into extreme sectarian tensions and violence, one can predict that women's issues will continue to be played out at the core of sectarian and ethnic conflicts against the backdrop of militarization and religious conservatism.

BIBLIOGRAPHY
Iraqi Constitution. 2014. Permanent Mission of Iraq to the United Nations in New York, November, https://iraqmission.us.

31

Waiting for the Revolution

Women's Perceptions from Upper and Lower Rural Egypt

LORENZO KAMEL AND MAHA EZZAT ELKHOLY

While covering Egypt's uprisings, media outlets mainly focused on transmitting developments in major cities but often left out events that they considered "too local." A clear, but not unique, example is the uprising that took place in Qasr Al Basel (Adly 2011) a few weeks after former president Hosni Mubarak's resignation. Although it was considered a major event for the rural Fayoum governorate, it attracted little to no attention outside Upper Egypt. Many people in Fayoum protested, demanding redistribution of resources (such as land and water) and reparations to the marginalized classes. As in Cairo, women in Fayoum participated in these historic events. Of the fifty marches for women's rights that took place in Egypt in 2012, two events organized at the beginning of July 2012 were particularly symbolic: the Nasr City's Myself campaign focused on denouncing sexual abuses, and the Safe Tahrir for Women protest included thousands of women who gathered to shame "sexual terrorists" by spray painting those caught harassing women. Rural women's participation in these events was symbolic of much broader support for women's rights. Shrouk Gamil, a teacher at Cairo's Arabeya Center, who lost her brother in the demonstrations of July 2013, explains, "Most of the rural communities showed on many occasions a sense of solidarity with Tahrir Square, but they were often unable to participate because they could not afford public transportation, or, in many other cases, they were obliged to look after their houses" (interview with the authors, Cairo, December 12, 2012). Notwithstanding these and other obstacles, the interviews contained in this chapter, carried out mainly in Egyptian villages and with local activists between December 2012 and October 2013, support our main finding: the common perception that the 2011 Egyptian "revolution" did not pass by the countryside is based on a simplistic way of approaching the local reality.

Women's Activism in Upper Egypt and the Delta

In this chapter we argue that women tend to see change beyond the protest arena and tackle the widespread assumption that women from rural areas played a passive role in the 2011 Egyptian "revolution." We largely base our conclusions on empirical evidence such as semistructured interviews, informal talks, reviews of documents, social contact, and direct observations. As we shall see, Egypt's rural women do not represent in any way a homogeneous group, but their growing indoor and outdoor activism has a common goal: to ignite a cultural and social revolution. In this context it is important to stress that women's activism and engagement in resistance and reform is not a phenomenon that should be assessed only on the basis of public campaigns, or the presence of women in public places. The "reform process" is taking place first and foremost inside the houses of millions of Egyptian women, including, and perhaps especially, the ones residing on the "front line": rural Upper Egypt. James C. Scott would define their attitudes and actions as "everyday forms of resistance" that often "make no headlines" (Scott 1986, 8).

Upper Egypt and Delta women, who took to the streets in large numbers during the June 30, 2013, uprisings, believed that their struggle was not over. Poverty, in fact, is more concentrated in Upper Egypt than in Lower Egypt, in rural areas than in urban ones, and among women than among men. Egypt has one of the lowest female labor participation rates in the world and ranks 120 out of 128 states in terms of gender gap (UNDP 2010). Thus, women's activism in Upper Egypt bears a special meaning as women's empowerment continues to be paramount to improving the cultural, social, and political future of the ongoing and incomplete "Arab Spring."

Israa Said Thabet, a twenty-six-year-old mother of two who lives in Asyut, argues that women's activism must take into account women's growing awareness of their rights and agency: "Before the [2011] revolution most of the women were ignorant about anything that was happening in the country. After January 2011 they increasingly started to follow the news and to express their political views." Watching the revolution on the street urged women to turn the political revolution into a cultural and moral one: "We are witnessing a revolution against every traditional aspect. We are no more silent about abuses. Many women are taking actions, when necessary, against their husbands. I also noted an increasing number of divorces in our area. We still have a long journey ahead, but we are becoming increasingly aware that there is no more such a thing as 'a weak woman'" (interview with the authors, Asyut, June 4, 2013).

Women's increased self-awareness and attempts to break away from deeply rooted norms are issues that we registered in most of our field interviews. In our interviews with over ten women activist in 2013, we found that a growing number of people, in rural and urban Egypt, are becoming increasingly aware that the process of social and cultural change is much more complex than filling up squares and demanding the departure of a government.

Despite participating in protests, Egyptian women did not experience practical improvements on the ground. Although women's financial contributions to the household (due to employment) and their involvement in political activism were increasing, they did not enjoy greater power or more rights. In fact, harmful aspects of patriarchy, which have been increasing over the past few years, have in some contexts worsened (Bibars 2001, 155), while a new, more rigid patriarchal structure emerged, in which strong women were often discredited and victimized. Samah Anwar, a twenty-four-year-old woman from the outskirt of Tahta (Sohag Governorate) claims that women's suffering is increasing and that "their conditions were indeed better before the revolution." Because of their association with the former regime, "The charitable organizations established by Suzanne Mubarak [that] were perhaps not so big or effective, but . . . at least able to offer some opportunities" became immediately censured (interview with the authors, Tahta, June 10, 2013). After the end of Mubarak's regime, "These organizations almost disappeared. People started to look at them as remnants of the past regime." Samah laments, "I am afraid to dream of a better future and I do not have trust in anything that is currently happening in this country."

This powerful fear, which is common, constitutes a hindrance in the path toward further participation in indoor and outdoor activism. Huda

Saber, a twenty-four-year-old woman from the Sohag Governorate, admits that despite having female friends involved in activism, she did not participate in any demonstration because she feared the thugs' harassment that usually takes place in such gatherings. It would be naive to overlook the drastic increase in crime since Hosni Mubarak was forced out of power. It is enough to mention that due to continuous assaults and gang rapes of women, Tahrir Square, which had once attracted electrified crowds, has become a no-go zone for women, especially after sunset. Huda is pessimistic about the future: "The main change that I can currently see is related to the deterioration of security that now is extremely bad" (interview with the authors, Sohag, June 4, 2013). Yet, the pressure exerted on women remains constant, as Huda explains: "In Upper Egypt, more than in other parts of the country, the reputation of women is always under question." They have become an easy and vulnerable target.

Women's acceptance of this type of pressure is very closely linked to their low educational attainment and confinement to the home (UNDP 2010). Lower-class men in Upper Egypt often prefer to marry uneducated women, who do not interact with strange males, over women who attend secondary schools or work. Likewise, some parents from poor rural areas are still loath to obtain birth certificates for their daughters because they do not see them as worthy of the lengthy process or expect them to interact in the public sphere. As a result, many young women are deprived of public health services and are unable to attend school. This dramatic trend, however, is slowly changing, and, thanks to UN women's initiatives and powerful projects such as *Rising Voices*,[1] local families are becoming increasingly aware of the damages caused by these choices. Women too are changing their attitudes, according to Eman Abd Al-Aziz, a twenty-four-year-old woman residing near Manfalut (Asyut Governorate): "Here in Asyut an increasing number of girls study medicine or pharmacy and they are strongly committed students that frequently obtain very high grades" (interview with the authors, Manfalut, June 9, 2013). Despite the numerous difficulties, Eman believes that these women will persist in their resistance: "Women in Upper Egypt are very patient and never surrender to the status quo. Their tenacity and determination represent powerful weapons."

Women's Resistance in Rural Lower Egypt

In rural Lower Egypt, engagement in resistance and activism is, to a certain extent, easier than in Upper Egypt. The relatively short distance to Cairo guarantees more opportunities and easier access to information. During the "utopian eighteen days," as Ahmad Kadri called it, of January 2011, rural communities in Lower Egypt were quick to mobilize with a growing number of initiatives and to create local councils to fill the security vacuum that threatened to take over the country.

Local women quickly learned how "resistance" could have impacted their lives. Reham Mohy, a twenty-three-year-old woman from Kafr Algemal, shares that "during the revolution there was an unusual respect for women. People looked at women not only as mothers, daughters, or sisters, but also as persons fully capable of sharing the magic feeling of the revolution. This also helps to explain why there were no harassments during those eighteen days" (interview with the authors, Kafr Algemal, April 10, 2013).

Women redefined resistance to mean standing up against all social and cultural restraints, Eman Awad, a twenty-three-year-old woman from rural Lower Egypt, confirms, "The first thing that comes up to my mind when I hear the word 'resistance' is the struggle against the rules imposed by our society, against flawed ideas and customs, but most of all against our parents' mentality and the one of most of the people of their generation" (interview with the authors, Giza, July 12, 2013). Eman feels that she gives voice to an entire generation of women who were denied such privilege: "My relatives in the countryside only live to get married, produce babies and then to die. Freedom, for Egyptian women, is in most cases just an empty word."

She is strongly determined to fight for her rights, and believes that the fruits of her efforts will be seen in the future: "In the era of Internet and the social networks, we have the duty to reach any Egyptian woman, especially those in the countryside. We have to explain to each of them that divorcing from a violent husband is not the end of the world. But it will take time. In a few decades, women's conditions will improve and finally there will be a new generation fully aware that women are independent human beings and that they don't belong to anyone, except to themselves."

Like many women in Central and Lower Egypt, Eman participated in a number of protests in January 2011. as well as in June 2013. Most of them took place in Cairo, either on the Six-October Bridge or in front of the Law Syndicate building. Overcoming her fear of violating social norms, she admits, "I felt the necessity to do something practical and not just sit and fear for the future of my country." Although they were viewed as two "revolutions," some Egyptians differentiate between the January 2011 and June 2013 uprisings. Eman believes that the first uprising was about freedom, justice, and dignity, while the second was about defending Egypt's unique identity from being totally taken over by the Muslim Brotherhood's conservative ideology: "The one in January 2011 was a revolution in which the whole people marched together united: a dream that has quickly evaporated. The second revolution, on the other hand, is mainly directed against one faction that works to erase the true face of our Egypt."

Quest for Social Justice

Several women were convinced that obtaining national independence was connected to achieving social justice. Dalia Yousif, a twenty-three-year-old woman from the Maadi suburb, agrees (interview with the authors, Maadi, July 15, 2013). She took part in and organized many initiatives before and during the two revolutions. She was part of the group Nazra for Feminist Studies, an organization inspired by the firm belief that feminism and gender are political and social issues that affect society, and she worked in Cairo with the teams Operation Anti–Sexual Harassment/Assault and Tahrir Bodyguards: "I noted many differences between the two revolutions, in terms of participation as well as motivations. Despite the differences, we, the women of Egypt, have tried to participate in every initiative alongside men, not against them, in the fight for national independence and social justice."

Many activists focused on raising rural women's awareness of their rights in relation to the role of religion in their society. Gender inequality in the Muslim world and Egypt is widely blamed on Islamic ideology and teaching (Abdel Kader 1987). Because Islamic interpretations of gender equality have not changed since the seventh century, Fatima Mernissi posits that "in analyzing the condition of women in the Muslim countries it must never be forgotten that ideologically the year 622 still lives in the formulation of future strategies" (1987, 84). However, women's status in Egypt, and in the Eastern Mediterranean area, cannot be attributed to the presumed intrinsic properties of religion. Such conceptions are facile (Shukri 1999, 3) and obscure the fact that Islam is neither more nor less patriarchal than other major religions—all of which idolize women as mothers and wives (Moghadam 2003, 5). Moreover, using a singular term to refer to Islam obscures the fact that more than a billion people practice and interpret "Islams" differently (al-Azmeh 1996). Indeed, Om Zyad, a thirty-year-old mother of three children from Qaha, claims that "the real issue is not related to your religious background. It is a matter of who surrounds you, and if these persons encourage you or push you back. Yet you need to be sure of your dreams if you want to realize them" (interview with the authors, Qaha, March 9, 2013). Likewise, Dalia Yousif stresses that it is a priority to provide women with "a broader awareness of their rights as well as of the campaigns and the activities that are currently taking place in many villages. Nowadays I am also more aware of my rights." Awareness and education, she points out, "will play a vital role in defusing the effects of ignorance and religious fundamentalism."

Paradoxically, divorce is increasingly becoming a potential expression of resistance. In Lower Egypt as well as Upper Egypt, the most symbolic but also difficult face of resistance is closely connected to private indoor struggles. Doaa Salah, a twenty-three-year-old mother from Sandibis (Qalyubia Governorate), represents in this respect another powerful example. She got married after finishing high school, but soon after her divorce, she plunged into a fierce struggle against old traditions that stem from "one-sided rules" (interview with the authors, Sendibis, June 16, 2013). In these areas, arbitrary divorce is often a form of social violence against women. It is not uncommon that a husband divorces his wife without her knowledge, or for reasons not permitted under Islamic Sharia. Doaa represents a different but not isolated case: she decided to divorce in order to regain her freedom. "I totally disliked," she claimed, "the cultural impositions and the routine imposed on me by this society. More than everything, I continue to wonder why a married woman cannot work and have a normal life as it happens in the main cities and for virtually any men of this country." She commutes almost daily from

Sendibis to Cairo, spending many hours in traffic. She pointed out how people in her village consider her taboo. "Men," she noted, "treat me and the other divorced women as if we were public properties." Despite the huge pressure exerted by her family and community, she is determined to continue to fight for her rights. "I chose what I wanted," she concluded with pride: "I am a free woman."

Conclusion

Rural areas in Lower and Upper Egypt have been neglected for decades, and are therefore viewed as "static" and not worthy of much attention, even today. This "static perception" represents, mutatis mutandis, an updated version of what happened in many national uprisings of the past: Shafiqa bint Muhammad, Aisha bint Umar, Hamida bint Khalil, and many other women who paid with their lives for their commitment in the Egyptian revolution of 1919 have been largely ignored by historians until the relatively recent past (Shaarawi 1986, 118). Struggling against these prejudices, Egypt's rural women continue to move forward. Rural women do not represent in any way a homogeneous group. Still, they are, in many ways and forms, taking part in a process of growing awareness that aims at finding alternative ways of "resisting." Uprisings, in fact, are not the only means of achieving change. Improved education, cultural activism, and creating economic opportunities and public spaces for women's participation do not have immediate effects. But in the long term and thanks to deeper shifts, they have better chances to tarnish the "*hogra* attitude," which condones and propagates discrimination, especially against women.

NOTE

1 *Rising Voices* is a film series on education by UNICEF. The documentary films focus on personal stories of students at schools that implemented particular policies to ensure the best interests of the children.

BIBLIOGRAPHY

Abdel Kader, Soha. 1987. *Egyptian Women in a Changing Society, 1899–1987*. Boulder, CO: Rienner.

Adly, Amr. 2011. "Ela Ay Muaskar Yandam Al Falahon?" *Shorouk News*, September 17, http://www.shorouknews.com (accessed July 2, 2013).

Al-Azmeh, Aziz. 1996. *Islams and Modernities*. London: Verso.

Bibars, Iman. 2001. *Victims and Heroines: Women, Welfare, and the Egyptian State*. New York: Zed.

Mernissi, Fatima. 1987. *Beyond the Veil*. Bloomington: Indiana University Press.

Moghadam, Valentine. 2003. *Modernizing Women: Gender and Social Change in the Middle East*. Boulder, CO: Rienner.

Pound, Ezra, and Clifford Hugh Douglas. 1935. *The Social Credit Pamphleteer*. London: Stanley Nott.

Scott, James C. 1986. *Weapons of the Weak: Everyday Forms of Peasant Resistance*. New Haven, CT: Yale University Press.

Shaarawi, Huda. 1986. *Harem Years: The Memoirs of an Egyptian Feminist (1879–1924)*. New York: Feminist Press.

Shukri, Shirin J. A. 1999. *Social Changes and Women in the Middle East*. Aldershot, UK: Ashgate.

UNDP. 2010. "Egypt Human Development Report 2010." Cairo: Institute of National Planning, http://hdr.undp.org (accessed July 19, 2013).

32

New Media/New Feminism(s)

The Lebanese Women's Movement Online and Offline

NELIA HYNDMAN-RIZK

We have built our own alternative [online] Beirut, and it's a
beautiful Beirut.
—Nasawiya Activist, May 2012

Since the start of the Arab Spring in 2011, the upsurge in citizens' rights
campaigns across the Middle East have highlighted the role of women
among the new social movements and revived feminist scholarly debate
over the relationship between citizens' rights and women's rights in processes of social transformation. While the critical role of new media
technologies in facilitating new social movements has been widely
debated, fewer studies have collected empirical data on online campaigns in the Arab uprisings or asked activists themselves their views on
the efficacy of online versus offline modes of social mobilization. This
chapter contributes to the conversation by comparing online and offline
women's rights activism in Lebanon and examines two campaigns that
employ both modes of social mobilization. The chapter asks whether
new media technology has enabled the Lebanese women's movement
to enter a new phase in its development. Through analyzing the online/
offline efforts to promote the recognition of civil marriages in 2013 (Aziz
2013) and a law that criminalizes domestic violence in 2014 (AFP 2014),
I argue that the iterative dynamism between the two modes of activism
has led to significant reforms in women's rights despite Lebanon's state
of political paralysis.

Methodology

This chapter uses mixed methods research design and draws on qualitative and quantitative research strategies, including interviews and
surveys. I interviewed women across the spectrum of Lebanese women's
organizations, exploring key issues related to digital media technologies,
including use patterns, consumption, and digital divide issues, as well as
the application of digital media technology for women's activism. I also
distributed through e-mail and Facebook an online survey on women's
rights activism and social media use in Lebanon. With 110 responses, I
collected statistical data on online activism and on activists' ranking of
the most pressing women's rights issues in Lebanon today.

New Media, the Arab Spring, and Women

"New media" is a "catchall phrase used to distinguish digital media forms
from old media, such as newspapers, magazines, radio, and television"
(Hirst and Harrison 2007, 234), whereas "social media" refers to digital
media—either web or mobile based—that integrate telecommunications
and social interaction and are based on web technologies that allow the
creation and exchange of user-generated content (UGC), including
Skype, Facebook, Twitter, MSN, YouTube, LinkedIn, and WhatsApp, to
name a few (Fisher 2009).

While some scholars have linked the digital revolution and the process
of democratization (Noueihed and Warren 2012, 44–45), authoritarian
and democratic regimes alike are sensitive to the power of social media
and have attempted to regulate it, to control it, or even to shut down the
Internet. Other scholars even questioned whether social media technology was primarily responsible for bringing about the Arab uprisings.
While Barkawi (2011) argues that revolutions are caused by human agency,
not new media technologies per se, Perry (2011) suggests that though
ideas spark revolutions, social media technologies help sustain them by
accelerating the circulation of revolutionary ideas, thus circumventing
censorship. Contrary to the technological determinism thesis (Hirst and
Harrison 2007), Howard and Hussain (2013, 48–49) found that information infrastructure, especially the mobile phone, was central to the success
of the Arab Spring and caution for a nuanced approach (2013, 50).

If the role of technology in the success of the new social movements has been a contentious issue, so has the role of women. Indeed, the Arab Spring has revived feminist debates over the relationship between campaigns for citizens' rights and campaigns for women's rights and how each facilitates the other (Cooke 1994–1995). Mohanty (2011) calls for further research into the role of women in the Arab Spring, while Wolf (2011) reminds us that throughout history, periods of uprisings and campaigns for civil rights have been followed by campaigns for women's rights, as with the abolitionist and suffrage movements in the United States during the nineteenth century.

The Case of the Lebanese Women's Movement

The first women's organizations in the Arab world and in what is now Lebanon were founded in the early 1900s (Arenfeldt and Al-Hassan Golley 2012, 13), and women's organizations played a significant role in the Lebanese decolonization movement (Stephan 2012, 114). A second wave of women's rights activism emerged following independence in 1943, as part of the women's charitable associations of the post–World War II era, which were firmly part of the *haute bourgeoisie* and were embedded in the sectarian family structure of Lebanese society (Stephan 2012, 114). This wave of feminist activists focused on women's suffrage, the right to female mobility, and female reproductive rights and access to contraception. Stephan characterizes their approach to feminism as "family feminism," which worked within the kinship structure of Lebanese society and often involved wives working in conjunction with their husbands (2010, 535). The third wave of the Lebanese women's movement emerged from the ashes of the Civil War in 1990. The women's movement flowered, therefore, after the United Nations International Women's Conference in Beijing in 1995 (UN Women n.d.), which led to the ratification of CEDAW, the Convention for the Elimination of All Forms Discrimination against Women (UN Women n.d.), by Lebanon in 1996 (Stephan 2010, 539). In this period, organizations like KAFA (Enough Violence Against Women) were first formed. These women's rights organizations have links to international agencies, such as the United Nations and its Millennium Development Goals, which include gender mainstreaming and equality as measures of human development, but which are translated into the local context, through women's rights organizations on the ground (Sabat 2015).

In 2010, however, a fourth wave (Stephan 2014) of younger, technologically savvy women's rights activists emerged in Lebanon, led by the organization Nasawiya, an online feminist collective. Naber and Zaatari (2014) traced the nascent emergence of Nasawiya and the new wave of activists in their research on the impact of the 2006 Israeli invasion of Lebanon on feminist and LGBTQ activism. They argue, though, that the state of emergency imposed by the war foreclosed activism, while saving lives, not challenging sexualities, became the priority, as patriarchal social structures were accentuated in the context of war and imperialism (96). But this was only a pause, and the state of emergency that has become the new normal (Hermez 2011) did not foreclose the development of a new and more radical wave of Lebanese feminism, as the founder of Nasawiya explains: "This period 2010 to 2011 is a new wave of Lebanese feminism. I think it's been changing so much, it is becoming a lot more focused on change, real change. Before 2010 the women's movement never talked about sectarianism. But now, it is becoming a lot clearer that we are against the sectarian system, and the warlords" (interview, Beirut, May 2012).

This new wave of feminist activists in Lebanon transcended the malaise of the secular Left in Lebanon, which struggled to develop a new politics in the aftermath of the decline of the Soviet Union, the rise of the Islamic resistance, and the emergence of the NGO agenda (Hermez 2011). Most importantly, new wave activists recognize the intersectional relationship between women's rights and secular citizenship rights in Lebanon as their core project. As I will argue, new media provided the platform for the development of a more radical feminist critique of Lebanese state and society, which first gained momentum ahead of the official start of the Arab Spring. A distinctive Lebanese feminism is being articulated, therefore, that defines itself as being both feminist and antisectarian. In the online survey I conducted, I asked respondents whether Lebanese feminism could be classified as liberal, socialist, radical, or faith based. The majority of respondents felt that none of these classical divisions from Western feminisms applied to Lebanese feminism. Seventy-three percent of the 110 respondents identified as feminist

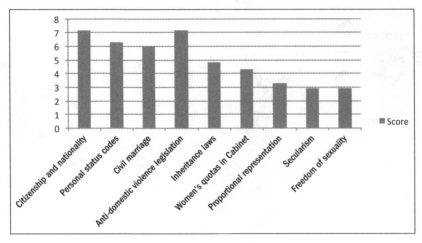

Figure 32.1. Ranking of the most important women's rights issues in Lebanon

and favored an intersectional approach that recognizes the intertwined nature of the woman question in Lebanon. Consequently, in ranking the most important women's rights issues in Lebanon, respondents identified the top four issues as citizenship and nationality rights, followed by anti–domestic violence legislation, personal status codes, and civil marriage (see figure 32.1).

In explaining their views on why Lebanese women need feminism, the Nasawiya feminist collective states on its website that "we're not really Lebanese citizens; we're just the daughters of Lebanese men. Because if we really did possess a Lebanese citizenship, we'd be able to pass our nationality to our husbands and children; but we can't" (Nasawiya 2012). This explanation sums up the core of the gendered citizenship puzzle in Lebanon. Without full citizenship rights, Lebanese women do not belong to the nation, and as long as the nation denies women their full citizenship rights, Lebanon will remain a nation divided by sectarianism. But how should the gendered citizenship puzzle be resolved?

Strategies for Online Activism

The most important new campaign strategy utilized by the new wave of feminist activists in Lebanon is the extensive application of new media technologies, both mobile and web based. In the survey, activists

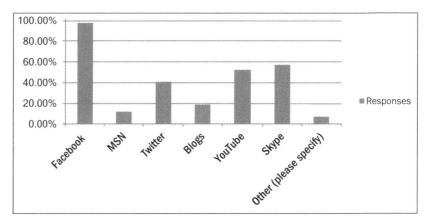

Figure 32.2. The use of social media

reported using smartphones at 45 percent and the computer at 55 percent for their online communication activities. The iPhone accounted for 57 percent of smartphone users, Windows and androids 26 percent, Blackberries only 17 percent. The high cost of home-based Internet plans and their slow speed has, therefore, led to the increasing reliance on mobile smartphone technology for activism.

The other key finding regarding use patterns of online media is that English is by far the dominant online language among respondents, with 79 percent reporting using English and only 15 percent reporting using Arabic and a small 6 percent reporting using French. English, therefore, is the dominant language of the Internet and in Lebanon, especially among the younger generation of women's rights activists.

The most popular form of social media is Facebook, according to the online survey (see figure 32.2), because it is free, is unregulated, rivals traditional media, and has a broad potential audience in Lebanon and abroad, as the founder of Nasawiya explains: "We cannot pay for traditional media, or billboards, or TV ads, or radio ads, or magazine ads, etc. But social media is free. And all the traditional media are following us to social media. We started using social media because we didn't have another choice" (interview, Beirut, May 2012).

This activist felt that the most important aspect of the online campaign is its democratizing potential to provide open access to information. That is, if it is "online," it is published, read, and distributed and the ideas are shared, and this is a threat to the mainstream media.

As for the technology and social change debate, is human agency or technology the driving force behind social change, according to online activists themselves? The founder of Nasawiya puts forward her view on this debate and argues that new media technologies are just a new tool to build mobilization for social change: "I think it would be naïve to think that social media brings about social change, in the same way a telephone cannot bring about social change or a microwave. These are tools. They can support you immensely, but in different ways. You have to have work on the ground, so social change would manifest" (interview, Beirut, May 2012).

The critical link, as this interview demonstrates, is that the online and offline campaign has to be synchronized with and materialized in social action on the ground, in the form of street demonstrations and, ultimately, legislative change. In fact, the survey supports this view, with 97 percent of respondents supporting the proposition that online campaigns need to be followed up with action on the ground, though 46 percent thought that online campaigns were very successful and another 45 percent thought they were moderately successful.

From Online to Offline Activism: Two Key Campaigns

Building on these findings, I argue that the ability to use the online sphere to promote real change in the offline sphere, and the iterative movement between the two, are crucial to the success of the new wave of feminist activism in Lebanon. The recursive relationship between online and offline social movements and their synchronization and mobilization with new movements has also been noted by Turner (2013, 380). In the case of Lebanon, online activism has been a particularly significant tool to overcome the perennial security problems that foreclosed the possibilities for activism in the past (Hermez 2011). Hence, the iterative movement between online and offline activism enables a strategic movement forward, despite the prevailing circumstances. If conditions on the ground do not permit offline activism, due to security reasons, for example, activism can continue online and then return to the streets when the conditions improve.

The success of two key online and offline women's rights campaigns in Lebanon in 2013–2014 are cases in point. Firstly, the recognition of Lebanon's first civil marriage followed years of offline and online campaigns by a wide range of women's rights organizations that culminated in a series of protests in downtown Beirut. Civil marriage in Lebanon refers to a marriage contracted outside of a religious court and often involves a couple from different religious sects. Until 2013, civil marriages have only been recognized if they are contracted outside of Lebanon, usually in Cyprus, where there is a civil marriage tourism industry servicing Lebanon, but a recent civil marriage contracted inside of Lebanon ("Sectarian Shackles" 2013) has reignited the national debate ("A New Lebanon" 2013). While the president supported the move, the prime minister and prominent religious clerics, including the then grand mufti of Lebanon, Mohammed Rashid Qabbani, opposed it, with Qabbani issuing a religious edict (*fatwa*) that any Muslim politicians and supporters of the legislation would be declared apostates. In counterpoint, protesters in support of civil marriage carrying signs at a protest in downtown Beirut responded, "Civil marriage, not civil war" (Maroun 2013).

There is a broader sentiment that Lebanon's family law system needs reform, as noted in the online survey findings, including the introduction of a unified civil status code and civil marriage, to advance women's rights in Lebanon. This interview with a Maronite Catholic, who undertook a civil marriage with his partner, who is a Sunni Muslim, explains the broader sentiment on why civil marriage is important for women's rights in Lebanon: "I had a civil marriage for two reasons, the first reason is ideological—I believe in the separation of state and church. The second reason is that I believe that religious institutions are short in giving rights to children and their mothers. It is important, because the laws that govern a relationship between men and women when you get into a civil marriage are equalizing the rights of men and women. I think it will be beneficial for the whole judicial system" (interview, Beirut, November 2013).

However, the first civil marriage contracted on Lebanese soil by two Lebanese citizens was the final push that galvanized the national debate in Lebanon on the issue of civil marriage, as both a civil rights and women's rights issue. The marriage was contracted using the French civil law LR60, from the mandate period, and received extensive media coverage in Lebanon and across the Arab world. In this interview with a civil marriage couple, in which one is Sunni and the other is Shi'ite, the wife explains her views on the advantages of civil marriage for Lebanon:

> Firstly, civil marriage is a door to communicate with the other sect. Actually we have married from the same religion. . . . First if we are going to talk of the sectarian regime, it opens the way among people to talk more about the other, to live together, and sometimes maybe to live in different regions in Lebanon. Civil marriage allows you to see Lebanon as all yours, not just a part of it and, especially in our case, when you want to go for civil marriage you have to drop your sect from the ID. . . . [T]his will open more doors for you to be a real citizen. (interview, Beirut, November 2013)

With support from the president, the Ministry of the Interior recognized the first civil marriage contracted on Lebanese soil on April 25, 2013 (Aziz 2013). Since then, fifty civil marriages have taken place in Lebanon, but the minister of the interior, Machnouk, declined their registration in 2015, referring them to the civil court. Meanwhile, street rallies returned to the streets of Beirut in March and April 2015 to push for the recognition of civil marriage in Lebanon and the passing of a new civil marriage law (Obeid 2015). The recognition of Lebanon's first civil marriage in 2013 set the precedent for further change on this issue. However, Lebanon's first civil marriage couple moved to Sweden, due to the media publicity their case attracted, the continued opposition of religious leaders, and the government's decision, ultimately, not to recognize any further civil marriages (Sukkarieh 2018). The civil marriage debate continues and, no doubt, will be revisited, as demonstrated by a civil marriage in 2019 that also utilized the LR60 law (Chulov 2019).

The second case is the passing of Lebanon's anti–domestic violence legislation, Law 293, which followed years of online/offline advocacy by KAFA (Qiblawi 2014), which first introduced the draft law in 2010, with support from a wide range of other women's rights organizations in Lebanon, including Nasawiya (a feminist collective) and ABAAD (Dimensions: Resource Centre for Gender Equality). Following a year of inertia in Lebanese politics and the highly publicized murder of three Lebanese women in domestic violence cases, one activist and respondent to the online survey describes the operation of the online campaign: "During the last two months we were monitoring regular news about gender-based violence and women's rights violations, and posting them along with pictures and videos, invitations to events, and articles on Facebook."

Meanwhile, she went on to describe how other activists and NGOs working on this issue were informed about the campaign by building a sustainable relationship through social media, with fifteen thousand people viewing her posts on Facebook and three thousand people sharing and liking the posts. Additionally, she sent personalized messages through an e-mail mailing list to twelve thousand members. Offline, a record number of protesters attended the International Women's Day demonstration on March 8, 2014, in downtown Beirut (Al Saadi 2014), which placed pressure on lawmakers at the first sitting of the newly formed cabinet to pass the law.

Despite the decision to remove the marital rape provision, a move heavily criticized by ABAAD and Nasawiya activists (AFP 2014), the law was passed as the first act of the new Lebanese government on April 1, 2014. The legislation was also criticized by human rights organizations for failing to address the family law question, including women's divorce and child custody rights, which make leaving a violent relationship more difficult (Human Rights Watch 2014). A year later, activists reflected that the law, while a first step, still has a way to go before it is fully implemented (Sidahmed 2015). Nonetheless, following the introduction of Law 293, several violent male spouses have been arrested and tried.

Conclusion

This chapter explored the utilization of new media technologies during the fourth wave of the Lebanese women's movement (Stephan 2014), which has led to a new phase of heightened activism. Online strategies have enabled women's rights activists to reach a wider audience for free by self-publishing and circulating their ideas, which diverts the flow of information from traditional media to new media sources, while offline strategies have seen record street demonstrations in Lebanon, which resulted in legislative change. The renewed push for the advancement of women's rights in Lebanon draws on an intersectional approach, which links women's rights and civil rights, as evidenced by two key campaigns:

the recognition of Lebanon's first civil marriage in April 2013 and the passing of Domestic Violence Law No. 293 in April 2014. The success of the two campaigns demonstrates how the iterative movement between the online/offline modes of activism has enabled women's rights activists to bring about legislative change despite the country's broader state of political paralysis.

Acknowledgment

The author wishes to acknowledge the contribution of the research assistants, Sara Al Mokdad and Sibel Atasayi, who worked on this project.

BIBLIOGRAPHY

AFP. 2014. "Lebanon Passes Law against Domestic Violence." Yahoo News Maktoob, April 1, https://en-maktoob.news.yahoo.com (accessed August 13, 2015).

Al Saadi, Yazan. 2014. "Thousands Renew Fight against Patriarchy on International Women's Day." *Al Akhbar*, March 8, http://english.al-akhbar.com (accessed August 13, 2015).

Arenfeldt, Purnille, and Nawar Al-Hassan Golley. 2012. "Arab Women's Movements: Developments, Priorities, and Challenges." In *Mapping Arab Women's Movements: A Century of Transformation from Within*, ed. Purnille Arendfelt and Nawar Al-Hassan Golley, 1–7. Cairo: American University in Cairo Press.

Aziz, Jean. 2013. "Lebanon's First Civil Marriage a Sign of Change." Al Monitor, April 28, http://www.al-monitor.com (accessed August 13, 2015).

Barkawi, Tarak. 2011. "The Globalisation of Revolution." Al Jazeera, March 21, https://www.aljazeera.com, accessed October 25, 2019.

Bryman, Alan. 2008. *Social Research Methods*. Oxford: Oxford University Press.

Cooke, Miriam. 1994–1995. "Arab Women Arab Wars." *Cultural Critique* 29: 5–29.

Chulov, Martin. 2019. "Society Couple Said 'I Do'—but Lebanon Won't Accept That They Are Married." *Guardian*, August 25, https://www.theguardian.com, accessed October 25, 2019.

Fisher, Ken. 2009. "Social Media versus Social Technology: Refining Definitions." *Web 2.0 Blog,* April, http://www.Web2oblog.Org/2009/01/04/Social-Media-Vs-Social-Technology (accessed May 2, 2011).

Hermez, Sami. 2011. "Activism as Part-Time Activity: Searching for Commitment and Solidarity in Lebanon." *Cultural Dymamics* 23, no. 1: 41–55.

Hirst, Martin, and John Harrison. 2007. *Communication and New Media: From Broadcast to Narrowcast*. Oxford: Oxford University Press.

Howard, Philip N., and M. M Hussain. 2013. *Democracy's Fourth Wave? Digital Media and the Arab Spring*. Oxford: Oxford University Press.

Human Rights Watch. 2014. "Lebanon: Domestic Violence Law Good but Not Complete." April 3, https://www.hrw.org (accessed August 20, 2015).

Maroun, Bachara. 2013. "Place des Martyrs, le «oui» au mariage civil." *L'Orient le Jour*, February 5, http://www.lorientlejour.com (accessed August 13, 2015).

Mohanty, Chandra T. 2011. Foreword to *Transnational Borderlands in Women's Global Networks*, ed. C. Roman-Odio and M. Sierra. London: Palgrave Macmillan.

Naber, Nadine, and Zeina Zaatari. 2014. "Reframing the War on Terror: Feminist and Lesbian, Gay, Bisexual, Transgender, and Queer (LGBTQ) Activism in the Context of the 2006 Israeli Invasion of Lebanon." *Cultural Dynamics* 26, no. 1: 91–111. https://doi.org/10.1177/0921374013510803.

Nasawiya. 2012. "What Is Feminism?" http://www.nasawiya.org (accessed August 13, 2015).

"A New Lebanon." 2013. Editorial, *Daily Star*, January 21, http://www.dailystar.com.lb (accessed August 13, 2015).

Noueihed, Lin, and Alex Warren. 2012. *The Battle for the Arab Spring: Revolution, Counter-Revolution, and the Making of a New Era*. New Haven, CT: Yale University Press.

Obeid, Ghinwa. 2015. "Civil Marriage Activists to Revive Protests." *Daily Star*, April 17, http://www.dailystar.com.lb (accessed August 19, 2015).

Perry, Mark. 2011. "Ideas Kindle the Fire of Revolution, Not the Internet." *Daily Star*, February 21, http://www.dailystar.com.lb (accessed November 17, 2011).

Qiblawi, Tamara. 2014. "Women Decry Lebanon's Domestic Violence Law." Al Jazeera, April 15, http://www.aljazeera.com (accessed August 13, 2015).

Sabat, Rita. 2015. "Campaigns for Gender Equality in the Family." In *In Line with the Divine: The Struggle for Gender Equality in Lebanon*, ed. Rita Stephan, Guita Hourani, and Cornelia Horn, 15–39. Warwick, RI: Abelian Academic.

"Sectarian Shackles." 2013. Editorial, *Daily Star*, January 30, http://www.dailystar.com (accessed August 21, 2019).

Sidahmed, Mazine. 2015. "Domestic Violence Law Still Not Fully Applied." *Daily Star*, April 3, http://www.dailystar.com.lb (accessed August 19, 2015).

Stephan, Rita. 2010. "Couple's Activism in Lebanon: The Legacy of Laure Moghaizel." *Women's Studies International Forum* 33: 533–41.

———. 2012. "Women's Rights Activism in Lebanon." In *Mapping Arab Women's Movements: A Century of Transformations from Within*, ed. Purnille Arenfeldt and Nawar Al-Hassan Golley, 111–33. Cairo: American University of Cairo Press.

———. 2014. "Four Waves of Lebanese Feminism." e-International Relations, November 7, http://www.e-ir.info.

Sukkarieh, Kholoud. 2018. "The Journey of Change." TEDxKarlskrona, December 14, https://www.youtube.com/watch?v=4-Fr3DqgXF0 (accessed February 4, 2019).

Turner, Eric. 2013. "New Movements, Digital Revolution, and Social Movement Theory." *Peace Review: A Journal of Social Justice* 25: 376–83.

UN Women. N.d. "Beijing and Its Follow-Up." United Nations, http://www.un.org (accessed August 13, 2015).

Wolf, Naomi. 2011. "The Middle East Feminist Revolution: Women Are Not Merely Joining Protests to Topple Dictators, They Are at the Centre of Demanding Social Change." Al Jazeera, March 4, http://www.aljazeera.com (accessed June 4, 2012).

PART V

How They Organize

There is a strong debate in the social movement literature over whether disruptive tactics are more likely to have an impact than sustained non-confrontational actions.[1] While disruptive tactics are more likely to produce comprehensive change, they are harder to organize and achieve. Alternatively, nonconfrontational actions are easier to achieve but less likely to produce a notable impact. Women's activism before and during the Arab Spring varied tremendously in context and consequences. Some women organized widely to challenge authorities and modify oppressive norms; others focused on changing regimes, norms, or culture.

Fatima Sadiqi shares the story of her success in gradually changing norms and establishing the first women's studies research center at the University of Fez in Morocco, whereas, influenced by stories of European revolutions, Dina Wahba reflects on the confrontation style of the Egyptian revolution she helped shape. Marwa Shalaby and Ariana Marnicio examine how, regardless of their political stance, Bahraini women overcame their ideological disagreements and worked together over time to introduce reform, much like Kuwaiti women, who tore down taboos in defense of their dignity, as described in Emanuela Buscemi's piece. Writing from Japan, Namie Tsujigami shows how Saudi women transformed the power dynamics of political and religious authorities by driving, while Manal al-Natour compares intellectuals' activism to that of those who were compelled to fight injustice in Syria. Finally, Layla Saleh captures the perspective of the university-educated mother of seven who saw the uprisings as tearing down her "wall of fear" in Syria, and Emily Regan Wills highlights how women living in the diaspora participated in the Arab Spring.

NOTE

1 Marco Giugni, "How Social Movements Matter: Past Research, Present Problems, Future Developments," in *How Social Movements Matter*, ed. Marco Giugni, Doug McAdam, and Charles Tilly, xiii–xxxiv (Minneapolis: University of Minnesota Press, 1999), xvi.

33

Genesis of Gender and Women's Studies at the University of Fez, Morocco

FATIMA SADIQI

Launching the first gender studies program in the conservative University of Fez was quite a challenge. Obstacles and glass ceilings come to mind: What to call the unit in Arabic? What to include in it? How to legitimize the program as worthy of academic attention? The university finally settled on "*dirasat al-ajnas*" (study of genres) as the closest to what would constitute an "acceptable" name, a name we had to accept lest the program be refused. We also agreed to link the contents to our own specializations and avoid "taboo" topics like homosexuality or sexuality altogether. The whole experience has been a kind of university activism that is now changing minds in ways we did not think were possible!

It all started in 1997 when a small group of female colleagues and I went through the long and challenging process of convincing our university administration to set up a center for studies and research on women as a preliminary step to the creation of a graduate gender studies unit. We perceived the center and the unit as spaces for discussing Arab and Berber women's agency and as venues for us to make our voice heard and allow our students to claim their own voices. The rather conservative nature of our university made the process long, but we were persistent.

The day the Center for Studies and Research on Women was created, March 23, 1998, was memorable. The process of setting aims was exciting. We finally picked two main aims for the center: promoting women professors at the University of Fez and sensitizing the faculty and students to women's issues and their academic importance. To achieve these aims, we organized workshops, roundtables, and international conferences on women and gender. We wanted to create fora where ideas on gender topics could be discussed among scholars and students from Morocco, the region, Europe, and the United States. The center changed perceptions among our colleagues on the concepts of justice, equality, and promotion of women's issues in our university, especially among female students. We had to put up with criticism, and sometimes attacks, but we continued to be persistent.

My colleagues and I felt the center was not enough. We were fully aware that some of the tenacious stereotypes and attitudes about women were deeply rooted in Morocco's past; and some were new ideas and movements that contributed to setting the clock of development back. Going beyond these stereotypes, and reflecting from within our academic disciplines, we started to realize that the formalization of disciplinary boundaries in the human sciences—that is, the division of teaching and research into history, geography, sociology, psychology, philosophy, Islamic studies, literature, and linguistics—prevented collaborative projects between researchers from these different fields. We felt that the fragmentation of the social sciences within disciplinary boundaries constituted a genuine hurdle in this respect. Epistemological and institutional obstacles impeded the crossing of disciplines and the creation of new modes of research. We thought the expansion of our educational system was bound up with the growth of specialization within every branch of knowledge.

As a result, we began to toy with the idea of micro-level studies to restore the social sciences to their role of examining the social process as a complex mosaic in which many processes are interconnected, especially gender and women's studies, which play a major role in this respect. Luckily, the Ministry of Higher Education in Morocco was then interested in reforming higher education. We started to think about creating a graduate gender studies program instead of women's studies because we did not want to be exclusive of men. Indeed, the process of orchestrating gender studies, and the long process of reflection that led to its establishment, showed us that it is not possible to address the needs of women students and teachers (who constitute the core of the educated and militant elite) without rethinking the fundamental assumptions behind Moroccan scholarship and teaching, and the way Moroccan universities are structured.

We raised questions about women professors' contributions to transforming higher education in the preceding fifty years. A compelling reason for asking certain questions is the steady increase in women in education, with women teachers comprising more than one third of the teaching staff of some universities. Likewise, women students are increasingly forming a significant segment of the university student population, some 60 percent at the Faculty of Letters in Fez, for example. My colleagues and I questioned our role as academics and reflected whether we managed to transform curricula, scholarship, and practices—or whether we succeeded only in transforming ourselves in isolation.

These reflections led us to focus our concerns and desire to create a research unit on gender studies as a way of contributing to the democratization of Moroccan higher education. We explained that our activities in the center needed an "audience" that would, in the long run, ensure continuity in including women's contributions in curricula and focusing on social action projects.

Our success was realized when the Gender Studies Unit started to function in September 2000. More than 175 male and female students registered for the program courses, but we could take only twenty, so we selected ten males and ten females. The university had almost no books or articles for us to use; so we provided our own. We asked the university to provide us with a cupboard for the books, and we took turns supervising the book rentals.

One major objective of the Gender Studies Unit was to invigorate the liberal arts curriculum by redesigning courses that would reflect the scholarship on women. The unit was open to all researchers, both men and women, who were interested in gender and women's issues. We decided to introduce gender studies by rooting it in Arab culture. For example, in my class, I provided students with copies of a book by a twelfth-century grammarian, Ibn al Anbari, who was the first scholar to highlight the gender category in Arabic in his book *al-Mudhkkar wa al-Mu'annath* (The Masculine and the Feminine). In whatever grammatical definition he used, he would state whether the rules applied to women or not. As the students reacted, I explained that we needed to contextualize this and that Ibn al Anbari was the first Arab Muslim grammarian who allowed women a place in his writings.

Other colleagues used similar approaches appropriate to their disciplines. They too explained gender within the Arab and Muslim culture and value system, before launching into comparisons with other cultures. By the end of the year, students asked us to teach topics we could never have dreamt of introducing ourselves. Some wanted to address taboo topics like sexuality and homosexuality; others came up with diverse ideas about creating environments shaped by women, such as gender and women's studies courses/gender centers. Together, we recognized the rich legacy of these centers, and our knowledge of this rich heritage allowed us not to reinvent the wheel but to build upon these centers' experiences and successes.

As a gender training and research unit in a "developing" country, the gender unit offered courses that contributed to knowledge building about Morocco and the larger MENA societies. It highlighted the communities' problems, underlined the progress of human rights, and broadened the horizons of research. The unit also participated in programs that sought the full development of human resources. The impulse toward wholeness reflected not only the interdisciplinary nature of gender and women's studies but also the salience of the lack of objectivity in knowledge production.

Together, the center and the graduate unit broke out of the molds that constrain so much of Moroccan higher education. Attracting both male and female students, the courses offered engaged students new and passionate questions and introduced voices that push the limits of understanding. The programs also brought to the University of Fez "experts" whose knowledge combines activism and research.

Thanks to these efforts, the Ministry of Higher Education considered implications for gender when examining research proposals. The graduate unit (and its PhD branch) contributed significantly to bridging the gap between the university and civil society, as students often conduct fieldwork with women NGOs. Before 1998, such activities were simply viewed as programs through which knowledge was extended to various sectors of society. Today the concept of community service is a *condicio sine qua non* for the postgraduate program's accreditation; and it is meant to include activities that could influence, or provide solutions to, particular social problems in Morocco.

Our gender programs have been instrumental in democratizing higher education. More national and international colloquia are devoted to women's issues and more books by and on women are introduced in the university curriculum, as well as in other Moroccan universities. The current move in the Moroccan women's movements, from a predominantly political discourse to academic discussions, focuses on building up scholarship and fieldwork, bridging gaps between academia and activist civil society, and, most importantly, preparing students who will ensure continuity. As a result, gender is used as an analytical tool for understanding men, women, and society in Morocco and beyond. Today, the number of graduate students is growing in a steady way, opening novel venues in academic research in Morocco and the region. We have come a long way!

34

My Revolution!

DINA WAHBA

It was the best of times, it was the worst of times, it was the age of wisdom, it was the age of foolishness, it was the epoch of belief, it was the epoch of incredulity, it was the season of Light, it was the season of Darkness, it was the spring of hope, it was the winter of despair, we had everything before us, we had nothing before us, we were all going direct to Heaven, we were all going direct the other way.
—Charles Dickens, *A Tale of Two Cities*

Like my father, I have been obsessed with Charles Dickens's novel *A Tale of Two Cities* from a young age. A socialist revolutionary who is infatuated with the French Revolution, my father used to read Alexandre Dumas's novels to me as bedtime stories. I grew up believing in "liberty, equality, fraternity" and dreaming of my own revolution. The following is a mere account of my personal experience during the 2011 revolution in Egypt. It is not a conventional political analysis of the revolution, unless "the personal is political." I can't remember why exactly I decided to join the revolution, but I did so one day, alone, after dark. It was my first protest and I never forgot this experience, especially when it turned into a revolution.

On that momentous day, January 25, 2011, walking into Tahrir Square, my mind was racing because I was scared of thugs, police, men with beards—or maybe it was just men in general. As I walked towards the square, my heart was pounding. I didn't know what to expect but definitely it wasn't what turned out to be a revolution. Even in my wildest imagination, I wouldn't have dared to dream what I witnessed. It isn't easy to describe, even after so many years. I stood then at the corner afraid to mingle with the crowd, primarily scared of harassment or sexual assault, until I met some friends who became my comrades as events unfolded. I felt safe enough being with them to enter the square. There, I was in the middle of thousands of people chanting, "Down with the regime!" It was my first protest!

The more I intermingled with the crowd, the safer I felt. I went to a higher ground just by being among so many people. There was a breathtaking yet strange feeling of harmony and acceptance. In one of the gardens in the square some people were praying, others were smoking; some were chanting, others were singing—yet everyone was at peace. It was as if we realized for the first time that our real problem wasn't each other, but the oppressive structure that ruled us.

In the streets, we sat, sang, and slept; we practically owned these streets. I was reminded of a song from one of late Egyptian director Youssef Shaheen's famous revolutionary movies, "The Street Is Ours," which captures liberal youths' reclamation of their rights to the "street" (i.e., public space). Sadly, Shaheen wasn't there to see his song sung in the streets of Cairo.

For many years, El Sheikh Imam's songs were banned in Egypt. One of the most talented revolutionary singers had been erased from Egyptian history. His songs skipped a generation but they didn't die off. They were sung daily in Tahrir Square, defying years of oppression. During those eighteen days, I felt like I was in a euphoric trance. I can't remember eating or sleeping much, although there was an abundance of food. Those who had any food distributed it among the protesters; no matter how simple or little, it was always enough. Sometimes we would buy food ourselves just to give it away with joy. No one was ever hungry or thirsty.

When I reflect on those days, I don't remember details, only flashes of colors, feelings, and sounds. However, some scenes I remember in vivid detail, as if they happened yesterday. My favorite memory was going through lines of people on both sides of the street as we entered the square. Men, women, and children were singing and clapping, welcoming us: "Welcome to the free, welcome to the revolutionaries." We were free, at least for that moment. During the eighteen days of our revolution, I not only felt safe but, more importantly, I felt empowered. The square was an egalitarian and inclusive space; I felt I was accepted and that I belonged.

So many years after the revolution, some claim that we failed. Failed to do what? To bring a truly democratic regime to power? Maybe. To democratize society and promote a culture of diversity and human rights? Probably. My revolution didn't fail. I might be deeply disillusioned, but, for purely selfish reasons, I don't regret it. This is the most significant experience in my life. Sometimes, I feel ashamed of this feeling because many people lost their lives, some lost their loved ones. In the larger scheme of things, I wonder if it was worth it. Certainly, on the personal level, I feel it was. The sense of hope, pure love, freedom, elation, transcendence, altruism—and many other feelings that I won't be able to put in words that I felt—was worth it. The sense of limitless possibilities, and of dreams coming true when life surprises us in unimagined ways, is also worth it. I would do it all over again. I feel lucky to have been alive, able, and young in that particular historical moment.

I have never written these words before, or told them to anyone, even to myself. It was overwhelming; it still is. Several years have passed and it still hasn't sunk in yet. I still don't fully realize the magnitude of emotions. Nevertheless, I am grateful that I was present at the beating heart of humanity, among the crowd, just a small dot at the heart of the square.

35

Women's Political Participation in Bahrain

MARWA SHALABY AND ARIANA MARNICIO

Bahrain is at a major crossroads. With the unmet demands of the Pearl Roundabout protests in 2011 and the failure of the ensuing National Dialogue to introduce tangible political and constitutional reforms, the Bahraini regime has managed to maintain the status quo while making minimum concessions to the opposition. The culmination of this gridlock is manifested in Bahrain's parliamentary elections that took place in November 2014—notable for the absence of opposition forces—and the dominance of independent voices (thirty out of forty seats) with no clear ideological or political affiliation in the 2014 Lower House.

This political stalemate impacts the country's balance of power and the status of women's rights. Notwithstanding the steady government efforts to promote Bahraini women's educational and health outcomes (UNICEF 2011) over the past decades, numerous obstacles persist due to the conflict between tribalism and modernity (Al Gharaibeh 2011), on the one hand, and the struggle for power between the rival political forces, on the other. Despite the long history of women's cross-sectarian political activism through both formal and informal channels, the country's increasing political fragmentation has led to a deep schism among women's groups, dividing them into "loyalist" or "opponent" camps, with little or no attention paid to issues of particular importance to women in Bahrain.

We examine the transformation of Bahraini women's roles before, throughout, and after the Arab Uprisings while placing it in the context of the dynamics of women's activism in both formal and informal venues since the inception of Bahrain's brief period of political liberalization, between 2000 and 2011. Through semistructured interviews with politicians, activists, and scholars conducted in 2014, we explore the impact of the political situation on the status of women in the aftermath of the Pearl Roundabout events and prospects for women's political empowerment in Bahrain.

Political Context of Bahrain

"[Bahraini women] have been shoulder-to-shoulder with men fighting the [British] occupation in the 1950s and 1960s," remarked a Bahraini activist and journalist (personal interview, November 26, 2014, Houston, Texas). The period of the 1950s witnessed the birth of a unique moment in Bahrain's history, with the rise of a nonsectarian political movement challenging the ruling power of Sheikh Salman bin Hamad al-Khalifa and his British advisor (Coates Ulrichsen 2013). Mounting discontent concerning British policies in Bahrain and the sweeping Arab nationalism served as potent catalysts to mobilize Bahrainis for a unified cause and eventually to seek Bahrain's independence from Britain in 1971.

The newly formed government set in place a constitution in 1973 that guaranteed universal suffrage, though it denied women the right to vote. Women were viewed as a means to strengthen the nation, and their education and participation in the country's development were considered necessary elements for a modern state following independence (Al Gharaibeh 2011, 96). From independence until the turn of the century, however, women achieved minor advances in the realm of formal politics, whereas women's education, economic capability, and organization flourished (Pandya 2012; Seikaly 1994).

Between 1994 and 1999, political and social unrest rocked Bahrain once again with the Uprising of Dignity, in which both liberals and Islamists joined forces to demand employment opportunities, social justice, democratic reforms, and a stronger role for the Parliament (Coates Ulrichsen 2013; Seikaly 1997). Central to these demands were the political rights and participation of women (Al Gharaibeh 2011, 97). Indeed, women themselves mobilized to fight for their rights and started a petition in 1995 that articulated their concerns about the state of Bahraini society and their desire for concrete reforms that would include women in the political process (Seikaly 1997, 125).

Protests erupted once again in 2001. In response, a National Action Charter was proposed as an attempt to appease opposing voices and make the government more responsive to citizens and inclusive of women. Remarkably, it was the precursor to a new constitution in 2002, which called for the establishment of elections for the Parliament and gave women the right to vote and participate in public affairs (Fadhl 2008). "The Bahraini women were participating in protests, participating in life," remarked a member of the Gulf Center for Human Rights (personal interview, December 3, 2014. Houston, Texas). A scholar researching Bahrain at the time of the first elections reflected on that historic moment, saying, "They were so excited to be able to actually participate. It was the participation that got women charged up. And that moved on to activism in other areas" (personal interview, December 3, 2014, Houston, Texas). While the National Action Charter and universal suffrage opened doors in the formal political realm, women continued to face challenges that curtailed their advancement.

Decades of Activism

Numerous legal restrictions prevented women from voting in elections and holding office until the advent of the twenty-first century, though women participated in informal venues (personal interview, December 3, 2014, Houston, Texas; Pandya 2012). Organizing within religious and charitable organizations, Bahraini women were able to voice their opinions, become active in the community, and push for positive change. They mobilized primarily through religious institutions such as the Shia Ma'tam, or congregation hall for Shia Muslims. These congregation halls transcended their religious purpose and became forums of debate for women. Sunni women also found a space to articulate their aims and goals and gain social capital through institutions of religious learning such as Umm al-Darda' (Pandya 2012).[1]

In addition to religious organizations, following the National Action Charter in 2001, several government-affiliated institutions were established to promote women's political participation. In 2001, the Supreme Council for Women (SCW) became the primary governmental body responsible for promoting women's rights and political participation. Such government-sponsored organizations have power because of their proximity to the ruling elite (Joseph 1986). The king's first wife, Sheikha

Sabika bint Ibrahim al-Khalifa, has led the council since 2008 and acted as a role model for women on the pro-government side.

The Bahrain Women Union, also established in 2001, is an umbrella organization that encompasses several women's organizations and groups, including the Awal Women's Society and al-Reef Young Ladies' Society—both have been active in the country independently since the early 1970s. Ideologically, the Bahrain Women Union is seen as independent, though sympathetic to the cause of groups opposed to the Bahraini regime (personal interview, November 7, 2014, Houston, Texas). The union describes itself as a consortium of associations with a democratic character and a focus on the empowerment and development of women and families ("National Cooperation" n.d.). Alternatively, other women voice deep mistrust of these organizations and chose to become political activists outside of Bahraini government and/or political parties' control through organizations such as the Gulf Center for Human Rights and the Bahrain Center for Human Rights (BCHR). Established in 2002, the BCHR is a powerful civil society organization that reported on human rights abuses in Bahrain, including women's rights. A notable BCHR member shared some of the challenges in being an activist: "I am working as a human rights defender and activist. The moment I join a political party, automatically I will be serving that party, not others. . . . I contribute and participate as an individual and try to raise the voice of women [at] international conferences" (personal interview, November 28, 2014. Boston, Massachusetts).

The 2011 Pearl Roundabout Protests

Bahrain was the only Gulf Cooperation Council (GCC) state that experienced extended waves of demonstrations after the onset of the Arab Uprisings. Starting from February 11, 2011, Bahrain experienced one of the worst outbreaks of popular dissent since the Uprising of Dignity in 1994. Organized and led by the February 14th Coalition—a cross-sectarian underground youth movement—the Pearl Roundabout (PR) demonstrations were heavily influenced by the protests taking place in Egypt and Tunisia. However, scores of unfulfilled political reforms since the National Charter, and decades of social injustice, immensely contributed to these uprisings (Matthiesen

2013). Despite the fact that the Peninsula Shield[2] managed to stifle the demonstrations by March 18, 2011—as well as the fact that the international community has turned a blind eye to the situation in Bahrain—the Pearl Roundabout events left a lasting imprint on the country's modern history (Coates Ulrichsen 2014) and dramatically transformed the political landscape for women's mobilization and political participation.

Notwithstanding their long history of political activism, the courage of Bahraini women at the February 14, 2011, Day of Rage protests was unprecedented. Unlike incidents of political mobilization in previous decades that involved mainly urban and middle-class women (Seikaly 1997), these uprisings included women from different sects and ethnic backgrounds who came to the very forefront of the political arena. Both men and women, mostly youth, reiterated demands similar to those made during the uprisings in the 1950s and 1990s: political and social reforms, and specifically the full enactment of the National Charter, electoral reforms, and an empowered Parliament. In the beginning protesters never called for a Western model of democracy; rather, they wanted "reform" and a "voice" (personal interview, December 2, 2014, Houston, Texas). However, the regime's excessive use of violence to suppress the revolts, and the negative media framing of the protesters and their demands, led to the emergence of more radical calls for the ousting of the regime and the establishment of a republic led by the Al Haqq party[3] (Jones 2012), the Shia supporters (Louër 2014), and the coalition of February 14th youth.

Not only did female activists take a leading role in the PR events, but their modes of participation have vastly transformed in comparison to their previous acts of dissent. Despite the fact that about a quarter of the female protesters during the first few weeks of the uprisings were arrested—and even tortured—women were assertive and unyielding in the face of security forces and intimidation. As a leading Bahraini activist said (personal interview, November 7, 2014, Houston, Texas), "Women were joining the revolutionary youth and clashing with the police. . . . I found it very hard to believe because the Bahraini society is traditionally conservative, but families were allowing their women to go and participate not only in the demonstrations but also in the clashes. There was a change in people's views there."

Yet, the ideological polarization that dominated the political arena prior to and throughout the protests has also affected women's groups. Whereas groups of female activists were at the forefront of protests taking place on February 14 and afterward, and many others worked to inform the international community of the regime's abuses and use of excessive violence, other women's groups were actively against these protests. Pro-government movements witnessed increased participation of prominent women such as Sawsan al-Shair and Samira Rajab, who advocated widely for the regime, both domestically and internationally. As a result, women's groups were trapped in the pro- versus antigovernment camps. Any prominent female figure or women's group working with the government would be instantly placed in the pro-government camp, with little or no cooperation from other women's groups who share similar interests. This caveat has also played a major role in the first parliamentary elections after the Pearl Roundabout protests.

Women in the Legislative Arena: 2014 Elections and Beyond

In theory, there is no equivalent to Western political parties in Bahrain. Instead, there are a variety of religion- or sectarian-based political societies. Political associations were strictly banned until the advent of the twenty-first century and the onset of the political liberalization process brought about by the accession of Sheikh Hamad to power. Despite the fact that women have been allowed to vote and run for elections since 2002, the country's ideological fragmentation has significantly circumscribed their role in the legislative realm.

Elections for the Lower House were held in 2002 for the first time in almost thirty years, and eight female candidates ran for office for the first time ever in Bahrain's history, though none won (Grewal 2010). The outcome of the 2006 elections was almost identical; of the eighteen females who ran for office, only one woman, Latifa al-Jawad, won a seat in the council representing the southern governorate. This victory was made possible as she ran unopposed in her constituency following the withdrawal of her two opponents. It is worth noting that political parties did not place female candidates on their lists, and their support of women was strictly limited to soliciting their votes (Al Ghareibeh 2011).

In 2010, nine female candidates ran for the third elections and only one of the nine, female legislator Latifa al-Jawad, succeeded in retaining her seat. Hence, the king appointed eleven female candidates to the Shura Council in an attempt to address the discouraging results. Later, three female candidates joined the Parliament in the 2011 by-elections when the Al-Wifaq party withdrew its members in reaction to the regime's excessive use of violence to end the PR revolts. The 2014 elections witnessed the absence of the opposition forces, which boycotted the elections in reaction to the failed reconciliation efforts with the ruling regime during the National Dialogue. This led many candidates to run as independents to maximize their chances of winning. In fact, three out of twenty-three female candidates successfully won seats by running as independents with no party support or political affiliation. Interestingly, they were elected from the northern governorate—one of the most conservative areas in Bahrain.

Unlike in previous rounds of elections, most of the female candidates in 2014 had a clear agenda with a gender-focused political platform. For instance, Fatima Al-Asfour (who won a seat) campaigned for family issues, social welfare, and unemployment. Rua al-Haiki's program focused on promoting youth and social programs[4] while Jamila al-Sammak called for improved health services and living standards. Since their election, female MPs have worked closely with the Supreme Council of Women (SCW) and were able to push for significant legislations benefiting women. They tried to lift some of Bahrain's reservations on CEDAW and succeeded in moving forward Law 17 of 2015 concerning protection against domestic violence. This period also witnessed progress in promoting women's presence in the Shura Council (upper house). Today, Bahraini society observes female MPs closely to see what changes they will bring to women's issues in Bahrain and the promotion of democratic and legal reforms.

Conclusion

Women have played a crucial role in the Bahraini political sphere over the past decades—through both formal and informal avenues of political activism. They were remarkably successful in shaping the country's political arena as they participated in the nationalist struggle against the British occupation, and in the subsequent calls for social and political reforms. Despite the regression of women's presence in the political sphere during the 1980s, Bahraini women have returned to the spotlight since the 1990s.

A close look at the political arena in Bahrain over the past two decades reveals that the deep ideological schisms among women's groups in the country have impeded their prospects toward achieving a unified front with a coherent feminist agenda—even following the advent of state feminism in the early 2000s. This lack of coordination between the grassroots initiatives and the state-sponsored women's organizations has further limited their ability to voice women's concerns and promote significant issues relevant to women in Bahrain. This polarization was evident during times of crisis such as the Pearl Roundabout events.

It might be prime time for the elected female MPs in Bahrain to work together to strengthen the role of grassroots organizations and promote cross-sectarian cooperation among these organizations, especially those interested in promoting women's issues. The fact that the three elected female MPs in 2014 are independents offers women a unique opportunity to push for genuine change—and to resolve many unsettled issues for women, such as citizenship laws, discrimination against women, women's presence in leadership positions, and personal status and family laws. These critical issues have been put aside due to the ongoing struggle for power. The time is ripe for female parliamentarians and women's organizations to address these issues and to push for a gender-focused agenda in a relatively less polarized legislature.

NOTES

1 The majority of Bahrain's population practices Shia Islam, though the Sunni al-Khalifa family has been in power in Bahrain since the late 1780s and occupies the majority of positions in the government.

2 The Peninsula Shield refers to the intervention of the GCC countries (Saudi Arabia, U.A.E., and Kuwait) in Bahrain on March 14, 2011, to quell the popular uprisings, causing significant sectarian tensions.

3 The Al Haqq party—headed by Hassan Mashima—was founded in 2006 to end the Shi'a repression and marginalization in Bahrain.

4 Habib Toumi, "New Women MPs Optimistic about Contributions," *Gulf News*, December 1, 2014, http://gulfnews.com/news.

BIBLIOGRAPHY

Al Gharaibeh, Fakir. 2011. "Women's Empowerment in Bahrain." *Journal of International Women's Studies* 12, no. 3: 96–113.

Coates Ulrichsen, Kristian. 2013. "Bahrain's Uprising: Regional Dimensions and International Consequences." *Stability: International Journal of Security and Development* 2, no. 1: 14.

———. 2014. "Bahrain's Uprising: Domestic Implications and Regional and International Perspectives." In *The New Middle East: Protest and Revolution in the Arab World*, ed. Fawaz A. Gerges. New York: Cambridge University Press.

Fadhl, Mona Abbas. 2008. *Bahraini Women and Their Position in the Reform Process*. Paris: Arab Reform Initiative.

Grewal, Sandeep Singh. 2010. "Election Quota for Women Plea." *Gulf Daily News: The Voice of Bahrain*, October 9.

Jones, Toby. 2012. "Bahrain's Revolutionaries Speak: An Exclusive Interview with Bahrain's Coalition of February 14th Youth." Jadaliyya, March 22.

Joseph, Suad. 1986. "Women and Politics in the Middle East." *Middle East Report: Women and Politics* 138: 3–30.

Louër, Laurence. 2014. "Activism in Bahrain: Between Sectarian and Issue Politics." In *Taking to the Streets: The Transformation of Arab Activism*, ed. Lina Khatib and Ellen Lust. Baltimore, MD: Johns Hopkins University Press.

Matthiesen, Toby. 2013. *Sectarian Gulf: Bahrain, Saudi Arabia, and the Arab Spring That Wasn't*. Stanford, CA: Stanford University Press.

"National Cooperation/Bahrain Women Union." N.d. Supreme Council for Women. https://www.scw.bh, accessed November 15, 2019.

Pandya, Sophia. 2012. *Muslim Women and Islamic Resurgence: Religion, Education, and Identity Politics in Bahrain*. New York: Tauris.

Seikaly, May. 1994. "Women and Social Change in Bahrain." *International Journal of Middle East Studies* 26, no. 3: 415–426.

———. 1997. "Bahraini Women in Formal and Informal Groups: The Politics of Identification." In *Organizing Women: Formal and Informal Women's Groups in the Middle East*, ed. Dawn Chatty and Annika Rabo, 125–46. New York: Berg.

UNICEF. 2011. "Bahrain: MENA Gender Equality Profile: Status of Girls and Women in the Middle East and North Africa." https://www.unicef.org.

36

Strategies of Nonviolent Resistance

Syrian Women Subverting Dominant Paradigms

MANAL AL-NATOUR

Fear brought us together, uniting us in the face of the on-
rushing unknown.
—Khawla Dunia, 2012

It appeared to all media that women disappeared from the
field of struggle, but that is not true. The women only left the
battles between the revolutionaries and the soldiers of Assad.
—Samar Yazbek, 2012

While fear motivated Syrian women like Khawla Dunia to participate in
the revolution, others, like Samar Yazbek, knew exactly what they were
getting into and which form of nonviolent resistance they adopted. Syrian women and men who are committed to advancing "a democratic,
human rights–upholding Syria that is bound by the rule of law" choose
the nonviolent, nonsectarian, noninterventionist path in their quest for
freedom (Kahf 2013, 2). Nonviolence was immediately recognized as the
shortest and most effective path to freedom. This chapter analyzes the
nonviolent strategies that Syrian women applied to contest, challenge,
and survive multiple oppressions, construct their "standpoints," and
gain power over their circumstances. It explores the practical approach
adopted by women like Khawla Dunia, and how other women developed
consciousness of nonviolent action and feminism in their resistance.

This study builds on Patricia Collins's (2000) theory of intersectionality, which examines the oppression of black women within the dynamic
interplay of the axes of "race, class, gender, sexuality, and nation," to
describe how these axes impact women's construction of identities. Spe-

cifically, I draw on two approaches to understanding power and resistance identified by Collins: dialogical and dialectical. In the dialogical approach, a transformation in thinking within an individual sphere or a group paradigm could lead to new actions when the lived experience is materialized into "a changed consciousness" (2000, 30). Alternatively, in the dialectal approach, activism comes as a response to oppression and does not require intellectual activity; rather, it emerges from daily experience (274). These approaches help illuminate how injustice generated by intersecting oppressions of gender, nation, ethnicity, and religion motivated women to participate in the 2011 Syrian revolution. More specifically, this essay explores how women employed different nonviolent approaches in their resistance, some gaining consciousness of nonviolent ideology and feminism, others applying practical tactics in response to injustice.

Dialogical Practices

Dialogical practices function as the fundamental basis for the resistance framework of feminist action, and they rely heavily on intellectual work that is based on theory and action (Collins 2000, 33). This weaving of intellectual work and activism is exemplified by Syrian women who had opposed the regime for many years before the 2011 uprising. These activists were outspoken women who resisted all forms of oppression from within the existing power structures. Aiming to effect a pragmatic change to Syrian society, they enforced what Maxine Molyneux calls "strategic gender interests," or what is termed "feminist" demands (1985, 233). In addition to their leadership role before the revolution, they played a major part in the revolution after its inception by combining their activism with theoretically informed revolutionary thoughts.

The dialogical approach is evident in the Syrian feminist and literary critic Mohja Kahf's description of the original grassroots revolutionaries who, she observes, come from diverse ideologies and geographic areas, but all share "a generational experience of disenfranchisement and brutalization by a corrupt, repressive, and massively armed ruling elite in Syria" (2013, 1). These activists believe in the power of nonviolent resistance to propel people and engage them in a revolution that demands political pluralism and secular society.

Mayya Rahabi and Sabah Hallak are two examples of women who have been fighting for women's empowerment since the 1980s, and have actualized strategic gender interests by employing the dialogic approach. These women reworked ideas and effected change within the arena of their relations to power. Mayya Rahabi is the coordinator of the Women Rally for Democracy and one of the founders of the Civil Society Movement. Previously a medical doctor, she has been working since 1989 on behalf of women's issues. In her intellectual work, which takes the form of books, articles, and short stories, she aims to find the Syrian woman's voice in her society and to place her on equal footing with the Syrian man. *Feminist Reading in the Personal Status Law: Islam and Women* and *Feminist Concepts and Issues* are two of her major books that are considered key references for the feminist movement in Syria. Her books have been very influential; many Syrian women consider her writing an inspiring source on feminist consciousness. Syrian and Arab women have joined Rahabi's workshops on gender equality throughout the past decades and during the Syrian revolution, as they learned how to work towards a secular society.

Rahabi also established the Women's Studies Center, which further sought to raise the banner of women's affairs. Despite the regime censoring her intellectual work, subjecting her to exhaustive security investigations for eight years, and banning her from traveling since 2014, Rahabi relocated to Beirut, where she works unceasingly to support displaced women inside Syria. Subsequently, Rahabi's aim to establish strategic objectives has crossed the borders of Syria, reaching Syrian refugees in Lebanon. Even in these refugee camps, she coordinated workshops to raise feminist consciousness and foster women's well-being through literacy sessions and craft workshops. These workshops sprang from the necessity to alleviate the intersectional economic, security, and political burdens that oppress women.

Rahabi established an electronic library that promotes feminist books and organized conferences on women and secularism, institutionalized forms of discrimination, and personal status law. Rahabi's work has been becoming progressively more vital, especially with the rapid radical changes in Syrian society that are affecting women's lives.

Armed with her ideological convictions, Rahabi became involved in forming a number of networks that work on implementing gender equality goals using strategic approaches. These include Syrian Women for Democracy, Syrian Feminist Lobby, Syrian Woman Network, and Syrian Women Initiative for Peace and Democracy. From these associations, many smaller organizations have emerged, such as Women Now and Syrian Women Journalists. The primary agenda of these organizations arises from prevailing modes of Syrian women's subordination. By finding innovative strategies to liberate Syrian women from the intersecting oppression they face and materializing feminist theory for their benefit, Rahabi has become a feminist pioneer in Syrian society. Today in Syria, the matrix of identity axes is becoming more influential in shaping Syrian women's lives and thus raising women's feminist awareness, especially for those who are displaced inside Syria.

Much like Rahabi's work, Sabah Hallak's advocacy is also grounded in implementing strategic gender interests and actively seeks to unseat oppression. Hallak is a feminist and activist who has been a member of the Syrian Women Association since 1987. As a political dissenter and a member of the Communist Labor Party, she was banned from traveling outside of Syria and subjected to security investigations. Her work has centered on women's rights and gender equality. She has conducted countless workshops on improving women's rights in the Syrian constitution and led many other seminars to empower battered women, stop child abuse, and foster women's leadership. Since 2013, Hallak has been working in Lebanon with Syrian refugee women. In order to advance reform in the disciplinary domain, through her work as a coordinator for the Syrian League for Citizenship, since mid-2011 she has been leading workshops on the concept of citizenship and its foundation among Syrian women. As a nonviolent activist, Hallak is an advocate for peace, and through her positions in the Syrian Initiative for Peace and Democracy as well as the Civil Society Room, she has been urging all parties to stop the violence. Such an action would bring peace to the country and women's lives.

As feminists whose work draws on subverting paradigms through creating effective gender strategies, Rahabi and Hallak recognize the heterogeneity that has been infiltrating Syrian society since 2011. Recognizing the differences among Syrian women, their ultimate goal has been for all women to benefit immediately from the rapid social change in the country. Thus, they focus their efforts on helping women by educating them on their rights, and insist that women's liberation must be enacted side by side with the political revolution. Rahabi and Hallak have challenged social and gender norms, even leaving their families behind and moving to Beirut to promote a real feminist revolution among Syrian refugee women. They also resist political oppression, and have been detained in the regime's prisons or subjected to exhaustive security investigations as a result. The modes of oppression they have endured are intersectional in nature, but so was their resistance. They have remained committed to furnishing the groundwork for a democratic and pluralistic society as well as achieving equal rights for women.

Dialectical Practices

Women who had no prior experience of active involvement in politics appeared on the scene with the outbreak of the uprisings, employing dialectical practices, according to Collins (2000), or what Molyneux terms "practical gender interests" (1985, 233). As noted, such practices emerge from daily experience, coming as a response to oppression and not intellectual reflection. Access to the Internet has allowed these women to express and develop a revolutionary stance that resists the status quo. Nonetheless, this stance emerged suddenly and was not based on an intellectual tradition or feminist thought that privileged freedom above all else. As a result, these women are divided into two groups. The first group began expressing revolutionary sentiments online, but then abandoned the uprising on the ground, or began oscillating between supporting it and opposing it. The second group became physically involved in the revolution. While not all of the women who employed dialectical strategies have used digital media to protest against the regime and the human rights violations, the majority did. Most of these women found that the immediacy and public nature of social media and online networks offered them digital space to express their counternarratives and involved them in creating political reform.

The Bayda women's rallies of April 13, 2011, are an influential example of Syrian women implementing "practical gender interests" through taking the path of the dialectical approach in their resistance. They were among the most powerful demonstrations that were led by women who had never engaged in politics. They demanded freedom for their imprisoned husbands and male relatives, who conventionally play the role of their protectors and the providers for their families. The regime forced these women to their breaking point; having lost everything, they were propelled to take action against the regime. In this context, we are reminded of Molyneux's (1985) claim that gender and class are two inextricable factors that influence women's mobilization. Announcing to television cameras that they are free women, many Syrian women who participated in the Bayda rallies demanded the release of prisoners and government action to provide food for their children; they succeeded in bringing about the release of several hundred prisoners (Damascenequeen 2011a).

Another example of Syrian women acting on practical gender interests through the dialectical approach is the Human Development Projects (HDP), which emerged as a response to the urgent financial need that resulted from the detention or loss of male providers and the declining economic situation in Syria after the eruption of the revolution. Most of the women who participated in these projects had never participated in politics before. Due to the internal displacement, HDP was established within cities such as Homs, Deir Atiyah, and Jurmana, as well as the Damascus countryside. It began aiding the displaced families through donations provided by friends, neighbors, or activists in the form of food, clothing, or shelter. However, with the rapidly growing number of displaced people, the resources became limited and finding a sponsor to help them became much more urgent. Women came together and formed instead Small Projects, an initiative designed to support handicrafts, canned food, tailoring projects, etc. The nature of its products depended on demand and available resources. Not only did Small Projects open new doors for women to provide for their families; it also assisted men in achieving more financial stability. Some men received loans to start a small project such as becoming a carpenter or a vegetable vendor. The loans were paid back through long-term payments without interest. These projects empowered women and armed them for their struggle against oppression by providing them with much-needed self-reliance. They brought Syrians together in their quest to be independent from the state and infused a sense of solidarity among Syrian women. Syrian women dissidents sponsored many of these projects and worked on finding markets for the products outside of Syria. Although called

Figures 36.1. Example of grassroots activism

"Small Projects," the initiative empowered women to contest a distinctive set of oppressions and endorse their own social equality.

Finally, Zabadani's schoolgirls wrapping their faces with the flag and painting them to cover their identities during the rally is another form of practical nonviolent resistance expressed in terms of artistic creativity (Damascenequeen 2011b). Much as with the Bayda women's rallies, these women left the home to advocate for their own issues. The streets of Syria became venues for these young grassroots activists to protest in an array of ways, including employing artistic creativity (Damascenequeen 2011b).

Some of these young grassroots activists have organized themselves into small coordinated groups, one of which is Saraqeb Walls, which includes both men and women. Saraqeb Walls is a nonviolent group that aims to deconstruct the state's propaganda through street art.[1] Saraqeb Walls promotes nonsectarianism and calls for pluralism: "Love it; it is a country for all of you."[2]

The group explicitly called its work revolutionary: "Because it is a revolution, we went to the streets and demanded freedom." The group engaged all Syrians in the deconstruction of state propaganda, and invited children to paint graffiti of flowers, ducks, and trees, symbols of their homeland, onto the streets of Syria. The graffiti spread a sense of solidarity among Syrians, whether they were imprisoned, injured, or displaced, and promoted nonviolent activism (AlAanTV 2013).

These examples show how Syrian women varied in mobilizing in the Syrian revolution and how their practical interests and financial or security needs politicized their actions. Their acts of rebellion come in the practical creative form of artistic expression and its political commentary.

Conclusion

This essay has illustrated how nonviolent resistance still stands as the backbone of the revolution. Syrian women have been actively engaged in the revolution and despite the escalating violence, they have continued to adopt nonviolent strategies of resistance. This chapter has analyzed women's activism and engagement in resistance through the lens of intersectionality and examined women's two main strategies for resistance: dialogical practices, which link intellectual work and activism, and dialectical practices, which link experience and ideas.

Syrian women engaged in dialogical practices in order to wield their intellectual, professional, and vocational capabilities to resist oppression, linking intellectual work to activism. These feminists continue to employ dialogical practices most centrally in resisting the multiple forms of oppression that Syrians and especially the disadvantaged face. While the essay did explore a few examples of well-known activists in this sphere, the other Syrian women who have been able to bring about change are too numerous to mention.

Women in Syria also engage in dialectical practices, which link direct experience of oppression to revolutionary ideas. Social media attracted many of them to participate in the public sphere to resist the multiple oppressions they face. Videos of demonstrations and news about the massacre of civilians, the use of chemical weapons, and human rights violations have all been spread on the social networks. News about detentions, prisoner releases, refugees, donations, and displaced people have been published online. Media coverage of women's projects that seek financial stability through handicrafts, canned food, and coordinated groups has been uploaded online as well. These modes of resistance are a remarkable feature of the Syrian feminist movement, in general, and the Syrian revolution, in particular. The approaches and the strategies actualized by Syrian women in their nonviolent resistance complement each other. On a daily basis, Syrian women are resisting injustice in its complicated manifestations, including the patriarchy within societal institutions. Syrian women's journey toward freedom and social justice is still ongoing, regardless of the interlocking spheres of oppression that they act within and seek to dismantle.

NOTES

1 The group takes its name from a small town in Idlib in Syria.
2 All quotations of Saraqeb Walls's graffiti are my translations.

BIBLIOGRAPHY

AlAanTV. 2013. "Saraqeb Walls in Idlib Are Becoming Paintings Calling for Freedom." YouTube video, 3:03. January 13, https://www.youtube.com/watch?v=4oZuaNZnkX8#t=12.

Collins, Patricia. 2000. *Black Feminist Thought: Knowledge, Consciousness, and the Politics of Empowerment*. New York: Routledge.

Damascenequeen. 2011a. "Women Rock the Syrian Revolution." YouTube video, 4:47. November 11, https://www.youtube.com/watch?v=AKPtUWT_fiE.

———. 2011b. "Zabadani Women's Demonstration." YouTube video, 0:26. November 11, https://www.youtube.com/watch?NR=1&v=c7J5HRxL5ys.

Kahf, Mohja. 2013. "Then and Now: The Syrian Revolution to Date." Friends for a Nonviolent World, http://www.fnvw.org (accessed April 30, 2016).

Molyneux, Maxine. 1985. "Mobilizing without Emancipation? Women's Interests, the State, and Revolution in Nicaragua." *Feminist Studies* 11, no. 2: 227–54. http://genderandsecurity.org.

"Saraqeb Walls's Facebook page." N.d. Facebook.com, https://www.facebook.com/SaraqebWalls (accessed May 22, 2016).

Yazbek, Samar. 2012. *A Woman in the Crossfire: Diaries of the Syrian Revolution*. London: Haus.

37

Driving Campaigns

Saudi Women Negotiating Power in the Public Space

NAMIE TSUJIGAMI

In September 2017, Saudi Arabia lifted the ban on women driving. A myriad of factors and negotiations contributed to the removal of the ban on female driving, including women who continuously negotiated power and space to change existing political, social, and gender norms, despite often being faced with fierce public resistance. This chapter attempts to illuminate women's agency, strategy, and accommodation by focusing on Saudi women's fight for the freedom to move and drive, the backlash against them, and its impact on government policies.

Trajectories of Driving Movements in Saudi Arabia: The Gulf Crisis

The women's driving campaign in Saudi Arabia can be broken down into three phases. The first Saudi driving campaign occurred during the 1990 Gulf Crisis amid unprecedented tension between the neighboring countries of Iraq and Kuwait. In November 1990, as many as forty-seven women drove to protest the country's ban on women driving, believing that "in [a] national emergency, we need to drive for the safety of our families" (Wilson and Graham 1994, 65). The group of protesters included fourteen women with doctoral degrees, as well as several university administrators,[1] who alerted the office of the governor of Riyadh in advance about their intent to protest. The fourteen-car motorcade, which initially proceeded without any problems, was stopped within thirty minutes by so-called *mutawwin* (members of the Promotion of Virtue and Prevention of Vice), who surrounded the women. The women were taken into police custody, where their male relatives, or "guardians," were forced to sign documents agreeing that the women would never drive again. In the eyes of the state, the guardians, not the women, were held accountable for preventing any future violation of the law.

Soon after the incident, criticism of the protesters spread rapidly. The following day, accusatory leaflets were scattered throughout Riyadh listing the women's names, addresses, and phone numbers. More than twenty thousand people gathered outside the Riyadh governor's palace, enraged that the government was not able to prevent the women's driving protest. In light of this intense public pressure, the Ministry of Interior issued a statement warning against future protests, based on a *fatwa* declared by the Grand Mufti Sheikh Bin Baz. The Grand Mufti's *fatwa* expressed concerns about private meetings between a man and woman, *khulwa*, which would occur if women drive. These procedures demonstrate the strong alliance between the government and religious elites during that time. In addition to announcing the ban on women driving, the government prohibited female protesters from resuming their position as lecturers at the universities, and confiscated their passports as an additional punitive measure.

Despite these measures, the resistance did not end. In 2005, Muhammad al-Zulfa, one of a few Shia members of the Consultative Council (*majlis al-shura*),[2] tried to bring the issue to the then all-male council. He contended that granting women the right to drive would benefit the economy, as, at the time, Saudi households hired a million drivers per year at a cost of twelve billion Saudi riyals, most of which was remitted to the drivers' home countries. As a male government official advocating for Saudi women's right to drive, al-Zulfa's attempt was unconventional. It was entirely rejected by the rest of the council members, who refused to discuss the issue on the grounds that it was not approved by the chairman. In an interview, al-Zulfa revealed that some members secretly supported his proposal, but no one did so overtly in the council. Right after the Saudi government lifted the ban on women driving in September 2017, al-Zulfa reflected in retrospect that when he proposed at the council to allow women to drive, not only had he been disapproved of by his colleagues at the Consultative Council, but he also faced harsh criticism among his relatives and neighbors.[3] It is no wonder that a Shia female activist, Wajiha al-Huwaider, faced harsh criticism when she posted a video on YouTube of her driving on International Women's Day in 2008 as a demand to end the ban on women driving.[4]

Prevailing gender and social norms in Saudi Arabia were directed at denying women the right to drive despite the late King Abdullah's 2005 social reforms (Tsujigami 2017). Men as well as some women expressed their disapproval. It is particularly noticeable that what I call the "Anti-Cedawiyat," those who oppose CEDAW (the UN Convention on the Elimination of All Forms of Discrimination against Women), asserted that faithful women adhere to gender roles and gender norms (Tsujigami 2009), and their appeal resonated with a wider segment of the population, including men (Makboul 2017).

Reviving the Movement: The Second Phase of the Driving Campaign

The second phase of the driving campaign was inspired by the Arab Spring and spread through social media. As revolutionary movements swept across the Arab world, Saudi women regrouped and reorganized the protests to pursue different purposes. For example, on January 28, 2011, a woman took to the streets of Jeddah to demand improvement of the crumbling infrastructure, which had led to a spate of dangerous floods. Another group of women protested in front of the Ministry of Interior to free the alleged 9/11 bombers, who had been imprisoned for almost a decade without a transparent criminal investigation or trial.

Inspired by these protests, a driving movement resurfaced. The online campaign, called "Women2Drive," called for Saudi women to get behind the wheel on June 17, 2011. In contrast to the Gulf Crisis–era driving protest, participants did not drive together from a single gathering point. Rather, using the broadcast power of social media, movement organizers called for tens of thousands of supporters to drive by themselves in whichever direction they chose.

Manal al-Sharif, an information technology specialist with the state-owned oil company ARAMCO, decided to drive before the designated date. In support of al-Sharif's efforts, Wajiha al-Huwaider, an activist who had organized an earlier driving campaign in 2008, recorded al-Sharif's driving and uploaded the video to YouTube. When authorities became aware of the video, they arrested al-Sharif, and held her in jail

Figure 37.1. #women2drive campaign. Image Credit: Carlos Latuff.

for nine days. Her family was also harassed; her son was teased at school, and her brother was detained twice by the police. Al-Sharif ultimately had to leave the country partly because of the harassment and opposition she faced (Al-Sharif 2013). Her experience may have deterred those who were planning to drive on June 17. While some women did drive that day, organizers were unable to reach the level needed to mobilize reaction.

In her 2017 *Daring to Drive* book, al-Sharif disclosed why and how she engaged in the driving campaign. As a single mother and a career woman, she thought the driving ban was unreasonable. Contrary to some driving campaigners from wealthy families who do not have problems with transportation (Tsujigami 2017), al-Sharif sometimes had difficulties finding transportation. The fact that al-Sharif is a divorced mother is not a negligible issue when considering the needs of women driving in the kingdom. With one fifth of marriages ending up in divorce ("Saudi Divorce Rates" 2017) and 45 percent of Saudi women over the age of thirty remaining single (Batrawy2015), the number of women needing reliable transportation is increasing.

Resistance to women driving was reignited in December 2011 when a male Saudi academic submitted a report to the Consultative Council warning against the danger of increased prostitution, pornography, homosexuality, and divorce should women be allowed to drive (Usher 2011). Salih al-Luhaydan, a judicial and psychological consultant to the Gulf Psychological Association, fabricated "scientific" evidence that driving "affects ovaries and rolls up the pelvis" (Al Arabiya 2013).

The Third Phase: Women Driving Elevated to Public Debates

In 2011, King Abdullah had promised women that they would be able to participate in the Consultative Council and the Municipal Council in 2013 and 2015, respectively. Following on his promise, the king appointed thirty women to the Consultative Council, accounting for 20 percent of its membership. As he announced this decision, another online driving campaign was launched in 2013 called "Women to Drive on October 26." Following the campaign's inception, over eleven thousand women signed the declaration on the campaign website, www. oct26driving.com (Al Arabiya 2013). It was not easy for the monarch and the government to remove the ban, considering the existing opposition, but it was equally hard to ignore women activists' push for greater participation.

Although newly appointed female Consultative Council members described pros and cons of women driving, some female members, including Hanan al-Ahmadi and Latifa al-Shaalan, supported the driving campaign and advocated to end the ban on women driving. They filed a recommendation to the council on October 8, 2013, to lift the prohibition and requested that the council "recognize the rights of women to drive a car in accordance with the principles of *sharia* and traffic rules" (Agence France-Presse 2013). The council, however, rejected their proposal on the grounds that it was irrelevant to the current transportation ministry discussion (Al Jazeera 2013). Subsequently, the Ministry of Interior delivered a statement condemning the campaign (Jamjoom and Smith-Spark 2013).

The female council members continued the fight. In 2016, Consultative Council member Latifa al-Shaalan became recognized for her infamous statement, "We have been facing internal and external challenges since the state was founded by King Abdul Aziz." She criticized those who demonize men by characterizing them as animalistic beings who are always ready to harass women. Al-Shaalan argued that Saudi society is matured and sufficiently stable to accept these reforms. Being pragmatic, she did not criticize sexist patterns of thinking, but rather persuaded her audience on the basis of working women's needs for reliable means of transportation (Ukaz 2016).

Although female Consultative Council members' proposals were rejected repeatedly, the progress in including women in the council enabled them to act in an official capacity and suggest bills—which was a substantial involvement in the process of policymaking, including driving matters. This is proof that the appointment of female council members is not a matter of superficial participation in politics; rather, female members are bringing women's issues to the forefront of high politics.

While their appointments have been criticized by some as purely cosmetic, all the female members I interviewed insisted that they were working hard to address conflicts as a result of women's growing participation in the labor market, such as the increased push for greater freedom of movement. In a nutshell, the appointment of female Consultative Council members had an impact on Saudi political decision making. Women's issues were no longer exotic myths, but institutionalized as public, political, and social matters.

Vision 2030 and Government-Led Socioeconomic Reforms

While women driving debates were going through a seesaw process, the Saudi economy began to face serious deficits due to the sudden drop of international oil prices at the end of 2014. It also coincided with the shifting power politics resulting from the demise of King Abdullah in January 2015. Vision 2030 was announced in the midst of the political, economic, and social turbulence of 2016. The vision, which maps out a blueprint for the year 2030, mainly features a move away from dependence on oil and toward diversifying the economy. Vision 2030 also touches on social change, including changing gender norms. It also recognizes the people's need for culture and entertainment in light of the growing youth population. The vision clearly mentions, for the first time in the kingdom's history, that the government will support cultural and entertainment activities that suit the people's needs (Council of Economic and Development Affairs 2016, 22).

While repressing political freedom as symbolized by the corruption crackdown in 2017, the new Saudi regime is evidently liberalizing society by providing women with cultural, economic, and entertainment opportunities. Female members of the Consultative Council also showed confidence in bringing new perspectives and ideas on women-related issues to the council to improve legislation pertaining to women.[5] The driving ban was lifted within such political, economic, and social trends. The King's Decree, issued in September 2017, recognizes the negative consequences of not allowing women to drive, and states that female driving is now considered permissible by religious scholars. It is remarkable that a number of governors, Consultative Council members, and academics strongly supported the decision to end the ban immediately after the decision was announced, which stands in clear contrast to the fierce backlash that the Saudi society experienced earlier (Tsujigami 2017).

Conclusion: Is Driving the Goal?

Saudi Arabia's longstanding ban on women driving was unexpectedly lifted under new leadership and concomitant political, economic, and social changes. While the central power enabled the end of the prohibition, it should not be neglected that the Saudi female protesters and activists, in cooperation with female Consultative Council members and male advocates, have continuously negotiated power and space on various fronts despite often facing fierce backlash. As the three phases demonstrate, female driving campaigners gradually gained support, and eventually succeeded in winning the public debate when they were able to work together with female advocates among the Consultative Council members. Changing economic and social settings also boosted the move. Women's educational progress, gradually increased labor participation, and enhanced networks produced substantive needs for convenient, reliable, and affordable transportation. Vision 2030 recognized such needs among the young population and launched economic and social reforms, including transforming gender norms. Nonetheless, many challenges remain to be negotiated over gendered power and space in Saudi Arabia. Abolishing the male guardianship system, the other heated debate among Saudis, is still key for women to gain autonomy and power for decision making. Although the women's driving ban has been removed, the abolition of male guardianship in order for women to gain independent decision-making power is still needed.

NOTES

1 Author's interview with Aisha al-Manaa, March 9, 2013, Riyadh.

2 The Consultative Council is an advisory board to the king. Despite lacking formal legislative power, it functions as a quasi-decision-making body in Saudi Arabia.

3 Mariyam Al-Jabir, "al-Zulfa: Hhadha Mauqifi Mimman Hajamuni li-Qiyadat al-Maraa al-Sayyara." Al Arabiya, October 1, 2017, http://www.alarabiya.net (accessed March 17, 2018).

4 For Al-Huwaider's YouTube video, see "English: Wajeha Al-Huwaider," posted by LiesMustStop, YouTube, September 2, 2008, accessed on March 17, 2018, https://www.youtube.com/watch?v=q8GiTnb33wE.

5 Author's interview with female Consultative Council members on February 20, 2017, Riyadh.

BIBLIOGRAPHY

Agence France-Presse. 2013. "Saudi Shura Members Urge Lifting of Female Driving Ban." *Gulf News*, October 8, http://gulfnews.com (accessed October 27, 2013).

Al Arabiya. 2013. "Driving Affects Ovaries and Pelvis, Saudi Sheikh Warns Women." Al Arabiya, September 29, http://english.alarabiya.net (accessed October 27, 2013).

Al Jazeera. 2013. "Saudi Shura Rejects Women Driving Ban Move." Al Jazeera, October 10, http://www.aljazeera.com (accessed October 27, 2013).

Al-Sharif, Manal. 2017. *Daring to Drive: A Saudi Woman's Awakening*. New York: Simon & Schuster.

Batrawy, Aya. 2015. "Saudi Single Women Challenge Tradition in Love and Marriage." *Post and Courier*, January 24. https://www.postandcourier.com (accessed October 29, 2019).

Council of Economic and Development Affairs. 2016. *Saudi Vision 2030*. The Kingdom of Saudi Arabia, https://vision2030.gov.sa/en (accessed February 17, 2019).

Jamjoom, Mohammed, and Laura Smith-Spark. 2013. "Saudi Arabia Women Defy Authorities over Female Driving Ban." CNN, October 27, https://edition.cnn.com (accessed October 27, 2013).

Makboul, Laila. 2017. "Beyond Preaching Women: Saudi Dāʿyāt and Their Engagement in the Public Sphere." *Die Welt Des Islam* 57: 303–28.

"Manal Al Sharif: A Woman Who Dared to Drive." 2013. YouTube, 14:16. Posted by "TED," June 14, https://www.youtube.com/watch?v=vNpmq6Ok-QQ (accessed February 17, 2019).

"Saudi Divorce Rates Rise by 50%." 2017. *Gulf News*, October 19, https://gulfnews.com (accessed March 25, 2018).

Tsujigami, Namie. 2017. "Stealth Revolution: Saudi Women's Ongoing Social Battles." In *Arab Women's Activism and Socio-Political Transformation: Unfinished Gendered*

Revolutions, ed. Sahar Khamis and Amel Mili, 149–66. Basingstoke, UK: Palgrave Macmillan.

Ukaz. 2016. "Latifa al-Shaalan tafnid bi-'ladla' mubarrirat munawi i 'qiyadat al-maraa.'" Uukaz, November 29, https://www.okaz.com (accessed March 25, 2018).

Usher, Sebastian. 2011. "'End of Virginity' If Women Drive, Saudi Cleric Warns." BBC News, December 2, https://www.bbc.com (accessed October 27, 2013).

Wilson, Peter W., and Douglas F. Graham. 1994. *Saudi Arabia: The Coming Storm*. New York: Sharp.

38

Reclaiming Space(s)

Kuwaiti Women in the Karamat Watan Protests

EMANUELA BUSCEMI

A series of unprecedented protests occurred in Kuwait between October and December 2012 in response to the dissolving of the Parliament and the abrupt revision of the electoral law. Thousands of Kuwaitis joined the Karamat Watan (A Nation's Dignity) campaign demanding the resignation of Prime Minister Sheikh Nasser Al-Sabah. Following his resignation, along with that of the rest of the Parliament and the appointed government ("Kuwait's Prime Minister" 2011) in November 2011, due to the pressure of public mobilization and the revelation of corruption scandals, parliamentary elections were held in February 2012, marking the rise of an opposition majority. However, the Parliament was dissolved a few months later and an emergency decree was issued the following October.

On October 21, 2012, over fifty thousand people marched on the panoramic coastal Gulf Road for the first Karamat Watan demonstration. The following day, the Ministry of Interior issued a ban on any unlicensed public gatherings of more than twenty people. A demonstration followed on November 4, still without a permit. For the third protest, held on November 16, activists obtained a license. These protests sparked a widespread boycott of the December 2012 elections, effectively reducing voter turnout (Black 2012) and significantly affecting the composition of the new Parliament (Smith Diwan 2012). The present paper investigates the motivations of Karamat Watan women activists in two different arenas in which women protested: the physical space in the streets and cyberspace.

By means of intergenerational support, social media mobilization, and the breaking of preexisting taboos on activism, as well as experience from previous political campaigns, women were able to voice their dissent and articulate their political agenda. In doing so, they reached beyond "the stereotype of the silent, passive, subordinate, victimized, and powerless Muslim woman" (Charrad 2011, 418). These women's mobilization created in them a "new civic sense" (Kandiyoti 2011) that enabled them to counter their vicarious citizenship (Buscemi 2016) in their patriarchal society (Human Rights Watch 2015).

Findings are based on interviews with women activists that were conducted in Kuwait between September 2012 and May 2013, and between January and May 2015, as well as online data sources. In order to protect the anonymity of interviewees, real names have been changed.

Physical Space: Street Politics in the *Hirak*

During the Karamat Watan protests, women campaigned heavily to promote mobilization as well as boycott of the election. They became involved in decision making and choosing protest locations, logistics, and marching directions (Farah 2013). When stun grenades and tear gas were fired on protesters and violence ensued (Diwan 2014), women provided medical assistance and used their networks to call for emergency aid. They alerted other participants through Twitter to prepare masks for tear gas and to carry first aid kits (Farah 2013).

Whole families took part in the protests: some women activists participated with their brothers, while others participated with mothers and sisters, or with husbands and children. Intergenerational support of Karamat Watan was an important feature of the protests and gave women activists a validation for their civic and political engagement. Some skeptics of the *hirak*[1] voiced a fear that men were using women to inflate numbers and display a demographically representative movement (Nourah 2013). Such views discounted women's agency and the legitimacy of their presence. Several activists noted that men, fearing for women's safety, would often try to move them away from the center of demonstrations, where violence was likely to erupt.

In the course of a speech after the first Karamat Watan demonstration, Fatma, a liberal activist, addressed her fellow protesters, asserting women's readiness to bear the consequences of their actions, and demanding that men do not isolate them: "We are ready to get hit with you!" (Fatma 2013). Women protesters, whom police and security forces treated respectfully due to their social status and the potential outrage any physical harm to them would cause, deliberately offered to act as shields, as Zahra, a Muslim Brotherhood member and a university student, explained: "We noticed that while we are walking, police would get between us and the guys so that we're completely separated from them. We were never worried [for] ourselves—we're always worried they are starting hitting the guys—so for men's safety and ours we always try to stick with the guys for their safety" (2013).

When Zahra's brother expressed concerns about the physical dangers women could face in the protests, her mother argued that women must take part "so that men would not get hurt" (2013). Thus, the protest arena became a space for roles to be reversed in a society where men are traditionally the protectors of women.[2] The ensuing paradigm shift (Arshad 2013) was enhanced by women activists who negotiated social and cultural change beyond the political by asserting their agency politically through activism, and physically with their bodies.

Cyberspace: Using Social Media for Activism

Social media was significant for Kuwaiti activists, especially for youth and women, in voicing their dissent while simultaneously creating social capital and building networks (Howard et al. 2011; Dubai School of Government 2011). Youth-led protests in the region relied on social media as a tool for spreading information and raising awareness, breaking taboos, and enhancing women's visibility and demands (UNESCO 2014; Dubai School of Government 2011). Since the political debate in Kuwait is mainly confined to *diwaniyas* (local regular private meeting venues for men), social media provided women a *virtual street* (Kinninmont 2013, 3) beyond the traditional limits of state censorship. Fatma, an activist, notes,

> It used to be that men had massive networks through *diwaniyas* . . . [allowing them to access] networks, talk with anyone they want, whenever they want, without any restrictions. Getting into activism has helped expand our networks, and this is where social media came in for me. [As a woman] you are not sealed off anymore. . . . Now that I have information

because of my network . . . I can have an evolved thought and it's not a matter of gender. You know there's a communal experience, I feel like we're sharing that now a lot more than we used to. We didn't have access to that before. (2013)

Karamat Watan women activists campaigned heavily online in pursuit of democratization. Writing in English and Arabic, these women allowed a plurality of voices to be heard. In fact, activists who used blogs, Facebook, and Twitter to communicate with local and international human rights organizations[3] were contacted through their blogs by men organizers to mobilize in Karamat Watan demonstrations. Social media allowed for the emergence of a plurality of women's voices beyond cyberspace. Twitter was the main medium employed in organizing the *hirak*, and its penetration in Kuwait's society grew from 117,304 active users in 2011 to 225,000 in 2013.[4] Kuwait not only has the highest Twitter penetration rate in the Arab region, but #Kuwait was one of the top tweets in the region throughout the Arab Uprisings (Dubai School of Government 2011).

Reflections: The Arab Spring as Catalyst

The resentment caused by extensive corruption cases was a common motivation for protests throughout the Arab world. Protests across Arab countries like Tunisia and Egypt acted as catalysts for the growing dissatisfaction and disillusionment that had been mounting in Kuwait since the mid-1990s. Activists felt "empowered [and] inspired" (Aisha 2013) by the events taking place in the region.

The Arab Spring also showed that the Muslim community could be united and empowered through legitimate demands to the ruling elites: according to Zahra, "It made our [religious] community grow. It has changed the way we look at ourselves. . . . [We know we are] more powerful" (Zahra 2013).

As in other Arab countries, the government responded harshly and confrontationally, jailing activists, men and women alike. According to Human Rights Watch (2015), the government in Kuwait has reduced freedom of expression by accusing dissenters of insulting the leadership or religion, revoking licences to newspapers, and increasing censorship on the Internet and social media. Alternatively, the government has granted money allowances, free food benefits, an increase in salaries, and other financial measures in an attempt to increase its popularity among some segments of the population. Cyberactivism has been increasingly considered as a direct threat to the establishment and the status quo (Dana 2013).

After Karamat Watan, political contestation in Kuwait temporarily subsided due to the frustration brought about by arrests of young protesters, only to resurface later with more subdued tones and initiatives, but with the same goals. The tightening of state censorship on the Internet and social media (UNESCO 2014) has increased activists' self-censorship and caution. However, political activism has not ceased, having resorted to more informal venues and alternative practices.

According to a local political analyst, there is a profound disconnect between youth and the government (Al Sharekh 2013), recently exacerbated by the government difficulties in coping with and adjusting to falling oil prices and rising unemployment. Social and political reforms are possibly the only solution to a growing sense of restlessness and a crisis of identity. The role of women in influencing social change is not only unavoidable, but a growing feature of the political, social, and cultural landscape of the country.

NOTES

1 Arabic for protest.
2 For a more thorough examination of the complex relationship among citizenship, women, and the state in the Arab world and in Gulf countries, see Longva 2000.
3 The main international human rights organizations contacted were Human Rights Watch and Amnesty International (Aisha 2013).
4 Author's elaboration on data from Dubai School of Government 2011.

BIBLIOGRAPHY

Aisha. 2013. Interview with Samyah Alfoory and Emanuela Buscemi in Kuwait, April 20.

Al Sharekh, Alanoud. 2013. "Avoiding an Irreparable Disconnect in Kuwait." *Gulf News*, May 22, http://gulfnews.com (accessed October 30, 2015).

Arshad, Shazia. 2013. "The Arab Spring: What Did It Do for Women?" *Middle East Monitor*, March 25, https://www.middleeastmonitor.com (accessed October 26, 2015).

Black, Ian. 2012. "Kuwait Election Turnout Shrinks after Opposition Boycott." *Guardian*, December 2, http://www.theguardian.com (accessed October 15, 2015).

Charrad, Mounira M. 2011. "Gender in the Middle East: Islam, State, Agency." *Annual Review of Sociology* 37: 417–37.

Dana. 2013. Interview with Emanuela Buscemi in Kuwait, May 4.

Diwan, Kristin. 2014. "Breaking Taboos: Youth Activism in the Gulf States." Atlantic Council Issue Brief, http://www.atlanticcouncil.org (accessed October 30, 2015).

Dubai School of Government. 2011. *Arab Social Media Report. The Role of Social Media in Arab Women's Empowerment.* November, www.arabsocialmediareport.com (accessed October 10, 2015).

Farah. 2013. Interview with Samyah Alfoory and Emanuela Buscemi in Kuwait, May 15.

Fatma. 2013. Interview with Samyah Alfoory and Emanuela Buscemi in Kuwait, May 15.

Howard, Philip N., Aideen Duffy, Deen Freelon, Muzammil Hussain, Will Mari, and Marwa Mazaid. 2011. "Opening Closed Regimes: What Was the Role of Social Media during the Arab Spring?" Project on Information Technology and Political Islam Working Paper, www.pITPI.org (accessed October 30, 2015).

Human Rights Watch. 2015. World Report, www.hrw.org (accessed October 11, 2015).

Kandiyoti, Deniz. 2011. "Promise and Peril: Women and the Arab Spring." Open Democracy, March 8, https://www.opendemocracy.net (accessed October 20, 2015).

Kinninmont, Jane. 2013. "To What Extent Is Twitter Changing Gulf Societies?" Chatham House, February, https://www.chathamhouse.org (accessed September 30, 2015).

"Kuwait's Prime Minister Resigns after Protests." 2011. BBC Middle East, November 28, http://www.bbc.com.

Longva, Anh Nga. 2000. "Citizenship in the Gulf States: Conceptualization and Practice." In *Citizenship and the State in the Middle East*, ed. Nils A. Butenschon, Uri Davis, and Manuel Hassassian, 179–97. Syracuse, NY: Syracuse University Press.

Noura. 2013. Interview with Samyah Alfoory and Emanuela Buscemi in Kuwait, May 14.

Smith Diwan, Kristin. 2012. "Boycott Elections Distill Kuwait's Divisions." Atlantic Council, December 4, http://www.atlanticcouncil.org (accessed November 29, 2015).

UNESCO. 2014. *World Trends in Freedom of Expression and Media Development: Regional Overview of the Arab Region.* UNESCO Communication and Information Sector, http://unesdoc.unesco.org (accessed December 18, 2015).

Zahra. 2013. Interview with Samyah Alfoory and Emanuela Buscemi in Kuwait, April 23.

39

"The Factory of the Revolution"

Women's Activism in the Syrian Uprisings

LAYLA SALEH

> My young men, my family, my people
> Saw tragedies in your prisons
> I'm a Syrian, my head held high
> And I don't bow down except to the Lord
> You will leave, O Bashar
> We've declared it in the name of the people
> . . . .
> Our revolution is a humanist one,
> Muslims and Christians
> We want to defend the oppressed
> And demand freedom
> —Women's Protest Song, Zabadanee (Damascus), Syria[1]

"The Syrian woman is strong. She is resistant," asserted Um Ibrahim in an interview with me on April 28, 2013.[2] It was natural, then, for women to take a vital role in the uprisings against Bashar Al-Assad. Thus concludes Um Ibrahim, a Syrian woman whose life carries the scars of the oppression of both Assads, the late father, Hafez, and the son, Bashar. Forced to flee her country at age eighteen as political unrest against Hafez brewed, she was only able to return two decades later, in 2002, with her husband and children. After bearing witness to, and participating in, the peaceful protests that characterized the first stage of the Syrian uprisings, Um Ibrahim made the difficult decision to leave her home once again for a neighboring country, this time out of fear for her family's safety.

The centrality of women's activism to the Syrian uprisings is quite clear. Alongside men, women have been engaged in the "traveling" regional popular mobilization against authoritarianism (*harak*) in Syria and across the Arab world since 2011 (Sadiki 2016). Many have been pioneers of the revolution itself. Prominent activist Razan Ghazzawi notes that the first person to articulate the demand for the regime's downfall in Syria was Muntaha al-Atrash, in a telephone interview with *Al-Sharq al-Awsat* newspaper (2014). The first people to be arrested in what became the "revolution" were two women, as early as January 2011, as they reportedly dared to wonder out loud on the phone whether Bashar al-Assad would follow in Mubarak's footsteps as a dictator ousted by his people (Wedeen 2013). Given the precarious security situation and lack of comprehensive, reliable data gathering during a time of war, the number of female activists and participants on the ground or even outside Syria is difficult to estimate. From the earliest days in the spring of 2011, women have been both at the forefront and in the background in the march against the dictatorial Assad regime. Participating broadly and becoming victimized uniquely, women have served as "political activists, caregivers, humanitarians, and providers" (Human Rights Watch 2014), fulfilling a variety of roles as the peaceful uprisings degenerated into an all-out civil and regional proxy war. In addition to protesting, Syrian women became grassroots activists forming and heading organizations such as Syrian Women for the Syrian Intifada (SANAD) (Ghazzawi 2014), and providing medical care to local populations, as they did in the polio vaccine drives in Deir Ezzor and Aleppo (McGee 2014). Some, such as human rights activist Majd Shurbaji of the Damascus suburb Darayya, have risen to international prominence and been recognized by the White House for their "exceptional courage and leadership" (US Department of State 2015). They also worked as journalists documenting regime atrocities (and, more recently, extremists' crimes) and reaching wide audiences inside and outside Syria. Thus women's multifaceted activism reflects the inclusiveness of Syria's revolutionary popular mobilization that also transcended region, class, religion, sect, and ideology (Saleh 2017, 151–53) in the bottom-up uprising's initially peaceful phase.

The Syrian woman is thus present, even if not always physically visible, wherever one turns in the uprising. Um Ibrahim refers to women as the "factory of the revolution"—an essential part of its creation and sustained existence. Indeed, the role of women in the Syrian uprisings has been well documented by journalists and activists alike (McGee

2014). As the uprisings developed, the nature of women's involvement also evolved. Initially, women's protests were a regular feature of the first few months of the uprisings and continued a few weeks into the protests. One Friday was dedicated to women of the revolution, named by activists "the Friday of Free Women." As women increasingly participated and led protests, though, they became targets of the regime's crackdown: detained, tortured, raped, and murdered (Beaumont 2011).

Notable women activists include human rights lawyer Razan Zaitouneh—one of the founders of the umbrella opposition group that became the Local Coordination Committees (LCC), as well as the founder of the Violence Documentation Center (VDC), which tracks those detained, missing, and killed in Syria since 2011. Zaitouneh's husband and brother-in-law were detained by Syrian security forces in the early months of the uprisings, and she spent months in hiding (Sinjab 2012). Razan, her husband, and two colleagues have been missing since December 2013, after being kidnapped by a rebel group (Daraghi 2013).

Suhair Atassi, another human rights activist, was detained for more than two weeks after participating in a silent protest in March 2011. She remained in hiding for seven months after her release, then decided to leave Syria to serve the uprising from Paris, and was later appointed as the vice president of the now-defunct Syrian National Coalition. Of those who remained, many women have been active in the delivery of humanitarian aid across Syria, and in some cases, even joined the Free Syrian Army in what became the armed resistance against the Assad regime and its allies inside the country (Karel 2013).

In a *thawrat sha'b* (people's revolution) such as Syria's, though, the participation and contribution of women cannot be reduced or abridged to the activism of these well-known names, as herculean and awe-inspiring as their ongoing struggles against authoritarianism and tyranny are. Thus it would be more accurate to say that Syrian women in general—as *thaa'irat* (female revolutionaries) and *hara'ir* (free women)—have adapted as the needs and dynamics of the uprisings have dramatically shifted, remaining present and active in spite of the bloody plummet into full-scale war. One cannot begin to understand the uprisings in Syria, through its evolution and in all of its incarnations, without unpacking the role women have played since early 2011. This brief essay merely scratches the surface of women's experiences in the revolution, relaying the perspective of one participatory narrative, as the voices of the rebelling people in Syria's uprisings become increasingly drowned out by civil war, factionalism even among opposition forces, military and political, and the war against the Islamic State in a wider regional counterrevolutionary wave.

Um Ibrahim, a university-educated mother of seven, relays an account that gives unique insight into female participation in the Syrian uprising. She recalls how she waited for the revolution to reach her home country after watching the news about the uprisings in Tunisia and Egypt. "We had a feeling that this was for us; that it would come to us. It was time," she says (interview with Um Ibrahim, April 2013). Her perspective on the political and social situation in Syria before the uprising is important, as she was able to have a new perspective after having spent two decades living in exile. Women in particular had some level of freedom, but only at the margins—they possessed relative freedom of mobility, as long as they suppressed their actual thoughts or opinions. "We were living in duplicity, telling our kids two narratives," Um Ibrahim added, presumably referring to both Syrian men and Syrian women who, as Wedeen (1999) put it, were forced by the regime's domination to behave "*as if* they revered their leader" (1999, 6).[3] As the uprising unfolded, the so-called wall of fear was torn down and the two narratives became identical.

From the very beginning of the first protests, some women participated in hidden ways, such as handing out water to young men to counteract the tear gas, opening their homes to protesters being chased by the security forces, making signs bearing slogans that would be held at protests, and delivering goods and food to activists and, later, weapons to the Free Syrian Army, across town and throughout the country. Um Ibrahim describes an acquaintance of hers who was determined to participate in opposition activities despite her husband's insistence on inaction. Not only did Um Ibrahim's friend treat injured protesters in her own home; she also cooked large quantities of food and delivered it, along with weapons, to Free Syrian Army members. When her vehicle would be stopped at regime checkpoints, she would claim that she had an 'azeemah, or dinner party, to get to, and would offer the soldiers at the checkpoint tea so that they would let her through. This is undoubtedly just one story among many, demonstrating perhaps some of the added flexibility women sometimes have in Syria, because they can mask their opposition work under the guise of their everyday activities as women and caretakers.[4]

During the first months of the uprising, the stand against the Assad regime was less uniform in Damascus than in Daraa or Homs. It may be easy to forget, then, that some of the earliest protests in Syria did in fact take place in Damascus, and that these early demonstrations were women's protests.

Um Ibrahim describes her own participation in a protest, calling it a "small film," perhaps in reference to the surreal nature of the experience. She received a phone call from a friend, who asked to meet her at a particular place. "I understood" what she meant, says Um Ibrahim, "and I went at a certain time, to a certain market." Pretending to be shopping for housewares, she kept a lookout for other women. "We were all thinking like one another, glancing at each other." Suddenly, there were fifty or so such women, all wearing white shawls, some holding up pictures of the children of Daraa, others holding signs.[5] Careful not to chant, "The people want the downfall of the regime!" at this early stage, instead they chanted slogans like "Save Syria's women," "Save Syria's children,"[6] and "Break the siege on Daraa!" Many men gathered to watch, some expressing encouragement, others disapproval: How could these women, many wearing headscarves that reflected their religious observance, take such bold and public action? Very quickly, cars carrying security forces flooded the site of the protest. Some women were detained, and the protest was dispersed. Um Ibrahim, who had donned black sunglasses to disguise her face, was followed as she left the scene; she zigzagged in and out of several shops, bought items she did not need, and took a long, two-hour, circuitous route home to escape her pursuers.

Undeterred by the fear she experienced from being followed after the protest, Um Ibrahim speaks with passion and certainty when she narrates the episode. Being part of the protest is "impossible to describe. It felt like I had wings and was flying, like I was sure God was with me, that I was connected to something God loved." At the same time, she remembers worrying about her children, her husband, and all the people who loved her, who feared for her safety.

Despite participating in protests, Um Ibrahim was able to leave unharmed. She is now among Syria's millions of displaced, forced to leave the country with her family as the regime's crackdown became more and more brutal; she counts herself among the lucky ones, blessed in comparison with her "sisters." Millions of women in particular have paid a heavy price, losing fathers, husbands, brothers, and children to shelling, massacres, detainment, and torture. By December 2017, over 4.2 million women and girls had become affected by the uprising/war (United Nations Population Fund 2017), and their vulnerability to violence and displacement has heightened (United Nations Development Program 2016, 102). The Violence Documentation Center (VDC) reports that as of September 2014, out of a total of 105,220 deaths caused by the Assad regime that they have documented, 7,555 were women and 3,923 girls. At least 183 women and 92 girls are still missing (out of the 2,293 people documented by the organization). In Assad's notorious detention facilities, 1,554 women and 65 girls languish, a significant portion of the 55,285 documented.[7] As activist Razan Ghazzawi puts it, regime prisons were much more difficult for women than for men, as "jailing women also imposes a social stigma on them, not to mention the issue of sexual abuse" (2014). Ironically, many of the women on these lists went nameless and were given the label of either as "*Um*" or "*Mart fulan*" (wife or mother of someone).

Countless other women were victimized in other ways. Many were subjected to sexual exploitation, a particularly painful and sensitive violation. The sacrifices they have been paying for their country exact a steep personal and social toll, as Um Ibrahim notes. The United Nations Population Fund (UNPF) recently issued a statement highlighting the impact of what has become the war in Syria, in and around the capital in particular. Calling for "immediate and unhindered access to women and girls in need of life-saving assistance . . . especially emergency obstetric care," the UNPF has also drawn attention to the increasingly common phenomenon of "gender-based violence" and sexual exploitation, particularly among girls and women who have fled Syria (UNPF 2013).

The violent tumbling of a peaceful uprising into bloody carnage and unspeakable destruction has certainly taken a toll not just on women's security and access to basic needs but on their participation in the revolution as well. The mobility of female activists, for instance, has been limited not just by the ongoing ravages of regime shelling and the dropping of barrel bombs and, most recently, missiles launched by the US-led coalition against ISIS, but also by increasing numbers of checkpoints, particularly in areas under regime occupation. Women are being specifically targeted, harassed, and violated by extremist groups.

As the other essays in this volume confirm, the clear presence of women, as part of the broader citizen activism and engagement across the Arab world in the past few years, has undeniably confirmed their agency in this bottom-up popular uprising. Women are a *force majeure* that can no longer be ignored by authoritarian regimes, foreign governments and policymakers, or even academics and experts. And Syria is not an exception. Syrian women were part of the uprisings in a variety of ways, some similar to men: protesting, engaging in social media communication, and in some cases, even carrying arms against the regime. Others' activism was more specific to their traditional gender roles, including cooking for soldiers and activists and sewing protest signs and uniforms. As a direct or indirect consequence, Syrian women have also paid a heavy price and have been painfully victimized by the conflict. Sometimes they have been targeted in ways mirroring the abuse of their male counterparts seeking emancipation: detainment, torture, killing, and displacement. At other times their victimization affected them particularly *as women*: sexual exploitation and rape, widowhood, ending up as the sole breadwinners for their families.[8] Despite the steep cost borne by men, women, and children in their struggle for freedom, Um Ibrahim remains optimistic. To her, God has ordained victory for the revolution, a victory being forged by the steadfastness of the people of her beloved, beleaguered country. In the midst of an increasingly dubious and unpredictable resolution of a crisis whose death toll has climbed to almost half a million people, the hope and convictions of women like Um Ibrahim demonstrate that some parts of the Syrian population, at least, will continue in their quest for freedom.

NOTES

1 "الثورة السورية—الزبداني، أغنية للثورة إلى حلب," Michael Freeman, YouTube, January 16, 2012, accessed July 27, 2015, available at https://www.youtube.com/watch?v=7jEJwAg6e4k.

2 The name is a pseudonym used to protect her identity. The interview took place in Arabic and the translation throughout the chapter is my own.

3 Emphasis in original.

4 Waylen (1994, 338) makes a related point about women in Latin American demo-cratic transitions, where military governments (rather shortsightedly) "did not see women's activities as dangerous enough to warrant repression."

5 The Syrian uprisings began in Daraa when schoolchildren painted revolutionary graffiti on a wall. The children were detained and tortured by Assad's security forces. "Syria: Crimes against Humanity in Daraa." Human Rights Watch, June 1, 2011.

6 Author's translation of slogans relayed in Arabic by Um Ibrahim.

7 "About Us," Violations Documentation Center in Syria, available at http://www.vdc-sy.info/index.php/en/. These numbers are far from complete, though, as the VDC explains on its website: "We—by no means—consider [the three stages of documentation] as a complete mission due to the complexities of the Syrian situa-tion, the siege imposed on the areas and what the bad security situation the activ-ists are living, in addition to the separation of the Syrian cities and villages, the fear of the victims' families of providing us with more details because of security threats, and the cut-out of electricity and internet connection in most of liberated areas."

8 Men, too, and even boys, have been victims of rape and sexual violence in Syria, but given the social dynamics and the stigma discussed earlier, women suffer such violations in specific, and perhaps more excruciating, ways.

BIBLIOGRAPHY

Beaumont, Peter. 2011. "Syria's Defiant Women Risk All to Protest against Bashar al-Assad." *Guardian*, May 21, http://www.theguardian.com.

Daragahi, Borzou. 2013. "Syrian Opposition Activist Razan Zaitouneh Kidnapped at Gunpoint." *Financial Times*, December 10.

Ghazzawi, Razan. 2014. "Seeing the Women in Revolutionary Syria." Open Democracy, April 8, https://www.opendemocracy.net.

Human Rights Watch. 2014. "'We Are Still Here': Women on the Front Lines of Syria's Conflict." Human Rights Watch, July 3, https://www.hrw.org.

Karel, Asha. 2013. "'Mothers at Home and Activists on the Street?': The Role of Women in the Syrian Revolution of 2011–2012." *McGill International Review* 2, no. 3: 51–65.

McGee, Thomas. 2014. "Women's Activism and the Polio Epidemic in Syria." Jadaliyya, March 17, http://www.jadaliyya.com.

Sadiki, Larbi. 2016. "The Arab Spring: 'The People' in International Relations." In *International Relations of the Middle East*, edited by L. Fawcett, 324–55. Oxford: Oxford University Press.

Saleh, Layla. 2017. *US Hard Power in the Arab World: Resistance, the Syrian Uprising, and the War on Terror*. London: Routledge.

Sinjab, Lina. 2012. "Women Play Central Role in Syria Uprising." BBC News, March 13, http://www.bbc.co.uk.

United Nations Development Program. 2016. *Arab Human Development Report 2016: Youth and the Prospects for Development in a Changing Reality*. http://www.arab-hdr.org, accessed February 15, 2018.

United Nations Population Fund. 2013. "UNFPA Alarmed over Impact of Growing Violence in Syria on Women and Girls." August 26, http://www.unfpa.org.

———. 2017. "Regional Situation Report for the Syria Crisis." https://www.unfpa.org, accessed February 26, 2018.

United States Department of State. 2015. "Biographies of 2015 Winners." https://2009-2017.state.gov, accessed February 26, 2018.

Waylen, Georgia. 1994. "Women and Democratization: Conceptualizing Gender Relations in Comparative Politics." *World Politics* 46, no. 3: 327–54.

Wedeen, Lisa. 1999. *Ambiguities of Domination: Politics, Rhetoric, and Symbols in Contemporary Syria*. Chicago: University of Chicago Press.

———. 2013. "Ideology and Humor in Dark Times: Notes from Syria." *Critical Inquiry* 39, no. 4: 841–73.

40

Arab American Women and the Arab Spring

An Interview with Summer Nasser

EMILY REGAN WILLS

Women are central to community organizing in the Arab communities of the United States. In particular, they take on important roles in keeping organizations active and becoming spokespeople for their causes. During the tumultuous days of the Arab Spring, Arab American activists and community organizers of both genders refocused their efforts on the changes happening in their countries of origin. The role of women of all ages, but particularly young women, as leaders at these moments, is a testament both to the organizational centrality of women in Arab diaspora communities and to their investment in political change in their countries of origin.

Summer Nasser is a Yemeni American New Yorker who is a leader in the Yemeni American Coalition for Change, a New York–based organization supporting peaceful revolution and the end of the Saleh regime in Yemen. In the course of her activism, Summer has written for online publications, been interviewed for radio programs, and given speeches in front of rallies from Washington, DC, to Yonkers, New York. A student at Concordia College studying international relations and sociology, Summer has been involved in community organizations such as the Council on American-Islamic Relations and the Yemeni American Association of Bay Ridge, as well as working in Yemen at a school in the small city of Lahj.

In my interview with Summer, she gives her voice to explain how she understands the dynamics of gender and age in the revolution in Yemen and the transnational nature of this movement. I try to capture her passion for political change in the Arab world, and how diaspora Arabs relate to the Arab Spring, without attempting to construct a general narrative of women's participation in pro–Arab Spring activism.

Although the political changes of the Arab Uprisings drew from long-standing protest and dissent movements in the region, for many people who participated in street demonstrations or called for revolution, this was their first experience of being part of these movements. For others, it was a change and refinement in tactics from a previous interest in politics and social change. Summer narrates how her involvement in the movement was a sudden decision:

> Before getting involved with the Yemeni organizing against Saleh in 2011, I really wasn't involved with any other types of activism. Without thinking twice, I decided to get involved with a movement that inspired change in a country where such protests were never known. I felt that it was my obligation to get involved with what my people wanted in my home country. My role was as important (if not more) as any journalist covering the Yemeni revolution. The individuals that I have met along the way, since I decided to be active in such a historical moment, were new to me. Before 2011, I was not involved with my Yemeni community. There were new faces but eventually grew to a big circle of networks.

In the Arab world, youth were the ones who drove the revolutionary efforts in the Uprisings, particularly from the streets. Women were also a primary set of actors, on the front line of protest movements, speaking online and in the media in defense of revolutionary change, and becoming symbols of resistance. In Yemeni American organizing, however, Summer reports that both women and youth are sparsely represented:

> Many people were shocked with my activism and energy towards the cause. When the revolution first started in Yemen, it was around February/March (no official date) of 2011. I was only a junior in high school at the time. My roles at events such as conferences, rallies, and community meetings were not that of my young age. Most who are engaged are generally older people. Fortunately, my age hasn't stopped me to be in a position with others who were much . . . older and [more] experienced than I was. The genuine part was that I was the only high school student in the midst of men and women who have graduated with BAs, masters. A few women were involved in the making of protests and other events . . . while a few participated at demonstrations.

Summer's experience suggests that the absence of youth from the Yemeni American activist scene is connected to their relatively comfortable life, which is different from the experiences of young people in Yemen. Alternatively, she expresses puzzlement about women's low involvement. Summer's suspicion that Yemeni American youth are depoliticized because of their distance from events in Yemen may also explain the lower participation of women. Yemeni women in the United States may find themselves less directly connected to the reasons why women in Yemen are ready to take to the streets:

> It's very difficult to gather Yemeni youth in the US area just because our Yemeni youth in the US aren't into causes like revolutions. This is because they do not feel the waves of oppression and political/economic severity issues in Yemen. I hope one day that I and my fellow activists in the US area can change that soon. Takes time, but we will achieve!
>
> As Yemen is known to be a conservative region, it blew me away to find that those who were at the front line in dangerous times were women. In fact, women were most outspoken and the major players in organizing rallies for the revolution. I thought that the Yemeni women who were in the US would be out protesting just like (if not more than) the women in Yemen. It was disappointing to see that not happening in a region where we have our freedom to speak out. I found it to be odd seeing the women in Yemen give their lives in the name of freedom, since the government doesn't recognize such an expression, yet the women who were in the US and have a safe zone, were barely out at rallies. We, in the US, are guaranteed safety while the women in Yemen aren't.

Summer explicitly says that she felt obligated to advocate for the will of the Yemeni people and for "what my people wanted in my home country" and that her "role was as important (if not more) as any journalist covering the Yemeni revolution." Thus, she frames her involvement as separate from the actions of Yemeni activists. Her activism outside Yemen is about "supporting our people," not about being a driver within the movement. Her discourse about solidarity is similar to that of the Palestine solidarity activism that has emerged in the United States. Solidarity activism emphasizes the existence of identity-based differences between the activists and those they aim to support, and the importance of following the desires of those who are most closely affected by the issue. Summer frames herself, and the activist organizations of which she is a part, as in solidarity with activists in Yemen, although she frames herself as a Yemeni.

Summer's story shows that in organizing in the United States to support revolutionary change in their countries of origin, Arab Americans frame the distance between "here" and "there" in ways that make sense to them. They also create different ways of understanding actions and participation. The differences in the way organizations and individuals understand themselves in transnational perspective may come from personal relationships or experiences, from the other movements activists are a part of, or from larger structural elements of diaspora relationships and the nature of movements in the country of origin. However, these different framings serve to motivate action and engagement in both the home country and diaspora politics. Although it is still too early to tell how the generation of activists brought into politics by this historical moment will continue to interact with ongoing movements for social and political justice in the Arab world, this story will unfold over time.

ACKNOWLEDGMENTS

After many years of writing and rewriting, editing and reediting, we have many people to thank.

We express our appreciation to all our contributors who gave to this volume its unique character and made it a collection that includes the voices of activists, academics, artists, and politicians. Their patience, talent, and courage were invaluable. We are grateful to our dear friend and guide Ilene Kalish, executive editor at New York University Press, and her staff. Ilene gave us her support and shared her vast knowledge with us at every step.

Twice we had the privilege to present chapters from this collection on panels sponsored by the Association for Middle Eastern Women Studies (AMEWS) at the annual meetings of the Middle East Studies Association. The American Sociological Association also gave us an opportunity to present some of the work included.

We want to thank our research assistants Jana Suleiman, Samyah Al-foory, Zachary Cuyler, and Melissa Ajamian, who paid close attention to every detail of the manuscript. Last, but not least, our families, Michael Brenner, Camille Stephan, and Adele Homsieh, were there for us throughout the journey of the volume, as were Rony and Karla, to whom this book and the future belong.

ABOUT THE EDITORS

MOUNIRA M. CHARRAD (PhD, Harvard) is Associate Professor of Sociology at the University of Texas–Austin and a Non-Resident Fellow at the Baker Institute, Rice University. Her book, *States and Women's Rights: The Making of Postcolonial Tunisia, Algeria, and Morocco,* won numerous national awards, including Best Book in Sociology from the American Sociological Association. Her articles have appeared in major scholarly journals. She has edited or coedited *Patrimonial Power in the Modern World*; *Patrimonial Capitalism and Empire*; *Women's Agency: Silences and Voices*; and *Femmes, Culture et Société au Maghreb.* Her work has been translated into French, Arabic, and Chinese.

RITA STEPHAN is Research Fellow at the Moise A. Khayrallah Center for Lebanese Diaspora Studies at North Carolina State University and the Director of the Middle East Partnership Initiative at the US Department of State. After earning her PhD in Sociology from the University of Texas at Austin, she served as Survey Statistician at the US Census Bureau and a visiting researcher at Georgetown University. She is the coeditor of *In Line with the Divine: The Struggle for Gender Equality in Lebanon* and the author of several publications on Lebanese women's movement, social movements, social networks, and Arab Americans.

ABOUT THE CONTRIBUTORS

LINA ABIRAFEH, PhD, is Executive Director of the Arab Institute for Women at the Lebanese American University. Lina has over twenty years' experience in gender-based violence prevention and response in countries such as Afghanistan, Haiti, Democratic Republic of Congo, Nepal, and others. Her 2015 TEDx talk summarizes her experience. Lina completed her doctoral work from the London School of Economics and published "Gender and International Aid in Afghanistan: The Politics and Effects of Intervention" based on her research. In 2018 and 2019, Lina was listed as one of the Gender Equality Top 100: The Most Influential People in Global Policy.

NADJE AL-ALI is Robert Family Professor of Middle East Studies at Brown University. She has widely published on women and gender in the Middle East as well as transnational migration and diaspora mobilization. Her publications include *Iraqi Women: Untold Stories from 1948 to the Present* and *We Are Iraqis: Aesthetics and Politics in a Time of War*, coedited with Deborah al-Najjar, which won the 2014 Arab American book prize for nonfiction. Professor Al-Ali is an advisory board member of *kohl: a journal of body and gender research*.

ASEEL ALAWADHI is a former member of the National Assembly of Kuwait and the Cultural Attaché at the Embassy of Kuwait in Washington, DC. In 2008, she first ran for a seat on the National Assembly, losing the election but gaining the highest number of votes for a female candidate since women were allowed to run in 2007. She was elected in 2009 and held her post until 2012. Alawadhi earned her PhD in philosophy at the University of Texas and was a professor of philosophy at Kuwait University and a research fellow at Georgetown University.

ZAHRA ALI is Assistant Professor of Sociology at Rutgers University. Her research explores dynamics of women and gender, social and political movements in relation to Islam(s) and the Middle East, and contexts of war and conflicts with a focus on contemporary Iraq. Her publications include *Women and Gender in Iraq: Between Nation-building and Fragmentation*. She also edited *Féminismes Islamiques*, the first collection on Muslim feminist scholarship published in France, translated and published in German.

MANAL AL-NATOUR is Associate Professor and Director of Arabic Studies in the World Languages, Literatures, and Linguistics Department, West Virginia University. She earned her PhD in Comparative Literature and Cultural Studies at the University of Arkansas. Her research and teaching interests include modern Arabic literature and language, war narratives, postcolonial studies, contemporary women's writings, feminism, and the Arab Spring. Her most recent publications have appeared in *Arab Spring and Arab Women: Challenges and Opportunities*; *Alif: Journal of Comparative Poetics*; *Literature and Psychology: Writing, Trauma, and the Self*; *Journal of International Women's Studies*; *Comics through Time*; and *Women's ENews*.

ASAAD ALSALEH is Associate Professor of Arabic Literature in the Department of Near Eastern Languages and Cultures, Indiana University. He is interested in issues related to autobiography and personal voices in modern Arabic literature and culture. His interest in narratives about the political culture in the Arab world resulted in the publication of his book, *Voices of the Arab Spring: Personal Stories from the Arab Revolutions*. He publishes on diverse issues related to his background in Comparative Literature and Cultural Studies.

AMAL AMIREH received her PhD in English and American literature from Boston University. She is author of *The Factory Girl and the Seamstress: Imagining Gender and Class in Nineteenth-Century American Fiction* and coeditor of *Going Global: The Transnational Reception of Third World Women Writers* and *Etel Adnan: Critical Essays on the Arab-American Writer and Artist*. Her essay "Between Complicity and Subversion: Body Politics in the Palestinian National Narrative" (*South Atlantic Quarterly* 102 [2003]: 745–70) won the 2004 Florence Howe

Award for best feminist article of the year. Her work has appeared in many publications and was translated into Arabic and Persian.

GHIDA ANANI is Assistant Professor in the Faculty of Public Health at the Lebanese University. In June 2011, she founded and continues to direct the ABAAD Resource Centre for Gender Equality, which was awarded the Womanity Award. As an expert in gender-based violence and child protection, Anani has published a number of studies, articles, training kits and community educational materials on GBV & Child Sexual Abuse in Lebanon and the MENA region. In 2014 she received the Women Leadership Achievement Award given by The World Women Leadership Congress. She has led a number of public opinion campaigns, notably the latest #Undress522 which resulted in a historical parliamentary vote, repealing article 522 from the Lebanese Penal Code. In 2019, the campaign was honored with the first-prize UN SDG Action Award as the most impactful campaign globally.

MARGOT BADRAN is a senior fellow at the Alwaleed Center for Muslim-Christian Understanding at Georgetown University and a global fellow at the Woodrow Wilson International Center for Scholars. She has a DPhil from the University of Oxford and an MA from Harvard University. Her books include *Feminism in Islam: Secular and Religious Convergences* and *Feminism, Islam, and Nation: Gender and the Making of Modern Egypt*. She translated and edited *Harem Years: The Memoirs of an Egyptian Feminist, Huda Shaarawi*; edited *Gender, Islam in Africa: Rights, Sexuality, and Law*; and coedited *Opening the Gates: Over a Century of Arab Feminist Writing*. She is working on a book on women, gender, and revolution in Egypt.

SOUMIA BARDHAN (PhD, University of New Mexico) is Assistant Professor of Communication at University of Colorado Denver. Her research interests are interdisciplinary and informed by Intercultural Communication, Rhetoric, and Islamic/Religious Studies. By focusing on the intersections of culture, religion, and politics, she explores the multivocal discourses and discursive practices within Islam, the rhetoric of Muslim minority groups, and the role of new media/social media in the cultural-political transformation of Arab societies. Her work has appeared in the peer-reviewed *Georgetown Journal of International Affairs, Journal of Public Deliberation, Digest of Middle East Studies, Journal of Intercultural Communication Research,* and *Contemporary Islam.*

EMANUELA BUSCEMI holds a PhD in Sociology from the University of Aberdeen (Scotland) and teaches at the University of Monterrey–UDEM (Mexico). She previously taught at the American University of Kuwait (AUK) and conducted fieldwork in Kuwait. Her research interests include alternative social movements, informal activism and resistance, identity and gender politics, communities and belonging. Her most recent publications include "Abaya and Yoga Pants: Women's Activism in Kuwait," published in *AG: About Gender—International Journal of Gender Studies* (2016) and "Resistant Identities: Culture and Politics among Kuwaiti Youth," published in *Contemporary Social Science–Journal of the Academy of Social Sciences* (2017).

MICHELA CERRUTI is a PhD candidate in Social Sciences. Her dissertation, "Religious Awakening in Syria through Female Movements," has been funded by a Fellowship award from the Institut Emilie du Chatelet and the Region Ile de France. Her research interests are Gender and Islamic Studies. She graduated with honors in Islamic Studies at Ca' Foscari University, followed by a Research Master degree in Social Sciences at École des Hautes Études en Sciences Sociales. She was a visiting scholar at several universities in the Middle East and in the United States and consulted for UN Woman in New York and United Nations Relief and Works Agency for Palestine Refugees in the Near East in Syria.

NISRINE CHAER is a researcher who holds an MA in Gender and Ethnicity from Utrecht University. Her research interests consider the interplay among queerness, space, affect, and the political within the field of Arab cultural studies. She has published articles in the *Women's Studies International Forum, Kohl Journal for Body and Gender Research,* and *Global Dialogue.*

KEVIN A. DAVIS has a BA in Anthropology from the University of Washington with a special focus on the Middle East, and an MA with distinction in Contemporary Arab Studies from Georgetown University's Edmund A. Walsh School of Foreign Service. He has published various pieces in publications such as *Muftah*, *Washington Report on Middle East Affairs*, *Al-Qawl*, *National Yemen*, and *Warscapes*. Kevin currently works in refugee resettlement in the San Francisco Bay area.

MAHA EZZAT ELKHOLY graduated with a BA in English language, literature, and simultaneous translation from the Faculty of Humanities of Al-Azhar University. She taught Arabic at Arabeya, a school in Mohandessin, Cairo. Though she was born in the Sendbis village in the Egyptian countryside and is the daughter of uneducated parents, Maha's parents gave her the opportunity to study and work in Giza. She is strongly committed to giving a voice to what she calls the "forgotten girls and women" of the Egyptian countryside.

GINGER FEATHER is an independent researcher and is currently training Afghani ministry and university officials as a part of the Ministry of Women–sponsored Gender Awareness Program (GAP). She holds a PhD in Political Science from the University of Kansas and a master's degrees in Arabic/Islamic Studies and International Affairs from the University of Kansas and George Washington University. Her research focuses on the impact of discriminatory legal codes on violence against women in Morocco and Tunisia. Her first book project, titled "Torn between Bad Choices: Moroccan and Tunisian Women Battle Legal Discrimination and Violence against Women," is currently under review.

KAREN A. FOSS is Regents' Professor Emeritus of Communication & Journalism at the University of New Mexico; she received her PhD from the University of Iowa. Her research interests include contemporary rhetorical theory, feminist perspectives on communication, and social movements and social change. She is coauthor of several books, including *Gender Stories*, *Theories of Human Communication*, *Feminist Rhetorical Theories*, and *COLOR Up*. She has been honored with the Robert J. Kibler and Francine Merritt awards, National Communication Association; the Paul Boase Prize, Ohio University; Gender Scholar of the Year, Southern Communication Association; and Scholar of the Year, Humboldt State University.

SAMAA GAMIE is Associate Professor of English, Director of the Writing and Reading Center, and Assistant Director of the Writing Proficiency Program at the Lincoln University, Pennsylvania. She has her BA in English language and literature from the University of Alexandria, Egypt, her MA in Professional Writing from the University of Massachusetts at Dartmouth, and her PhD in English with a concentration in Rhetoric and Composition from the University of Rhode Island. She has published poems, reviews, essays, and book chapters. Her areas of research include digital rhetoric, postcolonial studies, and feminist theory, literature, and rhetoric.

THERESA HUNT is a University Lecturer of Humanities and Science, Technology, and Society at New Jersey Institute of Technology in Newark. She holds an MA in English and a PhD in Global Affairs, both from Rutgers University. Hunt's research investigates the use of gender, youth, and technology narratives in revolutions, as well as the history of youth organizing in transnational social justice movements. Her work has appeared most recently in the youth studies journal *Young*.

NELIA HYNDMAN-RIZK is a Cultural Anthropologist and Lecturer in Cross Cultural Management in the School of Business, University of New South Wales–Canberra. Her research interests include migration studies, with a focus on the Lebanese diaspora, and contemporary social movements in the Middle East, with a focus on the Lebanese women's movement. Her books include *My Mother's Table: At Home in the Maronite Diaspora* and *Pilgrimage in the Age of Globalisation: Constructions of the Sacred and Secular in Late Modernity*.

FATMA OSMAN IBNOUF is Assistant Professor at Development Studies and Research Institute (DSRI), University of Khartoum, Sudan. She holds a PhD in Development Studies from the University of Wales–Swansea in the United Kingdom. She is a prolific researcher whose work has appeared in several international publications and received international recognition. The recipient of the 2017 Social Science Research Council's African Peacebuilding Network's Book Manuscript Completion Grant and the 2016 APN-SSRC Individual Research Grant, Fatma is also a 2018 Rotary Peace Fellow at Chulalongkorn University in

Thailand. She has authored and contributed to numerous publications, policy documents, and reports.

MANAL A. JAMAL is Associate Professor of Political Science at James Madison University. She holds a PhD in Political Science from McGill University and a BA and MA in International Relations from the University of California at Davis and San Francisco State respectively. She is author of *Promoting Democracy: The Force of Political Settlements in Uncertain Times* (New York University Press, 2019), and numerous peer-reviewed articles and book chapters. She has held a number of fellowship appointments, including at UC–Berkeley's Center for Middle Eastern Studies and Harvard University's Kennedy School of Government.

SUAD JOSEPH (PhD in Anthropology, Columbia University, 1975) is Distinguished Research Professor, University of California–Davis; the founder of the Association for Middle East Women's Studies (AMEWS), the Arab Families Working Group, the Middle East/South Asia Studies Program at UC–Davis, the Middle East Section of the American Anthropological Association (MES); and cofounder of the Association for Middle East Anthropology (AMEA) and the Women and Gender Studies Program at UC–Davis. She was the president of the Middle East Studies Association of North America, and is General Editor of the *Encyclopedia of Women and Islamic Cultures*. She has edited and coedited numerous books and published over a hundred articles. She is the recipient of numerous awards, including lifetime achievement awards from AMEWS and MES.

MOHJA KAHF was born in Syria and immigrated to the United States. She has been a professor of comparative literature and Middle Eastern Studies at the University of Arkansas since 1995. Kahf is the author of a novel, *The Girl in the Tangerine Scarf*, and two poetry books, *E-mails from Scheherazad* and *Hagar Poems*, as well as the scholarly monograph, *Western Representations of the Muslim Woman*. In exile, Kahf joined the Syrian Nonviolence Movement (established in Syria in April 2011) at the invitation of its founding members.

LORENZO KAMEL is Associate Professor of History at the University of Turin and director of the Books and Research Studies series at the Istituto

Affari Internazionali (IAI). He has held teaching and research positions in several universities in the Middle East, the US, and Europe, including the Albert-Ludwigs-Universität Freiburg and Harvard University, where he was a postdoctoral fellow for two years. He has authored five books, including *Imperial Perceptions of Palestine: British Influence and Power in Late Ottoman Times*, winner of the 2016 Palestine Academic Book Award, and *The Middle East from Empire to Sealed Identities*.

AMINAH ALI KANDAR is a Canadian-born scholar with a bachelor's degree from Georgetown University's School of Foreign Service in Qatar (magna cum laude) and a certificate in Arab and Regional Studies. Having worked at the Centre for International and Regional Studies, Al Jazeera Media Network, Qatar Foundation, and with Georgetown University's Qatar Longitudinal Studies of Transnational Families research team, she participated in numerous academic and international conferences, and traveled extensively for community-engagement and conflict-management programs in Lebanon, Rwanda, South Africa, and Sri Lanka.

KARINA EILERAAS KARAKUŞ (BA, Wesleyan University) was the first PhD recipient of the Women's Studies Program at UCLA. Currently a Lecturer of Gender Studies at the University of Southern California, she has also taught at Berkeley and Pomona. Her research interests include nationalism and sexuality in the MENA; modest fashion, nude protest, social media, and revolution; sexual violence, fantasy, and visual culture; Islamic feminism; and film, music, and performance studies. Her book *Between Image and Identity: Transnational Fantasy, Symbolic Violence, and Feminist Misrecognition* explores women's representations of transnational trauma. Karakus is researching fashion and revolution in Turkey and editing a feminist "invisible archive" of Marilyn Monroe.

NICOLE KHOURY holds a PhD in Rhetoric, Composition, and Linguistics from Arizona State University. Her research focuses on Arab and Middle Eastern women's history, especially rhetorical discourse and public arguments for gender equality, with a particular interest in the intersections between gender and religion. She is currently a Lecturer at the University of California–Irvine.

ARIANA MARNICIO is Program Manager for Resilient Communities at the Harvard Humanitarian Initiative. She manages research on the response of communities to natural disaster and conflict. She holds an MPH from the Harvard T.H. Chan School of Public Health and a BA in Arabic from Georgetown University.

NADINE NABER is Professor of Global Asian Studies and Gender and Women's Studies at the University of Illinois–Chicago. At UIC, she is the founding director of the Arab American Cultural Center. She is the author of *Arab America: Gender, Politics, and Activism* and coeditor of the books *Race and Arab Americans, Arab and Arab American Feminisms,* and the *Color of Violence.* Naber is a cofounder of the Arab and Muslim American Studies Program at the University of Michigan–Ann Arbor; an international fellow with the Open Societies Institute; a recipient of the Stice Social Justice Award from the University of Washington; and a national council member of the American Studies Association.

RULA QUAWAS was the Founding Director of the Women's Studies Center and the Dean of the Faculty of Foreign Languages at the University of Jordan, before passing away in July 2017. She was a Fulbright Scholar-in-Residence at Champlain College in Vermont, recipient of the 2009 Meritorious Honor Award for Leadership and Dedication to the empowerment of Jordanian women, and nominee for the 2013 International Women of Courage Award. Her research focused on feminist readings of American and Arabic texts written by women writers. She published numerous essays, language textbooks, and books on Jordanian women short story writers and intercultural communication.

MARIA SAADEH has a bachelor's degree in Architecture, and an advanced diploma in Architectural Design from Aleppo University. In 1999, she earned her Diplôme d'études supérieures spécialisées from École Chaillot in Paris, France, and her doctorate degree from Geneva University in 2013. Between 2001 and 2010, Maria taught Architectural Design in the University of Damascus, while serving as an expert for the General Directorate of Antiquities and Museums and running her architecture and interior design firm. In 2012, she was elected to the

Syrian Parliament as an independent Christian candidate and unsuccessfully sought the Parliament's endorsement for the speaker's position in 2014.

FATIMA SADIQI is a linguist affiliated with the University of Fez who specializes in gender and women's studies in the Middle East and North Africa. Among her many publications are *Women, Gender, and Language* (2003), "Women's Activism and the Public Sphere: Local/Global Linkages" (*Journal of Middle East Women's Studies*, 2006), *Women and Knowledge in the Mediterranean* (2013), *Moroccan Feminist Discourses* (2014), and *Women's Movements in the Post-"Arab Spring" North Africa* (2016). Sadiqi has received numerous prestigious awards and fellowships from Harvard University, the Woodrow Wilson Center, the Rockefeller Foundation's Bellagio Center, and Fulbright.

LAYLA SALEH is Associate Professor of Politics and International Relations at Qatar University's Department of International Affairs. She holds a PhD in Political Science from the University of Wisconsin–Milwaukee, and is the author of *US Hard Power in the Arab World: Resistance, the Syrian Uprisings, and the War on Terror.*

SANA SAYED has an MA degree in English Literature from California State University–Fullerton and a BA degree in English Literature and a minor in Comparative Literature from the University of California–Irvine. She is a Senior Instructor in the Department of Writing Studies at the American University of Sharjah. Her areas of research interest are Victorian literature, gender and identity, and theories of assessment and accountability in teaching composition. Her most recent publication appeared in the *International Journal of Humanities Education* (2016), and she has an upcoming chapter publication.

MARWA SHALABY is the Anna Julia Cooper fellow and Assistant Professor of Political Science and Gender and Women's Studies at the University of Wisconsin–Madison. Her research areas are comparative politics, democratization, and research methodology. Her work focuses primarily on the intersection of the politics of authoritarianism, and women in politics. Her work has appeared in the *Journal of Compara-*

tive Politics, Political Research Quarterly, Parliamentary Affairs, and the *Middle East Journal.* She has coauthored an edited volume, *The Evolving Role of Women after the Arab Spring,* with Valentine Moghadam (2016).

NURULSYAHIRAH TAHA is an independent researcher, speaker, and writer who divides her life between Singapore and the Netherlands. She writes about the media representation of Muslim women and explores gender, race, religion, and other intersectionalities in the Nusantara. She started Crit Talk, a space for Muslims to discuss and deconstruct taboos. She is currently a PhD candidate researching obstetric violence in Singapore, and previously studied development at the International Institute of Social Studies in The Hague, Netherlands. She can be found on social media at @syataha.

NAMIE TSUJIGAMI (PhD, Kobe University) is Professor at the Faculty of Global Studies at Sophia University. She has conducted field research on women's movement, network, and agency in Saudi Arabia, and her research interests are in women's entrepreneurship and consumption. Her publications include *Higher Education and Changing Aspirations of Women in Saudi Arabia* (2017), *Higher Education Investment in the Arab States of the Gulf: Strategies for Excellence and Diversity* (2017), and *Stealth Revolution: Saudi Women's Ongoing Social Battles, Arab Women's Activism, and Socio-Political Transformation* (2017).

DINA WAHBA is pursuing her PhD at Free University, Berlin, in Politics, Emotion, and Affect within the dynamics of Tahrir Square. She completed her master's degree in Gender Studies at the School of Oriental and African Studies (SOAS), University of London. Dina graduated from the faculty of Economics and Political Science, Cairo University. She worked on gender issues such as sexual and gender-based violence, leadership, political participation, and empowerment, and she has worked in several countries, including the United Kingdom, South Sudan, Egypt, and Germany.

EMILY REGAN WILLS is Associate Professor of Comparative and American Politics at the University of Ottawa, Ontario, Canada. She holds a

PhD in Politics from the New School for Social Research, and publishes on Arab American studies, Middle Eastern politics, and transnational social movements. She is the codirector, with Nadia Abu-Zahra, of the Community Mobilization in Crisis project, which supports community mobilization education in the Arab world.

ANDY YOUNG teaches at the New Orleans Center for Creative Arts. While writing her essay for this volume, she was developing the course "Creative Expressions of Resistance," exploring how art responds to oppression, at the American University in Cairo. Her essays have been featured in *Waxwing* and *Unfathomable City: A New Orleans Atlas*, among others. She is the author of the poetry collection *All Night It Is Morning* and four chapbooks. She received her BA in Journalism and Mass Communication from the University of North Carolina at Chapel Hill and her MFA from Warren Wilson College.

MARO YOUSSEF is currently pursuing her doctorate in Sociology at the University of Texas–Austin. She received an MA in Middle East Studies from George Washington University with a Portfolio in Women's and Gender Studies and a BA in history from the University of California at Santa Cruz. She was previously a foreign policy analyst at the US Department of State, where she worked on political, economic, security, and social issues in North Africa and human rights and women's rights in the Persian Gulf and Turkey. She served at the US Embassy in Tunisia and the US Embassy in Turkey. She is focused on examining gender, civil society, Islam, and democracy in North Africa.

AMINA ZARRUGH is Assistant Professor in the Department of Sociology and Anthropology at Texas Christian University. She has coauthored "Equal or Complementary? Women in the New Tunisian Constitution after the Arab Spring," with M. M. Charrad, in the *Journal of North African Studies* (2014), and "'You exile them in their own countries': The Everyday Politics of Reclaiming the Disappeared in Libya," in *Middle East Critique* (2018). Her research interests include gender, nationalism, and religion in North Africa. She received her BA in sociology and government and her MA and PhD in sociology from the University of Texas at Austin.

INDEX

ABAAD: anti-domestic violence law and, 307–8; domestic violence and, 50–52; role of, 13

abaya, 219, 226, 286

Abaza, Mona, 186, 268

Abdul Aziz (King of Saudi Arabia), 343

Abdullah II (King of Saudi Arabia), 8, 341, 343, 344

Abu Nasr, Julinda, 208, 209, 216

Abu Salim Prison killings, 233–43, *239*, *242*

Abu Sammad, Aisha, 33

activism: Arab Spring and, 1, 363–66; Beirut with queer, 173–82, 182n9; with claim making, 13; collective action and, 6, 77, 149, 235; cyberactivism, 156–59, 352; cyberspace and, 198–202, 350–51; gender and, 102–3; grassroots, *336*; impetus for, 318–19, 364; in Lebanon, 215; LGBTQ rights and, 302; Mahfouz with challenges to, 122–25; minorities and, 62, 64; online, 73, 231, 303–5; online/offline, 299–309; in Palestine, 365; with political participation in Bahrain, 323–24; revolutionary, 76–78; 16 Days of Activism to End Violence against Women, 51; spread of, 5–7; in Syrian uprisings, 354–60; as taboo, 348; in urban spaces, 176–77; Yemeni uprisings and, 71–73, 76–78; by youth in US, 364–65

Adib, Najia, 13, 53–57

Adly, Magda, 250–51

advertisements, anti-domestic violence, 50, 51

Aesthetic Criticism in Arabic Literature (Ghurayyib), 208

AFTURD. *See* Association des Femmes Tunisiennes pour la Recherche sur le Développement

agency, 3–4, 9, 176, 195, 257, 360; bodily, 166; claiming, 120; collective, 235; expressing, 147; female agency, 201, 202; with gender violence, sectarianism and authoritarianism, 103–4; historical perspectives and, 99–100; human agency, 300, 305; intersectionality and, 98–99; Iraqi Baath Party and, 100, 101–3; political, 101, 350; in revolution, 58; with sectarianism and ISIS resisted, 104–6; spaces for, 105; state agency, 7; women's agency, 3, 9, 26, 98–99, 198, 212, 268–70, 279, 280, 291, 313, 339. *See also* graffiti, in Cairo

Ahmed, Leila, 166

al-Akhbar English (news publication), 74

Alawadhi, Aseel: as "Americanized," 42; with education and resulting victimization, 42; with Kuwaiti society and reaction of students, 41–42; on parliament and hopes for political life, 42–43; with YouTube accusation and reaction, 40–41

Algeria, 2, 3, 129–34, 151, 153; Arab Spring in, 2; Family Code, 131, 132; feminism with authoritarianism in, 129–33; laws for social and political rights in, 7, 8; Nationality Code, 132, 133; reform in, 2, 132–33

Mansoura-Spanish Company, 32
Mansur, Abd Rabbuh, 70
marriage: civil, 306–7, 309; divorce and,
8, 110, 131, 211, 241, 294, 296, 342, 343;
laws, 143, 306–7, 308; lower-class men
and, 293; polygamy and, 8, 87, 131;
practices, 211–12; rape and, 7–8, 54,
308; rights, 132
martyrs, 191–93, *192*, 218–19, 230, 243n2.
See also Libya, state violence in
The Masculine and the Feminine (*al-
Mudhkkar wa al-Mu'annath*) (Ibn al
Anbari), 315
masculinity, 51–52
Maspero massacre, 227
massacres, 110, 113, 151, 227, 234, 241–43,
337, 359
Massad, Joseph, 48
Matar, Ghiyath, 62
maternity leave, 8
MB. *See* Muslim Brotherhood
McCrystal, Stanley, 141
media: anti-domestic violence advertisements in, 50; Arab Spring with new,
300–301, *302*; digital, 119, 300, 334;
International Journalist Network, 73;
with journalists attacked, 30; labor
strikes in, 32; MB in, 127n2; pedophilia
in, 53; racism in, 151; Syrian Women
Journalists, 333; WJWC, 71; Yemeni
uprisings in, 71. *See also* social media;
specific outlets
Meem: defined, 182n1; with MENA-
situated queer politics, 174–76; with
protests and urban spaces, 177; role of,
173, 182
MEEM. *See* Majmou'at Mou'azara lil
Mar'a al Mithliya
Meltzer, Julia, 204–6
men: ABAAD and, 13, 50–52, 307–8;
against domestic violence, 50–52; with
gender injustice in workplace, 34;
gender roles and, 52; graffiti depict-

ing, 269, 271–72, 272, 274, 278, *278*; as
guardians of women, 339–40; loans for,
335; lower-class, 293; masculinity and,
51–52; in "Stop the Killing" campaign,
62; women as guardians of, 350
MENA. *See* Middle East and North Africa
region
Men's Center, 51
Mernissi, Fatima, 295–96
Middle East and North Africa region
(MENA): with Meem and queer poli-
tics, 174–76; social media and, 166
militarization, nonviolence campaigns
and, 61, 64
Millennium Development Goals, UN,
69, 301
Miłosz, Czesław, 140
minority activists, 62, 64
mobile phones, 254, 300, 304
El-Mogy, Ahmed Adel, 271–72, *272*
Mohammad (Prophet), 199
Mohanty, Chandra T., 301
Molyneux, Maxine, 331, 334, 335
Morocco, 2, 7, 8, 53–57, 153, 313–17
Morsi, Mohammed: criticism of, 127n4,
168, 187–88, *189*, 190, 192–93; fall of,
229
Moussa, Dalia, 32
MSN, 300
Mubarak, Hosni, 1, 30, 33; criticism of, 137,
193, 256; fall of, 33, 121, 187, 193, 225,
226, 271, 290, 293; party, 30; post-, 122,
267, 268, 269; regime, 1, 117, 125, 292;
support for, 122, 186, 355
Mubarak, Mais, 61
Mubarak, Samir, 61
Mubarak, Suzanne, 292
al-Mudhkkar wa al-Mu'annath (The
Masculine and the Feminine) (Ibn al
Anbari), 315
Muhammad, Shafiqa bint, 231, 297
"multiple consciousness," 119
museum, streets as, 195